STAGNANT DREAMERS

Stagnant Dreamers

HOW THE INNER CITY SHAPES THE INTEGRATION OF SECOND-GENERATION LATINOS

María G. Rendón

Russell Sage Foundation   **NEW YORK**

LIBRARY OF CONGRESS
CATALOGING-IN-PUBLICATION DATA

Names: Rendón, María G., author.
Title: Stagnant dreamers : how the inner city shapes the integration of second-generation Latinos / María G. Rendón.
Description: New York : Russell Sage Foundation, [2019] | Includes bibliographical references and index. | Summary: "Stagnant Dreamers captures the story of Latino young men often labeled "at risk" due to their race/ethnicity, gender, and zip-code, who are at a crossroad, attempting to integrate into the larger American context and carve out a space in its dwindling middle class. It follows the lives of forty-two male offspring of post-1965 Latino immigrants from two high poverty neighborhoods in Los Angeles as they transition into adulthood. This study shows how America's urban violence and social isolation in segregated contexts shape the integration process of young men, calling attention to underappreciated resources that exist in these communities that mitigate the negative impacts of growing up in America's poorest neighborhoods. It explains why some young men get ahead, while others sink deeper into poverty. In the process, it reveals how Latino immigrants and their young adult children alter their neighborhoods, becoming part of Los Angeles's resilient working class"— Provided by publisher.
Identifiers: LCCN 2019025820 (print) | LCCN 2019025821 (ebook) | ISBN 9780871547088 (paperback ; alk. paper) ISBN 9781610448901 (ebook)
Subjects: LCSH: Hispanic American young men—California—Los Angeles—Social conditions. | Children of immigrants—California—Los Angeles—Social conditions. | Inner cities—California—Los Angeles. | Problem youth—California—Los Angeles—Social conditions. | Social mobility—California—Los Angeles.
Classification: LCC F869.L89 S75665 2019 (print) | LCC F869.L89 (ebook) | DDC 305.23089/68079494—dc23
LC record available at https://lccn.loc.gov/2019025820
LC ebook record available at https://lccn.loc.gov/2019025821

Text design by Linda Secondari.

Cover illustration: *Bridging Generations* by Juan Chavez. © 2019 Juan Chavez.

RUSSELL SAGE FOUNDATION
112 East 64th Street,
New York, New York 10065
10 9 8 7 6 5 4 3 2 1

For Julieta and Gabriela,
who were patient and loving as Mommy wrote her book—
you are my pride and joy and the engines that keep me going.

CONTENTS

....

LIST OF ILLUSTRATIONS *ix*
ABOUT THE AUTHOR *xi*
ACKNOWLEDGMENTS *xiii*

Chapter 1. Introduction: The Inner City
and Second-Generation Latinos *1*

Part I. The Latino Immigrant Urban Context

Chapter 2. The Contested Immigrant City:
Navigating Violence, Family, and Work *35*

Chapter 3. Same Landing, Unequal Starts:
The Varying Social Capital of Mexican Immigrants *63*

Part II. Second-Generation Latinos in the Inner City

Chapter 4. Caught Up and Skirting Risk:
Young Latino Men in the Inner City *91*

Chapter 5. Collapsing into the Working Class:
Social Support, Segregation, and Class Convergence *131*

Chapter 6. Getting Ahead or Falling Behind:
The Impact of Social Leverage Ties and Social Isolation *166*

Chapter 7. Making Sense of Getting Ahead:
The Enduring and Shifting Cultural Outlooks
of Young Latino Men *188*

Chapter 8. Conclusion: How the Inner City Shapes
the Integration Process of Second-Generation Latinos *229*

METHODOLOGICAL NOTES *249*
APPENDIX: SOCIOECONOMIC CHARACTERISTICS
OF THE NEIGHBORHOODS *267*
NOTES *277*
REFERENCES *301*
INDEX *325*

LIST OF ILLUSTRATIONS

....

Figures

Figure 4.1. Exposure to Urban Violence and School Noncompletion *109*

Figure 5.1. The Class Convergence of Inner-City Children
of Latino Immigrants *134*

Tables

Table 7.1. Urban Latino Cognitive Frame Types *191*

Table A.1. Socioeconomic Characteristics of the Two Neighborhoods
and Los Angeles County, 2000 and 2010 *268*

Table A.2. Racial-Ethnic Composition of the Two Neighborhoods
and Los Angeles County, 2000 and 2010 *268*

ABOUT THE AUTHOR

....

María G. Rendón is a sociologist and assistant professor in the department of urban planning and public policy.

ACKNOWLEDGMENTS

....

I feel a deep connection to the places where I grew up, two communities in South Los Angeles. I spent my childhood in Wilmington, a predominantly Mexican community, and my adolescence in Lynwood, a black and Latino community then. Growing up in these communities shaped who I am and, not surprisingly, what I study. I am fascinated by the urban context and the ways in which Latinos—both immigrant and U.S.-born—have adapted to and transformed these neighborhoods. My parents are immigrants with modest levels of schooling, one having arrived without documents in the late 1970s. As a child of low-skilled immigrants, I subscribe to the "immigrant bargain" like the study participants in this book, intent on making my labor worthy of my family's sacrifice. Having grown up in a neighborhood affected by gang violence in the 1980s and 1990s and attended some of California's most segregated low-income public and underperforming schools, I was attuned to—and wrestled with—some of the challenges respondents describe in this book. I was fortunate in my youth to come across Chicano/Latino activists, inspiring teachers, and others who gave me the knowledge to understand my social context and the language to articulate the various issues of social injustice that plagued our community. I credit this early mentorship to my academic pursuits—the seeds of this book. It was during my own transition to adulthood, as I navigated America's system of higher education, including one of its most elite contexts, that I came to more fully understand America's drastic disparities in opportunities across race, class, and geography. The consequences of America's inequality have come into sharper focus for me as I have lived in different types of communities with vastly different resources; some communities have the resources to provide residents with opportunities to reach their full potential, while in others opportunity is denied because resources are lacking.

This book aims to show why it is that those who grow up in predominantly Latino and black, lower-income urban communities have a harder time securing a place in the American middle class. Though I share common ground with the Latinx millennials in my study, the book recognizes that these young men face a more brutal economic and housing context than did those who came before them. This generation has made great strides in educational pursuits, but the ladder they climb is steeper. Young inner-city men of color confront specific barriers that further complicate their efforts to get ahead, including a dominant narrative about them that overlooks their efforts. I hope that this book sheds light on their lives and the obstacles they confront, as well as on their resourcefulness and determination.

I have a village of people to thank—my support and social leverage ties have played a critical role in my journey to become an academic and complete this book. I have been blessed at every turn with individuals willing to invest in me and to take the time to guide, advise, and encourage me, even when I had doubts. Every step mattered. Antonio Portillo, whom I have known since high school, profoundly shaped my identity as a Chicana. I thank him for handing me invincible armor to wear when I have navigated spaces historically denied to people like us. I thank Cesar Sereseres and Ramon Munoz, two long-term champions of Latinx first-generation college students. Their dedicated service transformed the lives of many, and I thank them for nudging me into graduate school. These early mentors inspired me to dream big, pushed me, and opened up opportunities beyond anything I could ever imagine. I owe them in ways I can never repay.

People like me survive institutions like Harvard, a context starkly at odds with our lived experience, through the help of compassionate people, mentors, and advocates. I am indebted to Mary C. Waters, Xavier de Souza Briggs, William J. Wilson, and Robert Sampson, who encouraged and supported the initial study. My scholarship has been strongly influenced by the work of Bill and Rob, and I was fortunate to receive their guidance in developing this study. Both challenged me in ways that made my work stronger; Bill even provided line-by-line feedback at one point in graduate school. Xav was highly attuned to the experiences of black and Latino first-generation graduate students like me. He created safe spaces and made many of us feel that we belonged in the academy. I grew immensely as an ethnographer in the Moving to Opportunity ethnographic study he directed; he helped demystify the research process and, with his wife Cynthia and mother Angela, also warmly opened his home on several occasions—the kind of support one never forgets.

Perhaps Mary Waters knew what she was signing on for back when she encouraged me to do this study; in any event, I am eternally grateful and humbled by the extensive support she has provided over the years, for everything from my nascent ideas to the completion of this book. Mary has read and reread my work and helped it evolve. I thank her for her kindness, for not giving up on me, and for supporting my efforts to balance work and family demands. She has been generous and opened up opportunities, always reminding me that I have something valuable to contribute. This book could not have been completed without her unwavering support all these years.

Several people helped to broker access to the two neighborhoods in my study. Unfortunately, the need to maintain the anonymity of the study participants prevents me from naming them. You know who you are, and I thank you for making this study happen. Most of these individuals have played significant roles in the lives of youth and immigrant families in these communities. I thank them for their dedication to improving conditions in these neighborhoods and the lives of their residents. I can openly thank Diego James Vigil, who was highly instrumental in brokering some of these relationships. His scholarship on Los Angeles has garnered him great respect, and he opened doors for me. I thank my parents, Juan and Socorro Rendón, who welcomed me back home during the fieldwork, always supporting my efforts, and Xav Briggs, who arranged for me to have office space during my fieldwork at the Tomas Rivera Policy Center at the University of Southern California.

I received generous financial support to carry out both phases of the study. At Harvard, the Achievement Gap Initiative Fellowship and the Multidisciplinary Program in Inequality and Social Policy Grant provided funds for the first data collection. A dissertation improvement grant from the National Science Foundation (0703221) helped with the transcriptions. I was also supported by the Ford Foundation and the Public Policy Institute of California. I began discussions on a book proposal as a postdoctoral

Robert Wood Johnson Health Policy Fellow at the University of California–Berkeley/UC–San Francisco. Sandra Smith and Daniel Dohan were excellent mentors who were critical in my transition from student to independent scholar. Their candid and thoughtful comments elevated my early academic writings, giving it greater rigor. Both challenged me in ways that sharpened my thinking. Dan introduced me to the grant-writing process, and Sandra pushed me hard to exceed my expectations; I owe them greatly. The other RWJ fellows were the first to hear of my book idea, and I thank them for their early feedback. The RWJ program left an imprint on the book, shaping how I came to understand violence from a public health lens, and I thank that program for investing in me.

I began my second wave of data collection as a junior faculty member. I was fortunate to receive a New Scholar Grant from the Stanford Center on Poverty and Inequality to return to the field. At UC–Irvine, the Council on Research, Computing, and Libraries Cultural Research Grant (2013-2014-43) and the Hellman Fellowship also supported this effort. The Russell Sage Foundation extended a Presidential Award (88-15-03) for the analysis of these data. At RSF, Aixa Citron was instrumental in helping me bring clarity to the book proposal, and I thank the two anonymous RSF book proposal reviewers for their feedback; it strongly shaped the direction of this book. In the end, data became quite voluminous and several graduate and undergraduate students were hired to help me transcribe, code some of these data, and produce case reports of study participants. Laureen Hom and Kaitlyn Noli were reliably superb graduate students, as were Marina Corrales, Susan Guadarrama, Alma Zaragoza-Petty, and my postdoctoral fellow, Adriana Aldana. I had stellar undergraduates advancing the project, several of whom are now in graduate school. In particular, I thank Sonja Huang, Gabriela Manzo, Zaira Martinez, Yoselinda Mendoza, Brianna Ramirez, Orlando Ramirez, and Jacqueline Rodriguez.

The questions and comments I have received at the conferences where I have shared this work over the years also inform this book. Preliminary findings were aired at the Hispanic Poverty, Inequality, and Social Mobility Conference at the Stanford Center for Poverty and Inequality; at various colloquiums at UC–Irvine and at the Institute for Research on Poverty at the University of Wisconsin–Madison. Chapters of the book were presented at the Sociology of Education conference; the National Network of Hospital-Based Violence Intervention Program; conferences at UC–Davis, UCLA, and UC–Riverside; and several meetings of the

American Sociological Association, the Latin American Studies Association, the Latinx Studies Association, and the Society for the Study of Social Problems.

I am especially thankful to friends and colleagues who read chapters of the book and gave invaluable feedback. I thank each and every one of them for taking the time to help me sort out arguments and offering detailed editorial comments and constructive criticism. Among the many who helped me advance this book at one point or another were: Michael Calderon-Zaks, Leo Chavez, Susan B. Coutin, Silvia Dominguez, Laura E. Enriquez, Cynthia Feliciano, Glenda Flores, Cybelle Fox, David Harding, Luisa Heredia, Tomas Jimenez, Cecilia Menjívar, David S. Meyer, Laura Lopez-Sanders, Susan Smith, Natasha Warikoo, and, of course, Mary Waters. My colleagues in the Department of Urban Planning and Public Policy at UC–Irvine have been great and supportive. I want to especially thank Martha Feldman, Doug Houston, Nicholas Marantz, Walter Nicholls, Seth Pipkins, Rudy Torres, and Nicola Ulibarri, who also read my work and provided strong encouragement. Many others shaped the book through informal conversations over the years; I thank Adriana Aldana, Frank Bean, Irene Bloomraad, Susan Brown, Jeanett Castellanos, Victor Chen, Gil Conchas, Randol Contreras, Shana Gadarian, Roberto Gonzales, Laureen Hom, Helen Marrow, Joanie Mazelis, Richard Mora, Wendy Roth, Rubén Rumbaut, Frank Samson, Mario Small, Edward Telles, Van Tran, and Christopher Wimer. Kate Epstein provided immensely valuable editorial help at various stages of this process, as did the editorial team at the Russell Sage Foundation. Portions of chapter 4 appeared in earlier form in *Social Problems* (Rendón 2014), and chapter 7 appeared in *City and Community* (Rendón 2019).

Institutional support matters greatly. After the dean at the School of Social Ecology at UC–Irvine, Valerie Jenness, instituted funding for "book conferences" for junior faculty members, I was able to share my first draft with three great scholars—Cecilia Menjívar, Sandra Smith, and David Harding. They carefully read the first version of the manuscript and helped transform it in important ways. They pushed my thinking and were instrumental in reorganizing the book, helping me extract its main contributions. The RSF editor, Suzanne Nichols, was patient with me as I worked on this book. Suzanne and the three anonymous reviewers who read the manuscript provided incredible feedback that helped solidify my argument, expand my contributions, and ultimately helped me find my voice.

I began this venture with two children under the age of two and completed the book as a single parent. I have been blessed with a super family who facilitated this process in a multitude of ways. The book could not have been completed without the help and support of my closest kin. I have the best parents, Juan and Socorro Rendón, who never fail to step in when I need them the most. They cheer me on and encourage me—even as they tried to make sense of this road less traveled—and provide countless days of child care on weekends and during my times away at conferences. They never cease showing their love in the practical ways they know. My sisters, Yolanda and Rosa, step in as well. I share with them the fantastic experience of being a child of *our* immigrant parents, and there is never a dull moment as we navigate our second-generation in-between worlds and the endless faux pas that come with our cross-cultural experience, always ending in a good laugh. I am blessed with an extended family—grandparents, many *tias* and *tios,* lots of cousins—who keep me grounded: the entire Rendón clan, the Castros, and the Moraleses and Cerdas. In particular, I am grateful for my cousin and *comadre* Patricia Cerda-Lizarraga, who started college with me and rode the PhD roller coaster too. In Texas and across the border in San Luis Potosi, the Nietos have cheered me on from far away. I also have friends who are like family and who provide good times and endless moral support, including my Lynwood and UCI college friends and in particular Magdalena Cerda, Johnny Chavez (the book cover photographer), Cybelle Fox, Irene Gonzales, Luisa Heredia, Laura Kosek, Laura Lopez-Sanders, Miriam Nuno, Brisa Sanchez, and Angel Suarez. I am lucky to have all of you.

This book is dedicated to my daughters, Julieta and Gaby. They have grown up knowing Mommy was writing a book. I'm deeply touched that they take pride in my labor. I could not have asked for more patient, understanding, and encouraging kids. They have accomplished much more than I have during this process and become two incredibly loving, smart, witty, thoughtful, kind, and simply amazing girls. No words can capture the love and pride I have for you, Julieta and Gaby. You are my world.

I will always be indebted to the young men and their parents who gave me their time and opened their lives and homes to me, exposing their deepest scars and greatest dreams. I thank them for trusting me and hope that I have done justice to their stories. I also hope that readers come to better understand their world, including the hurdles they surmount as they carve out their lives in the United States.

CHAPTER 1

Introduction

The Inner City and Second-Generation Latinos

enaro was twenty years old when I first met him in 2007 and
enthusiastic about his future. He wore a short-sleeved, button-
down shirt and slightly baggy jeans and had a clean-cut "fade."
With a cheerful smile and an upbeat manner, Genaro was quick to share.
The day I first met him we sat on two old chairs in the front yard of his
parents' two-bedroom home surrounded by fruit trees, a warm breeze, and
an untamed garden. The home sat high on a hill, as if the family sat apart
from the social dynamics surrounding it. We were in the heart of one of
L.A.'s high-poverty Mexican immigrant neighborhoods. Genaro grew up
a few blocks away in the housing projects, which he described as the "war
zone." He remembered daily shootings, one of which took a playmate in
his front yard when Genaro was only eight. Genaro had run inside his
apartment to get his toy Ninja Turtle at the crucial moment. His family
lived there for ten years until the housing projects were demolished, and
they received government aid to purchase their home in 2000.

Genaro's parents and siblings tried hard to ensure that he did not slip
into a gang, and he never did. But at sixteen years old, Genaro was caught
in a brawl that broke out at a local park during a football game one summer
evening. He went to the hospital with caved-in teeth after receiving a blow
to the chin with a gun by a local gang member. After reconstructive surgery,
sixteen stitches in his lips, and months of recovery, Genaro sought to avoid
further problems with the gang members attending his school by switching

schools. Yet he was assaulted on his walk home on the first day. Ultimately, he stopped attending school altogether in his senior year. He was "never really into" school, he explained.

In much of the literature, as well as in the public imagination, the life of Genaro stopped when he dropped out of school. We assume that a life of struggle in the labor market followed, as well as continued exposure to violence and the close watch of law enforcement. Few studies examine the lives of inner-city young men past their adolescence, and exceptions rarely address the children of immigrants, who make up one-quarter of young adults in the United States today.[1] We know little about how they adapt to American city life and how urban neighborhoods shape their life trajectories, if at all. The inner city is understood as a risky place that can derail young men's achievement and attainment in school and the labor market by drawing them into criminal activity and local conflicts. As this book will show, this narrative simplifies life in these neighborhoods. It ignores how Latino immigrants and their children fend off urban conditions, altering the organizational and cultural context of these communities as they do so.[2] This dominant narrative of central cities also masks the less sensational, obscure ways in which urban conditions reproduce racial and class inequality. In this book, I show how America's poor, segregated neighborhoods reproduce the working-class background of children of Latino immigrants, specifically those of Mexican origin.

I capture the story of those young Latino men who are often labeled "at risk" because of their race-ethnicity, gender, and zip code and who are at a crossroad, attempting to integrate into the larger American context and carve out a space in its dwindling middle class. I follow the lives of forty-two male offspring of post-1965 Latino immigrants from two high-poverty neighborhoods in Los Angeles as they transition into adulthood. Their parents settled in the city between the late 1970s and early 1990s during a particularly turbulent time. Economic restructuring, failed policy, and government disinvestment had led to unprecedented concentrations of poverty in cities throughout the United States, and those levels of poverty brought deteriorating urban conditions in the 1980s, including a rise in violence that peaked in the mid-1990s. By that time, Latino immigrant communities in Los Angeles had become as poverty-concentrated and hypersegregated as poor, black urban neighborhoods.[3]

In 2007, I immersed myself in the two focal neighborhoods, among the most disadvantaged in Los Angeles. Close to 40 percent of their residents lived under the poverty line. I set out to understand the impact of the urban context on their integration process. I got to know these young men well, meeting them many times that year as I conducted in-depth interviews with them and their immigrant parents. I observed life in these two neighborhoods and learned how the urban context factored into their daily lives and, ultimately, how it shaped their social mobility trajectories. In learning how these young men made sense of their neighborhoods and how they made decisions that affected their life prospects, I gained a window into their understanding of American life and their chances of getting ahead. A year later, the Great Recession of 2008 set in, reinforcing poverty concentration in both of the focal neighborhoods. The signs had been there, from growing instability in the housing market to challenges in the labor market, and Latinos were especially hard-hit.[4] Then, in 2012–2013, I followed up with half of these young men—now in their mid to late twenties—and their parents to learn how they had fared. I wanted to learn how these inner-city Latino millennials had gotten by during this difficult time, the strategies they had employed to get ahead, and if and how their views had changed about the American opportunity structure and their chances to succeed.[5]

From the beginning, my aim has been to understand how conditions in American urban neighborhoods shape the lives of the children of low-skilled Latino immigrants. This study will consequently show how America's urban violence and social isolation in segregated contexts shape the integration process of young Latino men. I also call attention to underappreciated resources in these communities that mitigate the negative impacts of growing up in America's poorest neighborhoods. I explain why some young men get ahead, while others sink deeper into poverty. Finally, I also reveal how Latino immigrants and their young adult children change their neighborhoods and become part of L.A.'s resilient working class.

Children of Latino Immigrants in the American Inner City

The central city poses challenges to the Latinx second generation. Entrenched segregation isolates ethnic and racial minorities in high-poverty communities where they encounter failing schools, limited resources, a high incidence of violence and crime, and heavy police surveillance.[6] Studies are clear. Urban residents have worse physical and mental health than people living in more affluent neighborhoods, including higher rates of infant mortality and low birthweight and higher rates of obesity, anxiety, and depression.[7] Youth growing up in these neighborhoods experience worse life outcomes than youth elsewhere. Living in urban neighborhoods correlates with higher odds of being a victim of, and engaging in, crime and violence and of being incarcerated.[8] On average, youth in these neighborhoods obtain fewer years of schooling, score lower on achievement tests, and have higher odds of dropping out of school than their counterparts in more affluent neighborhoods.[9] Over the life course, they earn less than those growing up elsewhere.[10] In short, the American urban context dampens the social mobility prospects of inner-city residents and stalls the successful integration process of the second generation, particularly nonwhite children of low-skilled Latino immigrants.

The social mobility stagnation in American cities is not inevitable. At the turn of the nineteenth century, waves of poor and unskilled Southern and Eastern European immigrants and their children settled in the industrial slums of American cities. Despite the concentration of poverty, disease, and crime, these neighborhoods became stepping-stones in the integration process of these ethnic groups. Poor white ethnics were aided by a prevalence of manufacturing jobs, the rise of unions, strengthened workers' rights, and various forms of governmental aid, including access to low-interest housing loans and free or cheap college tuition rates that allowed them to climb the mobility ladder and build wealth to pass on to the next generation. Yet race matters greatly in America. People of color, including Mexican Americans, were denied such opportunities and confined to segregated contexts via restrictive covenants and other mechanisms of racial exclusion.[11] Although civil rights legislation outlawed blatant forms of racial discrimination, housing discrimination practices and a legacy of segregation persist across our cities, sustaining racial inequality.

It has also become harder to get ahead in American society.[12] Today's economic and political context does not offer low-skilled immigrants and their children the same kind of opportunities for social mobility that were available a hundred years ago; in fact, even white Americans are increasingly left behind. Neoliberal economic restructuring has led to the decline of unions and resulted in decades of flattened wages for all Americans except the highest earners. Government retrenchment now leaves low- and middle-income families with few support mechanisms to help them deal with rising housing and living costs. With rising inequality, the middle class has shrunk, and so have the number of middle-class neighborhoods.[13]

Spatial inequality is more entrenched now along class, racial, and ethnic lines. The affluent are more isolated than in previous generations, while the number of high-poverty neighborhoods in the United States—communities with 20 to 40 percent of the residents living under the poverty line—is higher than ever recorded. This poverty has spread into American suburbs, but the most extreme concentrated poor communities remain in historically segregated, urban neighborhoods.[14]

Rising inequality affects most Americans, but those in poor, urban (and, increasingly, suburban) segregated neighborhoods have a much harder time getting ahead.[15] We know some of the reasons why this is so, including the profound impact of institutions in urban neighborhoods on the life chances of residents. Today Latinx children are more segregated in urban schools than they were during the civil rights era, with the highest levels of isolation in California.[16] Spatial inequality results in a system of highly unequal schools that rewards those in affluent neighborhoods with quality education and opportunities for advancement but not others.[17] In central cities, poorly resourced schools struggle year after year to shepherd their students to a high school diploma and into institutions of higher education.[18] These schools face overcrowded classrooms and challenging social environments. While middle-class and affluent students benefit from having greater access to enrichment programs, urban youth must contend with a different kind of institution that can alter their lives: law enforcement. In urban schools, young men experience heavy police surveillance and criminalization that results in high rates of incarceration.[19]

At the same time, there is much we still do not know about urban neighborhoods and how they shape people's lives. More research is needed to understand the social processes and mechanisms within neighborhoods that affect life outcomes.[20] Research shows that some residents are more affected by their neighborhood than others. While few studies of neighborhood effects are longitudinal, those that exist show that neighborhood effects vary across the life span and depend on the extent of exposure.[21] The bulk of this research is focused on youth outcomes; we know less about the impact of neighborhoods into the adult years. More studies are needed to sort out why some urban residents are consumed by ill conditions, while others manage to thrive.

Latinx young adults, most whom are second-generation, are particularly underresearched. Their urban communities are not just poor and segregated, but also highly immigrant in character. The bulk of urban sociology and research on neighborhood effects remains focused on the poor black experience, and we know less about Mexican-origin contexts, as these have not historically concentrated in the Rust Belt cities that dominate this literature. Although some scholars suggest that immigrants revitalize poor urban neighborhoods, we know little as to why this might be so.[22] Moreover, few scholars have examined what happens if a community has a large undocumented population.[23] Despite the fact that Latinos are the largest minority group in the United States, we know little of how American urban neighborhoods shape their integration process.

The American imagination, as well as academic scholarship, fills the gaps in our understanding of how inner cities matter with dominant narratives. We see the inner city as a place of contagion. While some scholars highlight the role of institutions, others emphasize the socialization and acculturation processes that drive poor life outcomes there. These studies suggest that outcomes like dropping out of high school or engaging in crime function like epidemics, spreading through peer influence.[24] Seminal studies by William Julius Wilson and Douglas Massey and Nancy Denton once suggested that an "underclass culture" elicited antisocial behavior that reproduced urban poverty.[25] Such oppositional culture, they argued, was rooted in poverty concentration and social isolation. Urban scholarship on crime and violence has flourished since then, and many studies have documented the sweep of the crack epidemic in the 1980s and 1990s through these neighborhoods.[26] This heavy emphasis on crime and violence as the most dominant feature of these neighborhoods has resulted in a skewed representation of urban residents in the academic literature. Images in popular culture reinforce the notion that the urban poor are culturally distinct from mainstream America.

Segmented Assimilation and Downward Assimilation

In the 1990s, academics sounded the alarm about the future prospects of children of the Mexican immigrants who were settling in large numbers in America's urban neighborhoods. Today the dominant framework guiding our understanding of how the urban context factors into the integration process of children of immigrants is *segmented assimilation*.[27] The 1965 Immigration and Nationality Act had greatly diversified the flow of immigrants to the United States in terms of national and class origin, and Alejandro Portes and his colleagues projected *segmented* paths of integration for these immigrants' children.[28] Immigrants fare differently in American society given their national origin, race, class, and ethnic resources; some are embraced, while others are rejected. Segmented assimilation scholars projected that most children of highly skilled immigrants would experience automatic entry into the American middle or upper class, while they feared that those from humble backgrounds might be locked out.[29] They noted that those growing up in the inner city, like Genaro, were especially at risk of faring worse than even their low-skilled immigrant parents.

In line with urban sociological research at the time, segmented assimilation suggested that negative socialization processes in the inner city drove the poor outcomes of the Latino second generation there, such as their low educational attainment and high levels of incarceration. Immigration scholars have long deemed acculturation—the process of adopting the cultural outlooks, values, and norms of the host country—as the first step in the integration process for immigrants living in the American inner city. It has long been believed that American urban conditions corrupt children of immigrants. Citing Bonnie Kahn, Philip Kasinitz and his colleagues, explain, "Complaints that the children of immigrants were becoming the 'wrong kind' of Americans are also not new. As early as 1906, *The Outlook* magazine warned 'against rushing Italian children' into the 'streetiness' and 'cheap Americanism' which 'so overwhelms Italian youngsters in the cities.'"[30]

In the early 1990s, segmented assimilation scholars suggested that exposure to "downtrodden" U.S.-born racial minorities (African Americans or Chicanos) in the inner city caused children of immigrants to adopt an oppositional culture.[31] Alejandro Portes and Rubén Rumbaut hypothesized that "new cultural patterns" adopted by the second generation and their "entry into American social circles" in the inner city would "not lead to upward mobility but the exact opposite."[32] The Latino second generation was deemed at risk of *downward assimilation* by adopting an "adversarial" identity and a cultural orientation that dismissed school and work and leaned toward delinquency.[33] Herbert Gans labeled this "second-generation decline," explaining that nonwhite children of low-skilled immigrants "would reject immigrant-type jobs" but "lack the skills to do better."[34] Rumbaut pointed out that assimilation had its "discontents" and that, for children of low-skilled immigrants settling in poor, segregated neighborhoods, it would be devastating.[35] Tight-knit ethnic ties were said to enhance social control and buffer the second generation from risks in urban neighborhoods.[36] The problem was that some groups, like Mexicans, lacked such ethnic social capital. Mexican communities were seen not as resource-ful ethnic enclaves, but as *barrios* (segregated places of disadvantage), making Mexicans the textbook example of a group at risk of "downward assimilation."

Segmented assimilation remains a useful framework to explain diver-gent patterns of incorporation among children of immigrants. It high-lights how immigrants vary in their mode of incorporation and how this mode interacts with the context of reception.[37] Yet the framework makes only theoretical predictions of how urban neighborhoods matter. To date, few studies have examined how children of Latino immigrants are adapt-ing to the American city, how the local context shapes their acculturation process, and the extent to which the structural or cultural conditions of urban neighborhoods affect their integration.[38] Fewer studies examine how the growing presence of immigrants in America's cities has altered these communities, if at all.

Segmented assimilation theorists have rightfully identified the segre-gated urban context as detrimental for the incorporation process of chil-dren of low-skilled immigrants, yet they have mistaken the mechanisms driving poor life outcomes there. By following a group of Latinos from the inner city as they come of age, I have been able to take a close look at these processes that has led me to challenge key aspects of the dominant narra-tive. Segmented assimilation scholars underestimate the resources within the Mexican community that inhibit downward assimilation. The cultural outlooks and social capital of the Latino second generation are assets—not deficits—that nonetheless do not prevent class stagnation. My findings align with Vilma Ortiz's characterization of the Mexican-origin group in Los Angeles as "the permanent working class."[39] In the chapters that fol-low, I examine how American urban conditions reproduce the working-class background of the young men I interviewed. I also highlight the role of urban violence in derailing their prospects and detail how class and racial segregation denies Latinos opportunities to expand their networks and integrate into the broader American society. By focusing on violence and social isolation but also on the institutions and social resources of the Mexican community, I propose different mechanisms to explain outcomes among the second generation. Unlike the implication of the segmented assimilation framework, it is not the cultural attitudes of the second gener-ation that put them at risk; rather, violence, isolation, and lack of institu-tional support are the major hurdles.

American urban conditions weigh differently on individuals; not all young Latino men are similarly at risk in urban environments. Latinos' social capital varies and collides with urban conditions and the labor market to produce different outcomes. Although most of the young men in my study were positioned to remain working-class, some slipped deeper into poverty over the course of my research, while a few made the quantum leap into the American middle class.

The American Dream: Captivating Imaginations, Obscuring Structures of Inequality

Genaro jumped full force into the labor market after leaving school, convinced that he would work his way up in American society. A strong work ethic permeated his immigrant neighborhood, and aligning with this orientation gave him a sense of moral worth despite his lack of a high school diploma. His search for the job that would offer mobility led him to work in quick succession for Pizza Hut, UPS, a department store, and then a shoe store; all of these jobs had erratic hours and paid less than $8 an hour in 2007. When I met him that summer, he was three years out of high school and was ecstatic that he had just landed and started a job as a bank teller a few blocks from his home. A neighborhood friend had told him about the opening for the job, which paid $10.25 an hour for a forty-hour workweek, plus benefits. It was the kind of job his parents had hoped their children would get, a step up from the tedious and meagerly paid blue-collar work they knew. Genaro's eyes lit up as he voiced his lofty ambitions: he would move up the occupational ladder, take a managerial role, and perhaps become CEO one day. That was how one got ahead in American society—through hard work and effort.

Genaro would work that dream job at the bank for only a year; he lost his job in the Great Recession of 2008. For a year and a half afterwards, he sought work. Struggling to make car and cell-phone payments and hesitant to burden his low-earning parents, he developed what he called "bad habits"—check fraud and selling drugs. "I realized the length a person would go when they are desperate," he recalled when we met again years later. He fortunately eluded arrest before finding another job, and his family is still unaware of his short stint in crime. But his eyes welled up with tears as he explained that he knew at the time that his behavior "was hurting my whole family." Genaro voiced what upset him the most: "My parents come for the American Dream, and they want everything better, but they see us in these holes. It's like, was it really a dream, what [my parents] came here for?"

Same Dream, Different Opportunities

The young men I interviewed, like young Latinos in other studies, embarked upon their transition to adulthood with much enthusiasm. The second generation gains this optimism from immigrant parents whose narrative emphasizes hard work and sacrifice as a means to succeed in the United States.[40] Like their parents, the Mexican second generation adopts a transnational lens to understand their social position in the United States, and this informs how they understand their future prospects.[41] Even the most disadvantaged are optimistic. Of one young woman Portes and his colleagues note, "There is something truly moving in her [second-generation young adult] belief . . . that she can be 'master of her own destiny.' Against all odds, she keeps holding on to her dreams."[42] My study explores in part how young men sustain this optimism in the face of great adversity and stagnant mobility and why most inner-city Latinos remain strong believers in the American Dream.

The optimism of the second generation has led scholars like Richard Alba, Philip Kasinitz, and Mary Waters to suggest that the second generation is "mostly doing alright."[43] In their seminal study of young adult children of immigrants in New York, Kasinitz and his colleagues find that children of low-skilled immigrants (Colombian, Dominican, Chinese) fare better, on average, than their parents and native-born racial minorities, like blacks or Puerto Ricans.[44] Research on children of Mexican immigrants find they too fare better than their parents on important measures.[45] On average, Mexican immigrants arrive in the United States with an elementary education, but most of their children complete high school and many enroll in college, surpassing all other ethnic groups in educational gain from one generation to the next.[46] Robert Smith explains that Mexican immigrants hold their children to an "immigrant bargain"—the expectation that they will do justice to their parents' sacrifice—and he notes that the second generation tries to live up to this expectation.[47]

Still, there is little sign that the Mexican second generation is making enough gains to successfully integrate into the American "mainstream" middle class. This group continues to lag behind most other racial and ethnic groups in educational attainment and income. Their high school non-completion rates are still double the national average, and though Latinx high school graduates now surpass whites in college enrollment, they have the lowest college graduation rates of all ethnic groups.[48] Young Latino men fall behind their female coethnics in schooling and face above-average rates of incarceration, further complicating their prospects in the labor market. In addition, third-generation Mexican Americans do not show similar gains over the second generation and may be worse off in terms of education and income.[49] Thus, the American Dream of improved circumstances with each passing generation and eventual integration into the American middle class has been withheld from Mexican Americans.[50]

As scholars point out, the context of reception matters greatly. The young men in this study began their integration into the United States with a formidable disadvantage as their parents experienced one of the most hostile modes of incorporation. Portes and his colleagues identify three contexts of reception that welcome immigrants—governmental, societal, and communal—and shape the integration of immigrants and their children.[51] Portes and Rumbaut explain, "No matter how motivated and ambitious immigrants are, their future prospects will be dim if government officials persecute them, natives consistently discriminate against them, and their own community has only minimum resources to offer."[52]

The young men's parents to whom I spoke arrived in the United States as the government was taking an increasingly hostile stand toward Mexican migration. The government toughened its southern border in unprecedented fashion beginning in the early 1990s. And the political context in the United States has only worsened since then. By the time these young men were transitioning into adulthood, the country was experiencing the most massive deportation campaign in its history—a threat to the one-quarter of the young men in this study who were in mixed-status families.[53] The hostility experienced by the Mexican-origin group reached new heights by the end of this study as presidential candidate Donald Trump kicked off his campaigned labeling Mexican immigrants "murderers and rapists." During his presidency—and in the face of declining rates of immigration from Mexico—Trump declared a national emergency to secure funding for a wall along the U.S.-Mexico border, cut funding to three Latin American countries supposedly to "punish" them for the immigration of some of their citizens, and separated Central American asylum seekers from their children.

The disadvantage of the Mexican-origin group in American society has deep roots that extend beyond the immigrant experience. Mexican Americans have been incorporated into the United States as a nonwhite racial minority group and historically have experienced various forms of violence and exclusion similar to those faced by other people of color.[54] Prior to the arrival of post-1965 immigrants, Mexican Americans were racially segregated via restrictive covenants and denied access to fair housing. They were denied integration into schools and other American institutions as a function of race.[55] Precisely these conditions of racial exclusion and isolation gave root to some of the earliest Mexican American gangs in Los Angeles, who over time became institutionalized in their neighborhoods.[56] Studies show that discriminatory housing practices continue to steer Latinos to low-income neighborhoods and that predatory lending to this community, as in some other communities, exacerbated the foreclosure crisis of the Great Recession and left them devastated.[57] In poor and segregated urban neighborhoods and schools, young Latino men are criminalized, reinforcing their racialization and marginalization.[58]

The young men in this study came of age at a time when it is increasingly difficult to enter or remain a part of the American middle class.[59] The manufacturing sector that embraced generations of Americans, particularly low-skilled European immigrants and their children, is no longer the engine for upward mobility in the United States. Instead, young adults find a polarized labor market, offering well-paid, high-skilled jobs on one end and menial, low-wage service jobs on the other. Young adults are attending college at higher rates than previous generations, yet American institutions of higher education—from selective universities to community colleges and for-profit institutions—are failing these students, particularly those who are first-generation college students.[60] Today, only 40 percent of Americans earn an associate's or bachelor's degree by the age of twenty-seven. Outcomes are even more dismal for young people of color: only 30 percent of African Americans and fewer than 20 percent of Latinos in their midtwenties have an associate's degree or higher.[61] In our demanding economy, it is not more years of schooling that improve a young person's chances of climbing the social ladder, but earning a diploma or certificate, which most who enroll in college do not obtain. As a result, millennials are more educated than previous generations, but also more likely to live with their parents (30 percent) and in poverty (20 percent) than earlier generations.[62]

The young men in this study contended with rising college tuition, flattened wages, and a higher cost of living. These economic conditions have altered the transition to adulthood of the whole generation, who are now postponing marriage and childbearing and finding it harder to establish economic independence and financial security. As inequality has skyrocketed, the social safety net has thinned until it is nearly absent. In this neoliberal era, Americans—and particularly the poor—must increasingly fend for themselves.[63] Within this broader economic and political context, some scholars see a dim future for second-generation Latinos, especially those coming of age in disadvantaged neighborhoods.

In this book, I explain how American urban neighborhoods factor into Latinos' class stagnation. At the same time, I highlight the paradox of the American urban context: it denies residents opportunities to get ahead, while sustaining the concept of the American Dream. Despite rising inequality, most young men in my study kept faith they could get ahead, holding on to America's promise. America's urban residents, particularly the most marginalized, adhere strongly to a meritocratic ideology.[64] Latino immigrants and their children feed this ethos as they place their hopes and dreams in the promise of a better life.[65]

Genaro is no exception. Despite his setbacks, he found a job as a janitor at a swanky new hotel. Cleaning toilets "was horrible," but it "got his foot in the door"; he was determined to "use the opportunity to his advantage" and "squeeze" out of it what he could. By 2012, the twenty-seven-year-old high school noncompleter was a hotel representative earning $17 an hour on the swing shift. This was the same pay his older brother Pablo earned as a teaching assistant and community college student. At their age, they earned more than their father—a $10 an hour worker—ever did, a modest gain that gave them a sense of upward mobility, even if the actuality of upward mobility was lacking.[66] Most respondents were like Genaro, who lamented past mistakes but expressed a strong conviction that he would succeed: "I just see it from where we come from, we have overcome everything, you know? . . . There's no barrier for us. There's nothing holding us back. It all takes time, work, and effort, and if you mix those all up you can get yourself where you want to be. I know I am on the right path. I'm confident."

I challenge the idea that the cultural context of these neighborhoods and a lack of ethnic social capital are sources of vulnerability; in fact, I find the opposite to be true. Study participants had strong normative views of meritocracy, extolled sacrifice, adhered to the ethic of hard work that dominated in their communities, and relied extensively on social support from kin and community ties. Young men like Genaro leaned heavily on family in their young adult years. Kin support not only encourages young men but buffers them from the urban context and the whims of the economy. Many lived with their parents, took care of personal expenses, and sometimes helped their parents with bills. Kin and community ties ensured that they did not fall into despair. In a context of rising economic anxiety, government retrenchment, and hostility to immigrants, the young men in this study and their immigrant parents leaned on one another to get by and pull ahead.

At a time when they and their immigrant parents are charged with threatening America's cultural fabric, the Latinx second generation breathes life into the American Dream ideal—even as they encounter structures of inequality that relegate them to the bottom echelons of American society. The optimism and determination of the Latinx second generation contrast with the growing pessimism observed among the struggling white working class as they cope with economic stagnation.[67] Scholars suggest that American's social capital has declined, leading to fractured kin ties and disconnect from institutions and leaving many to indict themselves—or others—for their limited social mobility.[68] The efforts of young Latino men with a social support network are fueled by the concept of the American Dream, yet for those who are on their own—as are those most entrenched in the inner city—this ideology leads to self-blame. The American urban context does not debilitate because of an oppositional culture, but because it encourages meritocratic ideals that go unrealized, demoralizing the most vulnerable in a context of poverty and isolation.

Rethinking the Incorporation Process of Inner-City Children of Latino Immigrants

Urban sociology provides a theoretical backdrop to this study, as does the literature on immigrant integration, two bodies of work that have largely ignored each other. Segmented assimilation established an important rubric to conceptualize the integration process of children of immigrants. Building on this work, I advance the knowledge of how urban neighborhoods factor into this process by shifting attention to the structural features of American urban neighborhoods and the neighborhood mechanisms that complicate the integration process of the Latinx second generation. I examine why living in urban neighborhoods that are segregated by race and class matters.

Theoretically, I advance three lines of scholarship. First, I call attention to the urban neighborhood conditions and social processes shaping the lives of immigrants and their children.[69] I show how exposure to urban violence affects the second generation and how their social isolation impinges on their social mobility. In the process, I show how institutions and social networks moderate these effects. Second, I reconceptualize social capital in the case of the Mexican-origin group. I distinguish between social support and social leverage ties, highlighting the isolation of some, and show how the social context interacts with the urban context to produce divergent outcomes. Finally, I tackle the contentious debate around culture and acculturation in these inner cities. I examine closely how respondents make sense of their urban environment and the American opportunity structure and how these views inform their pursuit of social mobility. In doing so, I present the varying cultural outlooks of respondents to challenge the idea that acculturation drives poor outcomes in the group.

How Urban Neighborhoods Matter

Much has been theorized about the poor, segregated urban context and how it curtails social mobility, though few such studies have focused on Latinos. In urban sociology, the focus has been on the experience of poor African Americans and, sometimes, Puerto Ricans. Scholarship in the 1990s described the poverty concentration and segregation of Mexicans in the United States as "moderate," suggesting that the structural features of Mexican *barrios* made them less detrimental than black ghettos. Wilson noted "significant neighborhood differences" between Mexican and black communities, finding that Mexican neighborhoods in Chicago were "less poor" and featured "lower levels of joblessness and higher levels of social organization than comparable African-American neighborhoods."[70] Massey and Denton argued that because Mexican neighborhoods in Chicago were "considerably less segregated," they became less vulnerable to economic restructuring, and they pointed to the "moderate concentration of poverty" in these neighborhoods.[71] Drawing on these and other observations, several scholars then challenged the idea that an "underclass" culture existed in Mexican *barrios*.[72]

The social isolation of American urban residents has intensified since the 1990s and has now become particularly extensive among Latinos in Los Angeles. Today Mexicans are hypersegregated in the City of Angels and experience levels of poverty concentration comparable to those of many poor blacks.[73] As Massey now notes, we have moved into "an age of extremes," when class divisions are increasingly rigid as the geographic separation of the poor and the affluent amplifies and reinforces them.[74] Spatial inequality has risen, and the polarization of neighborhoods translates into growing isolation among the poor and the affluent alike.[75] Today in Los Angeles, Mexicans do not experience "moderate" levels of segregation and poverty concentration but rather "high" to "extreme" poor and segregated conditions.

Accounting for changes in Los Angeles, I draw attention to two features of the segregated urban context that immigration scholars have overlooked: urban violence and social isolation. I explain how these urban conditions affect the integration process of the Latinx second generation by constraining their social mobility prospects and shaping their acculturation. I also show how community institutions sometimes ameliorate these neighborhood effects but also sometimes aggravate them.

Urban Violence

American cities experienced unprecedented levels of violence in the 1980s and early 1990s. The violence was closely linked to the rise in poverty concentration in that period and the crack epidemic that swept through these neighborhoods. In Los Angeles, these conditions made local gangs, many with long histories in their community, much more violent than in the past. This violence declined beginning in the mid-1990s, but it remains one of the most crippling features of the American inner city. Violence threatens residents' sense of safety and mental and physical well-being to the point of causing post-traumatic stress disorder symptoms in some residents.[76] It negatively affects social mobility prospects by hurting educational attainment.[77] Violence also seeps into urban schools and impairs learning.[78] Urban violence affects the organizational and cultural context of neighborhoods; it encourages young men to adopt a "code of the street" and to structure their peer relations in ways that provide symbolic and physical protection.[79] Violence punctuated the daily lives of the young men I interviewed, complicating their efforts to get ahead and positioning some on a path to chronic poverty.

The immigrants in this study were taken aback by the violence in the 1980s and 1990s. They had left Mexico decades before the country was swept in the 2000s by an onslaught of drug cartel violence; the Mexico they knew was peaceful, especially for those migrating from rural towns. I discuss how immigrants' exposure to violence in American cities influenced how they established social relations and managed the context for their children. Immigrants responded to the violence and social disorder by imposing a moral order that made their urban neighborhoods culturally contested spaces for the second generation to navigate. Exposure to urban violence also influenced the way in which urban young men established social relations. Those who were highly exposed to violence and lacked kin and neighborhood support ties drew heavily on male peers' ties for protection. I show how this allegiance to peers influenced respondents' behavior in ways that were detrimental for their schooling. Urban violence impinges on the social mobility prospects of the Latino second generation, and I explain how it impacts their integration process.

Social Isolation

I draw on Wilson's definition of social isolation, which he describes as the "lack of contact or of sustained interaction with the individuals or institutions that represent mainstream society."[80] Wilson was especially concerned about the high rates of joblessness among black males, their marginalization from the labor market, and the impact of these issues on urban communities, including their social fabric.[81] Massey and Denton framed the social isolation of blacks similarly, couching it firmly within the legacy of racial segregation.[82] A consistent thread in these studies was the replication of poverty through the disconnectedness of urban communities from valuable opportunities—role models, information, institutional resources. Nevertheless, few studies have yet to examine the implication of Latinos' class and racial isolation and how this factors into their integration process.[83] In Los Angeles, research shows that spatial inequality along class and racial lines has resulted in the confinement of Latinos' social worlds primarily to Latinx spaces.[84] Not only do Latinos live in primarily Latino working-class or poor neighborhoods, but their schools and workplaces are also segregated by race and class.[85] The same is true for affluent whites in Los Angeles, who live, work, and spend their leisure time primarily in white, affluent spaces.

Immigration scholars have long noted that successful socioeconomic or structural integration occurs only when ethnic groups establish "primary" social ties with the dominant group through their cliques, clubs, and institutions.[86] Racial and class segregation stalls this process. In this study, I call attention to how Latinos' segregation reinforces insular working-class, ethnic ties, constraining their opportunities and social mobility. I point out that in the young adult years, most respondents' "social leverage ties"—those that help them get ahead—exist outside kin and neighborhood context.[87] Latinos' segregation limits their opportunity to establish these potential relationships.

Segregation matters in other ways. Latinos' social isolation shapes how they make sense of the American opportunity structure. Segregation insulates the second generation, reinforcing an inward orientation to the community in which the immigrant narrative and undocumented coethnics function as the main points of reference shaping the sense of opportunity in the United States. Their limited interaction with the middle and upper classes minimizes their exposure to racial and class inequalities, helping to sustain their belief in American meritocracy.[88] Respondents' beliefs shift as they are exposed to mainstream society, to whose "cliques, clubs and institutions" they have difficulty gaining access and which they find equally difficult to navigate. Loïc Wacquant explains that the urban poor experience "territorial stigma," that is, they are devalued, discredited, and tainted by the reputation of their neighborhoods, and Elijah Anderson notes that the "iconic ghetto" racializes blacks.[89] In Los Angeles, this effect extends to Latinos, as their association with the city's poorest neighborhoods informs others' perceptions of them, their self-perceptions, and their exclusion in everyday interactions when stepping out of their neighborhoods.[90]

Neighborhood Institutions

This study is not grounded in any given neighborhood institution; rather, it shows that neighborhood institutions weave in and out of the lives of young men to varying degrees and in contrasting ways. As noted, numerous studies on urban schools show the multifaceted ways in which these institutions often fail most of their students, positioning only a select few on a promising path.[91] In an era of mass incarceration, a plethora of studies have emerged that examine how law enforcement and heavy police surveillance have altered life in these neighborhoods, criminalizing young men of color in particular.[92] Literature on the school-to-prison pipeline further captures the intersection of these two institutions. Yet other studies draw attention to other types of community institutions, like programs that intervene in the lives of "at-risk" youth, such as sports leagues, boys' and girls' clubs, gang intervention programs, and church programs. The prominent role played by neighborhood institutions in the lives of urban youth is evident in urban scholarship as well as in studies on children of immigrants.[93] As I explain, some of these are also highly instrumental in helping immigrants adapt to and integrate into American society.

Neighborhood institutions moderate neighborhood effects. Throughout the book, I show how some of these institutions not only ameliorate the negative consequences of urban conditions but can drastically transform the life circumstances of young men. At the same time, as I show, trusted neighborhood institutions can reinforce disadvantage and collude with local conditions to lock young men in poverty.

Beyond Ethnic Ties: Reconceptualizing the Social Capital of Inner-City Latinos

I reconceptualize how we think social capital matters for second-generation Latinos. Immigration scholars suggest that the Mexican-origin group is vulnerable in the inner city because they lack social capital; the class homogeneity of predominantly low-skilled immigrants and presumed weak social ties are deemed to be sources of disadvantage.[94] Yet segmented assimilation muddles two types of social capital that I distinguish: ties that inhibit downward assimilation and those that facilitate upward mobility.

In emphasizing that cohesive ethnic ties function as a social control mechanism, segmented assimilation scholars suggest that strong ethnic ties reinforce parental normative controls and thwart adversarial cultural outlooks and behavior.[95] Portes, Fernández-Kelly, and Haller write:

> Community social capital depends less on the economic or occupational success of immigrants than on the density of ties among them. . . . Modest solidarity in communities can be a valuable resource, because their networks support parental guidance and parental aspirations for their children. . . . In densely integrated communities, where children have internalized the goals of occupational success through high educational achievement, the threat of downward assimilation effectively disappears.[96]

These scholars frequently reference Min Zhou and Carl Bankston's study, which found that strong cohesive ties in a low-income Vietnamese community in New Orleans allowed its members to reinforce conventional norms to discourage the formation of the oppositional identities associated with the American urban context.[97] Yet others point out that it is not just ethnic cohesion that matters. Waters and her colleagues explain:

> It is not the overall level of ties to the ethnic group . . . that leads to better outcomes. Rather it is maintaining ethnic ties within those groups which have significant numbers of middle-class, educated members that help children of poor immigrants. Ethnic embeddedness and social capital are helpful when they connect people to those with significant resources.[98]

Several studies support this claim, finding that cross-class ethnic ties help children of low-skilled immigrants get ahead in school.[99] Jennifer Lee and Min Zhou find that cross-class ethnic ties explain the Asian American paradox—that is, children of poor, unskilled Asian immigrants excelling academically above the norm.[100] Unskilled Asian immigrants, they observe, tap into the social and cultural resources of their middle-class or elite coethnics, while Mexicans, though they share similar values in regard to education, navigate America's educational system without such resources. In the absence of cross-class ethnic ties, these scholars find, low-skilled immigrants struggle to get ahead even when they have cohesive ethnic ties.

As they compare ethnic groups in their examinations of social capital at a community level, immigration scholars do not distinguish between the social ties that protect youth in the inner city and those that help them get ahead. I move away from this approach by examining social capital at the individual level instead, as "a resource for individual action that is stored in human relationships."[101] Taking this approach, Xavier de Souza Briggs finds two forms of social capital among the urban poor. One form of social capital is *social support,* which "helps one 'get by' or cope." Another is *social leverage,* which "helps one 'get ahead' or change one's opportunity set through access to job information, say, or a recommendation for a scholarship or loan." Social support stems from "bonding ties," those horizontal in nature, composed of similar individuals whose relationship is built on trust and reinforces norms and mores in the closed network, such as kin or neighbors. Social leverage is derived from "bridging ties" that typically lie "outside the neighborhood and, in general, [are] to people of higher socioeconomic status and different racial/ethnic groups."[102]

Second-generation Latinos vary in the extent to which they can draw on social support or social leverage, and this internal variation informs their social mobility trajectories. In this study, I also call attention to those who are devoid of *any* kind of social capital. These are the most socially isolated young men, the disconnected and marginalized *within* the disadvantaged neighborhoods. I show how institutions can alter the social capital of second-generation Latinos, providing both social support and social leverage.

Social Support

Segmented assimilation scholars suggest that the Mexican-origin group lacks ethnic cohesion, but research shows that their immigrant networks play a prominent role in their migration and settlement process. Scholars note that these ethnic networks help explain why the Mexican-origin group has the highest rate of employment.[103] Other scholars theorize that the "Latino health paradox"—the finding that Latinos are healthier than expected given their poverty rates—may be linked to their ethnic ties. The extent to which there is ethnic cohesion among the Mexican-origin group is inconclusive, as few studies examine how this changes over time and across generations. Yet numerous studies document the heavy reliance of the poor on kin and fictive kin to get by and to cope under challenging life circumstances, with varying success.[104] I find that kin and neighborhood ties helped respondents navigate the America urban context and the labor market and show that these bonding ties provide valuable and protective support.[105]

In particular, I show how the "ethnic cohesion" of Mexican immigrants is organized primarily around family and extended kin ties. Kin-based social capital in particular serves as an asset for young Latino men, and parents draw on this resource to buffer their sons' exposure to urban violence by limiting their time in the neighborhood and reinforcing conventional norms and values. In the face of limited job prospects and stagnant wages, immigrant kin instill optimism, a hard work ethic, and the norm of sacrifice to get ahead during the transition to adulthood. Intergenerational housing, links to jobs, and financial backing by kin soften the economic blows that can discourage others in poverty.[106] Heavy reliance on kin, however, comes at a cost, as kin stretch and exhaust one another's resources. In the absence of supportive kin, some immigrants and their children seek support via trusted community institutions, while others remain socially isolated. The bulk of the second generation, however, does not experience downward assimilation in large part owing to these support ties.

Social Leverage

Despite strong norms favoring education and social mobility, social support ties did not propel the Latinos I interviewed up the class ladder. By shifting the focus toward the American segregated context that sustains the insular ethnic and class ties of the second generation, I depart from scholars who focus on the lack of class diversity in their community.[107] Inner-city Latinos lack social leverage ties not only because they lack cross-class ethnic ties, but also because they are isolated from mainstream America, specifically from its dominant "cliques, clubs and institutions."[108]

Studies show that social leverage ties are critical for Latinx youth trying to access and navigate institutions of higher education.[109] Vivian Louie identifies these as "non-family ties," and others refer to them as bridging ties.[110] Ricardo Stanton-Salazar goes further, situating social leverage ties within institutions.[111] He identifies "institutional agents" as individuals "devoted to the empowerment of low-status youth . . . who act strategically . . . to provide institutional support." During the high school years, social leverage ties can be found in urban schools in the form of teachers, coaches, and counselors. They can also be found in programs such as those for the college-bound or in neighborhood organizations like boys' and girls' clubs. Still, Salazar points out, access to "institutional agents" is rare. A youth may be surrounded by these adults, but not all of them act to empower youth. The literature is replete with examples of adults in positions of power in urban communities functioning as "institutional gatekeepers," not striving to expand opportunities for youth but constricting them instead.[112] Moreover, where institutional agents can be found, not all urban youth are privy to them, as these agents are clustered in programs or classrooms that are opened only to the privileged few.

I build on the work of Stanton-Salazar, Louie, and Carola Suárez-Orozco and her colleagues. Complementing their focus on the transition from high school to college, I highlight the need for social leverage ties *throughout* the young adult years as the second generation navigates institutions of higher education and the transition into the labor market. In the young adult years, social leverage ties are increasingly found outside the urban neighborhood, primarily in institutions of higher learning.

Navigating these institutions is very challenging; community colleges can be byzantine, for-profit colleges fail to deliver, and elite institutions often fail the poor in particular. In this context, institutional agents are critical for brokering access to highly coveted sectors of the labor market and securing entry into the middle class. In their absence, even the most promising young men are pulled back to the constrained social networks of their kin and neighborhood.

Disconnected and Marginalized

Some young men in my study lacked both forms of social capital. With no social support or social leverages ties, they were disconnected and marginalized not only from mainstream society but *within* their neighborhoods. These young men—the truly socially isolated—were less likely to be connected to work and school and were also the most physically and socially entrenched in their urban neighborhoods. Disconnected young men are well represented in the urban literature and increasingly in immigration studies.[113] They get a lot of attention from scholars—and from the public at large—though they are a minority in urban Latino neighborhoods.

The literature on vulnerable inner-city youth often frames their fractured support structure along family lines. Studies on gangs show that young men who are more likely to join gangs come from single-parent homes.[114] Although single parents have fewer resources, framing support only in relation to the nuclear family is limiting—for instance, some married women with a husband at home find themselves alone in the parenting process. Moreover, support can derive from extended kin, community, and institutional ties. The social isolation of the young men I interviewed was deep-seated, with roots in their parents' migration and exacerbated by American urban conditions. Most Mexican immigrants—particularly those from rural areas—rely on kin to help them migrate and settle, but some arrive with minimal, if any, social support ties and remain isolated years after their arrival. Poverty and urban conditions strain what support ties they do have, and an inability to engage in social reciprocity can tax relations as well.[115] Some immigrants access social support via neighborhood institutions, but others do not. Socially isolated immigrants are on their own to manage the neighborhood for their children and to guide them in their adult years. It was their children, also disconnected from institutional support, who were the most vulnerable in this study.

Absent social support and social leverage ties, disconnected young men are "cut loose" to navigate the urban context and their transition to adulthood on their own.[116] Disconnected and marginalized Latinos are the most exposed to risks in the urban context and the most subject to the whims of the economy. They face the highest odds of getting caught up in negative peer dynamics in their urban context and of struggling in the labor market. These young men are more likely to experience "second-generation decline" or "downward assimilation" into chronic poverty, becoming locked into the poor neighborhood where they grew up.

Reassessing the Cultural Context of Inner-City, Second-Generation Latinos

Arguably one of the biggest issues with the concept of segmented assimilation was its emphasis on norms and values as a way to understand culture and acculturation processes in the urban context. The theoretical framework built on scholarship that presented homogenous cultural outlooks among the urban poor, suggesting leveled aspirations, hopelessness, or pessimism.[117] Yet growing research finds diverse cultural logics in the inner city consistent with mainstream norms and beliefs.[118] Some scholars sustain that a "street culture" deters urban youth from conventional paths.[119] Yet others find that these youth hold strongly to meritocratic ideals and are optimistic about their chances to succeed, even in the face of economic adversity.[120] This attitude is found not only among native-born racial minorities but increasingly among children of immigrants.[121] This research draws on distinct analytical tools—narratives, cultural repertoires, symbolic boundaries, and cognitive frames—to examine how urban residents make sense of their lived experience and the complex cultural context of their neighborhoods. In doing so, this research challenges depictions of a "culture of poverty," and I build on this work in several ways.[122]

First, I complicate how we understand the cultural context of the Latino inner city. Segmented assimilation scholars disregard how immigrants alter the organization and cultural context of these neighborhoods. Immigrants arrive in the United States with a strong family and work orientation that guides their migration and informs their everyday practices. When urban violence threatens the physical and social mobility prospects of their children, immigrants respond by making claims on these neighborhoods, building social relations and drawing strong moral boundaries against those believed to be responsible for the violence and social disorder—disconnected and gang-affiliated young men. I extend the research that examines how urban residents engage in drawing boundaries, the process that "defines a hierarchy of groups and the similarities and differences between them."[123] The Latino urban neighborhood is a morally contested space where those closely aligned with the immigrant "hard work ethic" are given moral worth. The second generation learns to navigate a complex cultural context that pits a stigmatized group against an immigrant community perceived as hardworking.

The segregated American urban context shapes the cultural outlooks of the second generation in other ways. I discuss how exposure to urban violence shapes peer relations, influencing the cultural orientation of young men, specifically how they navigate the threat of victimization. The young men most exposed to violence in these neighborhoods draw on male peer ties for physical and symbolic protection. I find that these young men do not adopt a "street orientation" so much as they privilege these peer dynamics, engaging in behavior counterproductive to their schooling. Not only does the Latino second generation differ in their exposure to violence and orientation to male peer ties, but they also diverge in how they make sense of their chances to get ahead in the United States. Thus, they conform to what Mario Small, David Harding, and Michèle Lamont call "different individuals perceiv[ing] the same events differently based on their prior experiences and understandings."[124]

As they assess the American opportunity structure and their chances to get ahead, young men differ in their "cognitive frames," which Small, Harding, and Lamont define as the "lenses" through which they "observe and interpret social life" or their "horizon of possibilities."[125] I introduce three types of young men in this study: resolute optimists, determined young men, and self-blamers. I examine the structural factors that result in these diverse outlooks, calling attention to how young men's social capital and their segregation inform their views. These distinct outlooks guide young men as they make school and work decisions, shifting as their social capital and degree of social isolation change over time. Young men's cultural outlooks are not only diverse but fluid.

Study Design: Second-Generation Latinos in Los Angeles

Los Angeles is the ideal context in which to study the integration process of the Latino second generation, specifically Mexican Americans, who represent the largest ethnic group in the city and a wide variation in generational status.[126] Los Angeles has long been a gateway for immigrants and the home of their children. By 2017, almost a third of California's residents were foreign-born (27 percent), and half of California's children had at least one immigrant parent.[127] Los Angeles has an even greater concentration of immigrant families: roughly 38 percent of its population is foreign-born, and 58 percent of all the city's children live in a household where another language other than English is spoken at home.[128] Half of Los Angeles millennials are Latinx.[129] Though most Mexican immigrants are legal residents or naturalized citizens, the city is also home to a large undocumented population. Of the two million undocumented immigrants in California, approximately half reside in the Los Angeles area.[130]

The forty-two young men in this study grew up in two of the most poverty-stricken neighborhoods in Los Angeles. These two neighborhoods, which I call Pueblo Viejo and Central City, lie within the bounds of the general area of East and South Central Los Angeles. The communities in these areas do not differ much, yet they do have boundaries and different high schools, churches, and organizations. I give the two communities pseudonyms and alter the names of high schools, streets, and organizations to protect the identities of my respondents. I selected these two neighborhoods on theoretical grounds (see the methodological notes). According to the segmented assimilation framework, children of Latino immigrants are especially at risk of downward assimilation in segregated, high-poverty neighborhoods where they are exposed to poor, native-born racial minorities presumed to have embraced an oppositional culture (African American or Chicanos).[131]

In Los Angeles, Mexicans experience hypersegregation and poverty concentration akin to what poor blacks experience in U.S. ghettos.[132] In 2010, residents in these two neighborhoods had a median income ($29,500) that was roughly half the Los Angeles County average ($56,266).[133] The 2000 census showed roughly 37 percent of residents living below the poverty line. By 2010, this figure had dropped to about 32 percent of the population, making these neighborhoods no longer "extreme poverty" neighborhoods, but they were still "high-poverty" neighborhoods, and the most disadvantaged in the county (see table A.1 in the appendix). Public schools in these neighborhoods are among the worst-performing in the state; highly segregated and underresourced, they rank in the bottom tenth percentile in the state. Both communities wrestle with entrenched issues of gang violence and are heavily policed.

The two neighborhoods share many disadvantages but differ in at least one respect: in their racial and ethnic demographics. As part of East Los Angeles, Pueblo Viejo is a long-established Latino community (92 percent) of primarily Mexican immigrants. This was reflected in its schools: Pueblo Viejo High was 98 percent Latino. Pockets of South Central Los Angeles are in rapid transition. A historically black neighborhood, Central City experienced black population decline in recent years, from 45 percent in 2000 to 37 percent in 2010. Yet the schools attended by most of the young men I studied there were racially mixed: Central City High was 45 percent Latino and 53 percent African American when I began the study. Comparing these two disadvantaged contexts by recruiting half my sample in each neighborhood allowed me to test an assumption underlying segmented assimilation—that neighborhood exposure to native-born racial minorities (blacks) hinders the acculturation process for second-generation Latinos. Readers will notice that I do not often compare these two neighborhoods, as I did not find that exposure to native-born minorities affected the integration process of young men in this study. Study participants in the South Central neighborhood absorbed certain cultural traits from their African American peers—mostly in terms of dress, music, and forms of speech—that distinguished them from Latinos from the East L.A. area. Nonetheless, most social relations in Central City were intraracial, including in the schools, where youth tended to self-segregate along racial lines.[134] Although some participants had cross-racial ties, urban conditions (gang violence) strained race relations in these communities.

Young Latino Men in Transition to Adulthood

I focus on Latino males because studies show that they are especially vulnerable in the inner city. In general, young Latino men fall behind their female coethnics in educational attainment, but especially in urban neighborhoods where they contend with entrenched issues of crime and violence and criminalization.

When I began this study in 2007, the study participants were between seventeen and twenty-three years old. Two-thirds of the young men were U.S.-born and one-third were foreign-born, having arrived in the United States at an early age, often by age five; only five remained undocumented when I interviewed them. Having been raised most of their lives in Los Angeles, foreign-born young men, like all of those in the study, identified as second-generation and not as "immigrants." I therefore use the term "second-generation" to describe both the twenty-eight young men who were born in Los Angeles to immigrant parents and the fourteen who were born in Mexico but came here as very young children. The term "1.5-generation" more accurately describes the foreign-born cases, but these young men did not identify as such.

Even the five young men who were undocumented identified as second-generation. Throughout the book, I discuss how being unauthorized impinged on these participants' life circumstances. In line with existing research, I found that they came to understand that their legal status blocked their chances to get ahead as they transitioned to adulthood.[135] These young men faced clear barriers to full integration into American society; several discussed being both physically and economically constrained by their inability to get driver's licenses and to work. But their views did not differ much from those of the rest of the young men in the study, and their school and work outcomes were not uniformly worse than for the rest of the sample; some of the U.S.-born study participants were also working in minimum-wage jobs (and a few had no work at all), were stuck in community colleges without a degree, and lacked a vehicle. This observation is worth further investigation. Roberto Gonzales suggests that illegality becomes the "master status" of undocumented young adults— meaning that it dominates their lives.[136] I found that participants could be equally affected by a criminal label, trauma, isolation, or acute poverty whether they had documents or not. After the Deferred Action for Childhood Arrivals (DACA) program went into effect during the follow-up study, some unauthorized young men in the study gained a temporary mechanism to improve their work and school outcomes. This benefit was under constant threat, however, during the writing of this book.[137]

I drew on personal contacts and knocked on many doors in schools and community organizations to find study participants who fit the selection criteria. Aside from their ethnicity, generational status, and age range, I purposely sought young Latino men from these neighborhoods with seemingly different social mobility trajectories. One-third were high school noncompleters, one-third finished high school and sought work and/or enrolled in community college, and one-third enrolled in four-year universities. I deliberately departed from the common approach of focusing on young men engaged in crime and violence, those who had dropped out of high school, or those who were disconnected from school and work. In fact, the majority of young men in urban communities complete high school and are not engaged in crime. In my efforts to avoid homogenizing young and urban Latino men, I tried especially hard to identify hard-to-reach young men—those who were disconnected from neighborhood institutions and thus easy to miss.

I focused on how the neighborhood mattered, if at all, in young men's lives—that is, its impact on their decisions and behavior, their identity and acculturation, their social ties, and their views on getting ahead in American society. My analysis benefited greatly from the multigenerational nature of the study. Interviewing the immigrant parents of participants allowed me to capture the migration journey and explore immigrant parents' relationship to their neighborhood, their social ties, and their outlooks on what the American opportunity structure made possible for themselves and their children. Thirty-two of the young men in the study grew up with two immigrant parents, six had a single mother, and only one was raised by an immigrant father and a U.S.-born Mexican American mother. Two young men were not raised by their parents but by relatives. I draw on multiple hours-long conversations with each young man and his immigrant parents over the course of a year. The result—approximately 160 in-depth interviews—coupled with ethnographic observations, gave me insight into the daily routines and worldviews of these young Latino men.[138]

Five to six years later, 2012–2013, I followed up with half of the respondents in the original study to account for the changing economy and the rising inequality then shaping the quest for upward mobility. The young men were between twenty-four and twenty-eight years old at this point, and some had graduated from college. Most but not all continued to live in the same neighborhood with kin. I set out to examine if and how the neighborhood remained relevant for these young men and how they were faring economically; I also revisited their views on the American opportunity structure and getting ahead. These additional interviews with the young men and their immigrant parents strongly enriched the existing data. This longitudinal component of the ethnography allowed me to account for the changes in circumstances and outlooks in the lives of these young men, avoiding a static representation of their lives and cultural outlooks. It also allowed me to study the impact of the Great Recession on the young men, who were members of the generation most hampered by the economic challenges of that period.

Overview of the Chapters in the Book

This book is divided into two parts. Part I draws heavily on interviews with the parents of the young men at the center of this book. Violence and social disorder emerge as among the most salient and consequential features of the two focal neighborhoods, and as among the most disruptive forces to the successful adaptation of the second generation. Yet the incorporation process for second-generation Latins is also affected by the ways in which immigrants alter the organizational and cultural contexts of the American urban context.

Chapter 2 captures the rude awakening that immigrants experienced when they arrived in Los Angeles. They quickly realized that America's violence and social disorder threatened not only the safety and well-being of their families but their children's future prospects. Because violence and social disorder evoked fear and distrust in immigrants, they found it difficult to establish community ties. Yet immigrants set down roots, established social relations, and made claims on their neighborhoods, disrupting some of the violence and social disorder. Two cognitive frames guided their migration and settlement process: work and family. These orientations filtered into the rhythm of their lives in Los Angeles neighborhoods and permeated the social fabric there, altering the organizational structure and cultural context of these communities. Drawing strong moral boundaries against an inner-city prototype of the idle, gang-affiliated young man, immigrants reinforced conventional norms and behavior. It was the second generation who would negotiate the morally contested neighborhoods of urban Los Angeles.

In chapter 3, I reconceptualize social capital in the Mexican-origin community. In general, Mexican immigrants have modest resources, but most count on a valuable asset: a support network rooted in kin ties that allow immigrants to get by, cope with challenging circumstances, and avoid second-generation decline. Kin ties drive Mexican migration to the United States and remain a primary organizing unit over time, extending between the first and second generations. Kin-based social capital ebbs and flows in Mexican families, and those with less capital tend to have more difficulty adapting to the United States and guiding the integration of their children. In its absence, some immigrants seek support by establishing institutional ties, with positive implications for the second generation. Others remain disconnected, and these were the most vulnerable families in the study. Social support varies across families, making some young men more vulnerable than others to urban conditions and the labor market.

Part II draws on the interviews conducted with second-generation young Latino men. In the first two chapters, I examine two features of the urban environment that interact with the social capital of Mexican immigrants to stall the social mobility prospects of the second generation: urban violence and social isolation. Chapter 4 discusses the negative impact of exposure to urban violence on the social mobility prospects of young men. The threat of violence encourages young men to seek physical and symbolic protection, but in doing so they become entangled in acts of reciprocity and these social ties with male peers compromise their schooling and increase their odds of risky behavior. Avoiding "downward assimilation" requires that a young man navigate the volatile urban context successfully, skirting not only victimization but also risky ties and behavior and staying committed to school or work. Young men in the study who successfully navigated this environment were those who were buffered from the violence in these neighborhoods. I show how parents employed various strategies to protect their children, drawing heavily on kin and community ties. Socially isolated parents who managed the urban context on their own had sons who were the most exposed to violence and were at greater risk of experiencing downward mobility.

While exposure to urban violence could set some respondents on a path toward "second-generation decline," for others it was their residential segregation that ensured their place in the social order. In chapter 5, I discuss why Latinos on seemingly different trajectories in their young adult years—some college-going, some high school graduates, and some nongraduates—converged to the working class. Segregation reinforces Latinos' insular social networks and ensures that even the most enthusiastic and high-achieving will remain working-class. I show that young men drew heavily on kin and neighborhood ties that allowed them to get by, but not ahead. Social support ties were especially valuable for the most vulnerable group—high school noncompleters. Not only did support ties encourage educational attainment and employment, but they provided skills and links to jobs that lifted these young men's labor market prospects. At the same time, their social isolation denies them access to social leverage ties. Young men in my study who were on a promising upward mobility trajectory were pulled back to their working-class community when the social leverage ties they did have disappeared.

The next two chapters take a closer look at these young men's divergent paths and their cultural orientations. In chapter 6, I introduce exceptional cases in this study—the most and least "successful" young men—to demonstrate how urban conditions factored differently for them, depending on their social support and social leverage ties. The least successful were those who navigated the labor market on their own, facing the greatest odds of joblessness and chronic poverty, while the most successful sustained social leverage ties that gave them access to a place in the American middle class.

In chapter 7, I explain why, despite the adversity that these young men faced in getting ahead, most remained optimistic that they would succeed in the United States. I explain the impact of kin and community ties, as well as their social isolation in segregated environments, on this optimism. I also explain why some young men changed their outlook. My respondents conformed to three types: the resolute optimist, the determined young man, and the self-blamer. Most were *resolute optimists,* strong believers in the American Dream and their ability to succeed. The obstacles they confronted were not daunting enough to alter their belief in the American opportunity structure or their determination to succeed. These optimistic young men relied heavily on kin in their young adult years, and their social world remained confined to their segregated working-class environment. Yet the obstacles young men generally encountered did not leave all optimistic. The *determined* young men were those who eventually lost faith in the American opportunity structure but persevered anyway, while *self-blamers* chastised themselves for not having the wherewithal to get ahead. Determined young men had the greatest exposure to mainstream society, which made them conscious of America's structural inequalities. Self-blamers stayed in their neighborhoods, navigating the urban context and labor market on their own and bearing the brunt of social stigma associated with their community.

I conclude the book by considering the integration process of inner-city second-generation Latinos in the light of America's structured inequality, and I call attention to the policy context that stalls their successful integration. My aim throughout is to illuminate the lives of these second-generation Latinos, a group who, I found, buck the dominant narrative of inner-city young men and sustain, rather than threaten, American ideals.

PART I

························

The Latino Immigrant Urban Context

CHAPTER 2

The Contested Immigrant City

Navigating Violence, Family, and Work

How do I know I've attained the American Dream? When I see it in my children.

ESPERANZA, Genaro's mother

Genaro's parents, Esperanza and José, lacked electricity, running water, and telephone service in rural Mexico. In 1992, they were living in Los Angeles in a crowded one-bedroom apartment with Genaro, who was four at the time, and his two siblings when they had the opportunity to move to a more spacious and affordable public housing unit. The couple was hopeful and optimistic about their move. Although they would be surrounded by other struggling families, they saw their new home as an opportunity offered by the United States to better leverage their scarce resources. But they quickly came to understand that this opportunity came at a high cost. The day the family moved into the housing project, a ten-year-old neighbor, Diego, instructed them: "When you hear gunshots, drop to the floor." They would live there ten years, although Esperanza wanted to leave that first night, when Diego's warning came true. That spring brought the riots in the wake of the video of the Rodney King beating. The family had to adapt to their volatile new social environment—the context in which Genaro and his family would attempt to forge their path to the American Dream.

Much has been written about gangs in Los Angeles. During the period when immigrants like Esperanza and José settled in the city and raised their children there, Los Angeles became known as the "gang capital" of the world: its approximately 1,000 gangs had over 200,000 members by the mid-1990s. In its peak years of violence, Los Angeles experienced over 1,000 homicides per year.[1] Many of that period's drive-by shootings were driven by gang disputes over drug territory and carried out increasingly by very young and lethal gang members.

The acute violence and social disorder that swept through the East Los Angeles and South Central neighborhoods in the 1980s and 1990s were rooted in a long history of public policy neglect, entrenched poverty, and persistent racial segregation, conditions predating the arrival of the immigrants in this study. Academics studying the integration of post-1965 Latino immigrant families into the United States suggested that such an environment, plagued with drugs and gangs, would hurt the children of immigrants. The fear was that immigrant children would acculturate to what scholars described at the time as the "underclass" culture of the inner city.[2] Segmented assimilation scholars projected that youths like Esperanza and Jose's children would be swayed by the gangs around them and adopt a "street orientation," then move away from school and work.[3] While Esperanza and José struggled to make ends meet as part of the working poor, their children would be at risk of pursuing a life of crime leading to incarceration, a course that would close off upward mobility to them as they became locked into place among America's chronic poor.

Yet not all scholars were as pessimistic about the fate of these Latinos. Urban scholars pointed to distinct features of Mexican *barrios* that set them apart from black ghettos. In his writings, Wilson noted that while poor black communities wrestled with high rates of joblessness, poor Mexican communities had a strong "work orientation."[4] Data reveal that Mexican immigrant males have the highest rate of employment of any group in the United States, including white males. Wilson suggested that this strong link to work made poor Mexican neighborhoods distinct in their organizational structure and cultural context, relative to the "underclass" communities he was studying. Others made bolder claims that immigrants revitalized American urban neighborhoods. They pointed not only to immigrants' strong attachment to the labor market but to their "strong family bonds" and ethnic ties.[5] Years later, as scholars tried to make sense of the sudden decline in violence in American cities, some pointed to immigration as having helped lower crime and violence rates.[6]

Research showed that immigrants are less likely to engage in crime and violence than the U.S. native population and that cities with more immigrants experience less crime and violence.[7]

The immigrants in this study settled in Los Angeles during its worse years of violence. Given these conditions, it is no surprise that scholars feared for their children. Yet segmented assimilation scholars ignored the potential impact of immigrants on the social organization and cultural context of these neighborhoods. Meanwhile, scholars studying poor black neighborhoods went on to challenge the depiction of a homogenous inner-city black culture, and after much debate, the "underclass" term fell out of vogue. What my immigrant respondents revealed was that after overcoming the initial shock of arrival in violent urban America, they put down roots and made claims on the city, pushing back against the violence and social disorder. What emerged were culturally and morally contested communities that the second generation learned to navigate.

Urban Life in the City of Angels

Immigrants like Esperanza and José were greeted by familiar sights and sounds when they arrived in the city. In the well-established Mexican neighborhood of Pueblo Viejo, the major streets are lined with small businesses—flower shops and ethnic fast-food restaurants, like *taquerias,* and hamburger joints. Murals expressing ethnic pride and the community's devotion to the Virgen de Guadalupe color the walls of some of these businesses, bringing life to otherwise drab and faded walls. On any given day of the week, it is common to see pedestrians on the street, especially mothers taking their children to and from school or running errands in the middle of the day with their little ones in tow. In the evening, the streets are filled with the rush of traffic and bus commuters returning home after a long day's work. Then, for a few hours, it seems that everyone in the neighborhood is outside—youth ride their bikes on the streets and play in the park, while high-in-demand youth centers wrap up busy after-school programs and then send the children home. In contrast with the depopulated urban neighborhoods often described in the urban poverty literature, Pueblo Viejo is a place of hustle and bustle.

Ethnic neighborhoods soften immigrants' transition to the United States, but adapting to the American urban context requires a distinct form of acculturation for immigrants like Esperanza and José; it is a place of contradictions, relentless struggle, and moments of lost hope. Social conditions in historically marginalized neighborhoods challenge new immigrants' enthusiasm and optimism about life in the United States. The daily struggle to make ends meet was evident in Pueblo Viejo. During the day, *mariachis* and *norteños,* musicians in cowboy hats and boots, carried their guitars or accordions in search of work. They joined *paisanos* in search of a day's pay, like the peddlers pushing carts and selling corn on the cob plastered with mayonnaise, cheese, and chile. Fruit vendors on the street corner quickly sliced mango, jicama, and cucumber, selling mixed-fruit cocktails to customers waiting in line. Others collected scrap metal from the trash to sell. Both the formal and informal businesses in Pueblo Viejo catered to its low-income Latinx residents—the stores were dollar stores or cheap clothing stores. Driving into the smaller residential streets, one skirted the potholes and noticed the old housing stock: dilapidated buildings had peeling paint and sheets for curtains, and there were signs of removed graffiti on almost every other wall.

Signs of conflict were ever-present in the neighborhood. A peek at the alleys revealed that there was simply too much gang tag graffiti to remove. *Veteranos* (non-active older gang members) could occasionally be spotted, and police patrolled regularly. A popular park frequented by youth after school was popular with loitering men, most often tucked away in a corner, drunk or high, and sometimes asleep; young men sometimes got jumped there. At night, particularly on weekends, you could see what locals called "ghetto birds" (helicopters) flashing their bright lights on the homes of Pueblo Viejo, searching for someone in the dark, usually a young male on the run.

Many of the sights and sounds of Pueblo Viejo could be found in Central City. Immigrants here also pushed carts, sometimes selling *paletas* or other frozen treats. They welcomed those exiting the freeways with rose bouquets or bags of oranges, making use of the still traffic stopped momentarily on a red light. Black men hawked their wares on these corners as well, typically selling other items, like sugar straw candy. They pitched their sale differently ("help a brother out!"). As a relatively new neighborhood for Latinos at the time of the study, Central City lacked the long-established businesses catering to the Latinx community that saturated Pueblo Viejo. Instead, mobile taco trucks positioned themselves in empty lots, competing with more established businesses like Louisiana Famous Fried Chicken and other Southern food. Like Pueblo Viejo, the streets of Central City became most alive during rush hour and shortly afterwards, as its residents came home from work. The streets filled with cars and full buses, and for that moment public transportation in Los Angeles appeared to be a viable form of commuting.

Central City had a good many more storefront churches and liquor stores than Pueblo Viejo—signs of the gross underinvestment in what had been a historically African American community. Both neighborhoods had gates around most of their homes, and steel bars covered windows and doors. The gates in Central City were noticeably taller, however; even fast-food restaurants there had bars on their windows. One could not help but experience an ominous feeling upon driving into the two local shopping centers that housed Central City's supermarkets, encircled by high gates as well; it was a fortified community that led to the impression of a hostile environment. Some said that most of the gates and bars were installed in these neighborhoods following the 1992 riots, but others claimed that fear of gang violence was responsible for this feature of the neighborhood.

Many of the signs of poverty concentration and social disorder documented by those who study poor, black urban neighborhoods were more common in Central City than in Pueblo Viejo. Vacant lots, piles of trash, and old furniture on the side of the street made up part of the scenery, reflecting the community's persistent neglect. There were more homeless men, pushing carts containing their belongings. They commonly occupied the benches of the local park and their makeshift homes were found along the edge of the freeway or in an underpass; they panhandled in the same high-traffic areas where others sold their wares. Whereas Pueblo Viejo was home to some of the oldest Mexican gangs in Los Angeles—some dating back as early as the 1930s—Central City had some of the oldest black gangs.[8] These gangs dated back decades, to times when Mexicans and blacks were excluded from living in other parts of Los Angeles and segregation was the law of the land. Oblivious to this local history of political neglect and social exclusion, the new arrivals in the city were primarily concerned with the entrenched violence and social disorder that threatened their family's safety and well-being, as well as the future prospects of their children.

Rude Awakening: The Violent American City

Esperanza shook her head repeatedly and then stared at me intently with her big, dark brown eyes, confessing that she remained in disbelief over what she had witnessed in the ten years she had lived in the projects in the 1990s:

> When I lived in the projects, that is when I realized that in reality there are a lot of *bad* people. I wanted to leave the next day. I lived amidst gangs, the sale of drugs, prostitution. They would prostitute behind my kitchen door. There was a little space; that was their hotel. I always had the curtains closed so that my children, who were young, would not see. *Dios mio!* [My Lord!] What is this?! To see drugs, to see gangsters who would beat one another and the *balaceras* [shootings]! We were constantly dropping to the floor.

Esperanza recounted vivid memories of young mothers running frantically with their children in strollers during drive-by shootings in the middle of the day. In addition to Genaro's playmate who was killed when he was eight, another child died while they lived in the projects. Bullets penetrated the family's bathroom walls on one occasion.

Esperanza and José had relatives in the Los Angeles area, but they rarely visited, and when they did, it was strictly between the hours of 10:00 AM and 2:00 PM. Esperanza's mother, who followed her family to Los Angeles, cried when she saw the conditions in which they were living. Esperanza herself seemed horrified in retrospect. "How is it possible that I lived there as long as I did, putting my kids through that danger?" Genaro was the youngest of three children, the oldest two having witnessed and experienced the most violence.

Immigrants in this study were shaken by the gang violence in Los Angeles that peaked in the late 1980s and early 1990s. Social disorder—drug use, drug sales, vandalism, assaults, and petty crime—accompanied this rise in violence. These social conditions shattered their romantic notions of life in the United States and shaped their adaptation to the city. They responded initially with shock, fear, and seclusion, all of which made it hard to establish trust and social cohesion in these neighborhoods and allowed these social conditions to flourish.[9]

Settling In: Fear and Distrust

"Well, you see, I came from a *ranchito,* very small, and I was very inno-cent," Isela explained. "When I got here I trusted everyone." She was twenty-one when she came to Los Angeles in 1991 with her two toddlers, joining her husband Carlos and her father-in-law, who had migrated years earlier.[10] Carlos's remittances had been enough to feed his family in their rural town in Zacatecas, but Isela migrated in order to reunite the family. She described her surprise at how "ugly" South Central was; the city she knew in Mexico, Aguascalientes, "was clean; everything was peaceful." Isela and her family lived in a crowded rented house with Carlos's father and his two siblings. Yearning for a place of their own, she romanticized apartment complexes, which she imagined as communities of trustworthy neighbors like those she had known in *el rancho*: "I imagined everyone introducing themselves and being *amable* [cordial]."

When the couple moved out on their own and landed in an acutely violent part of the area, in Central City, Isela regretted moving out of the house with her husband's family. She learned to yank her children to the floor at the sound of gunfire. The night a stray bullet pierced her bathroom window she wanted to flee. The neighbor upstairs was a gang member, and often the target of drive-by shootings, and they discovered that their next-door neighbor sold drugs and stolen items around the clock. "All night you would hear people knocking on the door," Isela said. She angrily asked Carlos, "*Si tu sabias que las cosas estaban así, porque nos trajiste?* [If you knew that things were like this, why did you bring us?]." But she ultimately con-cluded that he had been working too much to know about the neighbor-hood. "He goes from the house to work and from work to the house." Isela learned that the only strong ties in the apartments where she lived were those of the gang youth. Years later, it would be her sons who integrated into the social fabric of the apartment complex.

Jovita was the only mother in the study who was not an immigrant, and she consequently had a longer view of Los Angeles. Her parents had migrated from Mexico via Texas, and she was raised in Pueblo Viejo in a tight-knit community that she fondly recalled as peaceful. "When I was growing up in the sixties—very quiet—kids would go out and play. You [would] see couples taking strolls through the neighborhood. When it was summertime, everyone was out." Jovita had five sons, including two sets of twins, with whom she lived in the same apartment where she had grown up with her mother. Their immigrant father Luis was, she said, a "closet alcoholic." Their marriage had unraveled at the same time as the community, as she remembered it:

> In the eighties, that's when the drive-bys started popping out throughout the city and the gang members that were involved in the little street wars started becoming more violent. They weren't concerned about who they might hurt; they were in their fight, that was it. We couldn't sit outside in the evenings and enjoy a nice summer afternoon or evening because, quite literally, bullets were flying past us. . . . I was fearful for [my children's] lives, for all of us.

As the number of gangs grew and drugs filtered into the streets of Pueblo Viejo, not even morning walks to school were safe. Jovita and her five boys came to an abrupt halt one morning when a car sped by them, spraying an apartment complex with bullets. On another occasion, a brawl broke out between two rival gangs in their front yard, forcing the family to be on "lockdown." They emerged only after police declared it safe to do so.

Families learned to stay indoors at night and to be especially cautious on weekends, the peak times for violence. They avoided parks. Parents kept their children close, indoors, isolating them from the violence to their best of their ability. Jovita's sons were allowed to play only in the backyard of their duplex. In the housing projects, Esperanza and José encouraged their children's friends to visit and "play with the internet," but not the other way around. Genaro remembered riding his bike inside. "I'll try to go through the kitchen to the living room and then back." The need to keep children inside complicated parenting and added strain to work and family demands for all of the parents I interviewed. And they could not keep their children at home at all times; Martha and Jorge's three sons were assaulted on their way home from school one day and had their sneakers and jackets stolen.

Urban violence also complicated immigrants' work routines. Martha, an undocumented migrant from Guadalajara, had to catch a bus at around 5:30 AM to go to the affluent town of Palos Verdes, where she cleaned homes. She stood at the bus stop until the morning a man next to her was assaulted with a screwdriver. Since then, she had waited for the bus from the safety of her ground-floor apartment; she would watch for the bus to turn the corner, then run for it. Another migrant, Angelica, dreaded the walk to the rental office because she had to pass by the local gang. "*Mi corazón palpitaba a mil por hora*" [My heart beats a thousand per minute]," she recalled.

Urban residents who traversed the neighborhood by foot or relied on public transportation faced the greatest risk. Darío was a short immigrant man from Guanajuato, Mexico, who never learned to drive and regularly took the bus to work. He had witnessed and been victim to various assaults over the years. He said that he felt "*anger* because of the impotence of not being able to do anything. On one occasion, I was on the bus stop and two young black guys approached a young Latino from behind. . . . They pressed a cigarette on his back, and they took his shoes. . . . I couldn't intervene, I couldn't do anything."

Confronted by groups of young men, or young men with weapons, immigrants had a hard time putting up a fight. It pained Darío to feel so powerless and unable to defend his coethnics victimized on the street.

All of the parents I interviewed for this study reported that they had witnessed and experienced acts of violence. Most had experienced the threat of a drive-by shooting, and fourteen had been directly assaulted with a deadly weapon. Violence in Pueblo Viejo and Central City was especially pronounced in certain pockets of these neighborhoods, typically the housing projects or apartment complexes or blocks where gangs congregated. Most residents avoided these *zonas calientes* if they could.[11]

Residents of Central City often interpreted violence through a racial lens. Even before they immigrated, some had been told that blacks were violent. Martha explained, "Over there [in Mexico] you hear that blacks are very bad and well, you arrive with fear. People who lived over here [in Los Angeles] would say, blacks are mean, bad people, protect yourselves from them." While Jorge agreed with his wife Martha that "not all blacks are bad," he also said, "Look, over there [on the next block] you have lots of drugs. . . . It's dangerous. Not this block. This block has lots of Latinos, but those over there, there are a lot of blacks, lots of crooks." Many had been discouraged from moving into Central City by family and friends. Raymundo, an undocumented migrant, recalled that when he had bought their home, "there weren't many people who wanted to buy here. It was full of blacks, and in those days there was a lot of violence on the street. People judged us, told us we were crazy and didn't understand why we would want to live here."

Cross-racial incidents of violence reinforced these views. Flora and Marcos, also undocumented immigrants, moved a total of six times with their children in South Central, going from room rentals to converted garages. In their first neighborhood, the one thriving Latino gang in the area was at war with the black gangs surrounding it. Another neighborhood experienced a wave of muggings targeting women. In another neighborhood, their eldest son, Bernardo, witnessed a shooting. Then early one morning, Marcos was shot outside their apartment in Central City when he left for work at around 5:00 AM. Bernardo, then a junior in high school, recalled hearing the two gunshots. Flora was distraught; it was Bernardo who called 911. Marcos was shot once in the leg and in his back. His life was put in danger by the damage to his intestines as one of the bullets barely missed his spinal cord. He had to recover in the hospital for more than a month. The incident made the family warier of blacks. Bernardo, who had dark brown skin, confessed that he came to fear blacks even though he had spent his childhood playing with many black children. Things turned when he began to get beat up by black youth in middle school. After his father was shot, he said, "it kinda traumatized me. . . . [It] made my brain sort of like a black-and-white world. . . . I didn't like to step out of my house or walk to school. It took me several years to get over it."

Violence encouraged seclusion and dampened social relations for some respondents. In the ten years that Esperanza lived in the housing projects in Pueblo Viejo, she made only one close friend. Rufina, a working single mother who lived in one of the most violent housing projects in Central City, could not identify any friend after living there for over twenty years. Rufina and her children witnessed many acts of violence, including several murders, one the massacre of an entire family across the street from her apartment. Thirty years after her arrival in the United States, Rufina remained acutely distrustful of those around her.

A culture of silence worsened the isolation for some respondents. Esperanza's one friend in the housing projects advised her on the day they met: "If you see they kill someone, you didn't see anything. If you see a *cholo* [Mexican gangster] go into an apartment, you did not see anything. If you see them killing someone, you have to be *blind, deaf, and mute.*" The parents in this study feared retribution from gang members if they reported any crime or violence. Angelica said, "I did not get involved. . . . Once it got dark, we went inside. If we saw them tagging on the walls or smoking, we would act like we did not see anything. . . . I didn't want to get involved in problems." In those peak years of violence, participants claimed, police were corrupt and neglected their neighborhoods, and they saw little change even when they reached out for help. That would change over time as the police presence grew in both communities—oddly, as violence and social disorder began to decline.

Urban violence and social disorder threatened immigrants' purpose for having migrated: to work and to see their families prosper. Although initially shocked and afraid, immigrants sought to protect themselves and their children and to mitigate the influence of violence in their lives. Rather than succumb to the urban conditions in their Los Angeles neighborhoods, immigrants pushed back by putting down roots and making claims on these neighborhoods. They did so by building trusting community ties and asserting a narrative of a "hardworking community" at odds with the violence and social disorder.

Putting Down Roots: Building Community and Claiming the Neighborhood

Jesusita, a garment worker from Veracruz, Mexico, purchased a home in Central City with Damian in 1987 at a time when there was a lot of violence in the neighborhood. "Not one *paletero* [popsicle vendor] could pass by here without being robbed. He would get a beating and they would steal his money," she explained. But by the time I met Jesusita, twenty years after her arrival, violence had dramatically declined in her neighborhood, which was undergoing rapid demographic change. Jesusita described the strong sense of community that had arisen in recent years. She explained that she and her neighbors

> take care of each other. There are no problems. We all know each other. We all look out for one another. We protect each other. If we see something, a suspicious car, a strange person entering someone's patio and we don't know them, we immediately call. We get along nicely. When there are *fiestas,* we are united, we all celebrate. If people can attend, they attend. No one is calling the police [for noise complaints]. These are family gatherings.

Jesusita had directly experienced her neighbors' help when her family returned from a weekend camping trip to find that all but one bedroom in their home had burned to the ground. Her neighbors brought them food, clothing, and money.

Jesusita was convinced that this kind of social cohesion and mutual trust empowered her neighbors to deter delinquency and regain social control of their neighborhood. She explained that the key to living in peace is to *vencer el miedo* (overcome fear). "We don't allow any of that [vandalism]. . . . If we see youth [tagging], we call it to their attention, whoever happens to see it. We'll tell them to stop and that they have a few minutes to fix what they have done or the police will show up." Her husband had confronted a group of teenagers tagging their fence with exactly these words. As Jesusita said to me, "You can see for yourself, the fence is still up without one letter! Nothing! The thing is that one has to overcome fear. Otherwise, [gangsters] will dominate us."

Trust and Social Cohesion

Although researchers are not clear about the association between having more immigrants in a community and lower crime rates, the immigrants in this study suggested that establishing social relations—trust and social cohesion, what is known as "collective efficacy"—attenuated some of the violence and social disorder of their environment. Most of the participants slowly established amicable ties with neighbors over time. Ernesto migrated from Michoacán, Mexico, in 1977 and raised seven children in Pueblo Viejo during the peak years of violence. Though he lived in a neighborhood with entrenched gang violence, his trust in his neighbors helped him ensure his family's safety:

> The reason I trust the neighbors is because wherever I land, wherever I'm going to live, I start making friendship right away with the people around. I start to build a friendship, even though they don't know me or I don't know them, but I start to talk and talk and one begins to build trust. . . . Here, I sometimes forget to lock my van and nothing happens to it. One day the father of the *cholitos* [young gangsters] told me, "Listen, *compa* [my friend], don't be distrustful of my sons. I know my sons are this and that . . . but they will never do anything to you, your family, and your belongings."

Ernesto's amicable ties with his neighbors dampened his fear and distrust.

Even Esperanza learned to make strategic relations to enhance her family's safety, although she considered only one neighbor in the projects to be her friend. When her eldest son, Pablo, entered adolescence, he was repeatedly approached by gang members in the projects trying to jump him into the gang. Her daughter, Valeria, received a different kind of attention from the gang members in the form of repeated invitations to "kick it" (hang out). Esperanza took a bold approach. As she explained:

> I talked to the main guy who was in charge of the others. He lived in the apartment above us. There were shootings often targeting him, but they would hit us too. . . . One time my daughter told me, "Ma, the *cholos* are stopping Pablo all the time because they want him to join the gang because he lives in the territory with them." I replied, "Oh yeah?" So I went several times to talk to [the gangster upstairs] and told him, "Look, I want to ask you a favor. . . . Your friends keep stopping my son because they want him to join the gang because he lives in their territory. . . . I don't get in your business. . . ." He said, "No, *señora,* I know you don't, because the police give us the reports . . . and we have never had a report from you or the lady at the corner." I told him, "So, I want you to leave my son alone, in peace. Don't involve him and try to get him in the gang. If he wants to, let it be his choice, but not because your friends are pressuring him." He replied, "*Señora,* we won't try to get him in, he's fine the way he is."

Esperanza continued to turn a blind eye to the criminal activity of the gang and even covered for them. But she also used her relationship to prevent the gangsters from spending time near her apartment, citing the children at play nearby. The gang members retreated to another part of the projects. In a separate conversation, Genaro said that "they [the gang] had mad love for our family." Esperanza explained, "I learned to adapt to this life and learned to defend myself, not to get involved with others who are doing ill because it is their life."

Reaching out to neighbors and establishing relations was more challenging in Central City, not only because of language and cultural barriers, but also because some immigrants initially held the view that blacks were inherently violent.[12] These views would change over time. Humberto, an immigrant from the border town of Juarez in Mexico, admitted that he was afraid when he first moved to Central City in 1987. Humberto moved into a small apartment complex, which he managed for his brother Ramon. The brothers were among the first Latinos on the block, and Humberto recalled his hesitation: "I was afraid because all you would hear is that blacks were dangerous. I remember telling my brother, '*Oye, como nos va ir ahi?*' [How do you think we will fare?] Because blacks are very violent here. I don't know what will happen. He told me not to worry."

Ramon was right. In the twenty years Humberto lived in the neighborhood, he never had a negative encounter with an African American neighbor, and he noted that his children were well liked on the block. Immigrants in Central City came to understand that most of the violence was gang-related and not directed at them or other Latinos.[13] Humberto explained that "there are a lot of gangs here, between blacks, mostly all blacks. Here in this corner, they often shoot each other. We got used to it. I hear gunshots and I close the door. I tell my kids to go to the back room and not come out."

Cross-racial relationships emerged slowly over the years. Immigrants like Timoteo observed the dynamics on his block and learned to distinguish between blacks along class—and moral—lines. He said, "Some are from families who are of a higher category, and others are worse off. Those who fare better keep to themselves but are friendlier [if you talk to them]. Those who are of a lower class, you'll see them racing their car, burning tire outside [causing social disorder]." Drawing class distinctions allowed Timoteo not to make sweeping generalizations about blacks in his neighborhood. Respondents came to identify trustworthy neighbors, often long-term residents, who were African American. At times, they watched over each other's property and occasionally socialized over *carne asadas*. A number of participants, including both the young men and their parents, had established a role as handymen for some of their black neighbors, sometimes getting paid and other times providing the service simply as a friendly gesture, solidifying positive relations.

Even as they established a sense of community over time, immigrants still commonly kept to themselves. Humberto's neighbors "all knew him," and he listed those he liked: "those across the street, the other Latinos, the Salvadorans . . . the Korean lady from the liquor store." Humberto explained why he was especially fond of one of his black neighbors, Ricky: "Sometimes [Ricky] sees that I'm carrying bags of soil in my truck and he tells me, 'Friend, let me know when you need help.' He tells his sons to help me when they see me struggling. He says that is how it should be, helping one another, being good neighbors." As more Latinos arrived in the neighborhood, Humberto advised them: "*Llevenselo tranquilo* [Keep it cool]." He explained what he meant: "Don't give any problems, so you won't have any problems. . . . Don't get involved with these people [black gangs], don't offend them, and no one will offend you. That is how this *barrio* is."

Immigrants who established amicable ties felt like Jesusita—unafraid and emboldened to intervene in some of the delinquency in the area. Humberto took a friendly approach to the young men, whether black or brown, who every so often tagged his wall:

> I prefer to befriend them. *Oye, ven pa aca* [Listen, come here]. . . . I try to convince them in another way. "Look, I work very hard, and you come and write on my wall. I have to work to remove that graffiti. Would you like it if they wrote on your house?" Well, I tell you, they hardly tag anymore. It's good not to come out violent towards them. . . . Both races need to talk to one another. . . . It's better to take a positive approach than a violent one. If you come out shouting or with a stick in your hand, or I'm going to call the police, the sure thing is that they are going to break your car windows or your sons will take the hit or they'll tag more out of anger.

Humberto's approach evolved over time as he let go of fear and developed social ties on his block, where he felt some degree of social cohesion and shared values. Yet establishing cordial ties in some of the most violent pockets of these neighborhoods was not only challenging but dangerous at times.

Acts of Resistance

The immigrants in this study rarely engaged in violence, not even in self-defense. Yet during the peak of violence in Los Angeles, their efforts to establish amicable ties at times failed and police neglect left them with no other recourse but to defend themselves when victimized.

Humberto's brother Ramon got into the business of purchasing run-down houses in Central City and fixing them up to rent. He purchased what would be his long-term home in "the kind of neighborhood," Humberto said, "where you may enter, but you may never leave. Where you could see bullet holes all over the metal posts on the streets." Ramon's new purchase had been burned down, and in the process of rebuilding they discovered guns in the debris. Ramon had experience moving into predominantly black neighborhoods and was not fazed by the local gang present on his block. Yet only days after his wife and children moved in, their house was sprayed with bullets. Ramon had become fed up with the gang members' loud music and asked them to lower the sound; that was enough to provoke the shooting. Afraid for the safety of his family, Ramon called relatives for help, including Humberto. The Latino men showed up with guns but quickly realized that they were outnumbered. To prevent a tragedy, Humberto sought help from two policemen roaming in separate patrol cars, but neither agreed to help. Without much recourse, Humberto entered the street waving a white T-shirt, his knees buckling, and pleaded with the gang members to let him rescue someone who had been injured (a lie). The young men agreed and allowed Ramon and his family to vacate the home.

One week later, Ramon confronted one of the gang members outside his home: "You were shooting my house . . . we're fighting to the death, only you and I." Humberto recalled that other gang members showed up: "What does this Mexican want? To fight? Doesn't he know it's a grip [a lot] of us against him?" They laughed at Ramon then, but as Humberto related, they later came over and apologized: "'My friend, I'm sorry, we made a mistake. We thought you were going to shoot, we're sorry. Hey, you know how to do this [construction] job? You think you can do some work on my home?'" With this request, Ramon was folded into the block and went on to establish decades of friendship. Humberto laughed at life's ironies as he retold the story.

Other acts of resistance were not quite as risky, although they also reflected a lack of confidence in the police. Brisa, a Salvadoran immigrant living in Mexican-entrenched Pueblo Viejo, arrived in the early 1980s. She recalled a time when it seemed like "everyday there was a car with a broken window." In response, "all the neighbors, we decided to collaborate. My husband brought a sling shot from our country. . . . He would get rocks and sling-shoot whoever was in the car." The burglars would run into the alleys and hide. Sometimes Brisa's neighbors chased them down. She recalled, "We actually caught some who were inside the cars. One of the neighbors' sons chased them with a machete. They looked like snakes, sliding and hiding everywhere. We'd catch them and turn them in to the police, and they never came back."

Lucila, an undocumented Pueblo Viejo resident and mother of three, confronted taggers regularly, yelling at them when they started tagging near her apartment. Her husband told her that she was going to get shot one day, but Lucila told him, "No, no he's [tagger] not going to come shoot me! That's why the streets are the way they are, because we don't have the courage to report them. If they [police] don't catch them tomorrow, or sometime soon, God forbid, [gang members will] shoot that kid and he'll end up six feet under."

Immigrants pushed back against the violence and social disorder as they put down roots and built community, all the while hanging on fiercely to their purpose for migrating. Most were like Maritza, an undocumented single mother from Mexico City, who was undeterred by the violence. When she arrived at a house in Pueblo Viejo with thirty other immigrants, she was warned about the gangs and discouraged from navigating the city on her own. She described her response: "In my mind, I came to work. . . . The guys used to tell me, 'Don't go out because the *cholos* will do this and that.' I didn't even know what a *cholo* was. I only came to work. I don't want to know anything about *cholos*. . . . I left anyway."

Maritza did not heed the advice of her male coethnics and found a job as a babysitter. She saved her money and brought her children to the United States a year after her migration. Work and family guided these immigrants as they left their imprint on their neighborhoods.

Work as Moral Order

"*¿A que venimos a este país? ¡A Triunfar!* [What did we come to this country for? To succeed!]"

This is the refrain in the radio show *Piolín por la Mañana* (*Mornings with Tweety-Bird*). The show plays in Los Angeles during immigrants' ride to work. It emanates from radios in restaurant kitchens and on garment district floors, as well as the small radios of nannies and gardeners who quietly labor in the affluent parts of the city. The radio show openly caters to low-skilled Latino immigrants working in some of the most labor-intensive and meagerly paid jobs. Its catchphrase—meant to lend dignity to low-skilled immigrants' work—is repeated multiple times throughout the morning show, capturing and reinforcing the spirit of these immigrants.

The violence and social disorder in Los Angeles contrasted starkly with immigrants' daily lives in these neighborhoods, which revolve around work and family. Buses traversing these neighborhoods and the nearby Metrolink are full of workers making their way to and from their jobs. In segregated Los Angeles, Martha observed, "the buses are full of Latinos. At 5:30 AM, when I take the bus, it's only Latinos on their way to work." Octavio, an undocumented worker, noted that everyone on his block left for work at around the same time. Rosa, a full-time factory worker for twenty-five years, told me that there was no unemployment in her Central City neighborhood. "I think that everyone goes to work here," she said. "There are no lazy people here, no, you don't see that." Life was organized around work in Pueblo Viejo and Central City.

Even though the poverty in their neighborhoods was entrenched, immigrants declared them to be working-class or working poor communities.[14] Immigrants were well attuned to what statistics reveal: Mexican immigrant men have the highest labor market participation in the United States.[15] Mexican immigrant women's participation is not as high as it is for other women, but all but one of the women I interviewed had entered the U.S. labor market at some point. The high employment rate in the Mexican immigrant community is driven by well-established migrant networks that link these immigrants to jobs, at times even prior to their arrival.[16] But like most people who find any level of success in the United States, Mexicans attribute their high rates of employment to "hard work." This cognitive frame guides their understanding of their purpose in the United States.[17]

This cognitive frame of "a hardworking people" informed the moral order of these neighborhoods in ways that challenged violence and social disorder. As other scholars have found in urban poor contexts, immigrants drew symbolic boundaries in their neighborhood along moral grounds, the greatest moral divide being between those who were deemed hardworking and those who were not.[18] Immigrants in this study constructed moral boundaries against two archetypes: the gang-affiliated young man believed to be at the root of violence and social disorder, and the idle, "lazy" (American) young man unattached to school or work and a burden to society. In the minds of most of these immigrants, these two archetypes were one and the same—a reflection of what scholars might call "downward assimilation," or "second-generation decline." Those so characterized had departed from immigrants' strong work ethic—a symptom of their acculturation to the United States.

Inculcating an Ethic of Hard Work: Ganarse la Vida

Adhering to a strong work ethic was central to immigrants' sense of identity and regarded as a badge of honor. Angelica had been cleaning people's homes since she was eight years old. While she wished she had more schooling, she took great pride in her work ethic, saying, "That's what's beautiful about coming from Mexico. They've taught us to work because our parents were hardworking." Angelica worked in the informal labor market to make ends meet for her household of five and in order to send money to her elderly father in Mexico. Her husband, Gilberto, paid the rent and bills, but he was, she said, "*un poco codito* [stingy]." He sometimes withheld money for food when he got angry. To help her precarious situation, Angelica sold cosmetic and households products that were popular in her neighborhood, like Avon, Stanley, and Shaklee. She also sold *tamales, enchiladas,* and *flan,* which she towed up and down her neighborhood on her stroller, with her toddler on board. Angelica was an avid contestant in local radio shows and frequently won tickets to concerts that she would then sell in the neighborhood. She was used to the hustle, and she made sure that her three children were fed and that her father had medication. She had even paid for an upgrade to install a toilet convenient to his room and helped her sister make ends meet while she cared for him.

Parents were proud to model their ethic of hard work, and several put their sons to work at a young age. This practice was especially pronounced among the lowest-skilled immigrants, who regarded the work ethic as one of the few assets they could pass on to the next generation. Martha, for example, sometimes took her sons to her work as a housecleaner, and they helped her wash and fold clothes, dust, vacuum, and sweep. Timoteo, who had begun working when he was seven in Mexico, asserted that the peak age at which to cement a strong work ethic in a child was two to seven years old. He believed that "children are at their peak of learning" at this age and felt that he had successfully instilled this value in his son by paying him an allowance to help around the house when he was young. "That is how he learned on his own to carve a path for himself," Timoteo said. He was continuing the practice with his grandchildren. These immigrants understood that encouraging an ethic of hard work was their parental responsibility to ensure that their sons would be self-sufficient and productive members of society. Humberto said of his children:

> The best love is to teach them to *ganarse la vida* [earn a living/become self-sufficient through work]. Life is hard. We are not eternal. I wouldn't want people to feel sorry for them. If they know how to earn a living, if they are *acomodedidos* [accommodating of others] or they know how to work in something, they won't struggle, because in this life there is always work [opportunities].

As their sons entered young adulthood, parents advised them on being good workers and pleasing their employers. Adriana explained, "They need to be punctual and *echarle ganas* [give it their all], because if not, they'll let you go. And I tell them to obey [their bosses], because as my husband says, 'We are going to work. We are going to go do what they tell us to do. We are not going to go do what we want.'" Rosa said something very similar: "I tell [my children] to value their work and to be punctual, and I tell them they're going to work to be told what to do and not to tell others what to do." These lessons—being reliable and compliant at work—were in line with their working-class occupations. Most of the parents had held low-status jobs in Los Angeles for twenty to thirty years, many of them grueling and labor-intensive. They had worked as restaurant cooks, maintenance and construction workers, truck drivers, factory workers, nannies, housekeepers, garment workers, and more. Understanding that they were expendable, they intended to teach their children traits that employers valued to keep them on the job.

At the same time, parents were acutely attuned to the exploitation of their labor and the toll it took on them.[19] The day I met Esperanza in her living room she wore two black wristbands. Her hands rested on her lap, facing up to ease the pain that traveled up and down her arms and concentrated in her neck. For over twenty years, she had worked at a local factory, straining her hands from embroidering delicate towels and her arms from carrying heavy and hot pressed loads of them. "My hands are now damaged," she sighed.

> I feel the pain all the way back here [*points to her neck*]. All this gets swollen. My hands look like they're drying up, I have them very, very skinny, and I can't raise my hands to hang clothing on the clothing line. I struggle to raise my hands, to lift anything. They have to help me to shower, scrub my back. To think I worked all those years to be left this way. I am now disabled for life. . . . I sometimes ask, was it worth it?

Such reflections led parents to hope that their children would obtain jobs *donde no se maten tanto* (where they won't kill themselves or work their bodies so much). Ernesto worked twenty-five years polishing metal at a factory in Los Angeles before it closed. His wife was a cook at a lunch truck. Neither earned very much. He hoped that his children would have

> a job where they don't have to work a lot, like a receptionist, where they just pick up phones, take notes, be on the computer, pull out directions. . . .

I would hate to see [my son] picking up boxes of fruit at a supermarket, or sweeping or mopping. . . . That's what I tell [my daughters]: you would look so nice sitting on a desk . . . not flipping hamburgers.

Raymundo, who had climbed the occupational ladder to become a manager at an asbestos company, wanted his son to be

an accountant, a bank teller where they are nicely dressed, that they have a nine-to-five job. They won't earn a thousand or two thousand per week, but they're just sitting there looking at the computer, something like that. A lawyer, a doctor, what do I know? Perhaps I'm hoping for too much, but that's what I would like.

Parents understood that school was the route to such jobs. Like other immigrant parents, Brisa, who collected cans at times to make ends meet, concluded that "dreaming is nice, but here [in the United States], life is hard. I think it's very hard. Only those who study can reach that American Dream." Given their work histories and limited resources, these low-skilled immigrants strongly encouraged schooling while emphasizing an ethic of hard work—a cognitive frame within their reach—as the key to success. Frustrated parents whose sons wanted to leave school or decided not to continue after high school were quick to respond: *"¡No quisiste escuela, asi que vete a trabajar!* [You didn't want school? Get to work then!]."

"Sometimes Kids Go to Waste": Boundaries against Gang-Affiliated and Disconnected Young Men

I have described the lengths to which Esperanza went to keep her son out of a gang; other parents shared her anxiety. Like some scholars, parents in this study voiced fears that the negative context of their surroundings might corrupt their children, undermining their hard work and sacrifice. Claudia, who was from the border town of Tijuana, Mexico, saw migration as an enormous risk that threatened more than just her children's safety. As she explained, "Sometimes immigrants come [to the United States] and their sons *se hechan a perder* [go to waste]." Observing that not all youth succumbed to gangs, however, parents interpreted this possibility as a function of choice, which they sought to influence by imposing strong moral boundaries against those they saw to be at the root of the violence and social disorder: gang-affiliated, idle young men.

Parents were quick to blame disconnected young men on their blocks as the source of the violence, social disorder, and chronic poverty that plagued their community. From Humberto's point of view, idleness alone posed a threat, even for boys who were not formally affiliated with a gang: "If a group of guys gather there, by the liquor store, let's say they're not bad, that they're not doing anything, but they're hanging out in a group, a gang will come and look for a problem . . . that's what's going to happen, it affects the whole community."

Yet in many other parents' view, idle young men and gang members were one and the same. Rosa, a homeowner in Central City, felt that she could identify these young men in her neighborhood based on dress and demeanor alone. "No school. No work. Only the street!" she said. "I see these baldheaded guys . . . you can tell in their look."

In line with national figures, black men in Central City experienced higher rates of joblessness than Latino men.[20] The greater presence of young black men on their street corners reflected this, leading some immigrants to draw strong moral boundaries against them.[21] Agustina and Ricardo decided to sell their house in Central City because of the more visible presence of disconnected black youth on their block. Agustina explained:

These black guys—they weren't there [on the corner] before. Years back, when we got here [fifteen years earlier], they were my children's age, little, and they were no problem, but now that they're grown, it stinks awful out there . . . marijuana and God knows what else. . . . They sometimes fight, they've fought with bats and guns. . . . The police arrest them all the time but then let them go. . . . They just bring problems.

Similarly, Adriana attributed rising disorder on her block to a demographic shift:

It was all black [when she moved in], but it was different. There were more elderly than young people. . . . There were kids, but they wouldn't let them out like today. Now, I'm not really liking it here. . . . Those *chamacos* [young guys] are very disorderly, they have free rein. They don't educate them to respect, they let them be vagrants, that's what I think, and that is why I don't like it here anymore. In that house right in front, a bunch of guys get together to smoke, to drink and do drugs too.

In this context, moral boundaries against the gang prototype were aggressively exercised in families' homes. Parents intensely disputed their children's clothing choices that they thought might indicate gang involvement. Isela cringed as she thought back to the day when she returned from a trip to Mexico to find her two sons with shaved heads and wearing baggy shirts and pants. She later cut the clothes to ribbons. Her husband was indifferent, but Isela described feeling ashamed that her sons were embracing a lifestyle she detested, although neither of her sons was in a gang. Angelica admired her neighbor's sons for wearing more closely fitting clothing and keeping their hair tidy, lamenting her own sons' dress and grooming choices: "I wish you would dress that way, not with your *guanguras* [loose clothing]. They went to college, got married, and kept studying." Immigrants' general disdain for what was deemed gang attire filtered into the neighborhood. Salvador, a short, brown-skinned twenty-year-old with a shaved head, understood that despite not being in a gang, people viewed him as such because of the way he dressed. He said, "I mean, people see me and think, 'Oh look at that gangster walking by.' I don't pay no attention to that. They are always going to be prejudiced."

The appearance of gang membership alone was alarming and signaled to many of these immigrant parents a departure from work and responsibility. Parents of daughters worried as well. Estela, Timoteo's wife, was horrified that her daughters had gangster boyfriends in their teenage years. "You know that a gangster as a boyfriend is a problem. . . . A gangster has no future. Not with himself or for his children," she said. Their choice of boyfriends was a point of conflict in the home. Estela voiced harsh words to her daughters: "Instead of brains, you [the daughters] have rocks, trash, dirt, I don't know what you have in your head. . . . They don't get it." She held up their father's work ethic as the reason they had built a "future" together, as Timoteo and Estela too had become a couple in their teens.

Gang members were deemed morally deficient, unattached to work or school, a threat to immigrants' hard work and sacrifice. These immigrants gave little recognition to the reasons that underlay these young men's gang involvement or disconnect from the community, insisting that gang membership was a choice. Humberto explained, "There are jobs, but what happens is that they don't want to earn little and they don't know how to do anything. That's what happens." He asserted that ever since he "stepped into this *rancho* of Los Angeles, believe me that the day I don't work is because I don't want to, because I'm being lazy. Because yes, I can get work every single weekend, all the time." And Humberto did work most weekends on side construction jobs.

The Heightened Moral Order
of the Undocumented Immigrant Context

On one end of the moral spectrum were stigmatized, disconnected, and gang-affiliated young men; on the other end, held in much higher esteem, were undocumented immigrants. In the Los Angeles urban context, the Latino second generation found no room for the idea that "there are no jobs" in the United States. As several immigrants pointed out, jobs being filled by undocumented immigrant workers—who are technically not supposed to be hired because of their status—was proof that anyone who did not work chose not to do so. As Dolores explained: "Here, there are many people who don't have papers, but they are very *luchistas* [striving people]; they'll work doing anything. Like my husband says, there are many people who don't have jobs and have papers. They don't work because they're lazy, because looking for work you'll find it, even if it's picking up cans." Darío evaluated his three unemployed sons, ages seventeen to twenty-one, in this heightened moral context: "They must be allergic [to work] . . . because there are many people *without papers* who work."

In the Latino immigrant urban context, worse than toiling in the most meagerly paid and exploitative jobs was not working at all. Although immigrants strongly encouraged their sons to pursue an education, many expected their young adult children to work, even if, much to their dismay, they worked jobs in the low-wage sector. Rosita, a migrant from Mexico City, was greatly frustrated with her son Moises, who left high school, refused to work with his father, a mechanic, and then struggled to land a job.

> You don't want to go to school and you don't want to work with [your father]? . . . Pick a job: *tortillero,* baker, selling oranges on the corner. . . . [And he would respond,] "Mom! How can you say that?" Well, what do you know how to do? They're going to ask you, what did you study? He stared at me . . . *barrendero?* [street or floor sweeper]?

Moises found himself working alongside Rosita in maintenance, a job she saw as beneath him, so she would taunt him: "We're so studious, aren't we, son? That's why we do maintenance!" She hoped that this treatment would convince him to get a better job. Brisa had a similar approach to her son Simon's lackluster, part-time college pursuit: "You want to keep working like *burros,* keep at it! You want to be working like me, cleaning shit? I tell them with those [harsh] words so that they get it through their head that they have to do something in life."

Despite such fears and young Latino men's high rates of school non-completion, the children of Latino immigrants are *not* any more likely to be disconnected from school and work than others.[22] In fact, some studies indicate that the Latino second generation in central cities has a stronger attachment to work than most other young adults.[23] Still, some young men had bouts of unemployment, particularly during the Great Recession, and the contrast with their parents' steady employment created tensions. Darío had maintained steady employment in the United States for thirty years, even though he had relied on public transportation all those years to get to his job. His three sons were neither in school nor working when I first met them, causing him great frustration. "I'm tired of telling them to look for a job!" he exclaimed. His son Efrain, reported that Darío often lashed out at him and his brothers, cursing them off as *"¡par de huevones!* [lazy pair]." Disappointed, Darío explained that "the only thing they like to do is play on the computer, hear music, eat and sleep, like children. That's what they like. . . . They don't like either of the two, school or work." Dario's views of his sons would change and soften over time as he witnessed them make efforts to get ahead but struggle in a changing economy.

In line with their strong work orientation, immigrants reacted strongly to any suggestion that they seek public assistance. Despite the rhetoric in the immigration debate about immigrants migrating to seek public assistance, studies find that they are less likely to seek such help relative to other groups.[24] In keeping with their view that being idle represented a moral failure, respondents tried hard not to resort to public assistance, even when in great need. Brisa had been enrolled in Temporary Assistance for Needy Families (TANF) for a short time, but soon turned to juggling two jobs and collecting cans and scrap metal around the neighborhood to earn money instead of taking government aid. She said, "You know, when you get that money, it doesn't last you. I feel that way because when you don't work for it, you waste it and when you don't have anything, you don't have anything. So when I earn my money, I'm more aware how I spend my money and how I invest it." Others also emphasized that they had only received aid, whether welfare, food stamps, or food supplied through the Special Supplemental Nutrition Program for Women, Infants, and Children (WIC), "for short period of time," stressing that they did not like handouts and believed that accepting them made people lazy. Mexican immigrants have below-average rates of participation in these programs. So Franco, a migrant from Guanajuato, reacted strongly to the stereotype that Mexicans migrated to the United States to seek government help:

> This is an immigrant community. Those who come from Mexico don't come thinking about welfare. A lot of them don't know about welfare, they've never heard about that in their life. They come with the idea they're here to work. They arrive looking for work. They don't come looking for assistance. All of them, they either arrive here looking for work to send to Mexico or to pay the *coyote*. All immigrants arrive working.

Those who had never relied on assistance to get by took pride in it. Rosa said: "Thank God. It's because we [she and her siblings] all know how to work. . . . None of us have asked for help, none of that. We have advanced in life because we have all known to work." Such was her disapproval of government aid that she even connected assistance receipt to gang involvement: "People who go on welfare, that's like handing your kids to gangs, because they give them everything, it doesn't cost them anything." Timoteo and Estela's two granddaughters received public assistance after they became teen parents with their gang member boyfriends, which Timoteo and Estela lamented: "It's bad [public assistance] because I think it makes people *huevonas* [lazy]. *Atenidas* [loafers]." From the perspective of these immigrants, relying on public assistance, a characteristic they associated with the U.S.-born, was for "lazy people" who did not like or know how to work.

Despite tensions in some families, and fear that their son's departure from a strong work ethic was a real threat, parents generally expressed pride in their children as most attended school or worked or both. Jesusita, for example, had four children who were either in college or had graduated from college and were now working. She noted, "A successful life is that my children are people who contribute to the community. I would feel proud. Because if my children are *lacra* [leaches or bums], how am I going to feel? Like a failure." Even those whose children did not complete high school were proud of their children—so long as they had a job. These immigrants noted that raising a son in the inner city who escapes violence, completes school, and avoids gangs and delinquency "*es ganansia*" [is a gain]. Work was given moral worth in their communities—a cultural context that the second generation would become acutely attuned to as they transitioned to adulthood.

The Contested Immigrant Neighborhood: Navigating Violence, Family, and Work

The violence and social disorder that immigrants in this study encountered in Los Angeles when they arrived came as a shock to most, leading to a period of fear and seclusion. Immigrants quickly learned that the violence and social disorder in American cities not only threatened the physical safety of their families but the future prospects of their children as well. During the most turbulent years in Los Angeles, immigrants worried that their children would get entangled in local gang dynamics, be absorbed by its culture, and move away from school and work. For these immigrants, the American urban neighborhood was a place where their sacrifice, efforts, and dreams could quickly dissipate with their children. Such an outcome was also what some immigration scholars predicted.

Yet rarely do people allow their dreams to be stolen that way, and the Latino immigrants in this study were no exception. Through everyday practices extolling family and work, they pushed against the violence and social disorder. By the time I met the young men in this study, violence had greatly declined in these neighborhoods; in fact, by the time of the follow-up study, violence was at a record low. The decline of violence across American cities after the mid-1990s has stumped researchers, who offer competing explanations. One significant shift that took place at this time in the United States cannot be ignored: we entered into the era of mass incarceration. Whereas immigrants described pervasive police neglect in the 1980s and early 1990s, the young men in the study spoke of the growing presence and heavy surveillance of law enforcement. Yet this shift alone does not explain why crime and violence dropped. As Patrick Sharkey explains, the decrease also "came from within," as the "new guardians" looking out over the city included residents.[25] He attributes the mobilization of residents against violence to a growth in non-profit organizations. A few immigrants in this study had connected to these organizations, yet I found that they also displayed a subtler form of resistance to violence and disorder. In Pueblo Viejo and Central City, Latino immigrants responded to the violence and protected their children by managing social relations in their neighborhoods and enacting moral boundaries. In doing so, they altered the organizational structure and cultural context of these neighborhoods by building community and imposing a moral order that disturbed the violence and social disorder.

Children of Latino immigrants coming of age in these neighborhoods did not contend with a homogenous "oppositional culture" but rather navigated a context that was culturally and morally contested. Wilson was right that poor Mexican immigrant communities were distinct from poor black communities experiencing high rates of joblessness.[26] As I explain ahead, the strong attachment to work he noted in these communities was supported by migrant networks, primarily kin-based, that linked these low-skilled, often undocumented immigrants to jobs. These work networks are harder to come by for poor blacks, who face distinct employment discrimination in the labor market. As I show in later chapters, these immigrant networks concentrated in Latino urban neighborhoods facilitate the job search process of the second generation in a way that guards off unemployment or joblessness for this group, all while constraining them to lower tiered jobs. In a context of limited social mobility, symbolic and moral boundaries carry great meaning—and have consequences.[27] Immigrants exercised moral boundaries as a way to fend off negative influences and reinforce conventional norms. Yet doing so had the unintended consequence of reinforcing notions of an "undeserving poor." In this heightened moral context, immigrants often welcomed police, who became a formidable presence in their neighborhoods and had a profound impact on the most marginalized young men. Segmented assimilation scholars ignored how immigrants would respond to violence and social disorder, including how they altered the organizational and cultural context. As I explain ahead in part II of this book, these scholars also failed to recognize the most damaging features of the American urban context—its urban violence and segregation—and its impact on the children of these immigrants.

....

CHAPTER 3

Same Landing, Unequal Starts

The Varying Social Capital of Mexican Immigrants

Rosita's eldest son, Manolo, was shot and killed, at the age of sixteen, by rival gang members blocks away from her home in 1990. Rosita was surrounded by coethnics then but had few people to turn to for support when Manolo died. She explained that, "at that time my only *compadre* . . . was a priest. I didn't know anyone. . . . Aside from that, no, no one else." Rosita had migrated four years prior with her four youngest children to Pueblo Viejo, one of the most gang-entrenched neighborhoods in Los Angeles at the time. She left Mexico City to reunite with her husband, a mechanic, who sent for their three eldest children six months after her arrival. She had three more children in the United States, a total of ten.

Back then, Rosita's life was engulfed by the busy routine of the home. She recalled, "I need to mop, make the food, wash, iron, I have to run this errand, that errand. . . . I didn't go to church. I had to bathe them. I had to do this, do that, so what time did I have?" Rosita's sister flew in from Mexico City for a couple of days when Rosita and her husband lost Manolo. Rosita recalled that her sister recognized her social isolation. "I was indoors all the time. My sister would tell me, 'You're like those horses [with blinders on their faces]. You only see here.'" She gestured in front of her face. "'You don't see here or there.'" She gestured more broadly.

Rosita had tried to manage the risks of the neighborhood for her sons, at times walking the streets to search for them and beg them to return home after their alcoholic father's outbursts had led them to flee, but it was to no avail. Despite her concerted efforts, Manolo had joined a gang. And he had paid for it with his life.

Reconceptualizing the Social Capital of Mexican Immigrants

When considering who becomes absorbed into the violence and social disorder of high-poverty urban neighborhoods, scholars heavily emphasize the role of weak community ties, a particular lack of social capital. Neighborhoods with low levels of trust and social cohesion, or minimal collective efficacy, are associated with higher levels of crime and violence.[1] As chapter 2 explained, building trust and cohesion in violent neighborhoods is hard to accomplish and time-consuming, but the social capital available in the ethnic community can be understood as a potential resource for the second generation. Portes and Zhou suggest that dense ethnic ties in the central city can function as a form of social capital that protects the second generation from a negative type of acculturation and "downward assimilation."[2] Researchers believe that a tight-knit ethnic community reinforces conventional norms and social control, discouraging delinquency, gang formation, and tragedies like Manolo's death.

Examining social capital at the community level is useful when comparing neighborhood contexts (or ethnic groups), but it is less useful for explaining variation *within* communities. Even in the most gang-entrenched neighborhoods in Los Angeles—such as where Rosita landed—only about 10 percent of youth became involved in gangs in the 1980s and 1990s.[3] This internal variation is grossly overlooked in the existing literature on the Latino second generation. In later chapters, I examine why some young men, but not others, are drawn into negative neighborhood processes. To understand this I first reconceptualize the social capital of the Mexican case, calling attention to how migrant networks interact with the American segregated context to produce divergent outcomes for the second generation. In this chapter, I foreground the varied social capital of Mexican immigrants, calling attention to their kin ties as their primary migrant networks and source of *social support*—a kind of social capital that emerges through bonding ties.[4]

In the previous chapter, I discussed the role of building community in the decline of violence. Yet an emphasis on social capital at the community level ignores that the primary organizing unit of the Mexican-origin group is not the ethnic collective but the family or kin structure. A walk through Pueblo Viejo or Central City on any given Saturday or Sunday afternoon reveals families gathered in their homes to celebrate birthdays or engage in holiday festivities. Fellowship with family permeates these blocks, as do the music and food that lend their rhythms, tastes, and smells to these neighborhoods. Years after their migration, Mexican immigrants continue to socialize primarily with kin and to draw on them for social support. Rosita, for instance, was surrounded by a large ethnic community, but she found relief and support only when her sister flew in from Mexico City to be with her. Rosita lacked social capital because she had limited ethnic ties and no kin ties in Los Angeles.

Mexicans' strong sense of familism has long been documented, and this cognitive frame privileging family in everyday decisions and interactions has a profound impact on the integration process of immigrants and their children in the United States.[5] In addition to family being a value, family is a primary source of social capital. Coleman identified it as such, noting that family cohesion and family connections create a closed network that reinforces academic expectations.[6] The gang expert Diego Vigil has long noted that family support structures distinguish gang youth from non-gang-affiliated youth in Los Angeles neighborhoods.[7] In her comprehensive study of Mexican migration, Filiz Garip found that family ties factored prominently in facilitating migration during the mid-1970s and 1980s, the time period when most of my study participants migrated. Garip emphasized nuclear ties, writing, "Social facilitation . . . likely worked through immediate family members—who could be trusted and to whom the good deeds could be reciprocated—rather than extended family or community relations."[8]

Latino immigrants' social support—as a form of social capital—originates in the migration process and is unequally distributed across these families in the United States; thus, some are more vulnerable than others.[9] All families in this study reported a strong sense of familism, yet not all had similar access to kin ties. Study participants generally relied on kin— siblings, uncles, aunts, cousins—to facilitate migration by helping with housing and job-seeking. Kin ties continued to provide various types of support as immigrants raised their children in the United States and as they transitioned to adulthood. In the absence of kin ties, some immigrants turn to trusted neighborhood institutions, like a church. Others remained socially isolated years after their migration.

Kin-based social capital has limitations. Social capital depends not only on the availability of ties but on trust and reciprocity, which, as researchers have found, can erode with limited resources or taxing circumstances.[10] Although kin provide the poor with significant social support, poverty strains kin relations. Families in this study confronted numerous challenges as they juggled work and family demands, navigating risky neighborhoods, troubled schools, and, in many cases, ongoing financial distress as the needs of their growing families multiplied. I demonstrate here that kin-based social capital is an asset of the Mexican immigrant group that ebbs and flows throughout the life course of the second generation.[11]

In later chapters, I explain how kin-based social capital and social support via institutional ties inhibit "second-generation decline." In this study, young men who had socially isolated immigrant parents with neither kin nor institutional ties, like Rosita, were some of the most vulnerable in the urban environment. In the absence of kin or institutional support, immigrants and their children are especially vulnerable in American urban environments and struggle in the labor market. As I show in the following chapters, children of immigrants of socially isolated families are the most at risk of chronic poverty.

Unequal Starts: The Varying Social Capital of Mexican Migrants

The sociopolitical context impacts social capital. Distinct migrant types have dominated during certain time periods, reflecting the changing political and economic contexts in Mexico and the United States.[12] Male "sojourners" dominated until the mid-1980s, when women began to migrate in higher numbers than in the past.[13] As the Mexican migrant flow has diversified, so has the nature of their social networks and the social capital with which they arrive in the United States. Kin-based social capital has significant consequences for the integration process of the second generation: migrants' support network structures shape how they manage the urban environment and later mobilize resources for the second generation when the latter confront challenges in the labor market.

To understand the internal variation of kin-based social capital, I first distinguish between rural and urban migrants who arrived in the United States during distinct sociopolitical and economic eras and the impact of those differences on their human capital and the kin ties they have available. Immigrants' social support structure affects not only immigrants themselves but also the second generation. I also call attention to the way in which gender matters; female migrants who arrive in the United States without partners or other adult kin are especially vulnerable and often remain isolated. This chapter provides the backdrop to the contrasting experiences created by human and social capital of Mexican immigrants in the settlement and integration processes for them and their children.

The Last Wave Dominated by Rural Mexican Migrants

Two-thirds of the immigrants in this study, including Genaro's parents, Esperanza and José, grew up in *ranchos*—small farming villages or towns in the central-western region of Mexico—and came to the United States in the 1970s or early 1980s.[14] Migration to the United States from this region dates back to the late nineteenth century, when railroad lines gave U.S. job recruiters easy access to a population hungry for work.[15] U.S. employers' penetration into this region of Mexico resulted in an expansive and intergenerational chain of migration that continues to Los Angeles to this day, making it the longest-standing migration flow in the world.[16]

Strong communal norms and family ties in the United States encouraged Esperanza and José to seek work in El Norte. To describe their U.S.-born children as "second-generation" is to obscure the family's entrenched relationship to the United States. In reality, Esperanza's children would be the third generation in their family aiming to escape poverty and attain a version of the American Dream, although they were the first generation born in the United States.

Esperanza's farmworker father brought her to the United States in 1975, when she was nineteen, to help provide for the family in Mexico. She recalled her fear in making the journey, noting that her father, a *bracero*—a legally contracted temporary worker in the United States—was "practically a stranger" owing to the long periods of his absence when she was growing up.[17] When Esperanza arrived in northern California, she discovered that her father lived in a crowded trailer with other farmworking men. Seeing the arduous conditions her father toiled under to provide for their family—"with mud all the way to his waist," she vividly recalled—she was determined to work to supplement her father's meager wages and help the family get by. It was then, Esperanza noted, that "*work* became my American Dream."

In 1964, the United States had terminated the exploitative bracero program, under pressure from civil rights groups, and placed a cap on legal

Mexican migration for the first time ever.[18] The cap had not dampened demand for Mexican labor, and migrants like Esperanza's father remained in the United States to facilitate further migration. Thus, political changes did little to alter the flow of Mexican migration.[19] But they did alter the incorporation process that Esperanza and José faced, because, like most Mexican immigrants then, they had no documentation. Douglas Massey and his colleagues have referred to 1965–1985 as the "undocumented," or "de facto guest worker," era.[20] This was a period of minimal border enforcement and no employer sanctions against hiring undocumented migrants. These immigrants were not sojourners engaged in circular migration like their predecessors.[21] Many were "crisis migrants": in response to economic crises in Mexico, they turned to close-kin ties in the United States to facilitate their migration.[22] The rise in Mexican female migration during this time, also facilitated by kin relations, allowed them to establish family roots in Los Angeles.[23]

Immigrants from rural areas typically had only three to six years of schooling, at the most. Their low human capital relegated them to the unskilled, poorly paid labor market in Los Angeles. Yet by their own account, they had found it easy to find a job when they arrived, and some had a job upon arrival. Migrant networks eased their settlement process. Most lived with kin upon arrival and connected with jobs through them.

Cases like that of Ernesto, who arrived in 1977 from Michoacán with three male cousins, are well documented. Forced to leave school at ten years old to work in the fields "from sunup to sundown" to help provide for a family of ten, Ernesto arrived in the United States with ample experience in hard labor. A relative who was then a supervisor at a factory invited him and his cousins to come work there. Ernesto and his three migrant cousins lived with this relative and his young family for about two years before they rented a place of their own in Pueblo Viejo. He had lived in the United States for ten years when he met Patricia from Guadalajara. They married and would raise seven children in Pueblo Viejo. Ernesto worked steadily for many years polishing metal until his company closed in the mid-2000s, leaving him, now much older but also more skilled, to compete against a growing number of more recently arrived and still-undocumented migrants for meagerly paid jobs.

By the time this study began, immigrants like Esperanza and Ernesto had lived in the United States between twenty-five and thirty years—and some of their kin much longer. They had witnessed and weathered economic downturns and political transformations in the country, as well as changes in the urban environment. Most had documentation; half of those who had entered before 1986, including Ernesto, acquired authorization under the 1986 Immigration Reform and Control Act (IRCA), which gave amnesty to 2.3 million undocumented immigrants.[24] The other half, including Esperanza, acquired authorization through a family member as part of the U.S. immigration family reunification policy; Esperanza's father, a documented "circular migrant," was her sponsor.[25] Whereas recently arrived undocumented immigrants focused on their "lack of papers" as a barrier to upward mobility, long-term legal residents like Ernesto decried a changing economy in the United States that made it harder to get ahead, for both themselves and their children. Ernesto remained underemployed throughout the study, and when we spoke, he was contemplating moving to Las Vegas, where the cost of living would be lower and a cousin of his might help him find work.

Rural immigrant parents who arrived in the 1970s and early 1980s had experienced largely stable employment during most of their working years in the United States, and this work stability, albeit for modest pay, allowed about one-third of these parents to purchase a home. Esperanza and her husband received help from the government to buy their home in Pueblo Viejo when they were forced to move out of public housing upon its impending demolition, but most families relied on extended kin for help in establishing themselves residentially in Los Angeles.

Noel's parents, Adriana and Vidal, had also been part of the rural migrant flow. Like Esperanza and José, they were single when they migrated; they came from the same rural town in Jalisco in the mid-1970s. Though Adriana's father retired in Mexico, he and other kin had worked many years in the United States as *braceros*. Vidal's family had similarly deep roots in the United States, and both young people lived with extended family when they first came to the United States. After they met and married in the early 1980s, several family members combined their financial resources to help the couple make the down payment on their first small home. With Vidal's steady work in construction, they were able to pay their debt to their kin over time and to reciprocate with help throughout the years. By 1988, the couple had purchased a larger home for their growing family of eight in one of the quieter blocks in Central City.

Much of what we know about Mexican migration stems from studies on this well-established flow of migrants from the rural, central-western region of Mexico. The concept of downward assimilation was formed with rural, unskilled immigrants like them in mind; some researchers claimed that these immigrants had no social capital, partly because of their lack of class diversity.[26] Yet this assessment ignores the importance of "strong ties" and "bonding ties." In Los Angeles, many of these immigrants were linked to *paisanos*—ethnic ties from their specific rural communities. But the most significant help came from kin ties who provided migrants with a valuable form of social capital—social support—helping them migrate and get settled, and then, as I show later in the chapter, helping them navigate the American context for their children.

The migration flow from Mexico to the United States has been transformed since Adriana, Vidal, Ernesto, Esperanza, and José left their rural communities. Mexico experienced rapid urbanization in the last half of the twentieth century. Whereas only 42 percent of the Mexican population lived in urban areas (defined as municipalities with more than 2,500 residents) in 1950, this figure had climbed to 78 percent by 2010.[27] Many rural Mexicans migrated internally into Mexico's growing towns and cities or were engulfed by them, rather than migrating to the United States. By the late 1970s and early 1980s, this demographic shift in Mexico was accompanied by the country's economic restructuring, which would trigger the first large wave of urban Mexicans migrating to the United States.[28]

Immigrants from the New Era of Urban Mexican Migration

The urban migration from Mexico has given way to a distinct shift in the Mexican-origin population of the United States, as well as changes in their social support networks and human capital. The U.S. economy began to lose well-paid manufacturing jobs in the late 1970s as it liberalized and entered a global economy. During this time, Mexico underwent parallel changes. Beginning in the early 1980s, Mexico's economy was transformed from a closed, import-substitution industrialization model to an export-oriented and internationally competitive economy. Rubén Hernández-León explains that the high salaries and social protections of Mexico's urban working class eroded during this transition as Mexican national companies shut down, unable to compete in a global market.[29] Scholars have noted that Mexico's financial crisis in the early 1980s triggered a wave of Mexican urban migration.[30] Yet as Hernández-León explains, Mexico's economic restructuring also altered the character of

Mexican immigration to the United States by propelling an unprecedented flow from urban areas.[31]

By 2010, 70 percent of Mexican immigrants came from cities, like Monterrey, Guadalajara, and Mexico City.[32] This more urbanized migrant stream was also more regionally diverse, as fewer than half of these migrants originated from the traditional sending region. Mexico's economic restructuring and urbanization also opened the floodgate to new streams of migrants, including from the southern, much more indigenous region of Mexico. Migrants in this more diverse stream have spread throughout the United States, settling in destinations that did not previously receive many Mexican immigrants, like New York City and areas of the South.[33] In Los Angeles, this new wave of Mexican migrants has accelerated the traditional migration flow already in place.

One-third of the immigrant parents in this study were part of the new urban migrant stream, having arrived after 1986 and the passing of IRCA. With a growing backlog in U.S. immigration court cases and immigration reform efforts stalled, many immigrants in this stream remain undocumented.[34] Fifteen of the parents in this study were part of this undocumented population, despite having lived in the United States for well over twenty years. Five young men were also undocumented and two of their fathers had been deported. One-quarter of the families were "mixed-status": some kin were undocumented and others, having been born in the United States, were American citizens. With the rise of border enforcement to unprecedented levels, they could not leave the United States, unlike their authorized, mostly rural coethnics who occasionally visited family in Mexico.[35] Many study participants did not venture beyond Los Angeles and its surrounding areas owing to their status and modest incomes.[36]

Scholars are just beginning to untangle how this new migrant stream differs from the well-studied flow from the historical sending region. In general, urban Mexicans have higher levels of education relative to rural coethnics of the past and to nonmigrants of their own time.[37] Most urban migrants in this study had acquired at least a middle school education, and six of the parents had some post–high school education. Some experienced downward social mobility by migrating to Los Angeles and settling in its urban neighborhoods. Their greater human capital factored prominently in the lives of their children, particularly with respect to their schooling. As urban migrants, they were also more attuned to city life than rural migrants.

In keeping with others' research, this study found that, in general, urban migrants had more limited kin ties in the United States than rural migrants.[38] Rural migrants have access to a well-established migrant network that propels further migration and transnationalism. Although there is evidence that tight-knit migrant networks can emerge under certain conditions in urban environments, most urban migrants lack the kind of network infrastructure that rural migrants from the historical sending region can count on.[39] In this new era of high immigration enforcement, circular migration has practically come to a halt, as the cost of crossing without documents has skyrocketed and most migrants now require smugglers. Few relatives follow these migrants. With limited kin ties, urban migrants like Rosita experience more social isolation upon arriving in the United States.

Hector and Katia had also experienced social isolation. Two decades after their migration, they were the only members of their extended family living in Los Angeles. Both the eldest in their families, Hector was raised in Mexico City and Katia in Monterrey, Nuevo Leon, two of the largest cities in Mexico. Their parents divorced around the same time, and both moved to Irapuato, Guanajuato, to live with their respective grandparents. They met and married in Irapuato. Though Hector had a job at a radio station, they experienced downward mobility in a changing Mexican economy. In 1986, this impelled the newlyweds to search for better opportunities in the United States, to which they traveled on temporary tourist visas.

Unlike rural coethnics who drew on close-knit kin ties, Hector and Katia could only turn to acquaintances. These friends took them in initially, and they spent a few nights on an old mattress they found on the street when they first arrived. Katia explained that her family "never had the need to migrate," and she had no social ties in the United States. Hector had spent a couple of his adolescent years in Los Angeles prior to his parents' divorce, and he had high school friends in Los Angeles who gave them a temporary place to stay. These friends helped Hector find his first job. He later became a truck driver. The English skills he had acquired in his adolescence in Los Angeles were pivotal. Hector and Katia overstayed their visas and were undocumented until 2003, when they adjusted their status. Throughout this time, they longed for extended family, but only Katia's single sister followed from Mexico.

Although surrounded by coethnics, Hector and Katia felt partly estranged from their rural counterparts, of whom they heard stories that they had lacked "running water, transportation," and came from villages with "unpaved streets." This was a level of deprivation to which they could not relate. Though grateful for what she had, Katia explained, she had never lived in *"un barrio tan feo* [such an ugly barrio]" as Pueblo Viejo. Her siblings in Mexico were upwardly mobile, but she and Hector could not move beyond a small, two-bedroom apartment. Weak ties like Hector's friends could not replace kin ties, as those relationships lacked the trust, cohesion, and acts of reciprocity associated with strong ties. Hector had an advantage over some urban migrants in that he had spent some years in the United States and learned some English, but accessing social support through nonkin ties took time. Kinlike ties emerged only after Hector and Katia immersed themselves in a church. These church ties would help the couple and their two sons, Jesús and Sebastian, move out of their small apartment to a bigger home twenty-five years after they arrived in the United States.[40]

Marcos and his wife Flora were also dependent on nonkin ties. Marcos left the city of León, Guanajuato, when he was twenty-two and went to the border town of Tijuana because friends had promised to help him cross the border into the United States. He left behind Flora, who was eighteen, and their one-year old son, Bernardo. Flora reflected in 2007 that Marcos "thought he could count on his friends, but in our youth we could not see that they were 'friends' by word, but nothing concrete. He was stranded in Tijuana for about seven or eight months, waiting for someone to help him cross."

When Marcos finally arrived in Los Angeles, he could count on a place to live but could not rely on his acquaintances to find a job. Instead, he looked for open positions in newspapers, at times walking great distances in search of work. He ultimately found a job cutting leather, a job he had performed in León, the leather capital of Mexico. It took two and a half years for Marcos to acquire the financial resources to bring Flora and Bernardo to Los Angeles.

Life would remain a challenge for the undocumented couple as they raised four children on one meager paycheck; Flora had a short stint in the labor market but opted to stay home in order to keep a close watch over her children in Central City, where violence was rampant. Marcos would earn minimum wage for fifteen years, without a kin network to help; Flora supplemented his earnings by informally selling household products. She said that, within the network of people from their city in Mexico, "there is no 'let me help you find a job' or 'I'll take you [to an employment opportunity].'" Flora and Marcos remained in Central City, jumping from room to room and eventually apartment to apartment, skirting rising rents and violence until the morning Marcos was shot outside their apartment and they became acutely aware of their need for support.

Gendered Migration, Support Structures, and Female Isolation

The genderedness of migration has an impact on women's networks and social capital.[41] Historically, females have been "carried" by migrant networks to fulfill traditional family responsibilities.[42] In this study, half of the women migrated to follow their husbands, intent on reuniting with or maintaining their family structure. These women had expected to fulfill traditional gender roles as the primary caretakers of children and the home. The other half of the women, like Esperanza, arrived young and single because people in their families had encouraged them to migrate in order to support their parents or siblings. This meant working to send money to family in Mexico or providing child care and other household support for working kin, often sisters, in the United States. Brisa and Rosa, for example, came to Los Angeles as teens to care for their sisters' children and did not have the opportunity to attend school.

Even when immigrants are nestled in an extensive network, gender roles and expectations affect social capital formation. Angelica was embedded in a large migrant network from Michoacán, Mexico, one of the most established in Los Angeles, yet she raised her children in the housing projects in Pueblo Viejo with minimal social support. She arrived in Los Angeles as a single mother with three-year old Eddy in 1989, when she was twenty-three. He "crossed the line," she recalled, "dressed as a little girl, with a puffy baby-blue dress, using someone else's birth certificate." A male cousin helped her cross the border and Angelica made her way to Los Angeles, where she lived with her sister in an apartment where they had "nothing"—no furniture at all, not even chairs to sit on. At times there was no food and neighbors donated items, a gesture Angelica deeply appreciated. She had several relatives, including her brother, in the United States who refused to support her migration despite her dire need to provide for her son. Angelica began to sell food out of the apartment, *tacos, pozole,* and *sopes,* to pay the rent. She met Gilberto, a body shop worker, when he often stopped to eat there. He and Angelica married, and they had two children of their own. The sisters remained each other's main source of support, but their relations became strained over the years, leaving Angelica with a fragile sense of support.

For many women in this study, migrating to Los Angeles resulted in a period of social isolation. Whereas most men arrived to work and quickly integrated into the labor market, expanding their networks, women's gender roles often confined them to the home and neighborhood. Women who followed their husbands, like Rosita, at times had no kin in Los Angeles outside of their marriage; these women focused primarily on child-rearing and the home. Other women who did have relatives in southern California reported that they rarely visited. Isela had two sisters in southern California, but she hardly saw them. For years in the early 1990s, her husband Carlos refused to get a phone line, and Isela was locked into her neighborhood, not knowing how to drive or get around on public transportation in the sprawling metropolis. The same was true of Flora, who had only two elderly kin in Los Angeles; she rarely saw them, however, as she could not drive across the city. As noted, the urban violence also led these women to keep to themselves.

The women did expand their social networks over time, but the process was slow. Family demands exposed women to neighborhood institutions, principally schools and churches, and several built their social support system through these institutions. Their participation in the labor market also expanded some of their social ties, though not in the same way as happened for men.[43] Women juggled their jobs with their role as mothers and wives, striving to meet the well-ingrained gendered expectation that they would be the primary caretaker of their children; this expectation put significant demands on these women, who were raising boys in violent neighborhoods. Some, like Rosita, a mother of ten, opted out of the labor market when her children were young. Most others worked on and off as they raised their children. Although some women expanded their networks, their strong family orientation and consciousness of gender roles compelled most of them to continue to seek kin ties for socializing and social support. This would have implications for how well they could manage the urban context for their children.

Women who came with minimal or no kin ties to the United States were *pioneras* (trailblazers) who loosely followed a migratory flow with minimal help. Many had been uprooted from Mexico under desperate circumstances: migration was a response to challenging, intimate family circumstances there associated with fractured or strained kin ties. Scholars have documented such independent female migrants, but little is known about them, including why they migrated or how they fared in the United States.[44] In her study,

Pierrette Hondagneu-Sotelo found that these women often came from family with "more fluid" structures than the traditional patriarchal Mexican family structure.[45] Many had worked at a young age outside the home. They left independently, betraying the gendered expectations of migration. I found that their lack of support complicated their settlement process and their children's integration.

For example, Rufina migrated to the United States in the 1970s, alone, when she was nineteen. She had never attended school and had been working in the farm fields in Durango since she was six. Her mother died when she was fifteen, at which point, she explained, "everyone [in her family] did what they wanted." Her eldest sister had married, another was in prison, and kin ties were strained owing to violence in the family. Rufina moved north to the state of Sinaloa, where she worked on farms, as she had done since childhood. Ultimately, she arrived in Tijuana, where she lived briefly with a distant relative. She was anxious not to end up working in *cantinas,* as many women from her town, she claimed, did for "easy money." Instead, Rufina learned to sew and sold clothing for a living. She crossed to the United States in 1974 "out of curiosity" and as an "adventure" because "everyone was coming." She did not know anyone in Los Angeles.

Rufina landed in Compton, California, late in the day, about 5:00 PM, "because that is where the *coyote* [smuggler] left me." She began to roam the streets asking for help. The area was predominantly black, but she found an apartment complex with a large Latino presence. Approaching some immigrants who lived there, she said, "*Oigan,* what should I do? I'm lost. I'm looking for work." Someone led her to a woman who needed a babysitter, and Rufina found her first job, shelter, and food that same evening. In the next couple of days, Rufina walked miles searching for work while pushing a stroller; after making her way into the garment district, she would find a permanent job there. She was still working in the industry when we met in 2007. She was married briefly and had four children whom she raised on her own in Central City public housing during some of the most violent years in the city. Relatives eventually immigrated to Los Angeles, but they remained strained ties; she had no friends in her housing project, and at work she kept to herself to avoid problems, she said. Rufina remained grateful to the family who had helped her when she first arrived, but operating without support ever since had been an ongoing struggle.

Some *pioneras* were already mothers when they migrated, as Angelica had been. Like many others, Maritza began to work when she was eight years old to help her struggling family in Mexico City. At fifteen, she became pregnant and her father forced her to marry into what became an abusive relationship. At the age of twenty-one, with two children, Maritza separated from her husband. Two years later, she had a new partner and another child. However, Maritza's second union would quickly dissolve after she discovered in 1991 that her partner had sexually abused her oldest daughter, then eight years old. While she could support her children in a modest way with the income from her two jobs—one in a factory and another cleaning houses—she left her children with her sister in the hopes that they would be safe from their fathers there and she would be safe after migrating to the United States. A neighbor helped her migrate, and after arriving, she lived in a home with thirty other undocumented immigrants in Los Angeles until she found work as a live-in nanny for a Korean family. Maritza described herself as "locked in" for a year, meaning that she worked daily and had minimal exposure to the city. By saving her $150 weekly earnings, she was able to send for her children in 1992. She had no support system, however, and noted that "life became more difficult" as the family's trauma ultimately unfolded in Los Angeles. She too was one of the most isolated migrants in the study, and her children, including Salvador, had difficulties integrating successfully.

Ebb and Flow: The Changing Kin-Based Social Support of Mexican Immigrants

The social capital of families in this study varied not only across families but within the same family over time. Kin ties are not static, and neither is kin-based social capital. Rosita's second and third sons followed Manolo's footsteps into gangs, but her youngest three did not. A number of changes factored into the pattern among the boys. By the time the youngest three entered their adolescent years, gang activity had calmed a bit in the neighborhood. Benjamin, Rosita's third son, explained, "My mom really took care of [the youngest brothers]. My mom was like, 'I don't want them to be like the others.'" Rosita was now more aware of the risks in the neighborhood and had become more guarded. She had also lost her husband. Although she deeply mourned his death, it ended his alcoholism and abuse of her and her sons. In addition, Rosita's support structure had changed in the process—she found support in her adult children.

Rosita's daughters closely monitored the youngest children, but it was Benjamin who took credit for ensuring that his youngest brothers would not join gangs. He explained that one of his brothers "was starting to get in the same situation . . . hanging out with taggers.[46] But I said to myself . . . this is my position, where I need to stop the cycle. I'm stopping it with myself. I kinda talked to him." Benjamin said that he and his brother "got into arguments" about the consequences of gang membership, "but eventually he found out that I wasn't lying to him."

Benjamin left the gang only after he had been incarcerated and had linked with an organization helping young men transition out of gangs. Benjamin praised the organization, but concluded that his family's support was paramount to changing his life course: "Family is what makes me different than other people [who do not leave gangs]. . . . I'm fortunate to have that. I think family is very important." In the first wave of interviews, Benjamin said of Rosita, "She is the perfect mother. She made me good. My mom was always there for me." When we spoke again in 2013, he referenced his supportive family again: "My sister is always looking out [for me]. There were times I was broke, and she would just say, 'Here's $300, pay me back,' and I would pay her back. Same thing with my mother; we work like *that* in our family." Such acts of trust and reciprocity are a crucial part of the social support that buffered the second generation from some of the risks in their neighborhoods and helped them navigate the labor market.

Kin-based social capital can expand with marriage, with children becoming adults (as in Rosita's case), and with the arrival of new migrants, like the young women who often provide kin with free child care and other forms of support. It can also shrink, leaving families abruptly isolated, with death, migrants' return to their home country, and the straining of relations over time. Supportive kin relations rely on the careful management of trust and social reciprocity, which is difficult with limited resources, especially in a volatile urban context. At times kin ties that are supposed to be supportive prove taxing instead, as with Rosita's husband, who was abusive. In the absence of supportive kin, immigrant families faced two options: remain socially isolated or seek support elsewhere. Most turned to trusted institutions—usually church—where friends became fictive kin. At times institutions linked families to cross-class ties, but most often these community ties remained "bonding ties" between similarly situated families who helped one another get by. Families who remained socially isolated dealt with the weight of poverty, violence, and an unforgiving labor market on their own.

Growing Kin Ties, Expanding Opportunities

A greater number of kin ties creates the opportunity for more socializing with family, exchanges of information, and the social support that eases immigrants' settlement and their integration process over time. In this study, families with the most kin-based social capital were those from the traditional sending regions of rural Mexico, where husbands and wives often came from the same *rancho*. These immigrant families could often re-create traditional kin Mexican networks in Los Angeles. They socialized primarily within these networks and drew social support from them, and their children were also tightly embedded in these kin networks growing up.

Such was the case for Agustina and Ricardo, immigrants from a small town in Guerrero, Mexico. In 1980, when Agustina was sixteen, she joined her three older sisters and an aunt in Los Angeles; all four women were already sending remittances to their family. She lived with one of her sisters for a while after she migrated. Agustina's kin network multiplied when she married Ricardo, who had a longer family history of migration to Los Angeles. His father and uncles had worked many years in the city by the time Ricardo arrived in 1975. His mother and his ten siblings had also lived in the United States since 1977, and all were living in Los Angeles by the time he and Agustina married. Agustina described family visits every weekend that were like a party with "*un puño de gente* [a bunch of people]." Their two sons, Zacarias (Zach) and Elias, would grow up embedded in these dense kin ties that included many uncles and cousins. Zach and Elias spent minimal unstructured time in Central City, often socializing with family instead. Cousins attended Zach's musical performances—his "gigs"—and guided his college application process.

Sisters Dolores and Susana had almost no social support until Dolores married a man with a dense kin network. They had left Chihuahua, Mexico, for Los Angeles in 1981 after the death of their parents left them without many resources. Susana followed her boyfriend to Los Angeles, and Dolores, who was only seventeen, went with her. Several years later, Dolores was a single mother of two and expecting a third when she left her abusive partner and turned to her sister for help. Susana lived in a two-bedroom apartment with her boyfriend and their two children, and Dolores moved in, seeking relief. Financial strains increased, and the crowded living conditions created tension between the sisters. A neighbor, Ignacio, an undocumented migrant from Puebla who was younger than Dolores, took an interest in her. He promised her he would love and care for her and her children. Dolores moved in with Ignacio, and he proved to be an exemplary husband and stepfather. Dolores explained:

> For my youngest child, Ignacio is his daddy. My son adores him. Ignacio bought his first Pampers, his first sneakers. My other two sons have great respect for him. I love him very much. Everyone asks me, "Where did you find this wonderful man . . . ?" My husband pays the rent. He doesn't miss work, not one day. I think God had him destined for me because I had suffered a lot. He must have said, "Here's a little gift for you."

Ignacio's gifts included absorbing Dolores into his dense kin networks. Their home was often a stopping point for other relatives from Puebla migrating into the United States. Dolores fed them and washed their clothes, and in return they extended their support to Dolores and her children. Her eldest son, Raul, was a college student at one of the University of California campuses in 2007. Undocumented migrants who had benefited from his mother and stepfather's support helped Raul by buying him books and clothes and giving him gas money while he was in college. Their emotional support and pride in his accomplishments in college likewise meant a good deal to him. Dolores and Susana remained neighbors and supportive of one another throughout the years, both now part of a larger kin network.

Jesusita also found a rich source of social support through marriage. Her father had left her mother in Veracruz, Mexico, when she was fourteen to move to the United States. Jesusita's eldest sister followed their father to Los Angeles a year later, seeking work, and Jesusita joined them in 1974, when she was seventeen. She lived with her father's "other" family for a year and a half, a period when he sometimes denied her food and locked her in her room when he left the house. Fleeing his abuse, Jesusita moved in with her sister, who herself was in an abusive relationship. It was then that Jesusita got a job in the garment district and began taking an English class in the evening. Finding life with her sister and her sister's boyfriend an "*infierno*," Jesusita moved in with a friend she made in class. To pay her rent and living costs, she was forced to work more hours to provide for herself and had to leave school. But she met Damian, a native of Guerrero, at work, and they married by the time she was twenty-one. They had four children, including twins, one of whom was Leonardo. The couple continued to work in the garment industry, and they struggled financially for many years. Damian had a large extended family in Los Angeles, however, and as Jesusita said, they were "very united." Damian's twelve siblings had all settled in Los Angeles, and "there is not one day that we do not see them," Jesusita said, "and we get together every weekend." Jesusita still had strained relations with her own family, and as her nephews began to join gangs she kept her children at a distance from them. All of her children went to college, strongly encouraged by their father's relatives, with whom they spent a lot of time.

The Fragility of Reciprocity and Kin-Based Social Capital

Despite their strong sense of familism, various circumstances challenge immigrants' ability to support one another. Family issues arose even among the most supportive kin networks. In 2007, Ricardo had only recently resumed conversation with an estranged brother after not talking to him for more than a decade. In the late 1990s, his brother had offered to repay a loan of $6,000 by passing on the title of his property in Central City. The couple accepted his offer, considering it a great opportunity. The property was a large lot with one home in the back, where they would live, and a duplex they could rent out in the front. Ricardo and Agustina found out after the transfer that Ricardo's brother owed money for the property and they were stuck with the bill. He also failed to mention that finding reliable renters in a violent Central City neighborhood was difficult. They blamed Ricardo's brother for his lack of transparency and did not foresee seeking help from him, or giving it to him, in the future.

Other ties in Ricardo's vast kin network had been more productive. They had lived with kin when they first migrated and had provided living space for others who joined the family in the United States. Yet Agustina noted that living with family was "hell" at times: "There is no peace, no peace, you can't tell others' children to calm down. You can't reprimand them or tell them anything." Scarce financial resources led many immigrants to live with kin upon arrival in the United States, and relations were often strained in these crowded living conditions. Squabbles between young cousins strained ties among the adults, who struggled to maintain parenting boundaries with the children. This prompted families to seek independent housing as soon as possible. Yet with rising housing and living costs in Los Angeles and meager wages, it was not always feasible.

Grown children could be key sources of support when parents were raising younger children, as in Rosita's case, but large families could also create crowded living conditions. In 2007, I met Mina, a migrant from Puebla, who lived in a three-bedroom apartment with eleven other people, all kin. Mina had migrated in the mid-1980s, following her husband, Ramiro, who was also from Puebla and had extensive ties in Los Angeles. Her mother-in-law and sister-in-law shared one room; her brother-in-law's family of six shared another; and Mina and Ramiro shared the third with their youngest children, two teen boys; their three oldest children had coupled and moved out. One of the teenagers in the household might sleep on a daybed in the living room at times; in fact, I quietly sat next to a teen girl, soundly napping, the day I met Mina. There had been twenty-one people in the home at one point, but even with eleven, it remained extremely crowded. Mina was working full-time for $6.50 an hour at the time of the interview, but Ramiro only worked on weekends (a point of tension with Mina), filming *quinceañeras* and weddings.

Some relatives spent more time in the home, while others spent time working. This raised the question of what percentage of the rent and utility costs each should cover. An aunt had been "kicked out" because she did not contribute to the chores and often ate others' food. Trust waned often. Mina's eighteen-year-old son Mauricio said that his "relatives had money, but they don't want to help." He was also angry that his uncle had been slow to repay a loan. On the one hand, Mauricio noted, there "hadn't been a fight in a long time." In addition, the adults would share in monitoring the teens. Yet as the families aged and grew, splitting food, bills, and household chores became increasingly complex, and this broke down the sense of cohesion. Two of Mina and Ramiro's children, a son and a daughter, lived out of state, in Arkansas and New Mexico, respectively, and they encouraged Mina to come live with them. Ramiro resisted, however, as his entire family was in Los Angeles; several relatives even lived in the same apartment complex.

Adriana and Vidal acknowledged that it was a blessing to know they could turn to family for help, but like other study participants, they were careful not to overuse their family's support. For instance, Adriana said:, "If my car were to break down, or get a flat tire, my sisters' husbands are very helpful. If they're not home, they'll send one of the boys or figure out something." She was grateful to them for not having to worry that she might have to sit, alone and vulnerable, in a broken-down car, but noted that they helped her "because we are the same with them. They help us because we try to help them." Adriana avoided bothering her relatives on a routine basis, however, and took the bus when Vidal was using the car. She "never asked for rides," though she did not feel completely safe on the bus. "I've always left requests for help, for when it's really necessary," she noted. For example, her son, who has developmental disabilities, got lost one day in the neighborhood when he missed the school bus, and Adriana called the family for help. Immediately, uncles and aunts and cousins—whoever was available—mobilized in the area and they found him quickly. Adriana rarely visited these kin because "everyone works, we're all busy, and I don't like being *metiche* [a meddler]." Adriana noted that it was important to strike a careful balance with family and not tax one another. She generally saw them at family events—birthday parties, baptisms, weddings and other celebratory occasions, even funerals—where, because of the size of the family, there would be many in attendance.

Immigrants shared stories of strained and repaired relations over time. Some relations had been hard to mend, leaving immigrants socially isolated in Los Angeles. The most damaging strained ties were cases of abuse—domestic, sexual, financial, or drug use–related—that broke trust between family members and severed ties. Octavio and Pricila and their toddler, Federico, slept in a Central City park for a week soon after they migrated because of a rift with kin. They had departed Mexico City in 1990 with Federico, arriving at Octavio's sister's home, the only kin they had in Los Angeles. But after Octavio had intervened in his sister and her husband's domestic dispute, they were kicked out of the home. Octavio and his sister remained estranged twenty-seven years later.

Even after Octavio and Pricila were able to establish a relatively stable life in Los Angeles, they felt the sting of isolation. They were among the most highly educated immigrants in the study, as Octavio had completed one year of college and Pricila had taken nurse assistant courses. Octavio had started in menial labor in the garment industry, but his accounting skills allowed him to gain a factory position that he described as paying "between $25 and $30 an hour." The couple owned a home in Central City. They had migrated "out of curiosity," and they deeply regretted that they could not travel to Mexico and be with family because they lacked documentation. Pricila was angry that she had been unable to attend her mother's funeral services. Octavio lamented:

> What good is it to have what I have if I can't share it with my loved ones? What good is it to have a car if I can't take my mother for a ride? This is not an American Dream. It's not happiness. . . . We lost a lot. We lost the love of

our family, being there with them during Christmas, birthdays. Everything
I have [material goods in the United States] is nothing compared to family
unity we had [in Mexico].

The couple was determined to make their sacrifice worthwhile through
their children, both of whom enrolled in the university. The eldest, Federico,
however, was also undocumented.

Seeking Help or Going It Alone

In the absence of kin, immigrants expressed a deep sense of alienation in
Los Angeles, despite being surrounded by coethnics. Those without kin or
with strained kin ties had to seek fellowship and support elsewhere or go
it alone.

Fictive kin ties evolved over time, often via trusted community institutions, commonly a local church. Flora and Marcos experienced a dark
period of social isolation before they established a supportive network.
Marcos earned little as an undocumented worker and struggled to provide
financially for his family. He became an alcoholic in Los Angeles and began
to abuse Flora. Her only kin ties, two elderly uncles, discouraged her from
engaging with others in her violent neighborhood, but keeping to herself
left her completely isolated. The only help they offered Flora was a ticket
home to Mexico, but she turned it down, knowing that she would struggle there as a single mother of four, her parents both having died by then.
Desperate, Flora sought help at a local church when she began to have sui-
cidal thoughts and recognized the danger to her children. The church provided the family with support that helped Marcos give up drinking and the
couple to find new ways of relating. Flora joined the Bible group, volunteered at church events, and enrolled her children in the religious education program and the choir. According to Flora, the church became "their
second home." Another couple at the church, Manuela and Francisco,
became like family—like an older sister and brother-in-law. They socialized on weekends, celebrating birthdays and holidays together. The couple
frequently provided Flora and Marcos with support. Flora said:

> In my most difficult moments, I go to [Manuela], if we need moral or finan-
> cial support. When I least expect it, she gives me for my children, "Here,
> have this for the kids. Take them [out] for breakfast." It's not always, but she
> surprises me. They're a couple who have been in the U.S. for many years, and

I see that now that they have financial means, they give. Perhaps it is because at one point, they also had great need and someone helped them too.

Manuela and Francisco became Flora's daughters' sponsors for her first communion—a rite that formalized them as *compadres* and family.

Neighborhood institutions play a critical role in the integration process of immigrants. Immigrants in the study, especially the women, met others in the community via school, sports organizations, and after-school programs. As I explain later, these organizations helped parents manage their sons' exposure to the neighborhood, giving them great support. Yet the most sought-out institution that provided immigrants with personal support was the local Catholic church.

Churches play an important role in Mexican communities, offering an opportunity to practice shared beliefs that blend closely with traditional customs and cultural practices.[47] In Mexican culture, family festivities often involve the church—for baptisms, first communions, weddings, and *quinceañeras*. When families are in personal crisis, many seek moral support and guidance from local priests. Church life sometimes becomes a central part of families' lives, structuring their time and social relations, as in the case of Flora. The support that immigrants obtain from church then expands beyond the priest to include other parishioners, providing these immigrants with a strong sense of community. In both neighborhoods in the study, local churches were hubs of social activity. These vibrant churches connected immigrants to others, offering information and services. In this study, Protestant respondents, like Hector and Katia, drew in similar ways on their Christian churches—as a source of fellowship and support. Religious institutions are an essential source of support for many immigrants, alleviating the hardship and social isolation that come about with migration.

Years after arriving in the United States, however, others still lived in social isolation, which was a great disadvantage. Rufina's son, Ismael, described his father's abuse, but Rufina simply noted, "Marriage never worked for me." She had a brother in Los Angeles, but she saw him only occasionally, and they did not rely on each other. She also had no community ties. As her four children entered adolescence, she managed the risk of the neighborhood alone—with limited success. Her oldest daughter left home at the age of thirteen when she became pregnant. Ismael became drug-addicted and was incarcerated during the study. Rufina's eldest son, a gang member, had also served time. The youngest daughter had sought out alternative means of social support and was the only one of her children who had graduated from high school. She had attended a small new charter school to escape the violence at Central City High, and there she gained access to institutional resources that would be key to her college enrollment. Her mother Rufina, however, remained distrustful of most people around her.

Reconceptualizing the Social Capital of Mexican Immigrants

The academic literature has characterized the Mexican immigrant population as lacking social capital, in large part because they are primarily unskilled immigrants and lack cross-class ethnic ties.[48] Yet this characterization overlooks the fact that Mexican kin ties are the engine that sustained a steady flow of Mexicans into the United States even in the face of growing border enforcement. Kin networks link even undocumented immigrants to jobs, and they have historically eased the migrant settlement process. These ties can remain beneficial for Mexican immigrants as they integrate into the American context, providing them, under the right circumstances, with valuable social support over time. This kin-based social capital has significant consequence for the adaptation and integration of immigrants. It would also be vital for the second generation in their adolescent and young adult years.

The families in this study are part of an increasingly diverse flow of Mexican migrants that reflects the most recent socioeconomic and political changes in Mexico and the United States. Originating in diverse regions of Mexico, today's migrants are more urban, undocumented, and female than in the past, and they are not always well tied to kin or coethnics in the United States. These immigrants are less homogenous than the literature once acknowledged.[49] Researchers have begun to examine the impact of this internal variation on the social capital of Mexican migrants, but none, to my knowledge, consider its impact on the children of these immigrants.[50] I find that varying degrees of kin-based social capital help explain why some immigrants are better positioned than others to navigate life in the United States.

Twenty or thirty years after their migration to the United States, family continues to be the main form of socializing for Mexican immigrants and their main source of social support, despite changing needs over time. For the most part, kin provide the kind of social support that allows immigrants to get by on a day-to-day basis and to cope with life's challenges. This support is at times emotional, financial, and informational as immigrants seek guidance from their kin ties. In the absence of kin support ties, community institutions—primarily the church—can provide immigrants with an alternative form of social support. Some immigrants establish fictive kin through these institutions and find community within them. Being embedded within a kin-based social network—or an institutional support structure—allows immigrants to exercise their family traditions and customs and reinforce family-oriented values and practices. This serves as an important source of support for immigrants as they raise their children in the United States.

As noted, immigrant parents quickly come to understand that the American city threatens their children's future prospects. Cognizant of this risk, parents buffer their sons from the social dynamics in these neighborhoods by mobilizing their limited resources in their kin and institutional ties. Most immigrants succeed at this task. Yet Mexican immigrants vary in their social capital. The most socially isolated manage the urban context on their own, and their children are more likely to get caught up in neighborhood conflicts and male peer dynamics. Later in life, they are also more likely to navigate the labor market on their own. As I show in the following chapters, the social capital of immigrants has lasting impacts on the second generation well into their young adult years.

PART II

Second-Generation Latinos in the Inner City

CHAPTER 4

Caught Up and Skirting Risk

Young Latino Men in the Inner City

E frain's parents, Dario and Ester, moved several times. The first time they moved because there were drive-by shootings on their block. Their second move was precipitated by a man entering their home and stabbing Efrain's uncle in the leg. But they could not afford to leave the South Central area, and by the time Efrain was in middle school he, like many other boys his age, had joined a tagging crew, who offered protection from the neighborhood's violence. Midway through high school, Efrain quit the crew, recognizing that it brought him more conflict than protection. Yet Efrain had built a long record of truancy that put him behind academically, and as a result, he never obtained his diploma. By the time he was twenty-one years old, he had two children with his girlfriend. He tried several times to return to school to get the diploma. The last time was when he was twenty-two. Carless, Efrain walked to and from night school from his parents' home. Then one evening, around 9:30 PM, a man began shooting "like crazy" near him. The target of the shooting landed on the ground only steps away from Efrain. "The dude [the shooter] got up on top of [the victim] and just shot him, like, two more times. Just dead cold," he recalled. Glass shattered nearby as everyone ran for shelter.

Efrain had experienced violence before. He had been assaulted several times, even after he quit the tagging crew: one time with a gun at a gas station, and another time with a kitchen knife on his way to buy diapers. Yet the murder he witnessed on the way to night school affected him profoundly. Underemployed and with a growing family, Efrain's stress was already high. For two years after the murder, he had nightmares and would awaken in cold sweats in the middle of the night. The slightest noise made him jump. He took to drinking, and his girlfriend left him for a few months. He became aggressive toward everyone in the family, and he had alcohol blackouts and seizures that landed him in the hospital on several occasions. During these episodes, his brothers held him down, keeping him from hurting himself, while his mother fervently prayed over him. Doctors explained that Efrain had suffered trauma and now had succumbed to a severe depression. His PTSD symptoms shut down his school plans and further complicated his job prospects.

The Long Reach of Violence

The young Latino men in the study, like their parents, felt that violence and social disorder were the most salient features of their neighborhoods. They were the children who witnessed the drive-by shootings and the adolescents who withstood assaults. All forty-two young men who participated in the study had witnessed some form of violence growing up. Two-thirds of these young men were assaulted in their own neighborhood, and over half were beaten up at least once. Two-thirds witnessed a shooting at some point in their neighborhood, and four witnessed a killing. One-third were shot at or held at gunpoint, and six were hospitalized at some point. Aside from fighting back in self-defense, six young men confessed that they had assaulted someone themselves, and three said that they had shot at someone in their neighborhood. Their exposure to violence peaked in adolescence but had carried over into their young adult years for those who were most locked into their neighborhood—that is, the young men who were carless or jobless. Several of the young men suffered from anxiety and depression. Their exposure to violence also factored into their social mobility through its impact on their schooling.

Immigrant parents were shocked by America's urban violence, but it was their sons who faced the most victimization and experienced the collateral consequences of growing up in such an environment. An important body of research examines why some youth join gangs and engage in violence.[1] We know from the literature that the most severe forms of urban violence, such as homicides, ricochet back and forth through social networks of gangs.[2] Although urban violence is a "small world of conflict," exposure to it has a far greater reach beyond those directly entangled in gangs and those who become victims.

In this chapter, I explain how urban violence *punctuates* and *organizes* the daily lives of young inner-city Latino men and how these processes hurt their future prospects. A growing number of studies show that growing up in a violent neighborhood hurts a young person's social mobility by lowering academic performance, increasing school noncompletion, and dampening income.[3] Segmented assimilation scholars frame gang involvement or juvenile delinquency as a result of negative acculturation processes.[4] I demonstrate, here and elsewhere, that exposure to violence in fact explains much of the behavior associated with troubled inner-city young men: fighting, skipping school, delinquency, and school noncompletion. Violence prompted the young men in this study to establish social ties with other male youth to stay safe, both physically and symbolically, and to guard themselves from victimization—to seek, in other words, a kind of urban social capital.[5] In the process, some young men become entangled in obligations and acts of reciprocity that introduce conflicts and behavior counterproductive to their schooling. The social dynamics that emerge as a function of urban violence compromise the future prospects of the second generation.

I also explain the variation in these young men's experience. Parental practices and institutional structures buffered the majority of respondents from the neighborhood and its violence to some degree. Parents managed the neighborhood by leaning heavily on kin ties to limit their son's time in the neighborhood and reinforce conventional norms. Others relied on institutions for support. In the absence of kin and institutional buffers, urban violence drew young men into local conflicts and negative peer dynamics that increased their odds of high school noncompletion and incarceration.

Navigating Urban Violence

I sat with Simon, age twenty-one, at a local park in Pueblo Viejo one sunny weekday afternoon to learn from him what it was like to grow up in his neighborhood. A couple of feet from us were two mothers pushing their young children on swings. From where we sat, we could see a homeless man sleeping in one corner of the park and, in the opposite direction, a small group of young men in gang attire, one on a bicycle, when our conversation was suddenly interrupted. My notes captured what we witnessed:

> The young man on the bike got off and let it fall, and he and his two companions assaulted another young man, around sixteen years old. One hit him with a glass bottle and on the head and it shattered, then all three jumped on him as he curled into the fetal position, covering his face. The

young woman he had been walking [with], caught off guard, could only watch. Others who saw turned around, but no one visibly reacted. After a few minutes, the three attackers left the scene calmly. The victim sprung up, his white T-shirt encrusted with dirt, especially around his stomach where he was most hit. He limped away with the same young woman, in the same direction, impassive.

Homicides have long been in decline in American cities, but this sort of unreported violence remains a problem in inner-city communities. Simon turned to me. "It's always been this way," he said, then recounted the various acts of violence he had witnessed or fallen victim to while growing up.

Boys' victimization in these neighborhoods begins at a young age. They are first "hit up," asked to what gang they belong, in middle school. This is also when they are first "pocket-checked"—when a group of older male youth, usually with a weapon, assault and force them to empty their pockets. Contrary to popular imagination, most inner-city youth are not in gangs.[6] Yet they must all carefully navigate neighborhoods afflicted by gang dynamics. The threat of violence looms in everyday encounters. David described a typical encounter: "Usually they [gang members] ask me, 'Where you from?' I just look at them, like, 'No, nowhere.' But that one time [in high school], I looked back and they started running, getting closer, one of them pulled out a bat." David escaped that evening without a beating, but such incidents occurred time and again throughout his adolescent years.

Young men referred to the walk home from school as "a mission" because that was when most assaults took place, although the unstructured time they spent hanging out with friends in local parks or walking to and from friends' homes was also a dangerous time. Alfredo was first pocket-checked in seventh grade, when he was twelve years old. Once, gang youth assaulted him and his two brothers when they were on their way home from high school and took their money, jackets, and sneakers. Osvaldo described the two times he was "jacked" (assaulted and robbed) after school: "We were walking home from Central City High, and some *cholos* . . . just got in front of us with a knife. . . . It was a big *cholo,* fat guy, and he took my money and my pager. One day I was walking in the alley . . . a *cholo* held a gun at me and took two gold chains. He took my wallet and money."

Sometimes young men put up a fight when they are assaulted. Rigo was assaulted three times before he, in his words, "lost it." He was fifteen the first time five young men jumped him and demanded his money, but he wasn't carrying any. Another time three guys pushed him around and one socked him in the stomach in an attempt to take his iPod as he waited at the bus stop, but they ran away after an adult showed up. Several young men at school tried to take Rigo's sneakers another time, but school security chased after them. On the fourth assault, several guys jumped him on the street on his way home from school, and it was then that Rigo fought back, despite being outnumbered. He got lucky: a friend driving by stopped and came out of his car swinging a bat. Rigo jumped in the car and they sped away.

Young men learn to read and navigate their neighborhood carefully to reduce their victimization.[7] My respondents had figured out which blocks were especially problematic. Bernardo knew Central City well, having moved many times within the neighborhood. The college student described the geography of violence by pointing out problematic areas on a map I brought to an interview:

> Washington Boulevard is the borderline between the people here and the people there. There is stratification, if you can say it that way, as far as racial and gangs. East of Washington you have rival gangs. I lived here, and I lived there [*indicating two spots on the map*]. I saw both of the worlds. West of Washington, the racial tension was not as much. It was much calmer as far as the blacks and Latinos getting along; we would get along fairly well. Over here [*indicating the east side*] it was horrible. On the east side there is more poverty. A lot more places on the east side are apartments and from Chestnut Ave down here, this whole area is hot—you don't want to go in there! You go in there because you have been there before. I would see a lot of bad things around here as well [*indicating another area*]. I would see a lot of people get beat up, because when I used to walk from middle school to my house on this side, there was a lot of racial tension. It's like an area of gangsters that live there.

Bernardo longed to move out of the neighborhood. He never felt secure, and his views hardened after his father, Marcos, was shot outside their home. He found community through their church, but said, "Hell no, I don't have love for the neighborhood. . . . Why would I?"

Gang conflict in both neighborhoods ran deep. Conflicts during the study revolved around drug sales and turfs, but animosity between certain gangs traced back several decades. This local history structured how young men navigated their neighborhood. Eddy noted that certain areas of Pueblo Viejo were simply off limits: "You can't walk the streets." As a resident of a housing project, Eddy was associated with the local gang even though he was not in it. As such, he was careful not to walk through enemy gang territory. Staff in community organizations who understood local dynamics and gang conflicts backed up these accounts, allowing me to conduct interviews in their community spaces so as long as the youth did not live in rival gang territory.

At times, youth had no option but to cross through hostile blocks to get to school or work. Cristobal was chased home several times by assaulters who came to an abrupt halt on his block when the local gang stepped in. They protected him even though he was not a member; not only were his father, Humberto, and his uncle, Ramon, well liked on the block, but his brother, Felipe, had run with a local crew in his younger years and was close to the gang. Still, to avoid assaults, Cristobal drove Humberto's van to school his senior year, avoiding streets he knew to be racially tense and places where gangsters congregated. Other young men who relied on public transportation, like Genaro, experienced repeated assaults. For a short period, a gang member forced Genaro to surrender money—"taxes"—every time he waited at the bus to go to work. Genaro, who had already been sent to the hospital with a broken jaw after a football game, understood that he had no other option but to give the gangster money until he got a car or switched jobs, both which eventually happened.

Young men generally walked in small groups to ward off attacks, as many had been alone when first "caught slippin'"—assaulted and victimized in an off-guard moment. It was common for groups of young men, some of them high school age but others older, to congregate near street corners after school. Pedro explained that finding peers to accompany him home from high school was among the first things that came to his mind when the school day ended. "Walking to school wasn't as bad as walking home. Walking home is when you thought, 'All right . . . where is whatshisname and whatshisname?' Because we wanted to walk, like, in a group. And yeah, we wouldn't walk home, say, me and my brother. We wouldn't walk all by ourselves."

In these groups, young men had to appear calm and collected, strong and firm, so as not to appear weak—but not overconfident, as too much swagger could provoke hostility. Walking with his friends in Central City, Sergio noted that he "just had to get ready." Regularly, his body tensed while walking with his group of friends by a bus stop where forty or so young black men were waiting. There was silence as Sergio's group walked by, waiting to hear an insult or a shouted gang affiliation, waiting for violence to erupt. In his neighborhood, Sergio explained, "you can't back down . . . because they are going to punk you for life." He had seen it many times. "Once punked," he said, they "get your shoes, get your phone, take your clothes, because you didn't do shit." Returning the violence established a reputation: "Oh, don't fuck with this one!"

In this hostile context, male peers become an important resource. Drawing on such ties becomes what Ann Swidler calls "strategies of action."[8] These ties provide urban male youth with *urban-specific social capital*. Nongang youth typically establish neighborhood gang ties *without* joining the gang and/or alternative male peer groups, notably tagging and party crews.[9]

Ties to the 'Hood

Gangs occupy public space, like parks and green spaces around apartment complexes or housing projects. Given the presence of gangs, youth who spent time in the neighborhood often had gang ties, which often arose as the natural sequel to childhood friendships. Mauricio noted that six out of ten peers from his neighborhood had been "locked up," and he knew the gangsters who killed a young woman nearby. He explained, "They weren't really gangsters. I don't know what got into them. . . . A year ago we used to play soccer." They had nicknamed him "Racoon," but he had no interest in joining, feeling as most other nongang youth did—that "dying for a street name is dumb." Young men like Mauricio "didn't want others telling them what to do," and they "didn't want to kill anyone" or be killed.

Nongang youth like Mauricio were highly critical of gang activities. In spite of their ties to gang members, they did not identify with, much less glorify, gangs and gang behavior. They were nestled in an immigrant community that drew strong moral boundaries against gang youth, with parents who strongly discouraged any association with gangs, or even the semblance of association. This led to intense disputes at home over clothing and appearance. Zach complained about his father Ricardo not permitting certain clothing brands: "I had long hair! I'm tall, skinny, and I wear tight shirts." He insisted that wearing "Dickies," which are associated with gangs, was "not going to make a difference, but my dad was strict on it. No!" In the end, it was not parents' disdain for certain styles that discouraged young men from dressing a particular way. As Joaquin explained, "A friend who was not from any gang, he just dressed like that and ended up dead. He was walking through the projects, and some guys pulled up and shot him." On their own, young men came to learn that certain attire and gang membership increased their exposure to violence and incarceration.

Yet nongang youth "kept it cool" with local gang members, with measurable benefits. A young gang member unknown to Joaquin assaulted him one day, but older gang members reprimanded the youngster and beat him for his error. Joaquin explained, "Because they [the older gang members] know me for a while, they actually protect me somewhat." Joaquin's gang ties made him feel that he would not be "messed with." In a context characterized by gang rivalries and conflicts, nongang youth had a strong incentive to maintain these friendly ties, though young men walked a fine line with their gang-affiliated peers. Ezequiel was a thin, short, and fair-skinned Latino who associated with many gang members ("I used to hang out with the South Gang. I hang around with the Krazy Boys and the Broadway Gang") but was not in a gang himself. He eschewed gang activity "because I always thought, why give your life for a street name? It's not worth it. . . . I was kicking it with them . . . going to parties with them. If I had a party, I'd call them up, drinking together, smoking, but, like, bust a mission [engage in a gang shooting] with them—no." Ezequiel understood the consequences of engaging in gang activities and shunned the lifestyle. Like others, he felt it necessary to sustain amicable ties with local gangs. As Eddy asserted, "Of course I'm going to keep it cool. I don't want any beef with them." Among youth with gang ties, most reported drawing on them for protection at least once during their adolescence.

Residents of Central City, where most well-established gangs were black, had a harder time establishing friendly relations with gangs than in Pueblo Viejo, where most gangs were Latino. Often Latinos felt that they were targets of black gangs.[10] Pedro, who grew up in a predominantly black public housing complex, spent very little time in or near his home. Instead, he spent time on a predominantly Latino block in Central City. He said, "I see Hispanic kids with their bikes, just riding and having fun, playing out in the street. I guess that's why I went there a lot, because you didn't have to worry." But Pedro also noted that his friend on the block had a cousin who was in a gang, which offered protection from violence. Pedro's way of avoiding violence was just one of many such approaches taken by young Latino men to avoid victimization without the dangers of actually joining a gang.

An Alternative Means of Getting Respect

Although gangs receive more attention in the literature, more respondents in this study had joined "crews" than gangs. Seventeen youths out of the forty-two had been in a crew at one point; only three were formally in a gang. Gangs are long-standing, entrenched neighborhood institutions, whereas crews tend to be short-lived, loose associations of male adolescents who form an identity around partying or "tagging." These young men drink and smoke marijuana together, often during school hours. In a party crew, youth throw parties on weekends and "ditching parties" (skipping school) during the week. Tagging crews engage in graffiti art, gaining status by spreading their tags throughout the city. At parties some used other forms of drugs, like ecstasy. Although a few crews were involved in the occasional sale of drugs, young men in party or tagging crews were unlike gangs—which were territorial, bound to a block, and typically connected to prison gangs—in most other respects. Those who tagged said that they did so to make "their name known" and gain attention and recognition. (Some of the artistically inclined carry a sketchbook with their artistic "pieces.") Crew members did not typically carry guns, as gang members did, though many young men in the neighborhood carried other forms of protection, including knives or bats. Functioning like the boys' clubs or less violent gangs of an earlier era, crews were committed to protecting one another and showing that members could not be "punked."[11]

Among study respondents, crews became popular beginning in middle school, when gangs began to target them and assaults escalated. Gonzalo joined a tagging crew because his Pueblo Viejo middle school, where "everyone was fighting," made him feel like he was no longer a kid. He minimized the vandalism that members committed, saying that he never did any tagging himself and that "it was just a crew. If something would happen, they [members] would get in fights. That was pretty much it. They tagged, but it wasn't like an actual tagging crew." The crew helped him navigate his new context and gave him a sense of safety. Rigo also described joining a tagging crew even though he had no interest in tagging. He had lived in Mexico for two years just before going to middle school, so he entered middle school in L.A. without friends; he was also small for his age, and bigger boys often picked on him. The crew offered protection. Efrain formed a crew in middle school after being jumped several times. He explained that after he was assaulted a third time,

> I started . . . pumping up [lifting weights] and started getting confidence on
> my own. . . . I'm not going to let them punk me . . . 'cause I have [younger]
> brothers behind me that are going to come to the same school. I can't leave a
> reputation saying that, "This fool used to be punked, then we can punk the

brothers." Oh hell no. I'm going to get everybody that gets punked and start a crew, and that's the way we did it.

The collective allowed young men to find strength in numbers and signal to others that they could not be "punked." Jaime joined a tagging crew early in high school and explained its appeal:

People are like, "Yeah, I heard about you." . . . I got all of that [reputation and respect] 'cause of them [his crew]. 'Cause they were telling me, "Don't ever be a punk, because it's going to make us look bad." . . . See, if they come talking shit and you just let yourself [get victimized], that means . . . you're a punk; anybody can just come and step over you.

By joining a crew, young men like Jaime felt that they could avoid victimization.

Reciprocity and Excess Claims: The Downside to Urban Social Capital

Nevertheless, drawing on gang and crew ties for protection had a downside.[12] With time, these young men learned that there were consequences to "keeping it cool" with gang members on the block or to joining a crew. Although the older members of the local gang had made sure that their members did not attack Joaquin again, members of a rival gang, taking his friendship with the gang as membership in it, sent him to the hospital with three broken ribs, bruises all over his body, and a "messed-up face." Crews also found themselves in conflict with other crews, as their members postured themselves to gain respect and were challenged in return. Two nights before I first interviewed Jaime, his parents' house was sprayed by bullets by a local gang pressuring his crew to either join them or dismantle and no longer congregate on the block. Jaime's crew did not retaliate, but this incident escalated tension in his neighborhood. Youth with ties to gang and crew peers were constantly "watching their back." Rather than protect them from violence, these ties increased their exposure to violence, as it entangled them in local conflicts. In the process, young men engaged in ever-riskier behavior and became more likely to not complete school or to be incarcerated.

When I met Sergio, he was desperate to break ties with his gang peers. I could easily spot him in the sea of students exiting Central City High. Much to the dismay of his mother, Isela, Sergio projected an "old school" *cholo* look, wearing white, knee-high socks, Cortez sneakers, Dickies shorts, and a checkered flannel shirt, buttoned only from the top to display his white T-shirt underneath. He had picked up the style from the gang at his apartment complex, with whom he spent a great deal of time. When we met, he would always greet me with a quick raise of his chin. Sergio was at Central City High after having been expelled from a nearby school. He grew up in an extremely violent pocket of the neighborhood and turned to the local gang for protection. He often skipped school with them and was expelled for starting a "race riot."[13] As a result of being embedded in the local conflicts, Sergio "barely" graduated from high school.

Like other nongang youth in the study, Sergio was critical of his gang friends, stating, "They're low lives, just doing nothing, looking to see what to do because they are bored—same thing every day, going to the park, kick it." He then added, "I [was] raised to go to college and be something . . . even when I was with them, I still had that in my mind." I had not found Sergio hanging out on a street corner but rather in a physics course. He had been identified as "gifted" in fifth grade, though he never fit in with the college-bound kids. He said, "I couldn't relate to nobody . . . it was a different crowd, little nerd crowd, and people were like, 'Damn, you know, that *cholo* is smart.'" Despite his dress and demeanor, Sergio never joined the gang. He had no interest in "banging and fighting 24/7." Though his parents were originally from a rural town, his father, Carlos— who laid carpet for a living—had gone to college for a short period before dropping out because he could not afford it. Sergio had unfinished business to fulfill for the family. Yet he was scrambling to make up missing class credits in order to graduate his senior year, having had an epiphany that led him to choose the Marines over college. He explained his logic: "If I go to community college, I am still going to be in the streets. The homies are going be, 'What's up, let's go kick it [hang out], let's go smoke.' . . . That's how people don't make it. Yeah, you are going to college, but you are still *caught up*."

Sergio was on his way out of the neighborhood, soon to start military boot camp and then deploy overseas to Afghanistan. He understood that to get ahead he had to break from his social context or it would absorb him. As long as he remained in the neighborhood, he would be linked to his gang peers and, by default, embedded in their conflicts and risky behaviors. Given the entrenched conflicts in the neighborhood, he felt safer going off to war.

Getting "Caught Up" in Urban Violence

Drawing on male peer ties to avoid victimization makes demands on youth. Accessing social capital comes with "obligations" and "expectations" and this can weigh negatively on young men.[14] Some of this is social pressure—to "kick it" and party and sometimes to engage in delinquent acts, like tagging or "smoking out" (marijuana) in and out of school. Obligations can also involve providing backup to peers in conflict. As Sergio explained, in navigating urban violence with the help of their peers, some male youth become caught up in the male peer group dynamics of gangs and crews. Ultimately, these ties make "excess claims" on them.[15] The behaviors that enhance cohesion among gang or crew members and earn them urban social capital also compromise their well-being and jeopardize their future prospects.

Youth like Sergio who had ties to gang members or were in crews became caught up in the *dynamics of reciprocity*. While he drank and smoked with his gang peers who offered protection—"just to kill time"—Sergio also felt the need to reciprocate that protection and back them up, even though he was not in the gang. Despite holding strong views against their lifestyle, Sergio became involved in many gang fights because he felt the need to "get their back"—that is, support them—as they supported him when he was in need. He explained the logic:

> I had homies where I used to live in the apartments, and you can say that they were gang-related. They didn't try to get me in the gang . . . because they were more the family type. "I'll respect you if you *don't* do this [join the gang]." They actually told me, "Nah, don't do this. . . . I already fucked up, so you don't do this" . . . like [how] family just looks out for you. But if something happened, if somebody did something to one of us, then we all got his back, because we all kicked it together.

This dynamic led to Sergio's expulsion from school. Young men in the study who got caught up in local gang and crew conflicts often risked not completing high school as a consequence.

Education scholars pay ample attention to school-related factors that contribute to the limited educational attainment of urban youth, from punitive practices that punish and expel these youth to the overcrowded classrooms and poor-quality schooling they receive. Yet contextual factors outside schools matter; in Pueblo Viejo and Central City, getting caught up in obligations to gang and crew peer ties while navigating urban violence factored into the high rates of school noncompletion of young Latino men.

A common misperception of urban youth is that they simply do not value school or learning. Refuting this argument, however, are numerous studies that find that urban youth subscribe to both dominant and non-dominant cultural outlooks regarding education and strongly embrace American meritocracy.[16] The failure of the young men in these neighborhoods to complete school had much to do instead with the violence they navigated every day.

Collateral Damage: Violence and High School Noncompletion

Dropping out of high school is not a choice or an event but a *process*. High school noncompletion involves failing courses, falling behind on course credits, getting retained in school, and experiencing interrupted schooling.[17] Youth who fail to complete high school are the most likely to engage in certain behaviors that set them behind academically, such as repeated truancy and fighting. In the urban context, this behavior is often interpreted as "nonschool" or "street-oriented" behavior, and it elicits zero-tolerance responses from school authorities. When these young people are suspended, expelled, ticketed, or even arrested for their behavior, the odds that they complete school decline.[18]

Young men entangled in crew and gang ties, like Efrain, Sergio, and Rigo, faced higher odds of not completing high school. Efrain, held back in school owing to his truancy and failed courses, never graduated; Sergio and Rigo did graduate, but only after attending summer school and scrambling their senior year to get rid of demerits and earn credits. Young men who failed to complete school were set behind academically when their truancy and fighting caused them to be expelled from their local schools and interrupted their schooling. These young men were targeted by school authorities, punished for their behavior, and "pushed out" into "continuation" schools.[19] Rarely did youth report that they had skipped school alone or engaged in a conflict or fight that did not also involve neighborhood male peers. As such, school noncompleters were often youth who had become caught up in the dynamics of male peer group expectations and obligations or acts of reciprocity. They were truant *with* and suspended *for* peers.

Truancy, one of the biggest problems in both neighborhood schools, was central to the failure of these young men to obtain a diploma. For the most part, gang and crew ties pulled youth away from school for social reasons that strengthened cohesion among them, such as going to parties or drinking and smoking. Being perpetually truant made them accumulate missing credits and failed courses, putting them extensively behind in school. Some young men were retained a grade (or more), and others were expelled and rerouted to an alternative school, where they could pursue a diploma or GED but commonly failed to acquire either. Those who failed to complete school had bounced between several schools before they stopped attending altogether.

Angel, an ex-gang member and school noncompleter, explained that right before he stopped attending high school he "was taking care of business." He explained: "I was making sure I did my class work, but I was being sneaky. . . . I was also getting drunk, smoking weed, and hanging with the boys." Although most youth in this study skipped school at some point (and some did so frequently), youth who had gang ties or were in a crew were more likely to report skipping school to be with their male peers. Initially, their incentive to do so had been to maintain these ties to benefit from the presumed protection they provided.

Ezequiel offered a glimpse of how these neighborhood processes interacted with urban school practices. He got in a fight on the second day of high school, and that set the tone for the rest of his schooling. That day the high school was on lockdown after an incident of gang violence. Kept in their classrooms for several hours, some students "started acting stupid" by throwing paper balls and acting out. When a paper ball hit Ezequiel for a second time, he threw it back at the thrower, who then, Ezequiel recalled, "got crazy." A fight between them erupted. Both youth were kicked out of the classroom, and a group of students attacked Ezequiel in the hallway. Other boys who were gang-affiliated jumped in to back up Ezequiel, who was on the floor taking blows. Ezequiel became friends with these gang youths who stepped in to protect him, and soon enough his schooling took a nose dive. He explained, "That's when I started to hang around with everybody and just . . . stop caring, stop going to school. I was just going and looking for fights, you know, trying to prove myself in other words." Ezequiel—nicknamed Feisty—quickly built a reputation.

The schools in Pueblo Viejo and Central City were highly policed—an extension of the heightened surveillance in the neighborhoods. On several occasions, I witnessed police stops, interrogations, and ticketings of young males, as well as police chases, and these practices filtered into the schools. At Central City High, there was a "police station" on the school campus; a station was two blocks away from Pueblo Viejo High. Cristobal, a senior at Central City High, noted that "there are always police," while Fernando, from Pueblo Viejo, observed that the police station "keeps expanding, getting bigger and bigger. They have so many troopers now that they don't have parking for them." At these urban schools, ticketing for truancy was common practice, and police readily collaborated with security guards to keep order. Cristobal described the policing during school fights: "There are so many cops out here [in school], they mace them [the youth fighting] and that's it." As Rios explains, this heavy policing translates into the pervasive and ubiquitous criminalization of young men.[20]

It was in this context that Ezequiel was expelled after an encounter with the police, who "manhandled" a friend of his, a girl, after she had a fight and "was running her mouth":

> The black cop got her, twisted her arm, and put her behind her back like she was a dude, and [my friend] is like, "Why are you getting me? Why are you doing this to me? I didn't do nothing!" [And the policeman said,] "Oh just shut the fuck up!" Just straight out cussing at her! I am over here getting mad because I was raised, never hit a girl, and I can't stand if a guy hits a girl. . . . So I went to talk to him, I am over here trying to talk to him cool, you know. I tell him, "Officer, she didn't do nothing. Why do you got to hold her like that? She didn't do nothing, she is not the one that was fighting [started it]." [The policeman responded,] "You stupid little wetback,[21] get the fuck out of here!" Oooh! I was like, "Excuse me?! What the fuck did you just say?" I started getting into his face, and he pushed me . . . so what I did was straight out sock him.

Ezequiel received a ticket for "assaulting a police officer, intervening into a police investigation, and instigating a fight." This was the first ticket he had ever received, and he was put in handcuffs, though not arrested. When the principal showed up, Ezequiel recalled him saying: "It's you! I've been looking for a reason to kick you out and you finally gave me one."

Ezequiel was expelled and sent to a continuation school. In a textbook case of one disciplinary measure leading to more, he received two more tickets in the three weeks that followed. Police stopped him near the grounds of his continuation school and ticketed him for carrying marijuana and for truancy.

He was expelled again. At a third school, he got into a fight, got another ticket, and was expelled again. He enrolled in a fourth school but was there for only a week because he "didn't get along with" the gang at the school, TKB. Ezequiel insisted to me that conflict with the gang "was personal beef" and "had nothing to do with" his ties to a rival gang, but I had my doubts.

Ezequiel left school for several months after the last expulsion, explaining, "I was your typical lazy teenager." But his parents "hounded" him to return to school. I met Ezequiel at his fifth school, a continuation school where most students had similar stories of conflict, expulsions, and interrupted schooling. He was nineteen, and it would have taken him two years to get his diploma. He soon began to work full-time. Concluding that he had "too many missing credits" to catch up, he quit school for good without a diploma.

Schools fail youth like Ezequiel. Punitive practices like expulsion triple the odds of school noncompletion. Jumping from school to school interrupts learning and sets youth behind. Often continuation schools make matters worse by isolating young men labeled as problematic—often those in gangs and crews—from the rest of the student population and then concentrating them with each other. Young men in this study who attended such schools had to attend only half the day, a requirement that minimized their schooling and enhanced their exposure to the neighborhood.

At a personal level, Ezequiel, who was deeply embedded in his neighborhood, wrestled with his sense of obligation to gang and crew peer ties and remained trapped. Though disinclined to help friends who "started shit," Ezequiel felt that he had to do so: "It's like having a minor [child]. If he's out with you, he's under your responsibility. With my homies, if I'm out with them, they're not my responsibility, but I'm with them. What kind of a friend am I to stand right there and let him get his ass kicked?" This loyalty came at a high cost: the frequent fights that resulted had gone on his disciplinary record (though not everything on his record was related to fighting) and put him at odds with school administrators and police.

Young men who did not complete high school expressed no more disdain for school than others in the study, but they did uphold a distinct cultural orientation in relation to the violence surrounding them. Noncompleters privileged male peer ties and meeting the expectations and obligations that came with drawing on them to navigate the threat of violence. Some young men who managed to graduate, like Sergio and Rigo, moved away from this orientation toward their gang and crew peers. Efrain turned away from these peer ties too late and was unable to catch up. He had to resort to adult school, only to stop his schooling again after witnessing the shooting. For others, as a sense of obligation to gang and crew ties remained a feature of everyday life in their early adult years, school completion became ever more elusive.

Ties to gangs and crews carried consequences into adulthood. Jaime, a member of a tagging crew, became highly restricted to his neighborhood. Along with his peers, he was heavily monitored by police in front of his home. Jaime did not contest his two arrests for tagging but felt that most ticketing on his block was unwarranted. "The tickets are just bullshit," he said, "the tickets are just for walking around. Last time I got a ticket for being on the back of the bike!" Jaime felt targeted; he shared that he had been ticketed at least ten times and owed roughly $2,000 in fines, a debt that prevented him from getting a license and, in turn, a job. One "white cop" even took his bus pass, further restricting his movements to the neighborhood. At twenty-three years old, Jaime remained under probation, performing community service on weekends and making monthly payments. Others remained entangled in conflicts. Valentin, an active gang member, Salvador, a crew member, and Angel, an ex-gang member, landed in the hospital as young adults—Valentin after gang members broke his leg with a bat and Salvador and Angel after they were shot. Like Jaime, all three young men were closely monitored by local police officers, who were quick to stop them when spotted in the neighborhood.

Sidestepping and Succumbing to the Violence: Differential Exposure

The majority of inner-city young men graduate from high school, raising the question of why some young men manage to sidestep the violence and gang and crew dynamics while others succumb to it. To understand this we must recognize that inner-city young men vary greatly in their exposure to the neighborhood and its violence.[22]

Young men like Benjamin, Rosita's son, were highly exposed to violence in their neighborhood. After his brother Manolo was killed, Benjamin, who was well attuned to the gang conflicts, joined his brother's gang. Benjamin knew Pueblo Viejo "like the back of his hand." Pointing to the map I gave him, he showed me that his home was tightly nestled against several gang boundaries, only a block or two apart. With a kick of adrenaline, he excitedly sat up on his chair to describe how he got away from the police in his teen years "probably twenty-five times." He pointed his finger at the map, and I followed his index finger as it zigzagged across it.

> We knew our alleys *so* good. This is my house, and in the back of the house there was an alley, so we would chill here. But right here in back of the alley there is another house, these are the houses around them. We would chill in the middle of the alley, so if the cops came, we could go this way, that way, that way, this way, so I can jump to this house, to my house, well, this way and end up on this alley. I can jump to this house across the street and jump into that house and get into the alley, just keep the cops confused. . . . The cops never found our spot.

Benjamin recalled the peak of his involvement in gang violence, dictated by dividing street lines. One rival gang "would chill right here [*indicating a block away*], and we chill right here and [another rival gang] chill right here [*indicating a block away in the opposite direction*]. We could see each other. Sometimes we used to shoot at each other." Benjamin ultimately kept his youngest brothers from joining a gang, but he never finished high school and was incarcerated several times. When I met him, he took anxiety medication to calm his nerves; years of dodging bullets had taken a toll.

In these same neighborhoods are young men like Enrique, who spent so little time outside his home in Pueblo Viejo that he had no knowledge of the gangs in the area. Such was the social distance he felt from the gangs that he talked about them as if they were a world apart. I met Enrique at the local state university he attended. He felt comfortable talking there, out of his parents' earshot. As they had done when he was in high school, they continued to closely supervise Enrique, limiting his interactions. They went so far as to install a tracking system in the twenty-year-old's car to monitor his whereabouts, making sure he went only to college and back home. They were the strictest parents in the study, and Enrique was the most disconnected from his neighborhood.

Most young men in this study fell between these two extremes: Benjamin, an ex-gang member involved in violence, and Enrique, a young man quarantined in the neighborhood. Whether young men were highly exposed or buffered in the neighborhood had significant consequences in their lives and factored into their school completion.[23] Figure 4.1 shows how young men are differentially exposed to violence. Those not entangled in male

Figure 4.1 Exposure to Urban Violence and School Noncompletion

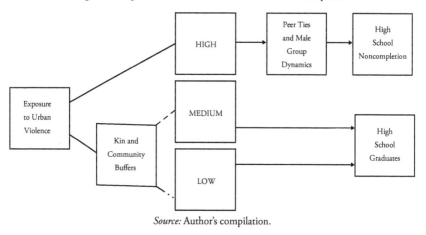

Source: Author's compilation.

peer group dynamics (gangs and crews) were buffered from the violence via supportive kin and institutional ties.[24]

Where youth attend school and where and how they spend their time when they are not at school influence their exposure to their neighborhood and to its violence. Youth buffered from the neighborhood experience less violence and bypass the opportunity and need to draw on male peer ties for physical and symbolic protection. Young men in the study who had no kin or institutional support spent a lot of unstructured time in the neighborhood and were more likely to witness and experience the threat of violence. These "exposed" young men were those drawing on male peer ties for physical and symbolic protection.

Buffered Young Men: Sidestepping Violence

Supportive kin and institutional ties buffer young Latino men from urban violence. While juggling work and family demands, some parents go to great lengths to maximize their supervision of their children in their neighborhoods or minimize their time there. Young men who were embedded in kin or institutional networks had an alternative social context, limiting exposure to the neighborhood, and these support ties reinforced family and community norms. Some youth found support from "institutional agents" in community organizations—adults who empowered them and helped them get ahead, not just stay safe.

Falling Back on Kin

Embedding their sons in the social support of kin ties was natural for migrants whose kin ties had been key to their integration upon settling in Los Angeles. Interacting with extended kin allowed these immigrants to practice customs and traditions and reinforce family values and community norms. A kin network that included aunts, uncles, grandparents, cousins, and a growing nuclear family provided the second generation with an alternative social context to the neighborhood.

Like other young men in the study, Noel was assaulted several times growing up. One day a gang member with a crowbar chased him down the alley behind his home, having thought Noel's school uniform—a white T-shirt and blue "Dickies" (pants)—identified him as a member of a gang. But his mother, Adriana, discouraged her children from making friends in the neighborhood, and he spent most of his childhood playing in the backyard of his home with his five siblings. When Noel's brother was assaulted after school one day when Adriana ran late to pick him up, she decided to take her children out of the neighborhood school. Noel started tenth grade at a small charter school that opened up a few blocks from their home. I interviewed him at age twenty, when he had a high school diploma and a job at a home warehouse store. He could identify only one young man on his block. Noel never felt connected to the youth around him. He never participated in sports or joined a community organization. Instead, he was close to his family.

In addition to Adriana and Vidal and his two sisters and three brothers, Noel had a large, tight-knit extended family who held frequent family events—weddings, *quinceañeras,* birthday parties, graduations. Without this source of support, he might have been more vulnerable to the neighborhood and its violence. During school breaks, he and his siblings often visited the *rancho* where their parents were born, in Jalisco, Mexico. Noel wished he had grown up in Jalisco, where he had greater freedom and was allowed "to go everywhere"; in Central City he was confined to his home and school. The extended family replicated the *rancho* lifestyle in Los Angeles; one cousin even had a horse in his backyard, which he would ride in the city of Compton. Although he was born in Los Angeles, Noel was highly Mexican-identified; he wore a *tejana* (cowboy hat) for his high school graduation and frequented Mexican dance clubs, looking the part. He took great pride in his ethnic background, and kin ties reinforced what his parents taught him: to value family, tradition, and hard work. Noel was especially close to his father and would join his father and uncles on construction jobs on weekends from a young age, sometimes having to get up as early as 5:00 AM. Vidal rarely paid Noel, but Noel valued the skill sets he acquired from his father. "I learned more with my dad than I did at school," he said. Vidal noted that all his children had a strong work ethic, explaining, "Ever since Noel was a *chiquillo* [a young boy], he's been with me everywhere. Here at the house, he's tore down walls, worked on the roof—several things. All of this has served him well." Noel, who opted not to pursue college, agreed, and he credited his father's teaching with his stable place in the workforce. He would join his father's labor union and secure a job in construction earning $30 an hour by the age of twenty-four.

Fathers and father figures played a special role in moderating young men's exposure to the neighborhood. Mauricio and Joaquin had extensive neighborhood ties, including gang ties, but their fathers kept them busy with work on weekends and occasionally during the week. While his father's close supervision did not protect Joaquin from getting a beating by local gang members, working with his father in construction, sometimes during school hours, helped him not get locked into conflicts. The same was true for Mauricio, who worked weekends filming *quinceañeras* and weddings with his father. Living in an apartment complex where other relatives lived, Mauricio also had more eyes on him. Uncles and aunts often monitored teens' behavior, and older brothers, such as Benjamin, were especially instrumental in monitoring younger brothers' whereabouts, helping them keep out of trouble.

Humberto's two sons, Felipe and Cristobal, had different levels of exposure to the neighborhood and its violence, in part because Felipe helped Humberto limit Cristobal's exposure. Felipe was one of the first young Latino men on his predominantly black block during the peak years of violence, and he experienced many assaults from a young age. He joined a crew and was expelled from seven schools for fighting. Predictably, he did not graduate with his class. In stark contrast, Cristobal was an honor student on his way to one of the University of California campuses when I met him. He too had been assaulted in the neighborhood, but Cristobal had the advantage of a brother who was seven years older. Cristobal explained that Felipe "always told me, 'Don't do this, I did this,' and talk[ed] me out of doing all the bad stuff." During his trying adolescent years, Cristobal "always had his brother and dad in mind" and admitted that he was "afraid of the consequences" if he misbehaved in school or got involved in the gang. Humberto and Felipe told Cristobal that if he joined a gang, they would "beat him up twice as bad as the gang [had]." At the same time, Humberto and Felipe's social ties in the neighborhood offered crucial protection for Cristobal. By then, Felipe had earned his GED and was moving up in the construction industry. Like Noel, Felipe picked up skills working with his father and uncles, but he was positioning his brother to aim higher. Felipe made sure that Cristobal "was on top of his game." Cristobal noted: "He's always bugging me, 'Are you staying on task [in school]? Are you doing this?' He says he looks up to me for actually going through high school without getting kicked out or getting in fights in school or anything, going to college. . . . He is proud of me."

The Important Role of Neighborhood Institutions

Not all young men had extensive kin ties that provided an alternative social context to the neighborhood, or an experienced brother looking out for them. Children of urban migrants with fewer kin ties were often at a loss. For these families, neighborhood institutions like the church, after-school programs in community organizations, community sport leagues, and church youth groups were particularly important.

As a single mother of five boys, Jovita turned to community sport leagues to keep her sons busy and out of trouble in their gang-affected neighborhood. Leo, her twenty-year-old middle son, recalled extensive gang violence but emphasized that growing up he had "a tunnel vision" because his social world was strictly structured. Jovita tightly scheduled her sons' weeks. She explained, "I knew they couldn't play in our front yard, so I involved them in sports here at the local park." From when her oldest son turned four until the last one graduated from high school, Jovita had a nonstop schedule that left her boys with little energy to do much else once they got home. Leo explained, "My mom kept us from wandering around the neighborhood and meeting friends that would get us in trouble. So it was pretty much home, school, go to practice, come back home, do our work, and that was it, and that was our daily, our daily lifestyle." Jovita reflected that she "ran herself ragged" making sure five children attended sports while she also held a full-time job. Leo gave a glimpse of their hectic schedule during their adolescent years when they played for a league in which the entire family volunteered:

> We'd line the field in the morning, set up the concession stand, cook, get ready for the game, play the game, and then after come back and cook some

more and then clean. And we'll be back to school on Monday and just do the same routine over, because we would practice during the week Tuesday, Wednesday, Thursday, and we were always involved.

In exchange for the whole family's volunteering, Jovita received free uniforms and a tight-knit social support system. Leo had fond memories of his childhood and spoke positively of the fictive-kin relations he developed through sports in Pueblo Viejo. He described the neighborhood as

a great place to be. You got to see, for what it's worth you got to get past the gang violence, you got to pass all the poverty and all the bullshit that goes on. If you hang out with a certain group of people or with anybody besides a gangster or people that do wrong in this community, you'll see that [Pueblo Viejo is] a real good place. There are a lot of family values here; there's a lot of closeness. I don't know how to say it, but people are very tight here in Pueblo Viejo, and we look out for each other a lot. You see a lot of people who have cousins who come here, brothers and sisters, and they stick together, they stick together real tight. That's one of the better parts of Pueblo Viejo, because it just creates a family atmosphere, and when you get more people acting like a family, then it's kind of like a disease—it catches on.

Jovita had a similar feeling: "We met such great people [through sports]. They are still our friends today, twenty years later. It was something that I thank God that I had the vision to get the boys involved in, because it became such a positive thing for all of them." Her sons found two coaches whom Leo referred to as his "father figures." When Leo briefly ran with peers engaged in delinquency, these coaches proved vital in encouraging him to stop. They came with his four brothers, his mother, and his uncle to get him at the police station when Leo was caught stealing sneakers from a store. The disappointment evident on his coaches' faces put Leo back on track. Years later, Leo would become a police officer serving Pueblo Viejo.

Alfredo and his two brothers were also kept busy in sports growing up. Their family was undocumented and struggled financially. For twelve years, his parents, Jorge, an underemployed salesman, and Martha, a domestic who cleaned houses, lived in Martha's sisters' converted garage. These were tight living quarters for the family of five; the couple had two sets of bunk beds for their three children, and Jorge and Martha slept on the floor. But the family was close, partly because Jorge had only a part-time job. The couple decided that Jorge would not search for a second job, although the family badly needed the money, so that he could supervise their sons after school. They set aside their own goals to prosper in the United States, reconceptualizing the American Dream as the successful adaptation and integration of their children.

When Martha's nephews joined gangs, the family moved out of the converted garage and into an apartment where they paid more rent. They distanced themselves from the only kin they had in Los Angeles. But they also aggressively scheduled Alfredo and his two brothers in numerous extracurricular activities, including piano lessons, swimming lessons (which Martha's employer paid for), and hockey. Jorge drove the boys to so many activities that, as Alfredo said, "We didn't have time to go out on the streets." Alfredo explained that his parents "*no tenian confianza* [didn't trust anyone]." For five years, they played soccer with a Christian church in the summer. Martha and Jorge volunteered their time on weekends selling chips and water at the games; in turn, the pastor reduced their fees. In high school, Alfredo and his brothers were on the varsity baseball and soccer teams. Practice occupied them during the week. On weekends, they played soccer with a community league. Alfredo knew that there were gangs in the neighborhood, but, as he explained, "I really don't go outside." Jorge and Martha felt that their decision that Jorge would not seek more work so that his schedule would remain flexible had paid off. "We can't claim victory just yet," Jorge noted, as the youngest was still in high school, but none of their boys were entangled in neighborhood conflicts even though they had at times suffered violence.

Parents like Jorge and Martha and Jovita enroll their children in extra-curricular activities with a mind-set very different from that of middle- and upper-class parents, as Annette Lareau discusses.[25] She explains that struc-tured activities are part of a strategy of "concerted cultivation" by the latter parents to help their children learn to manage time, navigate institutions, and question and challenge authority to ensure their place in the middle or upper class. Jovita, Jorge, and Martha had college aspirations for their sons, but their primary motive for engaging them in sports and other extra-curricular activities was to ensure that they stayed safe and out of trouble in the neighborhood; for these families, that was the first step to making sure that their children had a shot at getting ahead.

In most cases, the extracurricular activities took place in the neighbor-hood, and so these young men remained exposed to some degree of vio-lence. Sometimes sport team members got caught up in local dynamics and conflicts and fights broke out during practices or games. During the study, one young man was shot and killed at a high school football game. After-school programs walked a fine line: to ensure that they provided a safe space, they limited access by excluding some or all gang-affiliated youth. Extracurricular activities that took place in middle-class areas, like Alfredo's swimming or soccer league, provided safer spaces outside urban neighborhoods, but few parents had the knowledge or resources—of time and money—to sign their children up for these activities.

Young men's link to community institutions was not always brokered by parents but instead by school structures; this minimized the time they spent in the neighborhood. One of the most effective interventions that minimized young men's exposure to the neighborhood and its violence was the school busing and magnet program in the Los Angeles Unified School District (LAUSD). Designed to racially desegregate schools, the program shuffles students from disadvantaged urban schools to other schools. Although some of these host schools are racially mixed and higher-income, many are not. In this study, some Central City young men attended Pueblo Viejo schools, and vice versa. Researchers debate the academic quality of magnet programs and the extent to which they prepare youth for higher education, but restricting young men's exposure to their own neighborhoods is an advantage in its own right.[26]

Bused youth had to catch a bus at 6:00 or 6:30 in the morning to arrive at school on time. Because of the distance and Los Angeles traffic, they arrived home late in the evening, just in time for dinner, and had very little time to spend in the neighborhood and draw on gang and crew ties. Tomas had been bused out since sixth grade. He said that he knew no one in his neighborhood because he had no time there: "I would wake up at six-thirty, and I will get back like around five (PM) and eat, do homework. By that time it's already like seven. I just watched TV and go to sleep." Most of his friends from the magnet program were spread throughout the city. He felt disconnected from his neighborhood, but he also did not consider it to be nearly as violent as those who spent more time there.

Tomas's parents picked him up at the school bus stop—which they could not have done without the long bus ride delaying his return to his neighborhood—and that routine proved effective in reducing Tomas's exposure to the violence; he had never been "hit up" or "pocket-checked." Not all parents could provide this protection, but magnet programs themselves provided some protection just in being a barrier to students' ability to establish peer ties in their neighborhoods. Federico was also bused out of the neighborhood beginning in middle school. During high school, he was assaulted five times and beaten up once on his way home from the bus stop, but he had no ties to gangs or crews, and he finished high school.

The structure of magnet programs at local high schools also buffered youth from the neighborhood and urban violence in other important ways. Even those magnet programs that operated in schools that were experiencing urban violence isolated participating students from the broader student population. Forced to take the same courses in a cohort, youths in magnet programs were limited in who they spent time with, and how, by the structure of the programs. Most of the friends of the young men enrolled in magnet programs were also in the program, and many of them did not live in the same neighborhood. With less school and neighborhood peer overlap and their classmates living scattered throughout Los Angeles, magnet students were encouraged to participate in after-school enrichment programs to socialize with their friends, leaving less time to spend with non-magnet students in and after school or out in the neighborhood. Fernando explained:

> If I was in the regular track, I would have met all sorts of kids my age that lived around my block . . . and we would have hung out. I would have had friends that lived close by. . . . I didn't know anybody around my block. I didn't hang out with the neighborhood kids, and till this day, the people that's my age around my block, I don't know who they are.

Young men in the study also referenced a related advantage: the conflicts that flowed between the neighborhood and the school rarely entered the magnet classrooms, where magnet students were isolated. All of the young men who were on the college track had been in a magnet program—either in another school to which they were bused or in their neighborhood school with class peers from other neighborhoods.

Institutional program involvement correlated with having urban migrant parents with more years of schooling—the parents of Leo, Alfredo, Tomas, Federico, and Fernando all had some college education. On the one hand, these parents, with fewer kin ties to fall back on for support, sought the help of these organizations. On the other hand, these parents were acutely attuned to the important role that programs played in shaping their children's well-being and schooling. In short, parents who buffered their sons from the neighborhood and its violence did not manage the urban context alone but leaned on family and neighborhood institutions to provide their sons with an alternative social context. Spending time with kin working or socializing or in neighborhood institutions left less time to spend in the neighborhood and less opportunity to be exposed to violence.

Shielded Young Men: The Most Connected and Most Distant from the Community

Some young men were embedded in a supportive kin network *and* in neighborhood institutions. These young men had the most resources, not only at home but in the community, and the greatest protection from urban violence.

Leonardo, for example, grew up close to the paternal side of his family, surrounded by many aunts, uncles, and cousins. On his mother's side, kin relations were strained, and they worsened as his cousins joined gangs and left school, but his father's side was different. There were lot of relatives on that side, and they had many family parties. He was fond of two of his uncles, whom he helped in construction jobs at times. He could talk to them "about anything," he said, including things that he "couldn't talk to Dad about." His uncles had authority over him as well, and they disciplined him. Leonardo's mother, Jesusita, credited her husband for making time for their children: Damian "was always one of those parents that it didn't matter how tired he was, if they wanted to go shoot pool or something he would say 'Okay, I'll take you.' He'd shower and take them." Leonardo grew up camping, fishing, and going to museums with kin on a regular basis in southern California—"things," he noted, "that were free." His parents rarely allowed their children to go out with friends and prevented them from attending "flyer parties," where violence often erupted.

Leonardo also had institutional support. His mother volunteered at her children's schools throughout their tenure, adjusting the schedule for her full-time job to make time. Jesusita was especially involved in middle school, recognizing that things could go wrong then. She recalled: "Where my kids are, that's where I want to be. You need me to pass out lunch, that's where I'll be. You need service in the restrooms, that's where I'll be. I don't care where, but I'm volunteering my time to keep a close eye on them." Being at school also gave her access to information about college-prep programs, including the busing program that would eventually take Leonardo out of the neighborhood. In his magnet program, he would participate in various enrichment activities.

In addition, Leonardo's family was well integrated into the community, having started a community soccer league when Leonardo was only three years old. The league included cousins and children from across the neighborhood, and Jesusita and Damian were very involved in it. In the follow-up study, the family was still running the league, which now had ten teams and 250 youth. Long after their children graduated from high school, Jesusita and Damian continued to volunteer Saturdays from 6:00 AM to 6:00 PM, and Leonardo was serving as a coach. Jesusita explained, "We are also babysitters, parents, we are everything. We do it all. Some parents have to work Saturdays, and they leave their kids with us. The child is taken care of, he plays, he eats. We are happy to do it." The family was proud that many of these youth graduated from high school and avoided gangs in the area, and Leonardo expressed a deep connection and commitment to seeing his community thrive.

The dual forces of strong kin networks and institutional ties also provided Zach with a significant buffer, but he lacked Leonard's affection for his neighborhood. Like Noel, he was not allowed to play outside his own yard, but this restriction left him with only one playmate, his brother Elias. His parents had a high fence around their home, and their tall garden of corn, sugar cane, fruit trees, and other vegetables added to the sense of a highly guarded home. Agustina kept a close watch on her sons; in her own words, she was always *"detras de ellos* [after them]." Both parents spent ample time and energy discouraging their sons from being *vagos* (street-oriented). Ricardo felt attuned to the pressures that adolescent boys encountered, explaining, "Girls don't really peer-pressure each other, 'Hey come on, smoke,' or, 'Take this drug.' Men, if you don't have drugs, you're not a man. [Peers] get them hooked, they brainwash them to be macho. It happens all the time." So Ricardo often purchased gang movies for his sons to watch "to teach them right from wrong."

Agustina and Ricardo had the support of extended kin from each of their families in imposing expectations, values, and norms. For years, their family gathered at a local park every two weeks to play sports and to cook *carne asada* on the grills. Zach was especially close to some of his cousins, with whom he discussed his college plans. Neither of his parents had any formal schooling, but they enforced strict engagement in school. Agustina made friends with the high school secretary, who monitored her sons' school attendance. Zach also had institutional ties in the form of a magnet program and involvement in the high school band, and he often played at church and was part of a local rock band. Zach also used his musical skills to teach guitar in the neighborhood.

Unlike Leonardo, who expressed a strong attachment to his community, Zach voiced mixed feelings. He had also been assaulted on a couple of occasions, and during the study his block was experiencing a rise in gang violence. Zach and his Central City friends hung out mostly at each other's homes, doing "mostly indoor things." Zach avoided walking in the neighborhood to avoid violence. He described Central City as having "no unity." He said, "I personally don't like my community because of the pack of thieves, gangs, and this and that." He referred to gangs as "jokes": "Everyone sees them as those thugs in the streets. Mostly they are just people that are lazy and don't want to get a job so they just go and jack [steal]." His parents had put their house up for sale. Unlike Leonardo and his family, who worked to improve conditions in their neighborhood via their sports league, Zach and his family looked forward to getting out.

"Caught Up": Exposed and Marginalized

Immigrant parents of the young men who got "caught up" in male peer ties were often not much different from other parents in the neighborhood. Most were concerned parents who employed various strategies to keep their children out of trouble, encourage educational attainment, and help them become self-sufficient young adults. In a few exceptional cases, parents were absent to monitor their children's whereabouts. More often, however, parents of exposed youth sustained a strong sense of familism but differed in their social capital from the families of buffered young men. These young men were also less likely to be linked to positive institutions in the neighborhood. To the contrary, the institutions encountered by these young men—already the most marginalized young men in the study—often exposed them further to the neighborhood, locked them in, and served to criminalize them.

My focus on the social capital of families differs from a current emphasis in the literature on the structure of families to understand marginalized youth. Studies repeatedly find that young men who join gangs and become involved in criminal activity are more likely to come from single-parent homes.[27] Undoubtedly, youth from single-parent homes generally have fewer resources than those from two-parent homes. The presence of two parents is beneficial, however, only when both are playing a positive role in guiding the young man. In this study, several fathers were physically present but not actively involved in their son's life, and ties with some of these fathers were taxing and the source of family trauma. Rather than buffer their children from the neighborhood, their actions pushed their sons into the streets, as in Benjamin's case. Young men who became "caught up" were more likely to come from families where at least one of the parents, typically the mother, tried to manage the neighborhood context alone. These were the parents who had minimal kin support ties and were disconnected from institutions in the neighborhood that could help socially isolated immigrants—like Rosita was for a while.

On Their Own: Socially Isolated Parents

Among the most exposed young men were those whose parents worked excessive numbers of hours and struggled to provide close supervision; often these parents were disconnected from neighborhood institutions, as were their children. Ezequiel, who had been expelled from several schools and ticketed by police, often had nothing to do after school but get on his bike and "kick it." As he said: "When I had extra time, I would hang out in the street. Just walk up and down, talk to homies, homegirls, just kick it, do nothing. Just like that, when I had free time I would get home from school, have nothing to do, just walk around, ride my bike. Just kick it." The truth was that he often had extra time. Ezequiel described his immigrant parents as many other young men did, as "hardworking" and "very strict." His parents worked long hours, six days a week—Sunday was the only family time—and they taught him to be responsible for his actions and respectful of others. Ezequiel was thankful he had "good parents."

His grandmother was responsible for him after school, and sometimes he would stay inside, playing video games, but more often he went out on the streets. No one prevented him from spending time with his older half-sister, whose boyfriend was a local gang member; the boyfriend gave Ezequiel his first joint when he was twelve years old.

Struggling to rein him in, Ezequiel's parents sought a debatable source of support: law enforcement. When Ezequiel was thirteen years old, his mother turned him into the police after she caught him stealing money from her. The relationship grew tense. His parents reacted strongly against the multiple expulsions from high school and eventually pushed the seventeen-year-old to work instead. He felt that they "harassed" him and made him feel like a "lazy ass motherfucker," so he avoided being home. When money went missing at the house, his mother accused Ezequiel of stealing again, and he left his home for several weeks, although he and his parents had mended relations by the time I met him.

When Ezequiel turned eighteen, his juvenile record was erased, discarding the stigma he carried at home and in the community. As an adult, he was starting from scratch, without a record, and this motivated him. It was at this point that he re-enrolled (again) in school. When I met him, Ezequiel had a highly structured schedule that detached him from the neighborhood. He attended continuation school from 7:00 AM to 1:30 PM. At 2:30 PM, he began work at his job, where he worked for at least eight and a half hours. He was proud that, unlike many of his peers, he had no arrests or a criminal record as an adult, and he credited his parents for this. He said, "I love my parents. I thank God that he gave me parents like that, because if it weren't for them, I'd either be locked up, dead. . . . I didn't understand back then. I really didn't. I was like, 'Why are you on me so much?'" Eventually Ezequiel stopped attending school, opting to pursue full-time work. He took pride in his work ethic, which his parents had modeled for years, and put in overtime when possible.

Like Ezequiel, Jaime felt that he had good parents, but he recognized that they gave him "too much freedom" growing up: "They weren't that strict on me like they should have been." He said that when he has kids he will take a different approach: "You be here right after school! If you're not, I'm going looking for you!"

His father, Raymundo, worked long hours, while his mother, Leticia, stayed home to care for the family of seven. The family sometimes played soccer together at the park, but Jaime was never enrolled in extracurricular activities. They had extended kin in the area but kept a distance from them, as some of Jaime's cousins became gang members. Like Ezequiel, Jaime was not one to stay home: "I would hop on my bike and just go." His parents did not restrict where he could go in the neighborhood or which peers he could spend time with. They believed him when he said that he had no homework. In seventh grade, he began to skip school and stay out until dinnertime with his friends. Jaime's parents objected, but they didn't discipline him. Exposed to the neighborhood and the violence, Jaime joined a tagging crew early in high school.

To better monitor his sons and encourage them to hang out at the house with friends instead of in the streets, Raymundo tried to make their home more inviting. He converted his garage into a bedroom for Jaime and his brother, thinking that it would make a spacious place for socializing more safely than on the streets. Raymundo recognized that Jaime was in danger. He explained, "I always have to monitor him. . . . He's the one I've tried to keep closest because he's the one who has tried to get out more." Raymundo got to know Jaime's friends well, never missing an opportunity to reprimand the youth for their clothing or behavior. Some felt so comfortable at Raymundo's home that they crashed at his place for days; a foster youth and one young man whose mother abused him were often there. As Raymundo had hoped, the family's home became the "hangout" for Jaime and his friends—but most were in his tagging crew. The frequent congregation at the home of young men not engaged in structured activities garnered the attention of police, who kept a close eye on the house—as did local gang members.

Like Ezequiel's mother, Raymundo mistakenly turned for support to only one neighborhood institution, law enforcement, and that move had damaging consequences. At his wits' end over Jaime's behavior—his poor school performance and tagging—Raymundo allowed the police to take his son to jail when he was stopped and frisked on the street and caught carrying tagging materials in violation of his probation. Jaime was eighteen, so he spent several weeks incarcerated. Raymundo hoped that this experience would teach his son a lesson, but after Jaime was released the police increased their surveillance. "The other day they stopped and searched Jaime here," Raymundo said angrily, indicating the front of their house. When he questioned the police officers as to why they were stopping Jaime in front of his own home, their response was that Jaime "looked like a gangster." Raymundo retorted:

> I also have a shaved head, why don't you stop me? Did he do something? Do your job right! I'm also shaved and have loose pants. If you find something on him, I'll sign the damn papers so you can take him and arrest him. Why are you stopping him outside our home? If you see him tagging or breaking into a car . . . take him, but I need an explanation. Take his California ID. You don't have to handcuff him!

Raymundo was further upset when Jaime's thirteen-year-old brother witnessed the harassment and police threatened to handcuff him too. Under close surveillance, Jaime and his friends would be ticketed by police many times, and this would prevent him from getting a license. Unintentionally, his parents' well-meaning approach—to collaborate with police—locked him into the neighborhood further, making it harder to break his neighborhood ties. In the follow-up study, the twenty-three-year-old remained on probation.

Gender roles factored prominently into parenting, including how the neighborhood was managed and with what support structures. Typically, fathers managed the neighborhood context in ways consistent with masculine expectations, often taking their sons to work with them or keeping them busy with sports, although Jovita played that role in her sons' lives.[28] While hers was a single-parent success story, a father who did not help keep his sons out of gangs and crews was a disadvantage to his family. As well, gender roles assigned women enormous responsibility, as they were often charged with most, if not all, of the child-rearing and schooling responsibilities. Fathers were quick to acknowledge that they had no contact with schools, deeming this their wife's role. Often mothers managed the tricky transition to middle school alone. Even women in the formal workforce were expected to remain on top of their children's whereabouts and peer relations in order to keep their sons safe and discourage risky behavior at school and in the neighborhood. Without the support of a partner/spouse, other kin ties, or institutional ties, women left alone had a difficult time helping their sons navigate their environment and managing their exposure to the neighborhood.

Rosita's husband was hardworking and provided for the family. He was also an alcoholic who left her fully responsible for the household, including managing their ten children's peer relations and exposure to the neighborhood. Rosita explained, "*Yo era la que estaba al pendiente* [I was the one keeping an eye on them]." In the early years after her migration, Rosita was not fully aware of what to watch for in the neighborhood, or what she needed to protect her children from: "I didn't know what. I could not distinguish because I had no idea, because I did not associate with anybody and I wouldn't go out, only for the most basic needs." Rosita punished her children when they acted out with a spank or *el cinto* (the belt). She tirelessly gave them *consejos* (advice). Yet with conflict at home with her husband, she was unable to contain her adolescent boys inside the house. Rosita spent many evenings searching for them in the neighborhood, leaving her youngest children at home with their father passed out drunk on the couch, admonishing them to stay in the house and do their homework while she was gone. She recalled telling them, "Wait for me a little. Don't leave the house. Hurry with your homework. I'm just going right here, be right back." These fathers' passive parenting was not lost on the young men. Benjamin had harsh words for his father, while he praised Rosita for "always being there" for him.

Benjamin gravitated toward the gang because he "wanted to be part of something." He took refuge in the streets when his authoritative, "idiot" father was "power-tripping": "He'll get home from work and . . . he'll tell us to take off his boots. If we didn't take them off right, he'll fucking kick us in our face." Benjamin blamed his father for Manolo's death, and he spoke angrily: "He didn't teach me shit, honestly he didn't. He was a *pendejo* [fool]. Telling us we are going to *valer verga* [be worthless] when we grew up and we were fucking idiots." Thus, Rosita tried to steer her sons away from threats in the neighborhood as best as she could on her own.

Angelica's efforts to keep her sons out of trouble in the neighborhood created tension with them. Her eldest son, Eddy, rosy-cheeked and fair-skinned, was tall and wore oversized clothes and a shaved head. Eddy thought that Angelica did not understand what it was like for him to grow up in the projects. Some of the gangsters wanted to "check him in" and "rush him"—through a beating—because he "looked hard-core": "They wanted me *real* bad," he affirmed. Though he never did join a gang, he got "caught up."

The only support that Angelica felt she had in raising their sons came from her sister, but their relationship became strained when Eddy was a young man. Angelica tried to keep her sons at home, but they ignored her. Walking the projects as late as midnight in search of them, she carried a small, wooden corncob stick set for self-protection. "*Viera con que miedo . . . cargaba un palito de los elotes . . . si alguien se me pone, le pico un ojo* [You can't imagine my fear. I would take a corncob stick. If someone tries to attack me, I'll poke his eye out!]." Gilberto, Eddy's stepfather, disapproved of her approach and didn't join her on these searches, insisting that their sons were out looking for problems. Rather than help, he scolded Angelica. On her own, Angelica struggled to keep her sons out of the neighborhood. Eddy remained a handful, and Miguel began to "act hard" and "crazier" than Eddy; Angelica lamented, "*Miguel se me desvalago* [got off track]."

Eddy dropped out of school and wouldn't get a job. His brother, Miguel, who was fourteen, was arrested for stealing from another young man. The police reported him to the housing authority after finding $20 he had stolen. The family was evicted and moved into a two-bedroom home renting for $1,400 a month in 2007—a drastic change from the $214 a month they were paying for public housing. Conflict with Eddy escalated so much that at times Angelica feared that he might hurt her physically. Gilberto blamed Angelica for Eddy's failure to get a job and contribute to expenses. Miguel was caught in the housing projects, a violation of his probation, before the family had even unpacked. This time he was detained and put in juvenile hall. Angelica had recurrent migraines and clinical anxiety and depression as the neighborhood engulfed her sons. Though married, she felt alone in her parenting.

Ezequiel, Jaime, Benjamin, and Eddy could not fall back on a tight-knit kin structure to provide an alternative context to the neighborhood, and none were ever consistently enrolled in extracurricular activities. It took getting incarcerated for Benjamin to establish links to a priest and a community organization that the priest ran that would help him turn his life around. Most often their only institutional links were to local schools, which expelled them, and law enforcement, which detained them.

The Most Exposed: Co-occurrence Violence and Isolation

The young men most exposed to urban violence were those who came from the most socially isolated families in these neighborhoods. These young men lacked kin and institutional ties to buffer them from their surroundings as they grew up. Their families had no kin-based social capital, a situation that often did not change over time. (Benjamin was an exception.) The most vulnerable young men revealed strained and broken kin relations rooted in the trauma of having experienced multiple forms of violence, beginning from an early age and continuing throughout their adolescence in the neighborhood and into their young adult years.[29]

Salvador was only a boy when he witnessed his stepfather rape his sister. His mother, Maritza, migrated to Los Angeles in the hopes of making a life for her three children as a single mother, but she left them with a relative who sexually abused Salvador while she established herself. He remembered being overjoyed and relieved when Maritza returned to Mexico City for them.

Maritza had taken a job as a live-in nanny in an affluent home and arranged for an acquaintance to take care of her own children Monday through Friday. The children lived in a trailer with this acquaintance.

Salvador was about seven at the time. It didn't take long before the children began to act out, and their caretaker asked them to move out. Maritza quit her job as a nanny and took a job at a local bar. They were very poor. Salvador said, "It was a single, no bedroom, just a bathroom, a kitchen, and a living room [where they slept]." At the bar, Maritza met a man, and the family moved in with him in Pueblo Viejo. A drug dealer, he would become Salvador's main male role model, and the father of the boy's youngest sibling. The couple broke up after three years when Maritza became addicted to crack.

Salvador spoke of no other kin—no uncles, no cousins. His twelve-year-old sister was responsible for him and his siblings while Maritza and her boyfriend were working, but she often kicked Salvador out of the apartment when her boyfriend visited. When Salvador was ten years old, a priest at a local church found him stealing fruit from his tree. The priest learned that Salvador often had no food at home, so he gave Salvador canned food to take to his siblings and told him he could have $5 anytime he cleaned a window of the church. But this kindness did not prevent Salvador from establishing ties with gang youth. By age eleven, Salvador was smoking weed, drinking alcohol, and carrying a gun, practicing shooting with the "homies" from the projects. He began acting out at school and setting trash cans on fire, which led to his first arrest. Salvador was only eleven when he was first put "in placement" (juvenile hall).

Salvador and his siblings were placed in foster care for three years, except for the youngest, who was given to his father. Salvador joined a tagging crew. When Salvador and his siblings returned to their mother when he was thirteen, she was not noticeably less neglectful. Salvador had given up carrying a gun and doing drugs while he was in foster care, but now he resumed. On a couple of occasions, he took his mother's pipe and smoked her leftover crack, and he started using crystal meth. He was skipping school every day to go to the projects to get high. "Not a lot of people liked me," he said. He was in and out of juvenile hall and got kicked out of three different high schools. When the housing projects in Pueblo Viejo were demolished, the family moved to Central City.

Throughout his adolescence, Salvador was heavily exposed to the neighborhood. Maritza kicked him out of the house after he got arrested when he was fifteen. He recalled: "I started laughing, and she said, 'I am not joking, get the fuck out my house. You don't want to pay rent, you don't want to go school, you don't want to do shit, all right, get the fuck out of here.'" For two months, Salvador stayed out in the street in abandoned cars. He stole food from supermarkets and befriended drug-dealing pimps who would pay him for transporting drugs. Maritza let him move back in after two months, but there was often no food. He went to school for the free lunch, and he wasn't sorry to return to juvenile hall because he didn't go hungry there. He said, "I think that was like the best thing that could have ever happened to me because in there I was eating good. That's the only thing I love about being locked up. I used to get three meals a day, every single day." He regained some weight after drug dependency and undernourishment had left him bone-thin. By the time he was eighteen, Salvador had been arrested four times for "possession, sales, breaking and entering, stealing . . . destruction of private property." By then, he had also been hospitalized after getting shot at a party; the bullet grazed his side but did not penetrate. Maritza explained that she got him placed in juvenile camp for one year when he was eighteen years old for his safety. It was the longest time he served behind bars, and he participated more in education there than he ever had before, though he never acquired enough credits to graduate. Ultimately, his record got the whole family evicted from the housing projects in Central City by the time he was nineteen years old.

Salvador was one of the young men who was most exposed to the neighborhood and its violence. "Nobody cared," he recalled. "I would do bad stuff to people, you know, I didn't care." Apart from the priest who helped him, Salvador said that he had "no other positive person" in his life. The only other men who took an interest in Salvador were a group of black gang members in Central City who "took care" of him. "At that time, they were my mentors or something. . . . They'll talk to me, 'You are not going to be doing this shit. I see you and your family. You have good people around you. Go to school, get a job, do what you got to do. You don't have to be like us, you know, pimping women.'" Yet, he said, "I am telling you, there are no positive role models in my life." Salvador didn't listen to their advice. Even when he got a job, he sold drugs on the side.

Yet by the time I met him, when Salvador was twenty, he had been clean over a year and a half and felt that he was maturing. He had a complicated relationship with his mother. Salvador respected Maritza, but felt that he would have been in better shape if she had shown more concern for him and his welfare. He was attending night school in hopes of getting his GED and had A part-time job. The priest had helped Salvador get work and he was hoping for a brighter future. Certainly, he had reason to be grateful that he was not incarcerated or dead.

The Impact of Urban Violence on Second-Generation Latinos

One of the most consequential features of growing up in Los Angeles neighborhoods for young men in this study was their exposure to urban violence. In line with other recent research, I find that urban violence factored prominently in their lives, affecting not only their physical and mental health but also their social mobility prospects. Urban violence affects the schooling of young men in various ways. As it filters into schools, they become disruptive and feel unsafe. Urban violence also dictates young men's social dynamics. To stay safe they learn to affiliate with peers who offer them physical and symbolic protection. These social relationships originate out of the threat of victimization. Once entangled in these social networks, young men are implicated in acts of reciprocity that can be damaging.

In this study, urban violence played a prominent role in school non-completion because school officials severely punished behavior associated with involvement in crews and gangs—skipping school with friends or fighting to "back them up." Disciplinary measures, especially expulsion, frequently led to school noncompletion. Worse, the school-to-prison pipeline criminalized these youth, further entrenching them in the neighborhood by compelling them to pay tickets and court fees. Urban violence underlies various life outcomes associated with "second-generation decline," from school noncompletion to criminalization and later difficulties in the labor market. The lingering effects of urban violence on Latino youth are carried into their young adult years, impinging on their social mobility.

At the same time, most young men in this study were buffered from the neighborhood to some degree. As I discussed in chapter 2, many immigrant parents were alert to how violence and social disorder threatened their children, and for many of these children their parents' response had a positive effect, especially if they also had the support of kin networks or institutional ties. Most young men in the study did not join gangs or crews, or they left them quickly behind once problems ensued. Most of them graduated from high school. Although none of these young men was immune to the violence in these neighborhoods, most had some protection from the violence and from entanglement in local conflicts or group dynamics. Kin and institutional ties provided the young men with an alternative social context to the unstructured context of neighborhood male peer ties. Such connections provided some of the young men with a strong sense of community, despite the violence and social disorder. Others positioned themselves at odds with—and on higher moral ground than—gang members and disconnected youth in the neighborhood.

A clear picture emerges in this study: the most isolated families, those raising their boys on their own, without the support of kin and institutions, struggled to do so effectively. It is often these isolated parents who turn to law enforcement to help them manage their sons' activities in the neighborhood, but often such efforts are too late and they frequently backfire. These young men were the most exposed to the neighborhood context and the most affected by the violence; the most vulnerable among them hardly had a chance to survive as they battled trauma rooted in their early years and their entanglement in local conflicts and risky ties followed them into their young adult years. These youth faced the greatest odds of remaining in poverty.

The Mexican immigrant family is not devoid of social capital, as some segmented assimilation scholars suggest, but they are confronted with a challenging urban context that spreads them thin.[30] At times their resources are strained, and their sons must navigate the urban context on their own as best as they can. The contrasting trajectories of siblings reflect the fact that resources and social support are not static for families.

No one was left untouched by the violence in the East Los Angeles and South Central Los Angeles neighborhoods at the center of this study. All the young men were forced to contend with this reality in one way or another. Yet the violence in both communities declined over time, coinciding with these young men's transition to adulthood. As the majority of these young Latino men entered the labor market or institutions of higher education, most of them spent less time in the neighborhood, diminishing the chances that they would have to confront violence. Violence also became less salient in the everyday interactions of most young Latino adults as they disengaged from the peer ties drawn on previously for protection; local conflicts became a thing of the past, a feature of their adolescent years. Violence, gang, and crew ties remained relevant only for the minority of Latino young adult men who remained embedded in local networks of conflict.[31] Many of these young men were those who were most physically confined to the neighborhood, without a car or job, and who were closely monitored by law enforcement once they became entangled in the criminal justice system. The majority of the young men in the study skirted the threats of the inner city. But they had to shift gears as they transitioned to adulthood and focused on the next hurdle: getting ahead.

....

CHAPTER 5

Collapsing into the Working Class

Social Support, Segregation, and Class Convergence

Is [college] really that powerful? I personally think that it's based on *who* you know and *what* you know.

OSVALDO, age twenty-two

Hen I first met Osvaldo in 2007, he was juggling three part-time jobs that paid minimum wage. He was soon to be a father and was so desperate for a good-paying job that he "felt like shooting myself in the head." He had considered selling drugs— "at least for a little while so I can stack up some money"—and "thought about jacking people . . . someone with a nice car."

The violence and social disorder in American urban neighborhoods challenge the successful integration process of the Latino second generation, but Osvaldo had dodged most of the risks. He had avoided for the most part getting caught up in risky ties and behavior, he had completed high school, and he had an associate's degree. He was not among the nine participants who had been arrested. He was not "disconnected" from work and school and never had been, much like the majority of the young men in this study and the majority of second-generation young Latino men in the United States.[1] He was also typical in that he was struggling to establish a socioeconomic foundation that would allow him to prosper over time.

Osvaldo's mother, Rosa, had him bused out of Central City in middle and high school because she was concerned about violence at the neighborhood schools. As Osvaldo noted, rolling his eyes, she felt that "her kids deserved better." He hated the affluent schools where "stuck-up" students made "fun of the South Central kids with faded clothes," he recalled. He threatened to drop out of school altogether, so Rosa allowed him to attend Central City High in his senior year. While he reconnected with peers who were caught up in neighborhood conflicts, he did not get caught up himself. Osvaldo noted, "Out of all my friends, I was the only one to graduate . . . all either got kicked out, in jail, dropped out."

Osvaldo planned to go straight to work after high school, but in his words, Rosa told him, "If you don't go to school, *cabron* [fucker], you'll have to pay rent!" So Osvaldo attended community college for three years while working thirty hours a week at the airport earning $10.83 an hour. He earned his associate's degree in criminal justice. Although he had admitted to being tempted to engage in crime, he took after his parents, who took great pride in their work ethic. In fact, he was avoiding friends who introduced "a lot of problems," like "police harassing you, *cholos* messing with you." He looked down on his high school friends: "None of my friends work. They're all low lives, *huevones* [lazy]." Osvaldo felt different: "I'm not lazy. I work."

Osvaldo surmounted the risks of his neighborhood but still hit a wall in the labor market. He had left the job at the airport to follow a promising lead for a better-paying job that went nowhere. He and his wife were living with his mother, and he was eager to find a job that paid at least $15 an hour so he could pay rent and support his new baby. He had submitted over twenty applications to county and city jobs, including for the probation, customs, and animal control departments. Osvaldo wondered if part of the problem was his interview skills. He often got nervous, but asserted, "I'll go dressed nice. I shave, wear slacks, button-up shirt, sometimes a tie, [dress] shoes." He had thus far only been able to obtain temporary jobs he got through friends or work agencies—factory, clerical, and caregiving work that paid around $8.50 an hour in 2007.

Osvaldo decided to enroll at a state university, but he had little faith that a bachelor's degree would help his job search. He knew people without degrees getting paid more than he was. The case managers at the caretaker agency where he worked part-time were "earning good money" and did not have a college degree. A friend without a high school diploma took home $600 a week, much more than Osvaldo was earning. Visibly upset, Osvaldo said, "I have a high school diploma and a little bit of college and nothing! Shit!"

Osvaldo had a realistic understanding of the importance of social ties in the job market. He told me, "Jobs are based on who you know." He used the Spanish term *palancas,* which literally means "levers," to describe the importance of personal connections.[2] He had learned about the importance of networks in his teen years when his sister had helped him get a job at a pizza joint; coworkers had also found their jobs through friends and relatives. "Every single person that worked inside the restaurant knew each other," he recalled. Job applications were thrown in the trash if no one vouched for the applicant; jobs went to those with connections. "Look, if we both apply for the same position and we have the same ratings [qualifications] but they know one of us, guess who is getting the job? Exactly: *Palancas* [social leverage ties]!"

The Hidden Hand of Segregation

In the previous chapter, I described how exposure to violence derailed young men away from school and complicated their ability to get ahead. Those who had been heavily exposed to violence and had minimal kin and institutional support ties were more likely to experience what segmented assimilation theorists would predict—detachment from school and the labor market and engagement in crime.[3] Yet those who fit this profile were a minority. Most young men conformed to the story that emerges from the studies that contradict the narrative of downward assimilation: the Mexican second generation is not any more likely to be disconnected than others their age.[4] In fact, in Los Angeles, they have higher rates of employment than others, and most of the young men in my study were employed.[5] Like second-generation Latinos generally, they had made significant educational gains over those of their parents.[6] Contradicting key assumptions of downward assimilation, living in Central City and consequently being exposed to black peers did not put these young men at a disadvantage compared to those living in Pueblo Viejo, a predominantly immigrant community; young men struggled similarly in both neighborhoods.[7]

Most respondents were like Osvaldo. As they navigated their morally contested neighborhood, they sometimes identified with marginalized young men, but often distanced themselves from stigmatized peers, claiming moral worth through strong attachment to school and work. I began this study with three types of young men—the four-year college youth, the high school noncompleters, and those in between, typically high school

Figure 5.1 The Class Convergence of Inner-City Children of Latino Immigrants

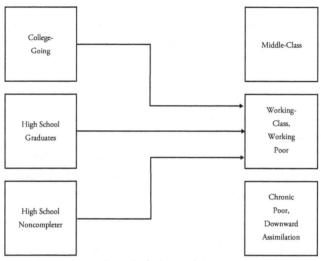

Source: Author's compilation.

graduates—but most young men converged over time, settling into the kind of jobs, with the kind of pay, aligned with jobs typically held by high school graduates or those with a year or two of a college education: their average pay by the end of the study, when they were in their mid to late twenties, was roughly $15 an hour. I expected that young men's educational attainment would translate into distinct social mobility paths, but as this chapter shows, I found that most fared similarly in their young adult years and were positioned to remain working class, if not working poor.[8] They typically earned pay in line with the median income of Pueblo Viejo and Central City.[9] Many of these young men shared Osvaldo's frustration because they had hit an invisible barrier as they tried to get ahead. Having skirted risks in the neighborhood and attained at least some level of higher education increased their frustration; these were investments that were supposed to lead to a stable life, but their incomes were significantly below the median income in the county.

The story of second-generation Latinos is both uplifting and somber, as shown in figure 5.1. High school noncompleters often fare better than predicted. Although some of the young men got caught up in negative peer dynamics in their adolescent years, most moved away from such ties and sought work or education. As this chapter will explain, kin ties and institutions were key to these success stories. At the same time, those on the most promising path, the four-year college-going respondents, were on a slippery slope: instead of moving into the middle class, they often slipped back into the ranks of their less-educated working-class peers. Most of them may have earned a bit more than their immigrant parents, but they came of age in an era of skyrocketing housing prices, ensuring that their modest gain was not good enough to improve their life circumstances.

Research suggests that the biggest social mobility obstacle facing people in the United States of Mexican descent is their limited educational attainment. Edward Telles and Vilma Ortiz conclude that "education accounts for the slow assimilation of Mexican Americans," describing it as the "linchpin" of their ethnic persistence.[10] At the population level, income gaps with whites do close substantially as this group moves up the educational ladder, but few make the climb—and those from the inner city are the least likely to gain entry. In my sample, even those young men who had entered four-year colleges realized few benefits, as being from the inner city overwhelmed any advantage that educational attainment could provide. Indeed, many studies have shown that growing up in a poor, segregated neighborhood makes it harder to get ahead at every level of educational attainment.[11] In this chapter, I explain how the urban context impinged on the social mobility prospects of the majority of the young men in this study.

As Osvaldo asserted, workers in American society need social networks in addition to credentials. Indeed, cross-class ethnic ties explain why children of low-skilled Asian immigrants have risen in U.S. society while their Latino peers have not, in spite of a strong work ethic and orientation toward education.[12] Research on this subject has generally interpreted the homogenous working-class networks of Latinos as a function of the ethnic community.[13] Scholars call attention to the fact that "non-family" ties and "institutional agents" are critical for the success of children of low-skilled Latinos immigrants in gaining entry to universities.[14] I extend this work by finding that social leverage ties are critical *throughout* the young adult years; these ties are essential for navigating and leveraging institutions of higher education and for brokering access to "middle-class" jobs. I depart from the aforementioned literature in one way. Rather than focus on the homogenous working-class ties of the Mexican immigrant community, I highlight the incorporation of this group into the American context of class and racial segregation. I reveal how segregation reinforces the working-class ties of the Latino second generation and constructs their social isolation, inhibiting their structural assimilation.

Beyond the Ethnic Enclave: How Race and Class Segregation Matters

In this chapter, I show how second-generation Latinos' social networks, bound to kin ties and a segregated context, collide with the labor market to position most on a path to a "permanent working class."[15] Immigration scholars recognize the role of race in shaping the integration process of immigrants, but few have examined how race factors into the integration process of the second generation.[16] Most evaluate the integration of this group through the lens of the ethnic enclave—a model only useful to understanding ethnic groups with class heterogeneity. The fact that for over one hundred years Mexican immigrants to the United States have been primarily low-skilled workers has shaped their class composition in this country. For even longer, Mexicans have been incorporated into the United States as a racial minority group. Race and class segregation is not new for this group, but it has reached new levels in a context of rising spatial inequality.

The segregation of Latinos extends beyond their residence. I have already noted that in California, Latino students experience the highest levels of segregation in schools, which concentrates them in America's least-resourced and most underperforming schools.[17] This alone put the young men in this study severely behind most of their peers in colleges and universities. Segregation affects these young men in other ways as well. Lauren Krivo and her colleagues find that in Los Angeles, "Latinos live in neighborhoods that are about 30 percent more disadvantaged than whites . . . and conduct regular activities [shop, attend church, work] in places that are up to nearly four times as disadvantaged."[18] In my study, immigrants and young men visited and ran errands in neighborhoods similar to their own and worked with others like themselves, remaining socially integrated primarily with coethnics even when they stepped out of the neighborhood. This kind of social isolation from the mainstream American middle class affected young men's social and cultural integration process in higher education. As I elaborate in a later chapter, it was at universities that young men came to discover that their association with the inner city "tainted" them, contributing to their social exclusion. Coupled with the social and cultural distance they experienced in these institutional contexts, their segregated, urban-neighborhood origins complicated their opportunity to connect with those unlike them.[19]

Segregation sustains class and racial inequality. It denies young men like Osvaldo opportunities for cross-racial and cross-class interactions and, more importantly, access to social leverage ties—*palancas*—that would facilitate their upward mobility. It isolates these young men from valuable resources found in more affluent communities—good schools, information, role models, mentorship, and links to jobs and various other forms of opportunities—and it leaves them at a further disadvantage by isolating them from the dominant culture, which shapes the norms and forms of social interactions among the American middle class. Institutions of higher education were ill equipped to provide these young men with the kind of resources that, in bridging them to the "cliques, clubs and institutions" of mainstream society, would have helped them navigate these institutions successfully and expand their social networks.[20] Inner-city young men in institutions of higher education are often disconnected and isolated. Schooling without the help of institutional agents leaves young Latino men with only their working poor and working-class ties to link them to the American labor market. This social isolation, rooted in their experience of segregation, pulls them into the working class, no matter how seemingly divergent their trajectories.

From Promise to Stagnation

Early in their young adult years, life looked promising for the young men in the study who had evaded violence and the risks of their neighborhoods. They eagerly jumped into college or work or both. Those in the sample, like their demographic group overall, had surpassed their immigrant parents' years of schooling. Even high school noncompleters made progress: three eventually obtained a high school diploma, and an additional six made attempts to do the same. It was clear that these young men understood that higher education enhanced their chances of a better job, and several of them enrolled in college after working for a few years.

Capitalizing on their English skills and acculturation, these young men moved away from the most labor-intensive, exploitative jobs in the city in which many of their immigrant coethnics were concentrated. The service-based economy allowed them to meet their parents' minimal expectations that they would avoid jobs *que maten tanto*—that "kill you along the way." Many parents in the study held the most physically demanding jobs in the city, such as in the garment industry, maintenance, construction, sanitation, and manufacturing. Their children often worked in the hospitality, retail, and entertainment industries. Some obtained jobs as bank tellers or in customer service; these jobs, if not actually white-collar, gave them the opportunity to sit at a desk. Others found jobs in schools as coaches or teaching assistants, or as caseworkers in community organizations. Those who worked in the construction industry or the trades expected to move up to supervisory or managerial positions. They also earned several dollars more per hour than their parents. The second generation's shift into the mainstream economy and away from "immigrant jobs" indicated that they were on an upward mobility trajectory.[21]

Over time, however, frustration such as Osvaldo's became common. As they grew older, these young men grew frustrated at continuing to live with their parents because they were unable to earn enough to live independently in Los Angeles. In line with county averages, three-quarters of young men in this study continued to live at home with parents or other kin in their neighborhoods into their mid to late twenties.[22] The insular, working-class ties of the Mexican second generation are akin to what other researchers have found among other Latinos, like Dominicans on the East Coast, who do not benefit from a class-diverse ethnic enclave.[23] In these communities, ethnic ties are a source of support, and relying on them animates young men's strong conviction to get ahead, but these ties ultimately prove ill equipped to reward their efforts. Mexicans rely heavily on ethnic ties, primarily kin—many of them undocumented—to access jobs, and their networks are saturated by low-skilled ties that pull them into bottom-sector jobs.[24] Young men in my study relied heavily on kin ties and sometimes on neighborhood ties to access and navigate both institutions of higher learning and the labor market, and this reliance constrained their opportunities.[25] That immigrants rely on kin ties to get ahead in a new country is not a surprise, but that their children, most of whom are American-born and embedded in American institutions, do the same indicates how great are the structural barriers they confront.

Converging to the Working Class: High Aspirations, Insular Social Networks

Young Latino men in the inner city who are on different educational trajectories converged into the working class via different social mobility routes. The bulk of young Latino men in Los Angeles urban neighborhoods are represented by the middle category in figure 5.1: they are high school graduates who take one of two paths: they go straight to work out of high school or they enroll in community college.[26] Those who went straight to work after high school prided themselves on their ethic of hard work, believing that their effort would translate into economic success. They typically rejected the schooling process—most described receiving a subpar education and being subject to punitive policies—but they also distanced themselves from criminalized peers. Those who went to college generally believed that it would pay off. Most enrolled in community college or a short-term vocational program at a for-profit college while juggling work. They stuck to meritocratic ideals and plugged away at school, but often with minimal institutional guidance and limited results.

Two other groups converge into the working-class category: university graduates lacking social leverage ties and high school noncompleters lifted by social support ties. University-going young men are on the most promising route to upward mobility, but their social capital can fade over time, leaving them to fall back on kin and neighborhood ties to navigate the labor market. High school noncompleters are projected to experience "second-generation decline," but most do not follow such a path because it is closed off by their support network.

Work as Virtue: High School Graduates

Rigo surprised his family when he graduated from high school, as he had failed three courses in his senior year alone. He had been in a tagging crew for the first two years of high school, which set him behind academically, but he had decided that the crew was not worth it. He said, "They didn't back me up like I backed them up." Rigo had also witnessed his eldest brother, an ex-gang member with a criminal record, struggle to find work, and he didn't want to end up like him. So the summer before his senior year, Rigo walked into a grocery store in his neighborhood and got a full-time job, earning $9 an hour.

When his senior year began, Rigo continued to work over forty hours a week. He said that he was keeping his "own self busy, just as some parents do with their sons." Rigo's father was deported when he was thirteen years old, and he lived with his sixty-two-year-old mother and his sister and brother-in-law and their three children in a two-bedroom apartment. Though he sometimes fell asleep in class, Rigo didn't want to end up "like everyone else." His family struggled financially, and he saw "EBT [food stamp] cards everywhere" in his poverty-stricken neighborhood. Rigo was critical of those without jobs: "They just don't want to work hard." He took pride in having a job and going to school, and he had moved up to a supervisor position by the time he graduated. At that point, he said, he was "tired of school" and wanted "to work and get his life started."

Though teachers and staff liked Rigo, he could not identify one who motivated him, challenged him academically, or told him he could succeed. Young men like him in the sample who took regular or remedial classes were rarely encouraged to seek more than the high school diploma; only those in honors or advanced placement courses received such encouragement. In a context that had few positive social relationships and "uncaring" teachers, students like Rigo rebuffed the urban schooling process and had minimal interest in college as a result. Indeed, they would have found themselves underprepared for college, as their high schools ranked among the lowest in the state in academic performance.

In a context where some young men are consumed by urban conflicts and gang dynamics, "hard work" carries moral worth that the immigrant narrative reinforces. Young men like Osvaldo and Rigo elevated their moral worth in these communities by emphasizing their ethic of hard work and drawing strong boundaries against the gang prototype, specifically those unattached to school or work. While a high school diploma did not carry much economic worth anymore, it carried symbolic worth in these communities. On the one hand, it was an educational milestone in a community that had few opportunities to reach this goal. On the other hand, it distinguished young men who were on the "right track" from those who had become consumed by the neighborhood.

Blue-collar kin ties informed the identity of these young men, their work orientation, and what they saw as viable and respectable jobs. Many had long admired the achievements of immigrant kin. Jaime's father, Raymundo, an undocumented migrant with a middle school education, worked his way up to a supervisor position in an asbestos company and owned a home in Central City. Jaime figured that if his father could get so much through hard work and sacrifice, surely he could too, especially given his advantage as a natural-born citizen.

> It's like [my dad] got all this, this is a lot . . . but he worked for it. So I think that if I work for it too that I may get something of what he got . . . even more . . . 'cause I was born here. It's more of an advantage. You isn't gotta worry about getting stuck, like there's no more jobs for you 'cause you weren't born here. . . . It's just up to me to do what I got to do.

Aligning himself with immigrant coethnics like his father provided Jaime with a sense of moral worth.[27] Likewise, Benjamin, an ex-gang member, set himself apart from others because of his work experience with immigrants: "Some U.S.-born Latinos are naive [about what the U.S. system demands] and that they are not hard workers, not because they are lazy, it's just that they are not used to hard work. . . . *I am,* because I worked with *paisas* [immigrants]." Jaime and Benjamin had criminal records, and neither had finished high school, but a strong attachment to work performed beside immigrants redeemed them in the eyes of their families and the community.

Young men's choice to work in the same types of jobs their fathers had done for decades frustrated some parents. Raymundo said he had told Jaime's older brother, who unlike Jaime had completed high school, "a million times to study instead, to go to college." He had even bought his son a car to help him get to classes, but his son preferred to get a job removing asbestos, as Raymundo did. Raymundo noted that most children of immigrants he knew were like his sons: "They work in jobs that their fathers got them, a friend got them. These are not good jobs, nothing professional. Something professional involves getting titles that allow you to work in the White House or at UCLA and USC," he said, citing the universities where he had worked removing asbestos. Raymundo wanted his children to be financially secure, "to have a good job, a nice car, a nice home," and not to "work every day like me." Raymundo often missed family events on weekends because he had to work. Even after he became a supervisor, he might get home from a job at 2:00 AM and have to be back to work at 5:00 AM. He wanted a better life for his children.

Rigo left the grocery store behind after he got his high school diploma, but he continued to get jobs through his kin and neighborhood network. His brother-in-law got him a job as a truck driver in which he hoped to earn $18 an hour eventually. Work slowed down after a year, so Rigo followed a friend's lead and applied for a job at LAX, the Los Angeles airport, where he started "from the bottom," loading and unloading, towing aircraft, and earning $9.75 per hour. He moved on to service the lavatories on the planes, and then, having done all the "hard labor," he became "a lead," earning $3 an hour more. This involved doing "all the paperwork," documenting what was loaded and serviced on the plane. Rigo did this for two years. He still put in long hours, sometimes working seventeen-hour shifts. He never showed up late, and he always came in when requested and stayed late if there was a reason. Some of his colleagues were in college, but he had the freedom to work around the clock. Rigo was an ardent believer that his strong work ethic would allow him to move up the ladder, and it did. After two years, he became a supervisor "overseeing the operation" and getting paid about $16.75. Eventually he was drawing a salary and working only forty hours weekly. In 2012, at age twenty-three, he was a manager in ground handling at LAX and earning $25.50 an hour, roughly $54,000 a year. He earned more money than any of the other young men in this study his age, and he earned more than his siblings and friends.

Rigo's family applauded his accomplishments, but he was not happy. He felt that his lack of a college degree put him in a precarious position in the labor market. He also recognized that steady, hard work in the blue-collar sector could not purchase a comfortable lifestyle. In order to live independently he followed the flow of Angelinos to the Inland Empire—a region southeast of Los Angeles—relocating outside the city in hopes of a better life, but poverty followed him there. He lived on his own in an apartment in an area that was more affordable than Central City but where the foreclosure crisis linked to the Great Recession had struck hard.

Rigo had to wake up at 3:00 AM because it took him over two hours to get to work. He was exhausted, and he looked older than his age. He thought of buying a home there with one of his sisters and a cousin, but both pulled out after finding it too much to handle financially. A home in Central City was out of the question; today even a home in the 'hood is out of reach for most second-generation Latinos in Los Angeles.[28]

When I spoke to Rigo, he sounded like most immigrant parents in the study. Imagining his future children, he said:

> I'm not going to let them work. I'm not going to let them go through what I went through. When I met you I was working graveyard shifts. I would get out of work, go straight to [high] school, and then I would go home, do my homework, and go to sleep. It was the same routine over and over. I don't want them to go through that.

He explained that he had worked hard "to get out of the 'hood," a place he associated with violence and concentrated poverty. He was proud of this, but he felt that he wasn't successful. "If you don't have an education, you're nobody. That's how I see it. I just have a stable job." Rigo felt locked into his job at LAX, with limited options:

> If I apply anywhere else, I won't get the pay I'm getting now. I worked for the pay that I have. I mean, I bust my ass, sometimes not sleeping, being tired,

back pains . . . all kinds of stuff. Going through some shit and you know . . .
it got me to where I'm at right now, but if I go apply to another job, they're
not gonna hand me this job like, "Here you go."'

Rigo felt that his résumé "said a lot" given his experience "but not an education." He said, "I haven't lost hope. It's never too late to go back to school."
But Rigo knew that some of his coworkers at LAX were college-educated
and could not find work relevant to their degrees. College was supposed
to pay off, but respondents' neighborhoods were replete with examples
of limited returns to higher education. This made Rigo nervous. "If I go
to college, I want to find something that I'm going to be able to get a job
with, you know?"

For Gonzalo, a young man with lofty goals of earning a six-figure
income, college did "not did make a lot sense." He explained that "the
wage that you're going to get [with a college degree] is not even going
to be spectacular. Now it's like you have to get more degrees just to
make more money. I'm going to school for four years and I'm going to
make like $40,000? That's still not a lot of money." Gonzalo enrolled in
community college halfheartedly, but it only took a fender-bender that
complicated his commute momentarily for him to stop his studies. The
guys in the neighborhood—a group of "thirty-year-olds" on the block—
advised Gonzalo to go to college because "that's where the money is
at," but Gonzalo dismissed them, as well as his parents. He had been
involved in a party crew for part of high school, when he had mediocre
grades and was almost kicked out of school. But like Rigo, he believed
that he could get ahead through hard work and effort. Gonzalo turned
to full-time work, distancing himself from friends who were still "trying
to figure things out" or "were just being lazy."

Gonzalo tapped into his networks to navigate the labor market. A
friend from high school linked him to a job with United Parcel Service.
The workday started at 4:00 AM; Gonzalo was there for only a month and
a half, concluding that it was too much work for too little pay. His sister
then got him a job at the department store where she worked in a middle-
class neighborhood. He noted that his white and Armenian coworkers
labeled him "the *cholo*" because he was from Pueblo Viejo. Gonzalo said,
"They think everything is gangster over here." He was earning $10 an hour,
but after a year he quit the job, figuring that "he could do more than just
hang clothes" and confident that he could find a better job on his own.
He was wrong.

For two years, during the recession, Gonzalo could find only "random," "bottom of the barrel" jobs through work agencies. He worked beside undocumented immigrant coethnics at jobs he found humbling, as he "was working [his] ass off for nickels and dimes." Work agencies were a last resort for young Latino men, sought only after kin and neighborhood ties were exhausted. These agencies provided temporary work for meager pay and offered minimal opportunities for advancement. Young men's kin and neighborhood ties produced better-paying jobs, even if they did not pay enough to establish a stable lifestyle.

Eventually, Gonzalo's sister helped him get a job at a home warehouse store where she worked, earning $15 an hour and working forty hours a week. He didn't really want to work as an "asset protection associate" tasked with catching shoplifters, but he took the job anyway because he felt pressure from his father. Gonzalo worked at the warehouse for two years, and then his other sister introduced Gonzalo to a friend, a successful realtor and life insurance agent in the community. Gonzalo began to sell life insurance on commission, but a year later he was still earning less than he had when he worked at the warehouse store. Yet he remained confident that he could succeed. He said, "I see other people that don't have any degrees and make a lot more [money than I do]. I know two people that only have high school degrees. It's just more work ethic and intelligence. So, I'd rather do that than go to school." Gonzalo was still living at home with his parents at the age of twenty-four and payed them $450 monthly in rent. He felt that "it's getting to the point that I have to move out" because he was "just too comfortable . . . eating their food and watching their TV." Moving out on his own would "force [him] to grow up," but living at home made it easier for Gonzalo to pursue his dreams and avoid feeling the full cost of living in Los Angeles.

Byzantine Paths: Community College and Vocational Training

At Pueblo Viejo High, Jesús had been an active student in the music program, a member of the Latin jazz group, and an enrollee in the magnet program. He stayed out of trouble in the neighborhood, spending evenings boxing at a gym when he was not playing with the band. Jesús was an average magnet student until he got "senioritis" and failed a few classes his last year. When it was time to apply for college, Jesús opted to take classes at the community college. Yet five years later, he still had not completed a degree.

He was not sure what major or career to pursue, or if and when he would transfer to the university. Like many community college students, Jesús was in limbo, unable to advance either through work or higher education. "College was more about finding myself," he said. "It doesn't always turn out the way you plan it. . . . Many are coming out with their degrees and there's no jobs. There are no positions for what they want to do, and they spend so much time and money preparing for something that is not available." That may have been true, but Jesús was having a hard time navigating the byzantine path that is community college. Most Latinos who enroll in college take this path, but few ever earn an associate's degree, transfer to a university, or earn a certificate. Years of school without a diploma do not boost job prospects or earnings; returns on higher education come only with diplomas or certificates.[29]

Young men in the study such as Jesús found minimal support at community colleges, and so they turned to kin and neighborhood ties for help navigating these institutions. Jesús's number-one resource was his aunt Sonia, an undocumented young woman in her late twenties who aspired to be a teacher and who lived with his family. Sonia had graduated from Pueblo Viejo High and enrolled in community college, following the advice of a high school teacher, Ms. Lopez. Since retired, Ms. Lopez was the only cross-class ethnic tie the family mentioned in our interviews. She had seen great promise in Sonia and helped her in high school. Jesús and his parents, recognizing that Ms. Lopez's help had been significant for Sonia, considered her responsible for Sonia's ability to help Jesús. He said fondly:

> The person who has supported me the most through college, even though I am stubborn and I don't listen to advice, has been my aunt. She kind of already went through the whole process, so she was the one that guided me. "You should take this many units, check the times, have breaks in between classes." She showed me my first two semesters, and then I took over, but I have to say, she was the one that guided me the most out of everyone.

Sonia was the family's only kin tie in Los Angeles. Katia and Hector, Jesús's parents, were urban migrants who, like other parents in this study, knew little about college or the application process.[30] Katia explained:

> We don't have a lot of knowledge of [community college], but my sister is very involved. . . . She guides [Jesús], gives him advice. She says he should

go to community college first so that he can figure out what he wants to do and because it's cheaper. She shares a lot and helps him with applications that come along. Orients him, but not me, I don't know.

Mexican parents navigated the American schooling system haphazardly. Even those with a high school education or a few years of college in Mexico were unclear about the application process and about the difference between community college, private or public universities, and for-profit colleges. They knew little, if anything, about financial aid. Their children were like all others in the neighborhood who navigated the transition into higher education with parental moral support and encouragement, but not much else.

Kin like Sonia who had trailblazed through institutions of higher education were incredible resources in these urban communities, but the support they could provide was limited. Sonia was never able to transfer to a university, as Ms. Lopez wasn't able to guide the undocumented student there. She also could not afford it. As Katia said, at thirty-four, Sonia was accepting "*migajas* [crumbs]" for her work and earning an "income that is laughable." Lacking university experience herself, she was unable to help Jesús transfer to the university. Her undocumented status also constrained Sonia in the jobs she could obtain, and she remained a teaching assistant. Sonia helped Jesús get a teaching assistant job where she worked, two blocks from their home in Pueblo Viejo. Jesús had no particular interest in teaching, but he found the job better than the shoe store where he had been working. He was still a teaching assistant five years later, earning $10.75 an hour or about $11,000 annually for the part-time job. He was also still living with his parents, as was Sonia.

Left alone to navigate the transfer process to a university, Jesús described what other young men in community college experienced: he was "all over the place." He said, "I never kept track of what I was doing, I just kept taking more and more courses." When he decided he wanted to transfer to a university for a liberal arts bachelor's degree, counselors gave him contradictory information about how many more classes he would need to take to transfer out. Jesús never found mentors at the community college; indeed, experts find that the lack of counseling is an acute problem in community colleges.[31] Jesús's commitment to college was fading by the follow-up study.

In this study, thirteen young men enrolled in community college at some point, but only one of them, Osvaldo, transferred to the university. Community colleges are more affordable than universities and give students who did not have high academic grades in high school an opportunity to enter the university by performing well in community college. In theory, students are supposed to attend community college for two years and then transfer to a university, but studies show that this rarely happens. In California, only 4 percent of community college students transfer in this expected time frame, and most students never transfer. Those who do, around 38 percent, do so typically after six years in community college; fewer than one-third of Latinx students make the transition. Various factors come into play in the low university transfer rate, but researchers point to the "maze" of typical community college systems, which are hard to decipher and navigate and which offer students conflicting information and poor guidance, particularly first-generation students.[32] These students advance slowly through coursework; three-quarters (and 85 percent of Latinos) take remedial courses that extend their time there. Many of these students attend part-time, as was the case with all the study participants who were in community college. Studies show that these students are more likely to come from lower-income households and to be juggling work and family demands, which prolongs their time in college. Community colleges appeal to students who see them as an affordable path to the university, but because of how long it takes most of them to transfer, some students end up paying more for college, on average, than traditional four-year university students.[33]

James Rosenbaum argues that part of the problem is American's "college for all"—or the "BA-for-all"—approach to higher education, which ignores and undersells the multiple paths to upward mobility, including vocational training and various certificates.[34] William Symonds, Robert Schwartz, and Ronald Ferguson explain that 27 percent of such middle-skilled professionals—that is, those with postsecondary licenses or certificates, credentials short of an associate's degree—earn more than the average bachelor's degree recipient.[35] Parents and young men in this study were highly receptive to these *carreras cortas* (short degrees), but were unsure how to navigate such institutions or programs and unclear about which ones were accredited and/or for-profit. Young men in this study were as lost navigating community colleges as they were universities—if not worse as they received even less guidance than those enrolled in four-year universities.

Studies show that a higher proportion of disadvantaged students enroll in for-profit colleges, which promise a career in a short time, with good pay upon graduation, but often leave students straddled with debt and without a job.[36] Jesús's brother, Sebastian, followed this path. Sebastian barely graduated from high school. He said he wanted to be a truck driver like Hector, but his father said, "What the hell is wrong with you? You can go to school and get a better job!" Katia objected to his dream of being a rapper: "For God's sake, a Christian man saying such foolishness!" Jesús and Sebastian were both musically inclined and put together "beats and tracks" to upload on YouTube. Participating in a music program at a community center got Sebastian excited about the music industry, and he enrolled in a music engineering program at a for-profit institution. He paid $30,000 for the nine-month program but could not find a job in the industry. At twenty-one, he was working as a valet attendant for an Italian restaurant Thursday through Sunday to pay off his student debt. Katia encouraged Sebastian to "donate his time" with a studio somewhere, hoping that with work experience he could break into the industry, as he longed to do. But Sebastian was losing interest in the field, which he felt didn't want him.

Katia and Hector sometimes worried that their sons lacked motivation. They did not understand why they did not seem to have clear direction. Katia asked me, "What did we do wrong?" While it was clearly a rhetorical question, it certainly seemed as though they had done nothing wrong. They made many sacrifices to ensure that their sons avoided the streets, filling their time with extracurricular activities when they were adolescents and strongly encouraging them to pursue higher education. When Jesús voiced an interest in aviation, Hector bought him a helicopter lesson, hoping to inspire his son. Jesús was enthusiastic after the flight, but the cost of aviation school with no financial aid—"$70,000–$80,000"—discouraged him. Katia and Hector recognized the shifts in the economy that Sebastian, Jesús, and Sonia faced. Hector stated, "Now the situation is harder than it was for us. Today the competition is stiffer; it's harder than it was ten or twenty years ago." They did not ask Sonia or their sons for rent.

In most cases, young Latino men in the inner city navigate higher education on their own and are left feeling alienated. Jesús said: "I don't know about the university life. It seems like you have to be so independent and so, like on your own, independent, in a way like friendship-wise. Nobody,

the teachers don't do anything . . . you just go in and listen to the professor."
Like most other young men in this study, Jesús studied alone and suggested
that he preferred it that way: "I like to do things on my own. I don't like to
depend on other people."

A school police officer where he worked in Pueblo Viejo called Jesús's
attention to an aviation program available through law enforcement. Jesús
applied to the academy but did not pass the initial interview. Two custo-
dians at the community college, both veterans, encouraged Jesús to pursue
aviation through the armed forces, but joining the military was never in
his plans. He received guidance from no one else—no one who might have
laid out other options for a path to a middle-class existence. As Stanton-
Salazar explains, accessing institutional support is an "extraordinary phe-
nomenon."[37] In his study, he found that only a select few Mexican-origin
youth had access to "empowerment social capital"—that is, "the resources
and forms of institutional support which are embedded in 'connections'
or relationships with high-status, resourceful, institutional agents oriented
to go counter to the *system*."[38] Jesús and Sebastian found no institutional
agents who could help them successfully transition to college or the labor
market. In the meantime, Jesús's networks remained bound to his very
small family and neighborhood. Several years later, when Jesús was twenty-
seven years old, I received an email from him. Voicing a sense of urgency,
he was hoping I could help him get into the university where I worked. He
was older now, he said, and in great need of a college degree.[39]

Falling from Grace: Struggling University Students

A subset of young men in this study were groomed from a young age for
the university and poised for success. Unlike most of their peers in their
neighborhood, they received significant resources from school personnel
and community members who invested in their future. In the sample, they
were among the most buffered from neighborhood dynamics and urban
violence. Typically, these young men not only could count on a supportive
kin network but were tightly embedded in school and community programs that gave them access to social leverage ties that provided key information and guidance to get ahead. They were a very lucky minority.[40]

Cristobal had been buffered from the neighborhood by Humberto, his
father, and Felipe, his brother, who made sure that he stayed out of trouble
and on task at school. He took advanced placement calculus, government,

and psychology as well as honors composition in his senior year. He was a member of his school's mathematics, engineering, and science achievements (MESA) program and the Coalition for Education and Justice and was running for homecoming king, a testament to his ease at school and his popularity. In middle school, Cristobal had been in regular courses, but a teacher took an interest in him. Humberto said, "This one black teacher said he was a good student. She put him in that program, and to this date he's there. She said, 'I don't want your son to be a worker at McDonald's. I want him to be a professional.'" Cristobal's teacher channeled him into honors courses and Upward Bound, a college preparatory program at a nearby state college where he received SAT prep, tutoring, financial aid information, and more. Cristobal "loved" the program: "If it wasn't for them, I wouldn't know a lot of things. . . . I was in tenth grade, and I knew so much about college that an average kid my age wouldn't know." The program linked Cristobal to summer college preparation residential programs in which he took courses that helped him stay ahead and that counted as college credit. Cristobal wanted to major in engineering or aeronautics, and a counselor in Upward Bound placed him in a program at a college in Arizona geared toward such interests. His family was very proud that Cristobal had been accepted into several universities.

Most young men who entered the four-year university straight out of high school had significant social capital. Many had been identified as "smart" or "intellectually gifted" from a young age, and they had been in programs that reinforced college-going norms and aspirations, like Upward Bound. This attention and treatment isolated them academically from the majority of the student population and facilitated a college-oriented peer culture, sustained through socialization in tight peer networks; most of Cristobal's close friends were other college-track students.[41] These young men received academic, motivational, and information support from various institutional agents, including teachers, academic counselors, and mentors in and out of high school.[42]

GETTING THROUGH COLLEGE

The challenges that young men in the study encountered at the university were multifaceted. Although they had received the best academic preparation their high schools offered, it fell drastically short of university expectations. "Gifted and talented" or "honors" inner-city students struggled in their writing and in math and science courses, at times ending up in remedial classes. Those who enrolled at affluent and predominantly white or Asian colleges experienced culture shock that made them feel disconnected and alienated. They had difficulties creating a supportive peer network and accessing institutional agents for guidance.[43] They found it hard to achieve college success.

Fernando, an engineering major at a California state university (CSU) campus, went from being in advanced placement (AP) classes in high school to academic probation (also AP) in college. When I met him in 2007, he dressed like many other young men in his neighborhood in over-sized clothes, a puffy bomber jacket, and a baseball cap, but he had acquired most of his knowledge of local gang dynamics from the neighborhood kids he tutored at a community organization. Growing up, Fernando spent most of his time at the local library or with friends in the magnet program. He was active in math-related clubs at school and deeply embedded in a college peer network. At CSU, he was enrolled in the Early Opportunity Program (EOP), a program designed to facilitate the transition to college for low-income, first-generation students. Through EOP, he received guidance on courses, took a time management class, and had access to tutoring. While the intervention helped him pass his classes, he was ashamed that he had a C average: "I'm not happy with my performance. I'm not. As soon as the first week that school starts, I'm already stressing out." Fernando partly blamed the magnet program at his high school, which he said "wasn't all that great"; like most young men in college in this study, Fernando did not feel academically prepared. Fernando said that he had "never learned to study" and admitted that he arrived unprepared for the tutoring sessions. "I would make something up. . . . I'm having trouble with so-and-so, even though I had not tried the problem." Tutoring felt like a waste of time, and by his fifth year of college he had a "hold" on his academic record, meaning that he could not enroll in any more classes without improving his grades.

As I elaborate in a later chapter, inner-city Latinos in predominantly affluent or white universities encountered a hostile environment; lacking the cultural capital to navigate these institutions dominated by the middle or upper-middle classes, they developed a sense of alienation. This sometimes unsupportive context affected their sense of belonging and could make them feel unwelcome. Yet when discussing their academic struggles, these college students identified a lack of study skills and time management skills as their number-one challenge.

Raul's transition to a University of California campus was difficult. He graduated with the second-highest GPA average in his class at Pueblo Viejo High, but said that he didn't "remember sitting down" to study much in high school. High school assignments had been easy, but fulfilling the demands of college classes didn't come "natural." Raul said, "I was not used to have to sacrifice to study that much. It was really hard in the beginning, and just the classes themselves, like they were a bit difficult." He was overwhelmed by the number of classes and the need to manage time for family, friends, and studying. He said, "I guess I underestimated the whole college experience." In those first years in college, Raul greatly doubted himself, and living away from home for the first time, he was homesick. As he said, "Yeah, instead of being like, 'I'm going to study to do better,' it would be like, 'I'm doing bad. I miss home.' It would just be in my head and would like keep me from studying and focusing even more." He earned Cs at best in most of his classes and failed some.

These young men were missing in college what they had in their magnet programs in high school: access to institutional agents and a cohesive peer group culture that helped them excel. Fernando contrasted his "successful high school experience" with his challenge at the university. In high school, he said, "I affiliated myself with people that were kind of the same track as me and had the same attitude about stuff." His high school peers supported one another in their college efforts; at the university Fernando was on his own, as none of his high school friends attended the same college. Fernando felt that studying in groups, as he had done in high school, might have helped. He said:

> Maybe some type of group tutoring, like have everybody just show up and do your work. I guess you get inspired by your peers. Like if you are going to Harvard or MIT your peers are kicking ass, so you're like, "Hey, I better get on the ball," you know? You don't expect anything less of yourself . . . because if some of these kids are whatever and they are getting the A, you are like, "Wait a minute, I can get an A!" Just setting the bar high on everybody and having them study together, pressuring each other to get As.

Though he lived near the college campus for four years, Fernando did not feel close to anyone. He named two friends he had studied with at times, but he never found a community there. He made a lukewarm effort to visit an engineering club, hoping to find friends, but instead he "felt like an outcast" in the majority white and Asian group. In his fifth year, Fernando could not identify one friend who was majoring in engineering and with whom he could study. He had moved back home by then and expanded his work hours at the boys' and girls' club and at his internship; commuting to campus amplified the disconnect he felt. He said, "I go to CSU. I don't talk to anybody. I just go there, go to my class, and that's it. I am completely separated from CSU. . . . I don't even feel part of the school, that's why I say CSU has no love for me." He never found a mentor. He did not connect with any professors. He felt that he "let them down" with his poor scholastic performance. Plus, he didn't see professors "go out of their way" to help students in need.

It was Fernando's eldest brother, Julio, a graduate of the Massachusetts Institute of Technology (MIT), who advised Fernando to seek an internship while at CSU. Despite his prestigious degree, Julio was not able to land an engineering job after he graduated—he was teaching at an elementary school when I met Fernando. Julio believed that an internship would have helped his engineering job prospects. Julio had focused his energy at MIT on passing his classes, giving little attention to his professional development. Julio never intended to become a teacher and tried to help Fernando avoid similar mistakes. Fernando followed his brother's advice; despite being on academic probation, he landed an engineering-related internship his fifth year that paid $11 an hour. Julio was proud of his brother but unaware of the extent of his academic struggles. Fernando was not one to share his troubles or ask for help.

A few months later, the university expelled Fernando. He recalled the email: "Bam! You're kicked out! You're no longer a student. You're no longer part of CSU." When I asked him why he had not sought more help, Fernando replied, "Isn't that what you are supposed to do? Just be on your own?" Hard work and effort, intelligence, and grit were supposed to be enough to beat the odds. As I elaborate in a following chapter, this was a theme—an ideology—that would often be repeated by the young men.

Raul was also on the verge of expulsion from one of the UC schools, but he managed to graduate in five years because he established a peer support network. Raul lived in the dorms his first year and observed students "always studying and stuff" and tried to follow in their footsteps. Shy by nature, he was nudged out of his shell. Raul recognized the stereotypes linked to his Latino identity and explained how challenging it was to ask peers for help:

> You feel like you're bothering them or you don't want to feel stupid, especially since maybe they are of different backgrounds. I'll be like, "Oh yeah, they might think I'm stupid, you know, me being Latino." So it's difficult to ask some questions, but there's times when you see people who are really helpful, and so you can go to them.

After two years of struggling in engineering, Raul dropped the major. He "wasted a year" transferring to business economics, but then found support with the Latino Business Student Association (LBSA). The LBSA brought alumni and professionals to speak about their educational and professional experiences, and Raul networked with them. Older peers in the LBSA who were "on the right path" pointed him toward school resources and advised him on which professors to take and what to look out for. The LBSA got Raul thinking about internships, and after two years with the organization, Raul became treasurer. Invested and supported, Raul graduated right when the Great Recession hit. Life would take a nosedive then, before Raul emerged victorious.

After Fernando was let go from CSU, he continued working at his internship site, and that position turned into a full-time job. After five years with the company, Fernando was earning $15 an hour and saw no opportunity for advancement. He felt underpaid and overworked. Despite his promising beginnings, he was unhappy and obsessed about returning to the university to complete his degree; he was afraid, however, that his work schedule complicated matters: "It was a lot of work, a lot of responsibility. I can't take days off on my finals or whatever, and I have to work all these crazy hours."

Fernando's social networks changed minimally during his time in college, and that had an impact on his job prospects. By the follow-up study, Fernando had sought better pay through a job recruiter who helped him find a better-paying job, earning $20 an hour, or $42,000 annually. As he said:

> I got hired because they said, "Wow, this is exactly the person we need. He has six years of experience. He knows all about a manufacturing company, how to read engineering drawings." I guess they are like, "Okay, this guy doesn't have his engineering degree, but he has everything we need and he

speaks Spanish. All the engineers are in Mexico. He's highly recommended, and we don't have to pay him as much as somebody who has a degree."

At twenty-seven, Fernando was still living with his parents and siblings in a two-bedroom apartment in Pueblo Viejo. He was soon to marry and stressed about returning to college, which he felt he needed to complete. Yet he felt even less equipped to "compete" with younger students than he had years before: "I feel like my brain has turned to mush." He knew a degree would help his career, but he was puzzled that college was not paying off for many people he knew.

COLLAPSING INTO THE WORKING CLASS: DEGREES WITHOUT *PALANCAS*

The first time I met Manuel, he was twenty-three and had graduated from an Ivy League college less than two years prior. We sat in a Central City park frequented by many homeless individuals pushing carts, a few blocks from his parents' home. Five years later, we met in the city of Downey, a middle-class community where Manuel spent his days at coffee shops and libraries, most recently submitting job applications. As we sat down at a local restaurant, he said, "I'm going to be your biggest disappointment." Manuel longed to live in Downey: "I hear what people are talking about . . . business, about education, about something productive. When I'm in Central City I don't hear that. I fit in here [in Downey] more." Manuel sighed. "I used to think that by going to college that I would get the job of my dreams, that easy, and that I would move out on my own." Manuel had a degree from an Ivy League college, but he was still unemployed after ten years struggling. He said, "If you had told me seven years ago, 'You're going to be without any savings again, without a real job, a stable job, living still with your mom and your sister,' I would have told you, 'You're crazy! There is no way that is going to happen.'"

A college degree alone does not guarantee that children of low-skilled workers from the inner city will obtain a stable, good-paying job upon their graduation. Making the quantum leap into the American middle class requires social leverage ties that are sustained *throughout* their young adult years, whether in the form of consistent social leverage ties or different social leverage ties over time. These *palancas* are needed not only to get through college but to broker the highly coveted jobs reserved for those with degrees. In the absence of leverage ties, even inner-city Latino college graduates with a prestigious degree fall back on kin or neighborhood ties, or they apply for jobs on their own and slip back into the working class.

In his recent book *The Privileged Poor,* Anthony Jack discusses how poor students navigate elite institutions and the particular challenges they present for students like Manuel, whom he would describe as "doubly disadvantaged"—poor and unfamiliar with the culture of affluence in elite institutions.[44] Unlike other poor racial minorities at his Ivy League school, Manuel had never been at a prep school; he went directly from Central City High, where fights broke out often. Manuel entered the Ivy League as an engineering major, but it took only a week for him to realize that his schooling had not prepared him for such a degree. He recalled, "Professors would go so fast, and I felt I never had time to catch up." He described both "culture shock" and "academic shock." He had been an A+ student in high school and taken advanced placement courses, but he considered dropping out of college. He threw himself into studying and made few friends. He felt socially isolated among upper-middle-class students with a vastly different upbringing from his, and studying all weekend did not help him connect with others. Such withdrawal from campus life is common among the "doubly disadvantaged." Manuel recalled, "That was one of the hardest things—not having people to relate [to]." When he returned to Central City the summer after his first year, chunks of his hair began to fall out from the stress.

In his second year, Manuel came to terms with his weak academic preparation in math and science and switched to Spanish literature. In these classes, speaking Spanish, Manuel felt more at ease. The major was not as easy as he thought, but Manuel managed to pass his classes. He also joined the Latinx student organization on campus, made "true friends" there, and began to feel that he belonged at his college. He started playing soccer again, and his soccer friends linked him to a fraternity in his third year. Eventually, Manuel became comfortable at his college, though he was often the only low-income Latino in the room, including in his fraternity, on the soccer team, and in his classes.

Graduating from an Ivy League was Manuel's greatest accomplishment, but it did not pay off as he hoped. In 2005, Manuel returned to South Central Los Angeles from the East Coast with his college degree but was lost searching for work. Few studies follow first-generation graduates from elite institutions after they complete their schooling. In their study of second-generation Asian American students, Hyein Lee and Margaret Chin found that institutional mechanisms, like career centers and job fairs, were crucial for linking this group to their desired jobs.[45] Manuel had no such help from his institution. Naturally, no one in his family knew anything about searching for a job with a college degree, and no one else he knew in the community could help him. As he explained, "My strategy for looking for a job, I was trying to come up with it by myself." Without institutional ties that could guide him after college, Manuel resorted to the internet in search of a job on his own.

Like Julio at MIT, Manuel was so focused on making sure he graduated that he missed opportunities that the university offered to help him transition into the labor market. When he was in college, he said, "I didn't know what an internship really was"—that is, he didn't realize that it was a stepping-stone to a job with the same company. He never visited his college's career center, assuming that a college degree was a surefire way to get a good job, and he had no mentors. He explained his logic: "My main goal was just to graduate. As long as I graduate with any degree, *ya Estuvo!* [it's done!]."

Manuel was shy about asking his college friends for help; the only time he had done so was when he was applying for a job as a bank teller and he asked for advice from a friend whose father worked at a bank. He confessed that he "didn't like to take advantage" of his friends' resources, adding, "I see them as friends before anything else." Manuel was embarrassed about seeking help—he was taught all his life that his individual effort would get him ahead. Over time, email communication with his college friends withered.

Manuel landed his first job out of college at a nonprofit organization in Central City after he walked in off the street one day and a security guard pointed him toward the director's office. The organization served a predominantly African American housing development and focused on improving race relations, providing resources to the community, and helping people find jobs. Manuel was enthusiastic when he started, but was paid only $8 an hour. A year later, he was earning only two dollars more. Manuel hoped his boss would promote him, but that never happened. Manuel left that job and took a tutoring job that promised him assignments that paid $15–$20 an hour, but he did not get enough hours to make a living. He also had to drive long distances to his few assignments, so he quit. He then landed a job at Univision, the television network, translating documents, assisting with planning and organizing community events, and answering telephone calls, among other office management tasks. Yet it too paid only minimum wage. When a conflict with his supervisor arose, Manuel quit.

Manuel then turned to a work agency he had heard about in passing at one of his jobs—Jobs USA. It was then that he came to recognize that the American opportunity structure was not tilted in his favor.

> The agency sent me to work around here at a steel factory. They had me cutting grass . . . it was thick . . . like palm trees . . . with the worst machines ever. At that point it really hit me: college graduate, Ivy League. There is nothing shameful about the work, but that was my thought at the moment—I'm cutting grass and it's ninety-five degrees. My back is going to start hurting pretty sure tomorrow, and only for a couple of dollars. . . . I just couldn't believe I was there. I never thought in my wildest imagination that I would ever be in that position. I had the gloves, the mask covering my mouth, the little helmet. . . . I thought to myself: *This is not where I'm supposed to be.*

After two hours on the job, Manuel turned to his coworkers, took off his work attire, and told them, "I'll see you guys later." There was no shame in the work, Manuel said, but he recalled thinking, "Everything I did to be here today. Everything I've been through. It just didn't feel right, but there I was and what could I do?" Manuel's chance to enter the American middle class had slipped through his fingers.

The college graduates in the study had more social capital than their peers who had only graduated from high school, but when their social capital ran out—in Fernando's case in college and in Manuel's as he entered the labor market—their relative advantage did too. Peers who helped them get through college often could not help them in the labor market, and their institutional supports were of little help beyond high school. Without *palancas* rooted in the university experience or the middle-class sector, these young men were left with only the social ties in their segregated neighborhoods that linked them to working poor and working-class jobs, with profound effects on their social mobility prospects. Even when they were on the verge of accessing the American middle class, these young men remained outside its "cliques, clubs and institutions," never having fully integrated without the support of institutional agents.

Manuel was not the only one to see minimal returns to his schooling. Fernando's family was the most highly educated in the study, but their insular social ties kept them locked into the neighborhood. Fernando's parents were urban migrants, with no close kin in Los Angeles. His father,

Fidel, attended college briefly in Mexico City and took community college courses in the United States. Fernando noted, "The thing about my dad is that he is really smart. He's always been thirsty for knowledge, and he reads a lot of books." Fernando's mother, Mariana, made the most of her time in Pueblo Viejo, taking English courses while raising her children and then more and more classes; ultimately she obtained a GED. With her daughters' encouragement, Mariana enrolled in community college and then, to everyone's surprise, transferred to a CSU. By the follow-up study, she had just earned her bachelor's degree in child development. Fernando's three siblings had obtained college degrees too—two engineers and one liberals arts graduate. Only Fernando lagged behind.

Fernando's family was still living together in the same two-bedroom apartment they had lived in for years. Fidel was the apartment manager and prepared income taxes for clients, mostly other immigrants in the neighborhood. Unhappy with being a teacher, Julio returned to school, and it was only after he acquired his master's degree that he landed an engineering job, with the help of a job recruiter, earning $90,000 a year; the recruiter took half of Julio's first check. Julio paid this steep fee recognizing that his personal networks confined him to working-class jobs—even after earning a master's degree from a University of California campus. Again, Fernando followed Julio's footsteps, and it was through a recruiter that he secured a slightly better-paying job. Fernando was convinced that paying a recruiter was necessary to advance, and he encouraged his sister, Helena, to seek one too. Helena had two degrees in engineering from a CSU but was unable to find a job in the field. She worked with her mother as a teaching assistant, earning $10 an hour, until her friend got her a billing job, which paid $15 an hour. The youngest, Carmela, got a liberal arts degree from a private college in Los Angeles. She was unemployed at the time of the follow-up study. By then, Julio had moved out on his own and the family was proud of his hard-earned success. Yet Julio had not found relief. His job was on a contract, and he was anxious, fearing that he could soon be unemployed.

In developing countries like Mexico where good jobs are hard to come by, it is common knowledge that *palancas,* or social leverage ties, are needed to advance in society. Yet the idea that social leverage ties are needed to get ahead in American society does not jibe with American principles of meritocracy.[46] Not knowing how else to explain his family's struggle in the labor market, Fernando concluded: "We don't do anything to better ourselves."

He blamed himself for his own predicament, "For six years [when he worked for $10 to $15 an hour], I could've looked for another job." Against all evidence, he suggested that he hadn't been taught to "push" himself. Fernando could not see that a lack of *palancas* was key to his frustration in the labor market.

His mother saw it differently. "Perhaps it's not discrimination, but it *is* harder. Those of us who are poor do not have the contacts. Who do we know who have jobs that can help us? Maybe an uncle who is a gardener can help, but no one else higher up." Mariana knew that her family was not the only one having a hard time accessing good jobs. She said, "It's been hard to find jobs for all of Julio's friends who were from this neighborhood, unlike his MIT friends, who did have contact[s] and found work quickly." She added, "I think it's like Mexico. You can only get into a company if you know someone. Well, it turns out that it's the same here too, *en serio* [seriously]." Without the right networks, the college-educated family was unable to leverage their education or key turning points in their lives.

Respondents in this study trying to get ahead via institutions of higher education found their social networks highly confined to their kin and neighborhood ties. These ties provided important emotional support, but they could not help them get through college or find middle-class jobs. As other immigration scholars find, second-generation Latinos' success relies heavily on the help of "non-family" ties, most often institutional agents willing to mentor and guide Latinx youth.[47] The working-class networks of the young men in this study constrained their efforts, but these same networks were the ones ensuring that the most vulnerable did not experience "second-generation decline" or "downward assimilation."

Inhibiting "Decline": Lifting High-School Noncompleters

High school noncompleters, especially those who had been entangled with the criminal justice system, struggled to get by in young adulthood. They were the young men who had been the most exposed to the neighborhood and were the most likely to have been caught up in the male peer dynamics that introduced conflict. Given their limited education and criminal records, these young men faced significant barriers in the labor market. Often lacking driver's licenses and cars, they were the most physically restricted to the neighborhood and had the most insular social ties. These young men were on the brink of second-generation decline; at best some would be lifted to the working class by supportive kin and neighbor-hood ties or institutional interventions.

THE VALUE OF KIN-BASED SOCIAL CAPITAL

Kin and community networks rarely propel the Latino second generation up the social ladder, but they do inhibit second-generation decline. Just as such ties offered young men a buffer from violence in their neighbor-hoods in adolescence, in young adulthood kin and neighborhood ties pro-vided skills and access to jobs, housing, and other forms of support. These resources were particularly valuable for young men with minimal school-ing, as they helped them stay afloat. These kin and community-based ties provided them with moral support to stay the course, a valuable kind of social capital that discouraged them from sinking into despair in the face of dismal prospects. In some cases, institutional agents could then provide these young men with a second chance to establish a stable, working adult life and essentially halt their spiral into chronic poverty.

Efrain did not have a criminal record, and he was able to find work through his personal networks. Soon after he stopped attending high school, kin linked him to construction work for a year. When work slowed, he found on-and-off work through a work agency for a couple of months. His brother-in-law helped him get a job at a game store, where he worked for a year and a half earning $8 an hour, working a little under forty hours per week. He loved this job, but discrepancies in the finance department resulted in several people being let go, including Efrain. By then, Efrain had his first child and he felt pressure to provide. His mother then helped him get a job as a yard supervisor at a local elementary school where she worked. He earned $10.50 an hour but worked only five hours a day and came home with a headache. Efrain was unhappy at the job but needed the money with a second child on the way. The Los Angeles Unified School District then entered a period of severe budgets cuts and teachers were "pink-slipped" and let go; Efrain's work was reduced to two and a hours a day. He quit and enrolled in a continuation school, hoping that a diploma would improve his prospects, but this was when he witnessed the murder and emerged with debilitating PTSD symptoms.

By the follow-up study, Efrain was married, a father of three, and living with his in-laws. After the shooting left him mentally distraught, his kin ties helped him by linking him again to some jobs. Efrain's undocumented father-in-law got him a job loading and unloading boxes, earning $8.75 an hour in the garment district. Three months later, he found a job that paid a little better, $10 an hour, working in maintenance at a hotel where his sister worked. This would be his steadiest job, lasting for three and a half years.

Throughout this time, Efrain's intergenerational household living arrangement alleviated many of his costs. Nonetheless, there were tensions. Early in his marriage, Efrain lent his in-laws his credit card to purchase a refrigerator, but they were subsequently unable to keep up with payments. Seven years later—Efrain's debt had gone into collection and remained a persistent point of tension. Efrain refused to pay his in-laws rent, arguing that he had to finish paying for the refrigerator first. He was angry that they had bailed their "good for nothing" son out of jail even though he did not contribute to the household. The family had also fallen behind on paying their utilities, and Efrain had to cover those expenses to ensure that his children had light and gas. Still, Efrain was paying only $500 a month, a fraction of what he would have paid anywhere else. His undocumented wife worked for minimum wage, and not only did they share living costs with her parents, but they often provided free child care for their grandchildren. Efrain was fully cognizant that he and his wife "could not make it on their own." Kin support allowed him to scrape by and ensured that Efrain and his young family did not slip into despair.

Intergenerational households were common in this study, immigrant parents having extended shelter for their young adult children as they struggled to establish themselves in the labor market. In 2013, Raymundo and Leticia had four young adult children living at home. Jaime, who worked at a factory and remained on probation, continued to live in the converted garage. Their eldest son had married and moved to Texas, where his in-laws had work prospects and the cost of living was affordable. The family was rearranging their sleeping arrangements in the home. Raymundo's eldest daughter was having financial difficulties because her undocumented husband, a construction worker, was underemployed; housing was much too expensive for the struggling family of six, so they were moving back in. Raymundo and Leticia were grateful that they could accommodate their daughter's family, but hoped that it would not be for too long, knowing it would strain resources. Raymundo sympathized with his wife commenting on how quickly her large batches of food vanished when their house was full. The couple braced themselves once their four grandchildren arrived— they would be the third generation growing up in Central City.

Social Support, Social Isolation,
and Converging to the Working Class

The young men in this study fared better than some scholars would have anticipated. Despite their exposure to urban violence, high rates of school noncompletion, and, for some, entanglements with law enforcement, they were strongly attached to school and work, much like second-generation young adult Latinos generally.[48] Although some scholars have characterized the working-class networks of the Mexican immigrant community as a source of vulnerability, I found these ties to be an asset for the second generation, as they were the primary ties that helped this generation avoid decline, even when they could not help these young people get ahead.

Like their immigrant parents who relied on kin when they first settled in Los Angeles, the second generation relied extensively—at times exclusively—on kin ties, and sometimes neighborhood ties, to broker and navigate institutions of higher education and the labor market. For most of the young men, these ties had buffered them from the neighborhood and its violence. In their young adult years, these ties alleviated the challenges that they faced as they tried to get ahead. At times young men helped kin; Rigo, for example, paid almost half of his sister's mortgage when he lived with her and contributed financially to his niece's private school education. Yet it was more common for parents to subsidize their young adult children's livelihood, offering free or cheap housing and covering food costs, college tuition, and other expenses. Resources were strained in some families more than others, owing not only to the size of paychecks but also to the size of families. Not surprisingly, tension mounted and relations became strained in families with more limited resources as kin leaned on and taxed one another. As scholars note, poverty makes otherwise tight-knit bonds fragile.[49] In this study, mixed-status families were especially vulnerable. As Frank Bean, Susan Brown, and James Bachmeier find, the concentration of undocumented immigrants has a dampening effect on Latinos' social mobility prospects.[50] I found that connections to jobs via undocumented kin weighed down possible earnings—as, for instance, when Efrain obtained work through his undocumented father-in-law. Being embedded in an undocumented network had a leveling effect on other respondents as well; Jesús leaned on his aunt Sonia to navigate college and work, and the undocumented brothers of Angel, whom I discuss later, could offer him only "dead-end" jobs.

Nonetheless, these support ties were valuable especially for young men with minimal schooling, as they helped them stay afloat and provided moral support to stay the course—they inhibited downward assimilation. Young men like Efrain and Jaime—both highly exposed to the neighborhood, both school noncompleters, and one with a criminal record—leaned heavily on their immigrant families to help them get by. Though both struggled, they remained firmly attached to the labor market and, as I elaborate in chapter 7, optimistic about their future.

Yet the social ties that protected these young men from downward assimilation did not facilitate their upward mobility. The segregation of Latinos allows them to obtain social support, but not social leverage. This leads to sometimes disastrous results when Latinx youth enter institutions of higher learning—whether community colleges, for-profit colleges, four-year universities, or the Ivy League—unless someone inside the institution, an institutional agent, provides them with social leverage. The extensive social capital that some of the young men in the study earned in high school that set them on the path to college was inadequate as they climbed the educational ladder. Many of them found themselves disconnected from peer and institutional resources that could help them achieve academically, navigate new cultural norms, and, as I elaborate in chapter 7, help them manage and deflect stereotypes often tied to their urban background. Without the support of institutional agents, young men on promising paths fell back on family and neighborhood ties and converged to the working class.

Many millennials share the struggles that study participants faced as they navigated institutions of higher education and the labor market before and after the Great Recession. But social isolation rooted in their upbringing in poor, segregated contexts made their experience more difficult and the likelihood that they would enter the middle class slimmer. Growing up in poor, segregated contexts amplifies class and ethnic differences that unfold in multifaceted ways. Urban schooling leaves many disinvested in higher education and most unprepared when they do arrive at institutions of higher learning. Rather than coming across caring educators who invest in their future, urban youth often encounter gatekeepers. This experience may lead them to step off the educational ladder and end up in lower-tier jobs. Those who continue on to obtain a bachelor's degree discover that their high school underprepared them for these institutions and they must take many remedial courses. The majority of these students will spend years in these colleges, without mentors and without establishing links to those who can guide them. Most in the four-year college group of the sample left with no degree. They then had to turn to family and neighborhood ties to link them to the labor market.

The hidden hand of segregation is particularly apparent in the lives of young men positioned early in young adulthood to be upwardly mobile. Their advantage relative to others in their neighborhood dissipates as they transition from the benefits of rich social capital in high school to the loneliness of their college path. They struggle academically for the first time, and while some find institutional or peer support to help them academically, most do not. The foreign social and cultural context of a prestigious university compounds their challenges. This first exposure to a majority-white, affluent community leaves them feeling dislocated and alone. They must contend with the alienation that comes with being one of the few who look, talk, and navigate the world as they do. They recognize that their upbringing in poor neighborhoods marks them. Racial-ethnic organizations on their campuses become vital, but are often insufficient. As the next chapter discusses, the culture shock of a context that feels unwelcoming leads many to withdraw from college.

As young men exit the universities, often without a degree, just how isolated they are from mainstream society becomes devastatingly clear.[51] Few acquire professional development networks that will help them in the labor market. Even Manuel, who had completed a four-year degree at an Ivy League school, had not built the social capital he needed to find the type of job that such degrees are supposed to ensure.

Existing research discusses the insular working-class ties of second-generation Latinos as a function of the ethnic enclave. Yet class and racial segregation hampers social mobility, facilitating the class reproduction of second-generation Mexicans into "the permanent working class." However, some do establish middle-class lives—and others fall deeper into chronic poverty.[52] The former cases illustrate the difference social leverage ties make in the lives of young men; those study participants who found social mobility had social leverage ties, typically outside the segregated context. The latter cases also reflect the importance of social capital. When young men lack social support as well as social leverage ties, they can fall deeply into chronic poverty. The next chapter discusses both the fortunate and least fortunate outliers.

CHAPTER 6

Getting Ahead or Falling Behind

The Impact of Social Leverage Ties and Social Isolation

Two types of young men diverged from the working-class path: those with social leverage ties (*palancas*) who managed to pull ahead, and those with no form of social capital, the disconnected, who most closely fit the idea of the downwardly mobile. These exceptional young men were like most others in this study in that they shared an upbringing in violent neighborhoods, attended urban schools, and faced the trials and tribulations of navigating institutions of higher education and challenges in the labor market. To be clear, receiving some form of higher education remained the strongest predictor of being on an upward mobility path, yet education alone did not translate into social mobility. All of the young men who achieved upward mobility and were best positioned to become middle class had received some education beyond high school, having obtained a college diploma, license, or certificate. But acquiring more schooling or more diplomas and going to better colleges made no discernible difference in outcomes. Beyond some degree of higher education, having someone in a position of influence who brokered their transition to the labor market was the primary factor that made it possible for these young men to get ahead. And though those who faced chronic poverty had all failed to complete high school, social support may nonetheless have played a stronger role in their fate; a lack of social support was behind their higher exposure to the neighborhood as well as their school noncompletion. Social leverage ties allowed these young men to circumvent the hidden hand of segregation. Those lacking these ties as well as social support became locked into these neighborhoods.

In this chapter, I discuss those young men who broke into the middle class, or who were well positioned to do so by the time I last spoke to them. These cases illustrate the role that institutions—and institutional agents—can play in raising the social mobility prospects of the most vulnerable young men. Some social leverage ties were found in community organizations, but more commonly these emerged outside the segregated context. In stark contrast, I show that a lack of social support made other young men vulnerable long before they had finished high school. Lacking support made it impossible for them to avoid gang and crew dynamics or to break away from detrimental neighborhood ties in their young adult years. As they became entangled in crime and detached from school or work, their world narrowed to the confines of the neighborhood. Rather than come across institutional agents, these young men encountered institutional gatekeepers who used punitive practices to punish and exclude them rather than provide them with opportunities.

Making the Quantum Leap into the Middle Class

When discussing upward mobility and joining the ranks of the middle class, the young men in this study imagined owning a car and a home in a nonviolent neighborhood and not scraping by. They imagined living in financial comfort that would relieve them of the stress of poverty and even enable them to take vacations. In the next chapter, I discuss how strongly these young men held to meritocratic principles and the idea that hard work would one day pay off. Despite their heavy reliance on kin and community ties, most young men spoke in individualistic terms, framing success as a function of their own effort and failure as a function of their own shortcomings. Yet it was not the most motivated or even those with the most education who did the best socioeconomically: it was those with social leverage ties—*palancas*—who fared best.

Social leverage ties provided these young men with access to "empowerment social capital": they guided these young men and connected them with information, resources, and others who could help them navigate institutions of higher education and broker the labor market for them. In this study, most of these social leverage ties were found in institutions that typically lay, as Briggs explains, "outside the neighborhood" and that led them, in general, "to people of higher socioeconomic status and different racial/ethnic groups."[1] As Stanton-Salazar notes, "institutional agents operate the gears of social stratification and societal inequality."[2] Connections to such agents had the capacity to transform young men's lives. They could reap the benefits of their hard work and investment in higher education only with the help of these ties who helped them bridge to the "cliques, clubs and institutions" of mainstream society, facilitating their structural assimilation.[3]

Successful Alternatives: Community College and Vocational Training

The two most successful young men in this study had each earned an associate's degree and gained vocational training. By 2012, Osvaldo was twenty-seven and earning about $70,000 annually, with good benefits, in a job with animal control in a nearby county. He also owned a duplex in Central City, across the street from his mother; he and his wife and two children lived in one unit and rented the other. He had plans to buy a home in a nicer part of town and was saving at the time. Osvaldo reported feeling successful and said he owed his success to his *palancas*.

Osvaldo had been just as lost as any other young man when he was navigating college. His parents had encouraged him to apply to college and told him to look on "the internet" for information. He ended up at a for-profit school to which his family paid $6,000 for him to attend for two months. Finding this unsustainable, Osvaldo enrolled in the nearest community college. It was by chance that Osvaldo met Yolanda at the computer lab. She was an African American woman whom he described as someone "who used to help out people, pretty sure she worked at the school in academic affairs." Yolanda looked out for Osvaldo and helped him transfer to a four-year university. He explained, "I really didn't know anything about [university]. . . . [Yolanda showed] me the ropes practically for everything. She told me about financial aid, how to fill out the application." He was "90 percent sure" that without Yolanda's help he would never have transferred.

Yet finding no support at his new institution, Osvaldo dropped out of CSU almost as soon as he started, after two academic quarters. He made no friends at CSU and sat in the back of his classrooms, where his doubt that a degree could help him get a job only rose. He also did not find someone like Yolanda—that is, an institutional tie to help him navigate this new environment. Instead, Osvaldo stayed focused on securing a job and submitted countless job applications. When the county called him for a job interview, Osvaldo almost passed on the opportunity. It was the third time he would interview for a job in animal control, and he had little hope of getting it. Moreover, "My savings were to ground zero, and they were charging $20 for parking, and no, I don't have this type of money." His wife encouraged him to try his luck anyway that day.

It turned out that Osvaldo was interviewed by someone he knew. At the affluent high school to which he had been bused, Osvaldo was required to volunteer and did so at an animal shelter. The job interviewer, Miguel, had been a supervisor at the shelter. He recognized Osvaldo and had a job offer for him the next day. Osvaldo figured that Miguel being Latino helped. His earlier interviewers with the agency were with white men who had not given Osvaldo a "good vibe." Miguel was willing to give Osvaldo a chance and vouched for him. Several years into his job, Osvaldo remained thankful to Miguel—the *palanca* he had been waiting for: "I tell him all [the] time, 'Thank you for giving me the job. I know it was you.'" Osvaldo's work experience reinforced his views about social leverage ties. Out in the field in different cities, he came across individuals with college degrees struggling to find work, and he counted his blessings.

Pedro, initially identified as a high school noncompleter, was earning over $75,000 annually and was a homeowner in Central City by the time he was twenty-seven years old. Pedro grew up in predominantly black housing projects with his mother and two brothers. His older brother joined a tagging crew, detaching from school and work. Pedro's own truancy caused him to fail ninth grade. But he spent time working with an uncle doing carpentry over the summers, and he attributed his work ethic to this experience. During his senior year, Pedro was waking up at 3:00 AM to be at work by 4:00 AM at LAX, where he earned $7 an hour. He put in three hours and was at school by 7:45 AM. He then returned to LAX after school to work an additional four hours, finishing at 7:00 PM. Disappointed that he did not graduate with his class, Pedro quit school that year but took a test to earn a GED. He remained at LAX for the next four years. While he once imagined that he could earn good pay there, he never made more than $12 an hour, and so he decided to pursue a vocational program.

Like most other young men in the study, Pedro pursued his higher education haphazardly. He followed a friend from high school and took air conditioning repair classes for two years but did not enjoy them. Following another friend, he took a test to sell life insurance but felt unsuccessful after trying out that line of work for half a year. Without any guidance, he then chose to pursue an area that had piqued his interest when he was a boy: "I kind of knew something about electrical because when I was a kid we would get toys and I would take the toys apart just to see what was in it and what made it work." His mother supported his decision to enroll at a for-profit college, and she took out a $15,000 loan to enable him to pursue an electrician's license.

Pedro was proud that he held a job and attended school simultaneously. He didn't think it was hard and could not understand people without jobs. "Like, for people that don't have a job," he said, "I don't know why. I mean, if they are going to school full-time, they have an excuse, but people that are not doing anything, I don't know. . . . I have a full-time [job] and go to school. It's not hard for me." Pedro earned his associate's degree in 2007 and quickly sought work in the construction industry, where he had ties. He was eager to complete 8,000 apprentice hours that year to receive his state license, but when the recession began he lost his job. Unemployed for several months, Pedro began to "feel depressed."

The recession pushed Pedro to seek work outside his familiar context. He went back to the career center at his college and submitted various applications through work search engines, like Monster.com. A meat processing company hired Pedro for $18 an hour, and he worked there for a year and a half. During that time, Pedro returned to college for programming courses. It was then that his instructor, a white male, informed him about a job opening at another food processing company; he knew the person hiring and told Pedro to give his friend a call. Pedro made the call and was hired shortly thereafter. He negotiated a salary of $25 an hour (about $54,000 annually). In 2010, Pedro threatened to quit after finding a job that paid more, but his employer made a counteroffer of $30 an hour (about $64,000 annually), and Pedro stayed for another year and a half. At work, he became close friends with two coworkers. Neither was Mexican; one was Portuguese and the other Vietnamese. Hearing that the company might close, all three of them found work at a pharmaceutical company. Pedro's new job paid $31.50 an hour; with overtime, he told me, he was earning about $75,000. The pharmaceutical company required a legitimate GED, and this was how Pedro discovered that his was not valid. Yet his Portuguese friend who had joined the company before him knew some of the hiring personnel. With his friend vouching for him, Pedro took and passed a valid GED exam while they held the job for him. Pedro felt more secure at the pharmaceutical company and talked about taking other courses to expand his skills. Like most young men, he stressed not the role of *palancas* in obtaining his jobs but rather his ethic of hard work. But his story suggests that Osvaldo's understanding of the importance of *palancas* was on target.

Making the University Count: A Diploma with Leverage

Raul wore a skinny tie, long-sleeved dress shirt, and slacks when I met him at a coffee shop in an upper-middle-class neighborhood near his job. He was living in a racially mixed, middle-class community with his girlfriend and another couple in a two-bedroom apartment, saving for the purchase of a condo somewhere nearby. He worked for the Social Security Administration office, earning $50,000 annually plus benefits, with many opportunities for advancement. A college friend who worked there, someone he met through the Latino Business Student Association, had told him about the job, and Raul was hired a year after he applied. He was happy and felt secure at his job with a promising upward mobility trajectory. But the UC graduate spent much of his time telling me about his "roller-coaster" labor market experience.

Raul graduated in 2008, at the onset of the Great Recession. Six months after graduating from college, he began to feel nervous: "I began digging for a job really hard, and then that's when I felt there really wasn't much out there. I would get a lot of interviews, but that would be it." The business major applied for jobs in "financing and banking . . . or any company that had an opening in their accounting department," but a year after graduating he still had no job. He explained, "People were getting laid off everywhere, every bank pretty much." So he began to apply for "just regular jobs" that he never thought he would consider to pay his bills, like "doing claims in automobile companies." He applied to sell cell phones but was told that "the college degree didn't have anything to do with what they needed." Given his lack of work experience, Raul got "denied a lot," and being unemployed for almost two years created a lot of stress.

> It got pretty frustrating. My family is pretty humble. They don't do very well economically. The excitement of graduating and moving forward was dying. It was getting to the point where I believed this degree didn't really pay off. Even the jobs I was applying for, they weren't paying very well. I felt like I was lowering my standard a lot of the time, but I still wasn't getting them.

Raul was becoming discouraged and it was hard living back at his family's apartment in Pueblo Viejo. His mother Dolores, stepfather Ignacio, and other Puebla Viejo relatives had enthusiastically cheered him on when he was in college. He was ashamed for his family—all of whom were undocumented—to see him unable to contribute without a job. His family never pressured Raul, but he felt desperate and recalled thinking, "Just do anything! Go work at the grocery store or something. It literally got that bad!"

In late 2009, Raul's college roommate reminded him about an internship program at Target. It was a managerial position and had nothing to do with Raul's major, but "the job paid well," around $45,000 a year. Raul was ecstatic when he was offered the job: "I was literally jumping on the bed!" At the training he met a lot of recent college graduates, but he soon discovered that he was not cut out for the job. He was expected to manage "20 to 30 sales floor people" and, worse, to lay people off. There were many procedures to follow and not a lot of decision-making, which seemed stultifying to Raul. He didn't like the irregular schedule and long hours. His supervisors initially encouraged him but ultimately agreed with Raul that "maybe this job isn't for you." He quit after a year and was unemployed again for "more than seven, eight months." He accessed job search sites through the UC Career Center but had no luck, and he didn't like the experience. Raul said that some of the jobs posted "didn't have titles. They don't tell you what company they are. They just give you a description of the job and maybe salary." That is how he found a job at a quick loan company. He took calls and tried to sell loans. Raul kept job-searching, and during that time he received the call from the Social Security Administration office. Starting his job there marked a new direction in his life.

Raul recognized that he had graduated at an extremely difficult time, but he wished that he had been warned there "would be problems" after graduation. Counselors, he thought, did not offer the kind of guidance needed by first-generation college students like him; Raul felt that Latinx students needed "their hands being held more in college than other people." He lamented that he was "just going with the flow" and noted, "I didn't have that support system." Ultimately, Raul's college friends linked him to jobs, but he never found a mentor to facilitate the process.

Gaining a strong footing in a middle-class occupation proved challenging for the college graduates. Pedro and Osvaldo earned middle-class incomes but remained in blue-collar jobs. University graduates sought to break into white-collar occupations in line with their credentials, but doing so required distinct social leverage ties to gain access to highly coveted sectors of the labor market. College mentors or institutional agents dramatically altered the kinds of occupations that these young men pursued, opening up opportunities to jobs where they could advance over time.

Cristian, a tall, thin, dark-skinned young man, earned, like most of the young men in this study, about $15 an hour, but he was also well positioned for a government job. The college graduate was juggling four internships when I followed up with him, and this made him feel "pretty successful." He said, "I don't think anybody's pulled four internships in a year." Cristian's experience in college was not exceptional. He earned a bachelor's degree in criminology with a minor in English from a CSU campus after struggling for six years. He failed many classes: "Pretty much every math course I had to repeat," he said, including remedial math. His first college term paper came back "all scribbled," and he took "four or five" remedial English classes. At times he wondered why he was not "booted out." He also had made few friends his age. He attended a "commuter campus" with many nontraditional students, so his "study buddies" were much older than him. In college, he became close to a white professor who had worked for the federal government, and she was highly instrumental in shaping his career.

On his own, Cristian submitted various internship applications to the L.A. Police Department and the Drug Enforcement Agency (DEA), but was having no luck. Then his professor recommended Cristian for an internship with the U.S. Marshals. "They picked me up in a month, I guess under the recommendation of my professor," he said. Cristian added, "It never crossed my mind to go federal." The internship was a revelation to Cristian, who said, "I was expecting white people. There's a stereotype that Latinos always go local, you don't have anybody going any higher. So that was cool, it shattered all stereotypes." Cristian "grew much from the program." The intern coordinator was an "amazing" and "passionate" African American woman who "put her heart into the program." After the six-month internship, Cristian was promoted to a lead intern position and remained there for another six months. He felt that it had opened connections for him to other jobs.

After the internship with the U.S. Marshals, "everything just started flying." He got a call from both the DEA and the police department. He trained with the police for a few months and volunteered sixteen hours per month there. Cristian also took the DEA internship, but was not too impressed: he did "a lot of filing" and had no access to confidential information. The internship coordinator there was less supportive, so he left the position after three months. He remained at the police department, however, helping with DUI checkpoints, traffic control, and city events. Then the same professor linked Cristian to his fourth internship, with the Immigration and Custom Enforcement (ICE) agency, where she had a close friend who was a special agent. The professor told Cristian, "The job is gonna be yours. You [just] need to follow the proper protocol and apply. I'll put it in for you."

Cristian had mixed feelings, knowing well that he had close friends and relatives who were undocumented, a fact he did not disclose to ICE.[4] Ultimately, Cristian justified his decision:

> I knew I didn't want to go after immigrants, the people who are trying to make a living here. The ones I wouldn't mind going after are the people who are actually criminals, who are doing all the wrong things. So even though I'm working for ICE, which is known for [going after] immigrants, they do have something that doesn't have to leave such a bad taste—human trafficking, child exploitation.

Cristian got the job quickly and began to work for ICE part-time, about twenty hours a week, making $12 an hour. After he graduated from CSU, Cristian got a full-time position earning a few dollars more. Initially, he did filing and worked in the mail room receiving and distributing cases to officers. He then moved "to the window," where he processed bail bonds and received the "list of all the illegal aliens, with their alien number"; he would look them up to "find out where they had to report for their court hearings." On a couple of occasions, he saw people get arrested for deportation. "It sucks," he said, "because some who get arrested are bailing out somebody and we have to get their information too." Cristian intended to stay in the paid internship for two years as he waited for opportunities to open up with the U.S. Marshals; he wanted "meaningful work." He was also losing interest in local police; he wanted "to go after the big fish": "sex offenders, child exploitations, human trafficking."

Cristian recognized the importance of the institutional agent who helped him: "I think you need that education, but at the same time, it's *who* you know. That's how I got my ICE job, the U.S. Marshals, by knowing people." Unlike most young men in the study, he found such a person in college, a professor. It also helped that Cristian had "great mentors," Latinos who had made the leap into the middle class. These cross-class ties originated through his local church, where he volunteered in his youth. They included Jonathon, a "radical" Latino PhD with "crazy" ideas about politics, and Jonathon's brother, Victor, a single, forty-five-year-old man who held a high position at a television network. Cristian spoke reverently of Victor's accomplishments: "He's like one spot from becoming the vice president. He makes a lot! He tells me that his taxes are like $40k a year—that's what he pays in taxes! He's Latino, but he's been all over the world." Victor treated Cristian and Jonathon to fine restaurants and concerts at the Walt Disney Concert Hall.

Cristian intended to follow Victor's advice: "If you want to get somewhere, you make sacrifices." He felt that being too embedded with family constrained his opportunities to succeed. He explained:

> If you've noticed, whites who are successful, they went [to] out-of-state schools, they went to a different state for work, they left their families behind, versus Latinos, we like to stick together, which is where I think it's kind of how we prevent ourselves from moving up. I know I'm eventually going to have to move to Washington, D.C. I'm going to have to leave my loved ones behind in order to become successful, at least the American way.

He didn't think it was fair that he would have to sacrifice family bonds to get ahead, but it was "what you've gotta do if you want that American Dream. You've got to make sacrifices." He turned to me, a newly minted professor originally from a nearby Los Angeles neighborhood. He knew I had spent years studying on the East Coast away from family. "Wouldn't you say that's the truth? Look at you."

Transformative Ties: The "Saved" Inner-City Young Man

The bespectacled ex-gang member was wearing a long-sleeved dress shirt and jeans when I met with him again in Skid Row. Benjamin worked there at a nonprofit organization as a case manager serving ex-convicts with mental health needs. He smiled from ear to ear when he saw me again. "I look like a square now, huh? I've changed a lot, right?" he said, as I noticed he had grown out his hair and no longer had a shaved head. In fact, he had already been out of the gang when I first met him, but not for long. He was working at another nonprofit then, earning $10 an hour. In the follow-up visit, he was earning $19 an hour (about $41,000 annually).[5] Not only was the pay better, but his fellow case managers were all college-educated.

A GED holder who was once undocumented, Benjamin felt lucky to work with them and counted his blessings.

Benjamin had been put through the wringer most of his young adult life because of his gang past. In his gang days, Benjamin recalled, he walked around the high school campus "thinking he was the shit" and often carrying a weapon he brought in by "jumping the walls" to avoid metal detectors. He was in the "fucked-up classes" because teachers thought that, as "a fucking gang member," he was "never going to get nowhere" but to prison. He gave his mother Rosita many headaches and was arrested five times. In eleventh grade, Benjamin was sent to juvenile camp, and it was there that he came across teachers "that really had a lot of faith" in him. He recalled that the program was "strict" and "structured." He said, "It actually shook me up a little bit, where I said, 'Wow! I like this program.'" They took him to a college campus and made him believe that he belonged there: 'I'm seventeen, I'm like, 'I like this shit!' and they were like, 'Man, you can do this!'" Benjamin turned his grades around, formed goals, and caught up academically. He felt that he was given a second chance, and after his release he was eager to graduate with his class.

But Benjamin was not welcome back at his school. Young men like him rarely come across social leverage ties to help them get ahead. Instead, they are more likely to encounter institutional gatekeepers—teachers, counselors, school administrators—who rather than provide supportive mentoring, respond to stereotyped ideas about their students that maintain inequality among them.[6] The dean at Pueblo Viejo High denied him reentry because, Benjamin said, he "didn't want his kind"—a gang member who was "gonna create problems." Benjamin pleaded to be let back in. The dean told him that he "wouldn't make it there" and that he "didn't belong." Benjamin painfully recalled, "My mom actually had to cry in front of me and him." But the dean had made up his mind, and Benjamin was defeated.

> I actually cried. I cried when I went home, of *coraje* [anger]. It was sad because I really wanted to do this. . . . He really closed the door on me, and I really, really sincerely 100 percent wanted to change my life. I said, "This is going to help me, not only to stay away from trouble, but to be successful and get my life [on] track at this time." I really had that motivation.

Proving the dean wrong had not helped Benjamin forgive him: "I hate that motherfucker for the rest of my life!" he said resentfully. The language and approach of gatekeepers like the dean—calling students "gangsters" (even those who, unlike Benjamin, had never been in a gang), "knuckleheads," and "troublemakers"—reinforced the moral boundaries of the community and the narrative that such young men were irremediable and unworthy of the time and energy of educators or other institutional actors.

With that door closed, Benjamin turned back to the streets, and for the next four years he "bummed and chilled in the hood," working odd jobs and earning minimum wage while gangbanging. For a short period, he worked with his father at a body shop but found the arrangement exploitative: "They didn't want to pay me like a regular job. They tried to give me a hundred bucks a week. What the hell is that?" Benjamin turned to a work agency, which linked him to a warehouse where he lifted and loaded boxes. For two years, Benjamin also sold drugs. He was then incarcerated, and a court order forced him to move out of the neighborhood. The relocation accelerated Benjamin's disconnect from the gang; he was already aging out as same-age peers were incarcerated or killed. As a new father, Benjamin turned to a nonprofit organization on ex-gang members to find work. He had briefly worked with the organization in the past, removing graffiti. He first heard about it through a priest, a white male, who held services at the jail. This priest and the organization he worked with would transform Benjamin's life.

This organization and the institutional ties Benjamin found there helped him navigate the stigma of his criminal past that was complicating his labor market experience. The job search process "stressed him out," and he described with deep frustration the discrimination he faced. He recalled one job interview at a restaurant.

> That guy just looked at me—I came in dressed up nice—he is like, "Nah, don't even sit down," he told me. That shit hurt me a lot. I think I shed a tear in the bus, but I was angry. I even took my fucking tie and I threw it away. You know my pants, I pulled them downer, my long-sleeve shirt, I unbuttoned it.

That job rejection created a negative cycle for Benjamin. For a short stint, he did landscaping, but he felt that his boss, an immigrant, also discriminated against him. "He saw a gang member," Benjamin said. The stigma still followed him.

Benjamin had no other male kin tie but his father to help him find work, but that had not worked. Benjamin returned to the nonprofit for a third time. The organization hired him half-time, then eventually gave him the opportunity to work full-time as a community service supervisor. Benjamin could not believe that he landed the job. He said, "I work in an office! I never thought and I never dreamt of it. . . . I never been a supervisor of nothing, and now I am. I oversee responsibilities and like, 'Oh! I can do this and I *am* doing this!' I never thought I was going to use a computer in my life!" Benjamin pictured himself in construction or as a mechanic, but having an office job changed his mentality: "I don't want to settle for whatever kind of job. It's not that I'm lazy, it's just that there's no future. It's like a dead-end job!" His office job "gave him hope" that it was not too late to get "his career going." Benjamin took advantage of the tutoring offered by the nonprofit and re-enrolled in school, earning a GED. While volunteering for the organization at an affluent high school, he got to talking to a youth who, after Benjamin inquired about his life, said that his father was an immigration lawyer. The youth promised to "talk to his dad over dinner," and soon the student's father was working on Benjamin's case pro bono to help him secure legal permanent residency.

A couple of years later, the priest running the nonprofit organization recommended Benjamin for an internship with the nonprofit organization in Skid Row. "Because of my personality, my great sense of humor, and my work ethic," he was told. "I can't blame them . . . that's me. I see myself as a warm-hearted person." Benjamin was immensely grateful to the priest, whom he had met in juvenile hall: "I was given an opportunity by him once again. The man [the priest] is always in my life." Benjamin saw "another door open up" and asserted, "I've seen so many out of him, but this one was not just an ordinary door. He opened a bigger door, like another chapter in my life. Those training wheels came off and he set me free; he let me go." By then, Benjamin's alcoholic father, with whom he never established a good relation, had died, but in the priest Benjamin found the father-figure he had longed for growing up. He said:

> The training wheels included love, support, encouragement, and a lot of guidance. Once he took off those training wheels . . . I took off and I realized how good I am at what I do. They had more faith in me than I had in myself at that time. [The priest gave me] a lot, a lot of encouragement, a lot of love, something that I wasn't really aware of, that made a difference. But you know, his love inspired me to love a little—to love myself a little bit, to have more motivation for myself.

The priest's nonprofit organization provided Benjamin with social support and social leverage throughout the years. He explained, "They give support that I never had, and that shit is priceless." He then listed the mentors he found there who provided encouragement, moral support, and the skills to leave the gang life behind.

The chance that Benjamin would have found a job on his own like the one he had with the Skid Row nonprofit was "low, low, low," as he acknowledged. He explained, "Either you have to be educated or your family member works there. That's it." Benjamin had neither advantage, but he was lucky enough to cross paths with a man who functioned throughout his young adult years as his institutional agent; the priest provided Benjamin with support and raised his job—and life—prospects. Benjamin often wondered what his life would have been like had he not met the priest, but it was impossible for him to imagine. He chuckled, "It's a big deal, right? It's a big upgrade?" He added, "There's no way I can turn back. I don't want to turn back. I love what I do. I work with very, very smart and great people here."

Disconnected and Marginalized: On a Path to Chronic Poverty

Benjamin's trajectory certainly at times seemed likely to lead to chronic poverty, given his exposure to violence and his incarceration. The fact that he avoided this path reflects the fact that he did not remain socially isolated but connected to kin and institutional ties who helped him along the way. Some young men remained social isolated, however, throughout the study. These young men could *not* fall back on kin for links to jobs, housing, or encouragement, and they were detached from community institutions that could provide support. In their adolescence, they had been highly exposed to neighborhood violence and entangled in conflicts and peer dynamics that cost them their schooling. In their young adult years, these young men were criminalized in their encounters with institutional gatekeepers instead of supported by institutional agents. Isolated without support and leverage ties, they navigated the labor market on their own, with little success, and were often shunned in the process. These young men were "cut loose" to navigate their transition to adulthood on their own with minimal, if any, social capital.[7]

One of these young men was Salvador, whose only meaningful social tie he discussed at length was his mother Maritza, who had grossly neglected him and his siblings growing up. Unlike others who could turn to kin ties to navigate the labor market, Salvador had none. It was only with the help of a community organization with which he was loosely associated that he was able to find work. He was hanging on by a thread, however, as he remained tempted to sell drugs to boost his earnings, and in fact he had a history of losing jobs because of his drug issues.

Several young men were incarcerated at some point, but only one, Ismael, remained incarcerated, having been sentenced to four years in prison by the end of the study. Ismael was also one of the most highly exposed to the neighborhood, having witnessed the most, and the most severe, incidents of violence. Entrenched in gang and crew dynamics, he was well connected in his neighborhood. Ismael's marginalization and social isolation were closely linked to his mother's. Rufina worked all her life in the garment district, raising her four children in one of the most violent housing projects in Central City. She acknowledged that she did not manage her children's whereabouts, saying that her own parents never enforced any rules and therefore she did not either. Rufina reasoned, "You can't tell a person what to do and expect the person not to do it." She also asserted, "I don't need to teach them anything; they see how I live." Having left her fractured family at the age of fifteen, she felt that her children's mistakes were their own: "If they want to make mistakes, those are their decision and they'll pay for it. That simple." Despite her loose parenting structure, Ismael felt that she was strict at times. She never allowed friends to visit their home and forbade any drugs or weapons at her house. When she found them, she confiscated them.

All but one of Rufina's four children had poor outcomes. Her oldest daughter was thirteen years old when she ran away with a boyfriend out of state and became pregnant when she was fourteen. Her oldest son got into many fights in his youth, and after being expelled from school, he became a gang member. As Rufina summed it up, "*Se hizo vago y ratero* [He took to the streets and became a crook]." He was incarcerated multiple times and, at age thirty, was living with Rufina when I first met her.

Ismael was first arrested, for stealing a bike, when he was thirteen years old. He was sentenced to probation. Ismael did not exactly follow his brother's path, as he never joined a gang; his brother didn't let him and Ismael was protected in the neighborhood. However, he tried marijuana and cocaine with friends when he was thirteen. He also joined a crew. Two years later, he had what he called an "episode" and was diagnosed by doctors as schizophrenic.[8] He was in and out of a mental institution for about five months. He shared that "it was crazy. A lot of screaming and a lot of fighting, people talking to themselves." He received medication, but he quit taking it the minute he returned home.

Rather than stay on his medication, Ismael turned to drugs. Without a job, he "slanged" (sold drugs) to feed his habit, and by the time he was seventeen years old Ismael was addicted to meth. His father, who lived apart, and his brother had sold drugs too. He felt that in his neighborhood, "you are raised to do drugs"; many of his neighbors, he said, smoked crack or weed. "I used to see it every day. . . . I used to see it everywhere in, around my house. People slanging, drugs . . . right next door they sell weed." Ismael rarely made a profit because of his addiction. His drug use led to theft and drug sales and multiple arrests. He violated house arrest, sleeping in the streets in empty cars and occasionally "crashing" with a friend, usually another drug user. His youngest sister noted that when he returned home, "the house smelled like a bum was living with us." He acknowledged that he "would do anything to get money to buy drugs." Often he would hustle in the Metrolink (Los Angeles rail system), asking people for their all-day passes (ticket) when they got off the train, which he would then resell to others for a few dollars. He also began mugging and breaking into cars to steal radios. He had been arrested six times by the time he turned eighteen. On several occasions, Rufina turned to law enforcement for help; she preferred him behind bars rather than drugged out in the street, so she reported him when he violated his probation.

Rufina believed that the violence Ismael had witnessed had caused him to develop schizophrenia. She remembered many murders that happened after they moved to the housing projects in Central City in 1987, including one that six-year-old Ismael witnessed as he looked out the window. Ismael also mentioned the incident: "I was looking out the window, and it was at nighttime. . . . I was the only one to see it." Ismael had also been with his father when his father was assaulted at a gas station. Ismael had a different opinion about the origin of his schizophrenia. He thought that he might have developed his mental illness because of his father, whom he remembered as having cut his wrist in an unsuccessful suicide attempt and having tried to choke Rufina with a wire when she was pregnant with her fourth child. After his parents separated, his uncle Chemo was Ismael's main male role model. Chemo was killed in the course of a drug transaction when Ismael was twelve.

Rufina was the most socially isolated parent in the study. She explained, "My children are important. After that, nobody else." Her only support tie was a priest, who offered her comfort and encouragement. During the study, Ismael received a sentence of four years in prison. When I last saw him in jail, his face was bruised and he was in a straitjacket. His talk was incoherent, but he was on antipsychotic drugs, which he promptly gave up in favor of crystal meth when he was released. Five years later, he was in prison again. Rufina visited her son behind bars weekly when he was in the Los Angeles County jail.

The social isolation of the most marginalized young men in this study originates in fractured social support structures that make them highly vulnerable to the neighborhood, whose violence compounds early traumas and hurts their social mobility, locking them in. This became apparent to me only after the most marginalized young men revealed deep wounds that had destroyed their sense of trust in those around them early in their lives. These scars weighed heavily on them, structuring their social relations with others and their engagement with the neighborhood. Once they were entangled in local conflicts, their social world shrank.

Valentin was six years old when his father made him point a rifle at his mother. "You wanna become a man?" his father said. "Just fuckin' pull the trigger. . . . This is how you become a man!" The boy wept and refused, so his father grabbed the gun and did it himself. That night Valentin's world collapsed with the sound of the clip.

Valentin was shuffled as a foster child between his grandmother and several aunts. They tried to set him on the right path, busing him out of the neighborhood to a Catholic school. During summer vacations, and like other immigrants, they took him to work beside them, at the local 99-cent store. Valentin appreciated their support but explained that he never felt understood by them: "They know what happened, but they don't know how I feel. They could know everything, but if they really don't know how I feel, then it's fuckin' useless to me. Straight up, they're fuckin' useless." Valentin often relived that horrific night.

> It always stays in your head. You could cover it up, but when you least expect it, it's gonna creep on you, like I was just there. I could just close my eyes and I could just picture exactly—the whole scenario. I could remember that shit like, like if I was there . . . the kitchen, it just, that little clip. It's just stuck in my head. There is no way I can get it out.

Valentin felt that his family had not addressed his trauma, and he grew angry over time. He took to the streets, and his entanglement in a gang further strained kin relations.

By the time he was eighteen, Valentin was no longer living with his relatives. When he began to spend the nights with his girlfriend, a relationship fraught with problems even before they had a baby, his aunt moved his things out of his room and rented it out. Valentin was hurt by this. When he broke up with his girlfriend, he had no choice but to continue to sleep on the couch in the overcrowded home, where he "babysat" while his ex-girlfriend was at work. He didn't like his living situation, feeling like an *arrimado* (freeloader), and he was hoping to move out when I met him. But Valentin could not find a place to go.

The first day Valentin and I talked, we sat on the stoop of the run-down house where he lived with his baby's mother and her kin; he was especially close to her brother, who allowed him to stay even after the breakup. Their gang congregated there, and police knew them all by name and kept a close watch. Valentin had already spent one year behind bars and remained locked in a cycle of violence. Like Salvador and Ismael, Valentin was afflicted by exposure to multiple forms of violence, first as a young boy and later as a gang member.[9] With his tags all over the neighborhood and daily "posting on the block," Valentin, as he acknowledged, "became known" to other gang members—and the police. Tagging "NK" (meaning "nigger killer") throughout the neighborhood, he said that he planned to kill some members of the rival gang, who were black, so that he "would be set for life." Such an act would prove his commitment to the gang, and Valentin believed that afterwards he would no longer be asked to engage in more violence. Somewhere down the line, Valentin slipped from being a victim of violence to a perpetrator in his neighborhood. Though accused of murder, Valentin assured me that he had never killed anyone.

Trauma and neglect were clearly implicated in Valentin's fate. His relatives had never been able to fill the hole that his parents left. He said that his relatives had never come to his school promotion ceremonies or otherwise suggested that they took pride in his scholastic accomplishments. He was embedded in a cultural context where familism was strong and individualism and hard work were touted as a means to succeed, but he felt that he had been cheated. Valentin understood what society—and his family—expected of him, and this motivated him to "prove people wrong."

He earned a high school diploma while in juvenile hall, and when we met he was at a community college.

It turned out that Valentin was a college student by day and a gang-banger by night. A prior girlfriend encouraged him to pursue college, and a few teachers in juvenile hall had done so as well. Valentin saw college as a necessity because of his lack of *palancas*; given his gang involvement, he felt that he could not turn to his family, with whom ties were strained, for jobs. Trying to fit in at college, he continued to wear oversized pants and shirts, but toned down his gang identity by avoiding certain colors and carrying his backpack with the college logo on it. Criminal justice courses caught his attention, and the Early Opportunity Program directed him toward a job at its office doing clerical work. "That's what is keeping me standing," he told me. "If it wasn't for the [job], it would be kinda complicated. They look out for me. I'm deep with this community college." Yet once 4:30 PM rolled around, Valentin left the campus and spent the remaining six to seven hours "posting it" (loitering) until midnight with his gang on the block and sometimes vandalizing. Valentin understood that he would have to break off these ties to advance in college, but his gang ties were his entire social world. He was passing his classes when I met him, but during the study I abruptly lost contact; he had been arrested once more.

Valentin was incarcerated for one year. He said that he had taken the blame for something he did not do, and he would remain angry at the gang member responsible, who disappeared from the neighborhood without ever acknowledging that Valentin took the blame. His ex-girlfriend moved on and had a child with someone else. After his release, Valentin struggled to find work. He followed an aunt to Arizona, where she had relocated. There he got a job at a cement company where he earned $600 to $800 a week. Yet when his aunt lost her home and returned to Los Angeles, Valentin was left completely on his own. He worked double shifts each day, using cocaine to endure long hours and avoid an empty apartment. Trouble followed Valentin, who struggled to let go of his gang persona, and one day a group of gang members pulled up in a car and attacked him with bats, leaving him unconscious with a leg broken so badly that he needed a metal rod insert to recover. Valentin returned to his neighborhood in Los Angeles only to discover that his gang had ostracized him; it turned out that leaving that gang was not a good idea, as they were unforgiving. He felt lost.

> After everything I did to put myself up there on the map, be the top notch of everything, I lost it all. I used to walk in the street with my head up like,

"What's up?" You see me now with my head down and shit, "Who's watching me?" because you know you're just a piece of shit, you're no good, you're a little bitch, whatever they want to call you. I learned that no matter what you're doing at the time to prove yourself, you get down with so many fools, put yourself up to be the best of the best, at the end, it didn't work.

Shunned by the gang, Valentin was more isolated than ever. Valentin had not seen his grandmother in two years, though she lived only blocks away. While grateful that his relatives had taken him in as a child, he felt that they were "fake," and he called them "hypocrites" who "talked shit behind his back." His involvement with local gangs and violence and his multiple arrests had taken a toll on the family who raised him. Despite their efforts to help Valentin, they found little support along the way and failed. Valentin became a taxing tie and, as he explained, a "bad example" for his cousins. The family slowly distanced themselves from Valentin, though they remained amicable with him, despite broken trust. Valentin figured that they thought he was "a loser, a piece of shit, no good, *bueno pa nada boracho* [good for nothing drunk]." Despite living close to his family and needing a job, Valentin refused to ask for help. He said:

> If they are my family, I don't need to go ask them, "Hey, *tia,*" or "Hey, cousin," or "Hey, whassup, you got a job and shit?" If they see me struggling, there's no point of me going to them asking for help, 'cause if anything, if they see that I'm struggling, how come they don't come forward or something? People want me to beg . . . but that's not me.

Valentin was then twenty-seven years old, carless and jobless, and living again in the same dilapidated house where I first met him sleeping again on the couch of his ex-girlfriend's brother. He was receiving general relief, a type of government aid for needy individuals unable to work (because of his leg injury), but he acknowledged that he was drinking all of it. Valentin had deep regrets: "I'm supposed to be somebody in life. I know. I'm supposed to be someone big, like a career. I know I had the qualities and skills before, but now . . . I just let everything go. I just . . . I don't even try."

Valentin was one of the few young men in the study who might be described as experiencing "downward assimilation," given his extremely precarious status. Ismael and Salvador could be described this way as well. All three young men experienced early trauma, having been exposed to repeated violence from a young age, starting at home and then in the neighborhood. Their trauma had often been multigenerational; Maritza and Rufina had migrated to get away from abuse, and Valentin's mother would die as a victim of violence. Their social isolation could be traced to fractured kin ties rooted in violence. Such fractured families were at a great disadvantage relative to others who arrived with or reconstituted a supportive network. Even when social support presented itself to these young men or their mothers, they often resisted it; distrust ran deep. Valentin refused the links I offered to nonprofit institutions that helped ex-gang members; once again voicing his distrust, he suggested that the organizations were connected to certain gangs.

The implication of "second-generation decline" is that immigrants fare better than their children. Rufina and Maritza both worked, while their sons struggled in the labor market and built a criminal record; in this regard, these young men did do worse. Yet both women carried traumas that informed their distrust of others and their social isolation. At one point, Maritza turned to drugs. I learned little about Valentin's parents, but his father was in prison for life. Although faring worse than their parents was hard to do, one factor was that these young men carried trauma, distrust, and social isolation similar to their parents'.

These vulnerable young men were the most marginalized in the study. They were labeled irredeemable, disconnected, and gang-affiliated, and the stigma associated with inner-city young men was imposed on them by both the community and the larger society. The burden of these expectations made a profound imprint on the psyches of these young men, who learned to blame themselves for their predicament, as I discuss in the next chapter.

The Value of *Palancas* and Social Support

Social leverage ties can transform or significantly alter the lives of inner-city young men, including the most marginalized, like Benjamin. Since I did not interview the people who provided social leverage, I do not know what informed their support. For some, like the priest who transformed Benjamin's life, it was a passion and a calling to heal and empower these young men. Others may have seen something special in these young men that was imperceptible from my vantage point. Yet respondents revealed that these were active institutional agents who were not only able but willing to help or act on their behalf and open up opportunities for them. These young men came across many adults, but only a few who either were in a position of influence or used it to expand their opportunities and empower them. As I showed in the previous chapter, higher education became a gamble for these inner-city young men without social leverage ties that make the difference between those who get by and those who get ahead. By brokering access to coveted positions in the labor market, social leverage ties can catapult young Latino men from the inner city into the American middle class.

Success stories like Osvaldo's and Benjamin's stand in stark contrast to the most tragic cases in this study. The lives of these disconnected and marginalized young men revealed that not everyone is fortunate enough to have a support structure—loved ones who encourage, guide, and help along the way—much less *palancas* willing to broker opportunities. I found that the social isolation of these young men was intergenerational: their parents were among the most socially isolated in these neighborhoods. Whereas most other respondents had kin or community ties via church or schools, the immigrant families of these young men, mainly mothers, had no such connections. They managed the urban context for their sons on their own, with little success, and were ill equipped to help them in the labor market. Looking more closely at these immigrants' lives reveals a fractured social support system, often rooted in violence and trauma. Most of these immigrant parents managed to work and get by in Los Angeles on their own, but they were highly vulnerable. It is difficult to say that their sons experienced decline rather than simply more of the same. It is certainly true, however, that poverty structured by violence and trauma is hard to overcome without meaningful support.

As I have already suggested, Osvaldo was one of the few respondents who clearly understood the role of social ties in his fate. As I elaborate in the next chapter, most of the young men remained committed to the American Dream ideal, believing strongly that the United States continued to offer opportunities to get ahead and that their hard work and dedication would eventually pay off.

CHAPTER 7

Making Sense of Getting Ahead

The Enduring and Shifting Cultural Outlooks
of Young Latino Men

W hen I first met Efrain, he told me, "If you aren't making $15 an hour, you are nobody, because rent up here is, wow, sky-high now!" By the time he was twenty-seven years old, he had overcome his episodes of PTSD but had yet to make more than $10 an hour, and at the second phase of the study he was unemployed. He and his wife had three children, and they lived with his in-laws. His wife was undocumented and working full-time doing clerical work in the garment district. Although as the wife of a citizen she might have qualified for a green card, the couple was afraid to start her authorization process for fear she would be deported.

I waited for Efrain at his parents' home. When he arrived, they had been telling me about their financial difficulties and the hurdles they navigated with several banks while trying to save their home. The balloon payments had kicked in right before the recession: $2,000 due one month jumped to $2,500 the next without notice.[1] Dario earned $8 an hour at the time, working full-time, and Ester earned a few dollars more, working part-time for $10 an hour. We observed Efrain park the car and walk up to the house. Then Ester walked to the front door to let him in. She then shared about the time a piece of the ceiling came crashing down where she stood, barely missing her. I looked up and noticed the smooth paint on the ceiling, which contrasted sharply with the rest of the dilapidated home, left untouched in the absence of resources. She explained that Efrain had helped pay for the new ceiling, a small gesture after living under their roof for years with his wife and children for minimal rent or, at times, for free.

Efrain struggled in the labor market and had felt moments of despair, but that day was promising. He walked into the house wearing a tie. He no longer wore his hair in a ponytail, as he did when I met him five years earlier. Instead, he had a conservative look appropriate for the job interview of the day. "I think it went well," he said with a smile as he sat down on the sofa. This was the third time that this hotel had asked to see him about a maintenance position, and he felt that the job was in the bag. The full-time job, which paid $12 an hour, would be the highest-earning Efrain had ever had. His dream was to manage buildings in downtown Los Angeles one day, and he had a plan:

> I have to work in the industry for at least a year, two years to get that hands-on experience, work with different companies on refrigeration and AC [air conditioning] or work in a building managing that. . . . I will go back to school and get my certificate for operations and engineering, which is about another year or two. Then I can manage everything. I deal with high-rises, big buildings, power plants. I can go there and do whatever I want. That's the main goal . . . to actually run downtown.

He imagined pointing to the downtown buildings and telling his kids: "Hey, look! That's where Daddy works!" Efrain had re-enrolled in adult education school because he needed a high school diploma to enter the trade school. He felt that his *ganas* (desire) would carry him forward and asserted that the American Dream is "achievable. You just have to know your *why* in life. Why are you here, why are you continuing every day?" He explained, "I've seen a lot of people be successful. . . . It's not that I *think,* it's that I *have to* achieve it. It's a must."

There is a narrative about inner-city young Latino men that leaves very little room for their struggle and perseverance, their optimism and hope. The academic literature has contributed to this narrative, historically depicting a homogenous cultural context in which young men like Efrain are expected to express leveled aspirations, hopelessness, or pessimism about their future; this narrative suggests that these young men give up.[2] Heavily emphasizing the inner-city young men who are engaged in crime and violence further sustains a skewed representation of these communities. The concept of "downward assimilation" built on these arguments to suggest that children of Latino immigrants develop "reactive identities" and "adversarial outlooks" in the inner city.[3] These young men were expected to become critical of the American opportunity structure, see obstacles to their opportunities for getting ahead, and opt for nonconventional means of getting ahead.

Other scholars consistently find that the most marginalized in high-poverty urban neighborhoods hold strongly to the American Dream.[4] Urban residents adhere to "abstract" meritocratic ideals and are optimistic about their chances to succeed, even as they face growing economic adversity. Most young men in this study were like Efrain, who continued to believe that the United States offers opportunities to get ahead, as long as individuals seek them out, exert effort, and persevere. Most remained confident that *they* would get ahead through hard work and effort, although they may have recognized that their group as a whole faced difficult odds. In line with others' research, I find that the concept of the American Dream is reinforced in the American segregated context and is especially pronounced among the most marginalized urban residents.[5] How and why some inner-city second-generation Latinos remain optimistic while others move away from this orientation is unclear. Immigration scholars have suggested that this "second-generation optimism" is rooted in their immigrant background.[6] I find support for this idea—as well as evidence that sustaining this optimism in the face of great adversity requires various forms of support. As I have shown, study participants without social capital faced significant forms of adversity—from having to navigate violence to meeting the challenges coming their way in institutions of higher education and the labor market—and some of them lost faith in their ability to get ahead.

Over the last two decades, urban scholars have challenged the idea that an "oppositional culture" reigns in the inner city, and specifically the idea that a "culture of poverty" flourishes there.[7] These and other studies find diverse cultural logics in urban neighborhoods and a strong embrace of mainstream norms and beliefs.[8] Here I extend these findings to second-generation Latinos. Concern over the integration of Latinos often hinges on whether this group is open and willing to "assimilate"—specifically, to acculturate—to the American way of life; popular rhetoric, including from political pundits and some scholars, suggests that this group refuses to learn English and self-segregates.[9] Of course, many studies show that this fear is unwarranted; most children of immigrants quickly absorb the English language and American customs. As Latinos move up the income ladder, albeit slowly, they move away from poor and segregated neighborhoods, a pattern described as "delayed assimilation."[10] The concern about inner-city Latinos has been that they might depart from mainstream norms, adopt a "reactive identity," and experience "downward assimilation."

In this chapter, I explain why most respondents remained optimistic or determined to succeed despite facing great adversity. To understand the cultural logics of these young men, I examine their cognitive frames—the "lenses" through which they "observe and interpret social life"—and specifically how they make sense of the American opportunity structure and their chances of getting ahead.[11] The cultural outlooks of second-generation Latinos are not homogenous; they varied among the young men in this study and shifted over time. Their cultural outlooks were fluid, changing with their structural conditions.

I find that second-generation Latinos are informed by two interrelated but distinct cultural logics: *their belief in the American opportunity structure,* which can be viewed as open or constrained, and *their faith in their own ability to get ahead,* which can be optimistic or pessimistic. Table 7.1 presents a taxonomy of four types of young men: resolute optimists, the determined, self-blamers, and oppositional pessimists. I found that structural factors underlie these distinct cognitive frames. In particular, I call attention to how the degree of young men's social isolation in the segregated environment informs their evaluation of the American opportunity structure and how the extent of their social support informs their belief in their ability to get ahead.

Table 7.1 *Urban Latino Cognitive Frame Types*

		More Segregated	Segregated
		←	→
		BELIEF IN THE AMERICAN OPPORTUNITY STRUCTURE	
		OPEN SYSTEM	CLOSED OR CONSTRAINED SYSTEM
More Support ↑ / Less Support ↓ — BELIEF IN THEIR ABILITY TO GET AHEAD	OPTIMISTIC	Resolute optimists ($N = 27$; $N =11$ at follow-up)	The determined ($N = 9$; $N = 7$ at follow-up)
	PESSIMISTIC	Self-blamers ($N = 6$; $N = 3$ at follow-up)	Oppositional pessimists ($N = 0$)

Source: Author's compilation.

Notably, not one young man in this study fit the theoretical category of oppositional pessimist—a dominant depiction of inner-city young men. The belief that racial minorities' poor school performance is attributable to their perception that the U.S. opportunity structure is blocked by racism once dominated the sociological literature.[12] Many studies, however, have challenged this argument, as do my own observations.[13] To the contrary, I find that young men who altered their understanding of the American opportunity structure—consciously coming to terms with racial and class inequality—did not give up faith in their ability to succeed and remained determined to achieve success.[14]

Most respondents (twenty-seven) were like Efrain: "resolute optimists" who were strong believers in the American opportunity structure and their own chances of succeeding. In line with existing research, I find that segregation enhanced their faith in the American opportunity structure—those who were most entrenched in the urban neighborhood believed most strongly in the achievement ideology. It was the young men who spent more time outside the segregated urban context whose views shifted as they confronted America's stark racial and class inequalities. Their greater exposure to mainstream America shattered their meritocratic ideology and made them lose faith in the American Dream; nevertheless, these nine young men in the study, "the determined," persevered against the odds and fell back on kin support ties. In contrast, six young men became "self-blamers": harsh critics of their own choices and behavior. These were the most entrenched in the urban neighborhood and the most socially isolated in their communities. They subscribed to American meritocracy but lacked the support of others, leading them to navigate their transition to adulthood on their own, with minimal success.

Making Sense of the "Resolute Optimism" of Young Men

Efrain looked back at his immigrant parents' journey and accounted for their struggles, sacrifice, and accomplishments as he assessed his own chances in the United States:

> I see ourselves [achieving] middle-class [status]. . . . [My parents] own their own house; they're pushing themselves. It's pretty hard raising seven kids. And my mom, from where she came from, and the steps she took working at the school district, going to [community college], doing everything

she could for us. It's pretty amazing. My dad taking all those shifts, night and day, and improving his English, not having any schooling. It's pretty amazing. . . . I've seen them achieve things in their life, not having a lot, and me? I only have three kids and I was born here! There's no way in hell I have to fail! Because if they struggled this much and they've gotten me to this point—to see me fail? Might as well just jump off a cliff and never have existed!

The internalization of their parents' hardship and struggle by respondents like Efrain discouraged them from giving up; well attuned to the immigrant bargain, they felt that they had to redeem their parents' sacrifice.[15]

Yet an immigrant narrative alone does not sustain second-generation Latinos' optimism, which is tested repeatedly in their young adult years. Efrain jumped back into the labor market with the support of kin but quit several jobs because he felt exploited for meager pay. His sister helped him get a job as a "runner" at a hotel, but it took a toll on his health. Efrain was stressed at the job because he was spread thin across departments; he not only did housekeeping but also helped with the engineering department, the restaurant, and the front desk at times. He worked overtime and stacked shifts. Then one day he woke up with his face partially paralyzed. For a month, food and liquid fell out of his mouth when he ate, leaving him deeply embarrassed and frustrated. For a couple of weeks, one of his eyes would not close, even when he tried to sleep, and it watered constantly, "freaking out" his children. He decided that he had to refuse overtime hours, which angered his supervisor. When the supervisor questioned Efrain's work ethic and threatened to "write him up," Efrain snapped back: "You know what? I'm gonna save you the paperwork. Fuck your job! I quit." That may have been a dramatic gesture, but in fact he left, he explained, because "I saw no future there. That's what it was. I saw no step-ups."

It was during this period of unemployment that I interviewed Efrain in the second wave of the study. I found that despite the challenges he encountered in the labor market, he was still optimistic. With three children to provide for on a meager paycheck and no social mobility, he might easily have become hopeless—or turned to crime under pressure. But he was able to interview for the maintenance job because his sister, once again, helped him arrange it. Without kin linking Efrain to jobs, he would have struggled a lot more than he did in the labor market. Although he was occasionally underemployed, Efrain did not experience joblessness for any prolonged period of time.

The support of kin ties extended beyond helping the young men navigate the labor market. Kin social capital was multifaceted and allowed the second generation to get by from day to day and to imagine brighter days; it propped up their American Dream. It also helped them focus on one another instead of on society as a whole, and this informed how they made sense of the American opportunity context.

Kin Support

Efrain benefited extensively from the support of his family as he leaned heavily on them for links to jobs, housing, and child care. Limited resources and overcrowded conditions complicated family relations, and life remained a challenge as these families were forced to pool their resources to get by. Despite tension, kin support eased life for second-generation young adults in Los Angeles. Paying minimal rent, if any at all, allowed Efrain to use his modest earnings to provide the other basic necessities for his family, including food, utilities, clothing, and the occasional toy for his three children. Both tangible and symbolic support cushioned the blow of economic scarcity, allowing the Latino second generation to get by and stay optimistic.

Even if the "immigrant bargain" alone did not encourage respondents to forge ahead, symbolic support mattered greatly. These young men also relied heavily on their immigrant parents and other kin for inspiration, encouragement, and moral support. Immigrant fathers and father-figures played a prominent role in shaping young men's perception of work, what it took to get ahead, and how they defined success. Most of the young men identified strongly with their fathers, emphasizing their migration story more than that of their mother. In Mexico, Dario grew up in dire poverty. His mother had nine children, but their father never took an interest in providing for them. This forced Dario to begin work at eight years old to have money for food and shoes. He sometimes slept on the streets, hungry and cold. At times he experienced abuse on the street. Efrain did not have a perfect relationship with his father, but he admired Dario:

> That's one thing—I actually look up to him. No matter, if life kicks him in the ass or whatever, like . . . he always picks up a job the next day no matter what. That's one thing that I like about my dad: that no matter how hard it gets, he always will go and get the money for whatever we [need].

Dario and Ester's home was overcrowded and on the verge of collapse, but it was a roof over their heads that they could call their own—a vast improvement, for Dario, over sleeping on the streets.

Their fathers' achievements, however modest and subject to setbacks, generated a strong conviction in the Latino second generation that they could succeed in the United States.[16] Many of their fathers struggled with low wages, and yet these young men were quick to point out their fathers' accomplishments. Cristobal, eighteen, was motivated by Humberto's acquisition of certain possessions, "like a couple of cars and a plasma TV," even though he was "not a millionaire." Given Humberto's poverty-stricken childhood, Cristobal saw him as successful:

> If my dad made it, it's because of all the work he's done. He never gave up. I'm not going to give up either! Especially me, I'm starting off at a higher level than him. I can do even way better. He tells me too, you must be dumb if you don't make it, you know what I mean? Any person must be dumb if they don't make it. It's true.

Pedro's role model was his uncle Javier, who arrived in the United States without documents. Javier worked in carpentry and owned a home on the outskirts of the city, where he often treated Pedro and his friends to *carne asadas*. Pedro felt that he could accomplish at least as much as Javier. In 2007, when he lived with his mother in public housing, Pedro stated, "I think anyone can [make it]. If an immigrant comes, like, not speaking English [like Javier] and [can] be successful, then I don't see why anybody else that lives here already, speaks the language, and pretty much gets a lot of help . . . can't." Most of these fathers and father-figures had achieved some modest form of mobility since their migration. Young men compared their father's socioeconomic status to their premigration years and accounted for their former unauthorized status.

While fathers inspired young Latino men, mothers provided a backbone that encouraged them to persevere as they experienced roadblocks. Ester worked two jobs, and the family credited her for doing what she could to avoid foreclosure. Ester's American Dream was having a house with at least five bedrooms to house her family. Instead, she had a two-bedroom home where at one point Efrain and his family of five shared one of the bedrooms, leaving the other for her and Dario; her two other sons slept in the living room, sometimes with their own children. It was not always a peaceful arrangement, but she moved the family forward and kept the family intact as challenges came their way. Despite being a working mother, Ester always managed to be there for her children. It was Ester who showed up at school to demand greater supervision and report when Efrain was beat up by other youth on and off campus. She was behind his multiple attempts to return to school. It was Ester who took her daughter's desperate midnight calls from Afghanistan, where she had been deployed by the army. It was Ester who sat for weeks in another son's classrooms to ensure that he did his work and then accompanied him to several therapists when he was diagnosed with attention deficit hyperactivity disorder. She stood beside her daughter in court when that daughter filed for divorce and a restraining order to prevent further domestic violence. It was Ester who financed her middle son's semester at a for-profit college—$11,000 that went nowhere. While frustrated at times, Ester was her children's backup and their cheerleader. When they said that they couldn't do something, she said that "the word 'can't' didn't exist." These young men identified strongly with their fathers and father-figures, but the unconditional support provided by their mothers consistently earned them the title of the "most important person" in the lives of most of the young men in this study.

Pooled resources brought relief to families and gave them hope for better days ahead. For some families, intergenerational support helped them get ahead, not just get by. After raising her five boys on her own on a teaching assistant salary, Jovita accepted her ex-husband Luis's proposal to reunite the separated family. Leo, her middle son, was not happy about this decision. The eldest, the twins, were off at a University of California campus when the remaining five in the family moved out of Pueblo Viejo with Luis. The move turned into a roller-coaster ride as financial problems ensued. As Jovita explained, Luis refinanced their home twice against her wishes, and the home went into foreclosure in 2007. For the next six years, the family lived cramped in an apartment.

Times got tough for everyone in the family during the recession. All of Jovita's sons were struggling. One of the twins graduated from the university with a degree in education but struggled for several years to land a teaching job. His twin brother dropped out of college and struggled in the labor market as well. Leo coached football for a few years, taking courses on and off at the community college. After all of Jovita's effort to keep her boys out of trouble in the neighborhood and to encourage them to go to college, her two youngest twins also opted out. Both worked as security guards at a nearby mall.

Then the tide turned for the family. Leo took a neighborhood friend's advice and applied to enter the police academy. By 2013, Leo was a school police officer earning an annual salary of $55,000. His younger twin brothers were following in his footsteps, waiting to come of age to apply for the police academy. His college-graduate brother finally got a permanent teaching position, while his twin also secured a steady job. As is the case with most of the young men in this study and millennials in general, Jovita's sons were postponing having children, even when coupled.[17] Jovita's family pulled together closely during those tough years to get by, and then they bounced back. In the follow-up study, I met them as Luis was laying kitchen tile in their new home, although he and Jovita were in the process of divorce.

Jovita was hopeful. I asked her if she believed in the American Dream, and her eyes teared up. Jovita had purchased the new home with her sons. "This house is a symbol of that—because we didn't give up. As I leave my house in the morning when I go to work, I thank God and I feel so blessed, 'cause I would never have thought we would be able to do it, after what we went through."

Jovita's sons had to let go of their desire to live independently, realizing that it was in the financial interest of all of them to live together. They discussed how their intergenerational housing arrangement would work. Living together, Jovita explained, was "working for us. . . . I think financially it's helped all of us." She noted that her sons "don't see anything wrong with it. They actually love this house, and they're very proud of it because they [had] a hand in getting it together." Jovita was certain that had they "decided to go separate ways," they all would have been worse off. She said, "Because we banded together as a family, we're shining right now."

Of course, not everyone in this study had a supportive kin structure. In the absence of kin-based social capital, some young men could sustain their optimism to pull ahead with the support of community ties. Community organizations—like the gang intervention program that helped Benjamin—played a significant role in preventing otherwise isolated young men from falling into despair. Community organizations offered various forms of support—from jobs and tutoring to mental health and substance abuse intervention to moral support, love, and encouragement. David was extensively exposed to the neighborhood and its violence in his teen years but in his young adult years hung on fiercely to a Pueblo Viejo boys' and girls' club where he had found great mentors in his youth.

David did not know his father, and his mother and two of his sisters had introduced him to crystal meth at home in his teens; they remained drug addicts who would be in and out of jail, and his mother had HIV. I found David, twenty-four years old, at the same organization where I first met him five years prior. He was staying with his eldest sister and sleeping in her garage. A high school noncompleter, David had earned a GED with the help of mentors at the community organization. His mentors helped David enroll in a firefighters' academy for "at-risk" youth, and he lived there for several months, training. After completing the program, David sought work, but he was having no luck. Still, he remained hopeful. The community organization remained David's sanctuary, and he continued to rely extensively on ties there.

David was unemployed and lacked a car, but he was confident he would do well. He explained that attaining the American Dream "is in the person's mind. Anything is possible. It all depends on what you want. If you choose to push yourself to . . . reach the highest point, then you can. The only thing that is stopping you is yourself. I learned that a long time ago." David referred to his drug addiction, which he managed to end—not on his own, but with the support of his mentors. Painfully, he had learned to disconnect from his taxing kin ties—his own mother and some of his siblings—and surrounded himself with fictive kin at the community organization. It was the only way he could stay positive and clean.

How Segregation Reinforces Meritocratic Beliefs

The American ideology that those who work hard can get ahead is widespread, inculcated in American schools and pervasive in the broader American culture. Studies show that this belief is especially pronounced in segregated low-income neighborhoods, where scholars find a strong adherence to individualism.[18] Most young men in this study expressed meritocratic views. In his early twenties, Leo was a strong believer in making wise choices and exerting effort as a means to obtain success. When I first met him, he said:

> If anyone has good work ethic, discipline, and determination, they will be able to reach their goal. I truly believe that's what it takes whether you are playing basketball, you are playing football, you're a lawyer, and you're a doctor, whatever it may be. I think if you put your mind to it, you can achieve whatever you want to achieve.

Years later, the twenty-five-year-old police officer would note that many young men his age "don't know what they want" or are "still fucking around." He was admired in Pueblo Viejo as a "poster child" for the community. Undoubtedly, Leo *had* worked hard to reach his goal. Yet he was also fortunate to have a supportive network that helped him through challenging times, including several mentors in the community and a police officer friend who encouraged him to apply to the police academy.

Although resolute optimists relied heavily on kin for jobs and to get by on a day-to-day basis, most emphasized their character and personal efforts as what carried them forward. Twenty-three-year-old Gonzalo, a high school graduate, was confident that he would one day earn "over six figures for sure," selling life insurance and real estate. Attaining success, he asserted, required determination:

> I think you can do anything, there's no reason why somebody can't do something. If you say, "Oh, I can't afford education," well, you can go to the library on your own. You want to learn how to do T-shirts or something. You can learn if you really want to. If you wanted to start doing real estate, you can get your license if you really want to. There may not be jobs, but there are opportunities.

Gonzalo admitted that the recession had made it "a little bit harder" than he had expected to find a job, but he remained a strong believer that opportunities abounded in the United States. Gonzalo also had extensive support from his family. With his two sisters married and out of the home, Gonzalo lived comfortably with his parents, his belongings spread between two bedrooms. Gonzalo paid rent but not an overwhelming amount. To the contrary, Gonzalo was free to explore various "opportunities," and he had launched a product, a designer T-shirt, to sell online with a friend.

Young men defensively held on to meritocratic ideals. In the abstract, these young men understood that, as Latinos, they had fewer resources than others to succeed in the United States, and as children of immigrants, they understood well their humble beginnings. Yet they minimized the structural barriers they confronted in American society.[19] In past research, I showed that most of these young men did not interpret their criminalization through a racial lens, but from a color-blind perspective.[20] Efrain, who left his crew midway through high school and had been ticketed numerous times by police in his neighborhood as an adult, said that he did not understand why: "Maybe I looked suspicious behind the wheel, or I looked too young driving that big old truck?" Though not a fan of police, Efrain seemed oblivious to how heavily policed his block was relative to other neighborhoods and did not articulate his experience as a function of racial profiling. Similarly, young men dismissed racial discrimination in their efforts to get ahead. Gonzalo ignored coworkers who labeled him as a *cholo,* explaining, "If you work hard and put yourself out there regardless of what obstacle you run into, you can do well for yourself. So yeah, discrimination plays a big part, but it depends on how people take it." Insulated in their segregated contexts, many young men shared Juan Carlos's feeling that even though he was aware of discrimination, he had never experienced it. Others were defensive, asserting that such a barrier would not get in the way of accomplishing their goals. Noel's father, Vidal, taught him to ignore racism: "Let them think like that . . . just keep moving on."

Reinforcing this ideology is an immigrant co-narrative that deemphasizes structural barriers (like discrimination and limited networks) and emphasizes instead hard work, effort, struggle, and sacrifice as the means to get ahead.[21] In this study, one immigrant after another repeated: "*El que quiere, puede* [If there is a will, there is a way]," suggesting that individuals could overcome any obstacle. Raul's mother, Dolores, who was undocumented, was like many immigrants in stressing individual attributes as a means to success:

> I think that if my son has the *ganas* [vigorous desire] to excel, he first needs to have the will and put a lot of effort in school. They say that money buys titles [privileged positions], but he has the capacity to develop and to get ahead. It does not matter that he is a son of a single mother, of an undocumented mother who was raised in Pueblo Viejo, attending its schools, one of the worse schools.

Dolores armed Raul with this defensive, individualistic outlook as he enrolled in college. She did not foresee his academic struggles or the difficulties he would face in the labor market after graduation. It took Raul about three years after he graduated from college to secure his well-paid job with the Social Security Administration.

In hypersegregated immigrant Los Angeles, the biggest barrier that second-generation Latinos perceive to getting ahead is a lack of documentation to work legally in the United States, which forces many coethnics into the most grueling and lowest-paid jobs. Efrain recalled, with some distress, an ICE raid he witnessed in the garment district: "Wow. That is some shit. These are people that are just here to work! They're here to make their life better for themselves." Efrain could see the barriers faced by undocumented immigrants, but not the ones he faced. He added, "It's sad. It just wasn't right. They were just discriminating [against] Mexicans." For many, the open antagonism toward undocumented coethnics and their work exploitation while being denied basic human and civil rights obscured other forms of discrimination.

The hypersegregation of the Latino second generation influences their reference point for understanding the American opportunity structure and assessing their own chances of succeeding. The presence of undocumented coethnics reinforces the idea that anyone with papers has opportunities and is thus responsible for their own success. When I first met Dario, he struggled with Efrain and his younger brothers, all who had left high school. Back then, Dario frequently reminded his sons about immigrants' higher moral character:

> I tell [my sons] that anyone who wants to get ahead in life works and goes to school. There are people [migrants] who come, who risk their life to come here, and once they are here, they work and study because they are interested in getting ahead, and they don't have papers. They [his sons] have everything, but what they don't have are *ganas* [a vigorous desire to succeed].

Respondents figured that if undocumented coethnics who faced the most severe barriers got ahead, there was no excuse why they could not do the same. With time, parents like Dario would shift their views as they witnessed their sons struggle in the labor market, despite their efforts.

In spite of their respect for undocumented immigrants, a number of young men were unwilling to tolerate themselves the exploitative working conditions that they witnessed being inflicted on people without papers. But by avoiding "dead-end" jobs, these young men experienced more periods of unemployment than their immigrant coethnics.[22] This cultural and behavioral shift introduced the notion that the second generation was not as hardworking as immigrants, and young Latino men consequently felt pressured to continuously prove their moral worth through their participation in the labor market.

Some young men in low-paying jobs found their optimism waning. Yet resolute optimists were tightly embedded in neighborhoods where an individual's ethic of hard work supported his moral worth and was touted as a means to success. It helped that these young men believed that vast opportunities existed. In the face of setbacks and structural barriers, they kept hope alive as they relied on kin to help them get by and forge ahead. The belief that choice and individualism explain social mobility minimized the role of structural barriers.

Shifting Cultural Outlooks: Stepping Out of the 'Hood and Those Locked In

Not all young men remained optimistic in their young adult years. Some of them shifted their understanding of the American opportunity structure as America's inequality came into focus for them. Those who spent time outside their segregated neighborhood, typically those on an upwardly mobile path, came across stark class and racial inequalities that shattered their sense of a meritocratic society. The handful of undocumented young men in this study confronted the consequence of their unauthorized status in these years, and they too developed a new understanding of America's opportunity structure. Yet these young men did not become pessimistic; instead, they were among the most determined to succeed and continued to rely extensively on the support of kin.

In contrast, the young men most entrenched in their segregated urban neighborhoods held most fervently to the American Dream ideal and America's meritocratic ideals. Physically entrenched in the neighborhood yet socially isolated within it, they lost faith in their own ability to succeed. The young men with the fewest resources explained success as a function of individual effort and failure in the same way, leading them to become pessimistic about their prospects as they blamed themselves for their life predicaments.

"Tanks of Steel": The Determined

At home and in the neighborhood, no one seemed to understand Manuel. Everyone knew that he had gone to a "good school"—an Ivy League school in fact. Most of his siblings worked in the garment district, but they had jobs. Surely he could do better. His family thought that he should accept an entry-level position that could provide him with steady income, and their strong orientation toward work resulted in much conflict. Manuel's father, who had been initially opposed to his college plans, often yelled at his son for not finding employment. As Manuel, then twenty-three, said:

> The other day I asked [my father] for five dollars. Uff! "*Que pendejo*" [What an idiot]. "*Que baboso*" [How stupid of me]. He told me I was an embarrassment because I had no money and I was asking for five dollars. "Look at the *pinche escuela* [fuckin' school] you went to and look at where you are." Things like that.

Manuel dismissed his father's insults, reasoning that he was an authoritarian, abusive alcoholic. "If I'm working, he gets mad because I am not working in a better job. I'm not going to worry about him," he said. Yet others in the family put pressure on Manuel as well. One brother who had gone to college after his military service had not given Manuel advice while he was in college, but now scolded him for getting a degree in Spanish literature. One of his sisters always nagged him when he was out of work to find another job. Manuel tried to "hear them out" and asked them to be patient, but he did not feel understood: "They didn't see what I lived through."

Whereas optimistic young men hope for opportunities, determined young men often had them. These young men were buffered from the neighborhood and avoided getting caught up, and they received ample support to achieve in high school and then transition into college. Manuel found enough support at his college to graduate. Despite their opportunities, however, these young men were having a difficult time breaking into the American middle class and running head-on into America's racial and class barriers. They learned that simply having opportunities, like going to college, and working hard did not guarantee access to the American Dream. Manuel took ownership of his missteps: "Having a child and taking on the responsibility of a marriage right after college, it's probably the worst decision that I could have made." Yet he pondered out loud, "I imagined doors would have opened for me, going to my college. Look at me! I went to an Ivy League and I'm not doing anything great." Manuel knew that his inability to find a good job was not for lack of effort, so he did not sit with negative thoughts for too long when they crept up. Even though he had missed his opportunity to expand his networks while at his elite university, he continued to feel resilient, saying, "The one thing that I do like about myself is that I've been able to adjust to some very difficult situations." Manuel believed that he would one day succeed, but he was quick to note that the journey was "tough" and required being a "tank of steel, unbreakable," to "take the hits in life."

Trials and Tribulations Outside the Urban Neighborhood

Life outside the segregated urban context gave young men a new under-standing of the American opportunity structure. There they encountered stark class disparities and experienced more subtle and blatant forms of discrimination.[23] College-going seniors at the beginning of this study were the most motivated to succeed, and all were optimists. Their enthusiasm, however, contrasted with the feelings of those already in college and those who had graduated. College itself disrupted respondents' faith in the American Dream, as they realized they had received a substandard K-12 academic preparation. Struggling, Manuel noticed that his peers breezed through college. "They used to tell me college was like high school to them," he said. "Are you kidding me? How can it be the same?" It was not just the academic rigor that made Manuel feel different from his college peers; he observed that they breezed through life in other ways as well.

At one of the nation's most elite universities, Manuel could not help but compare himself to other students there. He had a computer to do his work on, but no television or radio or money.[24] "*¡Que gacho!* [This sucks!]" he said. "I would see these kids' parents take them to Walmart, I mean, they had everything they needed." Manuel arrived on his college campus alone, and not once could a relative visit him or help him out financially during the four years he was there. Only his brother was able to join him at graduation. Manuel noted that most other students in his college "have things set in place for them—family structure, citizenship, parents have better jobs, and parents always teaching them. But for us, we have to do a lot, adjust to many things." As Anthony Jack explains, "doubly disadvantaged" students in elite institutions experience a profound sense of alienation as they become acutely attuned to their class background and are thrown off by the affluent cultural context, leading many either to withdraw or to become isolated in these schools.[25]

The determined young men in the study shifted their frame of reference, gaining a new perspective on the American opportunity structure. Manuel no longer referenced kin, neighborhood peer ties, and undocumented immigrants to gauge his sense of opportunity in the United States, but middle-class and affluent whites instead. The affluent college context made Manuel "feel out of his comfort zone" and painfully aware of his poverty. When he was growing up, the family of twelve had lived crowded in a small apartment in Los Angeles. All ten siblings worked long hours for meager wages in the garment district except Manuel, the youngest. This had an impact on him:

> I would see that they would not get paid much, not even minimum wage at times.[26] I could see that their income was barely enough to pay the rent and bills. I used to get sad. I don't know why we have to experience these situations. . . . I didn't want them to go work all those hours and return so tired, and they would get up every day [to do the same]. I felt it was a big sacrifice for them. It is very heavy work.

Manuel was raised without *lujos* (fancy things) and never had expensive clothing. He was embarrassed that his clothing was stained and ripped, though he tried to talk himself out of it: "I would see myself and tell myself, 'It's nothing to be ashamed of. I am a humble person. It doesn't matter if one has expensive clothes or cheap clothes. It's the person that counts.'" Poverty matured Manuel at a young age, and this informed his resilience: "Poverty makes you a strong person. When something hurts, you grow up." It also isolated him in the Ivy League. Most of his peers at college were from highly privileged backgrounds and did not find college as difficult as he did. They were not intimidated by the academic rigor and they fit in socially. Nonetheless, Manuel drew on his poverty and upbringing in the inner city to survive, characterizing his background as a source of strength. If he had grown up differently, "I would have been too soft," he said. "Here [in South Central Los Angeles] *como que te haces medio duro* [you become hard/tough]."

Their upbringing in poor, segregated urban neighborhoods mattered in other ways for these young men when they found themselves in diverse college institutions or stepped out of their segregated contexts. As Loïc Wacquant explains, urban residents experience the "territorial stigma" associated with the criminalized inner city.[27] Elijah Anderson similarly argues that the "iconic ghetto" racializes blacks.[28] It was outside the segregated, poor neighborhoods that young men encountered subtle and blatant forms of racial discrimination often linked to their association with the inner city.

College-bound Cristobal had been protected from harassment on the streets by his older brother Felipe, but he had no such protection in the suburbs when he attended a summer baseball camp at a private college. There a predominantly white group informed the Latino and black youth that they were not welcome: "Hey, you niggers, hey, you Mexicans, go back to South Central where you belong!" Cristobal and his peers were taken aback by these white teenagers, who "were just too racial," and staff had to engage the college-bound inner-city youth in an open discussion of the race and racism that they were bound to encounter more openly outside their community.

These incidents occurred as these young men entered mainstream society. Fernando, who would eventually get kicked out of his college, was shocked to learn that white people on his predominantly white CSU campus "walk around with all those stereotypes in their head." In the first phase of the study, he said that racism was "not a big deal." He had difficulty recalling any experience of discrimination because he did not "bother to store it in my memory." However, his views changed with time. In college, Fernando became self-conscious as he and other classmates of similar background struggled in class presentations that revealed to everyone who was from "the 'hood." He felt different from most other students; this made it difficult to form bonds with others and led him to withdraw, as he did after trying to attend the engineering club.

The more time my respondents spent outside their neighborhood, the more acts of discrimination they encountered. During college, Fernando worked with a Latinx youth organization in Pueblo Viejo. He noticed that on field trips, "everywhere we went, the white people would just stare us down, like, 'What are you doing here?'" A restaurant security guard who assumed that they did not pay for their dinner had chased his group down when they tried to leave, even though they had paid upfront. Fernando felt that discrimination like this happened "every time I leave my neighborhood." He recalled the time his Pueblo Viejo peers were threatened on a high school field trip at a mountain resort near Los Angeles. He noted that whites there "kind of live isolated from all the different minorities, so any Mexican that shows up, they feel like they are being invaded." After being told to "go back where you came from" and hearing what sounded like gunshots, the group ran back to their teachers. Fernando "thought they wanted to kill us just because we were Mexican."

Like Fernando, Leonardo, who was also buffered in the neighborhood, arrived at college believing that all ethnic and racial groups were afforded the same opportunities to succeed: "We all have the same opportunities. If you want to succeed in life, you better try hard to succeed." His beliefs were quickly put to the test: no matter how hard he studied, Leonardo kept getting Cs in his classes and was finding it hard to excel. By the follow-up study, Leonardo had shifted his perspective. Not only was the magnet student academically unprepared, but on his CSU campus he learned to avoid certain phrases to avoid sounding "ghetto." On his diverse campus, racial distinctions mattered all of a sudden—it was there that he was introduced to the concept of "acting white" and heard people of color described as "coconuts" or "Twinkies." He disliked ethnic labels and defensively identified as "human." Leonardo did not articulate it, but he was wrestling with being racialized. It was in college that he witnessed a blatant form of prejudice for the first time, when someone yelled at another student that she should "go back to your country." On campus, he felt criminalized by his peers and instructors: "You know, they might hold their purse a little tighter."

In his predominantly white, elite college town, Manuel was shocked by the many stares he received on and off campus. He heard racist remarks and experienced micro-aggressions. "I used to get mad," he said. "Why do they look at me? I'm just a person, why do they have to look at me as a Mexican instead of a person?" His fellow students were awed by his background but also suspicious of it. "People think that all of us [from the inner city] are the same," Manuel said with frustration. He came to understand that many people saw him as potentially criminal, and in frustration he shaved his head, reinforcing the image of a gang-affiliated young man—which was far from accurate. He reasoned, "I'm going to give them a reason to look at me."

By the time young men who went to the university reached their mid to late twenties, their experiences of classism and racism had shifted their perception of America's opportunity structure. Much more consistently exposed to white spaces than the rest of the young men in the sample, they came to understand that racism was not inconsequential and that the American opportunity structure privileged some over others. Unlike Efrain, who questioned why he was often stopped by police, Fernando, for example, was quick to label the policing in his neighborhood as racial profiling. Fernando was certain that it was prejudice that led police to be unnecessarily aggressive the day they "kicked his legs apart" and "smashed his fingers against the wall"; they suspected him of engaging in criminal activity when he was simply leaning into a car window to provide the passengers with directions. Fernando was also convinced that racial stereotypes affected Latinos' opportunities. He explained: "I feel like Mexicans do have it harder; even to succeed, you got to overcome people's prejudice because people are going to judge you."

Such experiences affected how some young Latino men navigated the labor market. After graduating, Manuel was hesitant to seek employment in "white areas"; he felt "judged" there, he said, "in the sense of skin color, the way you talk, everything." While Manuel had some fond memories of college, his time there had also been traumatic, and this trauma lingered years later. He noted that racism and classism were "just reality in America" and said that he felt safe seeking work only around his urban neighborhood. This limitation severely restricted his opportunities. When I first met him, he said, "I have this feeling that I never want to leave Central City. . . . In some places they make you feel less than."

Another young man from Central City, Alex, a dark, brown-skinned young man like Manuel, also avoided searching for work in certain parts of the city. Alex was raised by his grandparents, Timoteo and Estela, who told me that he had a developmental disability that made him "slow" and prone to acting younger than his age; "he's like a boy," they said. It was unclear whether Alex was ever diagnosed, and he graduated from high school not knowing how to read. His illiteracy made finding work difficult, and he sought help from a community organization linking youth to jobs. Timoteo taught Alex the value of hard work from a young age, and Alex was open to most jobs, especially if "he could work with his hands." When I suggested searching for a job in a diverse part of Los Angeles that was accessible via public transit, he shook his head and said that, since it was mostly all-white, he probably would not be offered a job. Mimicking a stereotyped form of white speech, he expressed what he thought he would hear: "Ah, oh my gawwd! Um, no—there are no jobs. Sorry." Instead, Alex turned to the community organization and worked occasionally at a local recycling center, convinced that he would be rejected elsewhere.

As it became clear that race and class factored into their chances of accessing certain jobs, these young men's views about American meritocratic ideology were shattered, to their profound disappointment. In this study, those hardest hit were "Dreamers": the undocumented young men brought to the United States as children and now enrolled in college. Undocumented young men faced the greatest barrier to upward mobility. Dreamers' resolve to get ahead in American society has drawn national attention, as it has spurred an immigrant rights movement, but the Dreamers among the study participants also commonly experienced pessimism and shattered dreams in their transition to adulthood.[29]

Bused out his neighborhood, Federico spent much of middle school and all of high school in an affluent school where he prepared for college. He was not eligible for in-state tuition or financial aid at the university, however, because of his undocumented status. His parents, Pricila and Osvaldo, urban migrants who longed to have family in Los Angeles, had placed all their hopes and dreams on their children. Pricila encouraged Federico to apply to a university instead of community college so that he would "be surrounded by people with similar aspirations." She reprimanded her son for crying when he realized how his status impacted the cost of going to his dream college. She explained, "I would cry when he wouldn't see me. Someone had to be strong. Apply [to college]. It doesn't matter if I have to work day and night. I don't care, but you have to go."

Federico was accepted to his top-choice college—a private university in Los Angeles—and the entire family beamed with pride. His parents refinanced their home to help fund his education. I met him when he was in his first year of college, and he was grateful and enthusiastic. Federico's rude awakening came after college graduation. He had a dual degree in urban studies and sociology but was unable to work legally in the United States. "There was this frustration of having a degree with a double major," he said, "and yet kind of falling back into the same working opportunities as my parents. I was just very, very angry and very sad. . . . It hit me. I was just faced with a lot of ambiguity. I was faced with a lot, a lot of personal struggle."

The psychological and emotional turmoil that arose as he came to terms with his undocumented status profoundly altered Federico's sense of the American opportunity structure. He said that he had gotten "disillusioned with the American Dream," which he felt was not "accessible to everybody."

> I think this country does provide opportunities. It is possible for you to achieve the American Dream of having upward mobility, but I don't think it's accessible to everybody. Honestly, I think I've gotten a bit disillusioned with the American Dream.

The determined among these young men who were U.S.-born called attention to other structural barriers to their social mobility. Leonardo earned a bachelor's degree in business from a CSU. Though he viewed graduating from college as his greatest achievement, he realized that his degree would not get him the job he once envisioned.

> When you go to college, you don't know what to do. It would have been helpful if growing up you had a role model, an idea of what you want to do. I didn't know anybody that worked in the finance district to help me, guide me on what to do, what to study, where to go.

Leonardo did not transition to the labor market as he had envisioned. After graduation, he worked full-time at a bank where he hoped to climb the occupational ladder. He was shuffled to various branches and became a "lobby leader," responsible for managing the floor of the bank. Although he had many responsibilities, including filling in for the district manager at times, he only earned $16 an hour. The twenty-six-year-old became frustrated at being passed over for managerial positions.

Feeling that he had reached a ceiling in his growth at the bank, Leonardo demoted himself to a part-time position at the local bank near Central City in order to pursue insurance certifications. He then took a part-time position at an insurance agency, where he hoped to build his career selling life, auto, home, and rental insurance. Leonardo came to terms with the fact that his bachelor's degree was not going to propel him forward. As he explained, his college degree had not purchased much: "First of all, in the bank, I worked my way up. With the insurance, yes, it helps if you have some knowledge, but we don't necessarily need [a college degree] because we're going to take [online] classes for that specific field [certification]." Given where he was, he figured he could have skipped college altogether.

"I Don't Give Up:" Falling Back on Kin Ties

Determined young men learned that hard work and higher education did not guarantee entry into the American middle class. They recognized the significant structural barriers to getting ahead—whether it was poverty, class, race, undocumented status, or a lack of social networks. Even though they came to terms with America's constrained opportunity structure in a period of disillusionment, they maintained a strong conviction that they would succeed. Rather than sink into despair as they struggled in the labor market, they bounced back in the face of structural inequalities, determined to persevere and succeed against the odds. This faith in their own ability to overcome significant barriers stemmed from the same support structure that gave others hope and optimism.

The determined fell back on kin ties as much as any other young men, and their kin-based social capital bolstered their perseverance. These young men also continued to live with kin, and the support they received at home was extensive; as with those who were resolute optimists, their family's support alleviated housing and other costs, stretching their modest incomes. A single father with full custody—and the only father in this group—Manuel received ample support from his mother and sister to help care for his son. In other cases, the tight household arrangements strained relations. Yet intergenerational households were normalized among the families in this study. In particular, having unmarried young adults at home was congruent with immigrant family expectations, even though the arrangement developed out of need.

Determined young men received extensive support from their kin. Leonardo and his siblings were fully supported by their parents to pursue college, strongly discouraged from working, and encouraged to live at home. His father, Damian, wanted his children to focus 100 percent on their studies, telling them: "I'm never going to ask my children to move, and I am never going to ask my children for money." School came first. Leonardo's mother, Jesusita, agreed: "It doesn't matter if we have to work day and night . . . you will be supported by us no matter how far you want to study." This encouragement helped Leonardo graduate after six years in college.

Jesusita and Damian did even more for their daughter. Jesusita quit her job when her daughter gave birth to care for her granddaughter, who was born with a severe physical and mental handicap, requiring care around the clock. Jesusita did not expect pay; instead, she encouraged her daughter, a teacher, to return to school and obtain her master's degree, which she did. The family built an in-law unit on their home's lot, and Leonardo's sister, husband, and two children lived there. Together the two families covered the mortgage.

Jesusita and Damian's children reciprocated their parents' help. Leonardo explained, "My mom doesn't want [my sister] to leave. She's my mom's shoulder to lean on." When the Great Recession hit, Damian's work hours were cut. It was then that he turned to his children for help to make his monthly $3,000 balloon mortgage payment. Leonardo paid $500 a month. This was a great help to the family and affordable for Leonardo, who was still able to save for a vacation with his girlfriend. His twin brother stopped attending college when he got his girlfriend pregnant and he felt the pressure to work. They lived with Jesusita and Damian as well.

Only one daughter lived outside the home: Elvia, the Ivy League graduate, lived with her husband in a middle-class community. Elvia earned a degree in neurology but was working at an insurance agency's headquarters as a multicultural recruiter. In linking Leonardo to the insurance agency, where he intended to make a living, Elvia was also helping her family members to succeed.

Even if kin ties could not link determined young men to white-collar jobs, the support they provided was meaningful. Though his family was often frustrated with Manuel's periods of unemployment, they still extended support. Before he and his wife divorced, Manuel's mother-in-law helped him get a job at Target, where he worked for three years and was in charge of payroll, scheduling, write-ups, new hires, and balancing accounts. He was forced to quit when he broke his knee at a soccer match and "had to learn to walk again." Without his income, the young couple struggled, and their worsening financial circumstances led them to go "on welfare." Eventually they broke up. Without a job, Manuel had "felt useless" and let the marriage go. Desperate to provide for his son, however, he took his brother up on the offer of a job at his small garment factory. His brother initially paid Manuel minimum wage but slowly increased his income. The job entailed ironing designer jeans, putting on the buttons, tags, and labels, making sure the jeans were not ripped or stained, and then packing them in bags and boxes to ship them to designer stores. Manuel worked steadily with his brother for three years. Living with his mother and sister, sharing the cost of housing, and receiving their help with child care allowed him to save some money, and he felt that he was on track to financial stability.

Despite setbacks, the determined bounced back and stayed the course. These young men remained committed to succeeding, though it often took a form they had never imagined. Tenacious, these young men adjusted their definitions of success and revised their long-term goals to ones they could meet through personal struggle and perseverance. At his brother's factory, Manuel hurt his back carrying heavy fabric rolls one day and stopped working there. His income had never risen above $12.50 an hour. He considered teaching at a college and applied to a master's program in Spanish literature at a CSU, hoping he could become a college professor—though he was unsure how one got such a job or whether he would need a PhD. He discovered that having worked in the garment district for a living made discussing literature feel frivolous—a luxury outside the realities of the working class—and he took a leave of absence after one semester, opting to enroll in a real estate license online program instead. Manuel explained, "Instead of giving up, I've always tried to do something with my life, regardless if it's not the greatest thing in the eyes of some people. I've always tried to do something productive." He felt that his experience in college gave him a "tough mentality" because it took him "out of his comfort zone." He had told himself back then: "This is going to be real life. You're always going to be out of your comfort zone, presented with so many challenges, so the more you build that mentality to get back up and become resilient, the better it's gonna be for you."

Likewise, Leonardo remained hopeful that he could be "his own boss" one day and earn at least $70,000. He was set on acquiring additional licenses to sell various types of insurances to the Latino community, where he felt he could carve out a future.

As these young men expressed their determination to succeed, they noted that their immigrant parents remained their source of inspiration and kin ties their main support structure. In 2012, Federico explained how he pulled through the low point in his life:

> I was able to empower myself and be like, "What the hell am I doing here feeling all depressed? Look at my parents, they're undocumented." I've come to the realization that I'm going to continue living my life. I don't care if I am undocumented. I'm going live my life like my parents, happy. . . . I am going to continue, go to graduate school. I am going to do what I want, and I am not going to back down.

After graduating from college, Federico found a temporary job working as a union organizer, and he remained stubbornly committed to getting ahead. The Deferred Action for Childhood Arrivals program allowed him to be legally employed in Los Angeles and pursue his career goals. By 2014, Federico had enrolled in a graduate program at a top university.

Manuel concurred, stressing the important of his kin network: "I know the whole world says this, but it's true. My parents sacrificed a lot. They risked their life crossing the border." Despite all his setbacks, Manuel stayed the course, noting that his father, now deceased, had worked too hard to get out of rural poverty in Mexico for him to give up. Like other young men, Manuel also looked back at his father's starting point and praised his accomplishments.

> He had ten of us. We always had food, clothing, and we received schooling. He never went to school; neither did my mom. Nonetheless, he came here, and he bought the house where I now live. He bought it! He was making minimum wage! Yeah, I'm proud of myself to some degree, but my dad was in a much, much, much more challenging position than I was. I feel so grateful. Even though I'm struggling still and all these things have changed in my life, I'm very grateful. I think that's the other thing why I always keep going, because I always think to myself, "Man, Manuel, you were like on this little ranch [in rural poverty]."[30]

This realization helped Manuel stay positive: "I think a lot of it has to do with my upbringing and seeing where my dad used to work, and my family, because they all worked at factories. You know, they all came to this country from Mexico in search of a better life, and they didn't give up." Also, given his personal struggles, Manuel felt that he owed it to himself not to give up. He told himself, "Manuel, you always believed in yourself and that a day would come that something positive would come your way." Manuel did this every time he had a personal setback. As we walked out of the restaurant in the Latino middle-class neighborhood he aspired to live in, Manuel handed me a business card, suggesting that I or someone I knew could be his first client. Without any guidance, he had launched into the real estate world on his own.

"It's All My Fault": Self-Blamers and an Unforgiving Meritocratic Ideology

Angel, an ex-gang member, saw challenging days in his youth. Yet in 2007, at age twenty-two, he was optimistic and enthusiastic about his future. He was undocumented and had been arrested four years earlier. He could not explain why he was not deported then, but he felt that God had given him "a second chance." He found mentors in an organization that served ex-gang members, and they helped him find a job and an apartment to rent. At that time, Angel was as optimistic as any other young man in this study: "I've always been told you can do whatever the fuck you want to do in life. I don't see why not—whatever you want to do in life you can accomplish. It doesn't mean it's going to be easy." But at the follow-up interview, he was very different. He was a single father, recently evicted, with no job and still undocumented. He told me then that he struggled "not to give up."

I met the twenty-seven-year-old in the studio apartment he shared with his five-year-old son, furnished only with a mattress, a couple of blankets, and three dressers. He was focused on getting by day to day—"surviving"—and trying not to "mess up." He and his son had been recently evicted from an apartment where he had been renting a room. Angel lost housing assistance when he stopped attending a substance abuse rehabilitation program; he had developed a drinking problem. He had also been wounded two months prior by a gunshot aimed at a friend, and he now had a limp. Wiping his tears with one hand and holding a beer in the other, he said that the "only right decision" he had ever made was taking full responsibility for being a parent, something his father never did. Yet raising a child on his own was very difficult. "It's hard . . . because, like, nobody wants to give me a job. I don't have a driver's license; I can't get an ID." Angel received food stamps to provide for his son.

Angel had no car and spent most of his time in the neighborhood. He did not emphasize the constrained opportunities there to get ahead but rather his personal shortcomings. Rubbing his knee back and forth to ease its pain, Angel admitted that he had made poor choices, disconnecting from people who could help him, like his "positive friends" and the mentors at the organization where I first met him. He said he repeatedly gravitated to negative ties in his neighborhood and suggested that his mother, Sandra, was right: "I have to get my shit together." Doubting his ability to get ahead, Angel painfully considered whether he should relinquish custody of his son; Sandra already stepped in to care for the child from time to time.

Angel did not seem to realize how many fewer resources he had than others. He had arrived in Los Angeles with his mother when he was eight. They had followed his teen brothers, whose first nights were spent on the pews of a church; they had left their father and had no other ties in Los Angeles. Angel's family further fractured when he arrived home from school in fourth grade to find that Sandra had returned to Mexico. He would not see her for the next four years, and his older sisters, then in high school, took over parenting responsibilities. Angel credited his siblings for stepping up to care for him, but it was then that he joined a gang, juggling school as he "began to act sneaky." His siblings continued to struggle financially, and their ties became strained along with their limited resources. Unlike most study participants, Angel did not evoke an immigrant narrative of success or striving and perseverance; his undocumented brothers struggled to provide for their families. Growing up, he had not worked side by side with these men—adolescents then—and had not acquired the blue-collar skills others learned from immigrant kin. In fact, Angel's family hardly saw one another or spoke on the phone. Angel was mostly on his own.

While most young men in this study were "resolute optimists" or "the determined," a few in this study lost faith in their ability to get ahead. "Self-blamers" were young men like Angel who could not draw on a supportive kin network to get by or to help them cultivate optimism or determination. With strained or broken kin ties, these young men had minimal kin-based social capital, if any at all. Angel was among the most exposed to the neighborhood, and his risky behavior continued into his young adult years. Although he found an alternative social context through the gang intervention program, he was in and out of the program, repeatedly pulled back into the surrounding context that had him mostly locked in.

As the most socially isolated, young men like Angel, Salvador, Eddy, Ismael, and Valentin were the most entrenched in the neighborhood. At the same time, they fully subscribed to an unforgiving meritocratic ideology and an ideal of rugged individualism that led them to "self-blame" as they struggled to get ahead and to become demoralized. Chastising themselves for not having the ability to get ahead, self-blamers contrasted sharply with the theorized "oppositional pessimists"—who were nonexistent in this study—who feel that life is "stacked against them." They were just as pessimistic as such theories suggest, but they blamed themselves.

Alone: Transitioning to Adulthood without Social Support

Social support for second-generation Latinos ebbs and flows over their life course. Some young men, like Benjamin, were once isolated and highly entrenched in neighborhood conflicts but found support through kin and community institutions that helped them transition successfully out of gang activities and into the labor market. Other young men who were not as lucky experienced prolonged periods of social isolation. Ismael, who became addicted to drugs and spent his adolescent years in and out of juvenile hall, could not name any kin support ties, aside from his mother Rufina; he didn't have institutional ties to guide him either. Ismael had never had the opportunity to work as an adult because he was incarcerated throughout his teens and as soon as he turned eighteen. Rufina remained as isolated as when she first arrived in the United States. She visited her son regularly while he was incarcerated, but they shared a small world.

Other young men could turn to extended kin—siblings, aunts, cousins, uncles, or other relatives—in times of need, but self-blamers could not do so as easily. Angel longed for family when I first met him, and five years later he was still longing. His family was "never tight," he said. "We don't really get together as we are supposed to," he lamented. He and his son stayed with a sister and then a brother for short periods after he was evicted, but things were tense when he did. Angel's sister objected to his smoking, though he did it on the porch, and complained that he ate her food. His brother struggled to provide for his own family, and Angel felt that he was a burden. Sandra had moved back to the United States when Angel was a teen but already in a gang. In spite of the drinking problem she had then, she provided him with the most consistent support. While Angel was in rehab, his mother took care of his son. She did the same when Angel was shot and hospitalized, staying with him for three weeks during his recovery, and she found the studio apartment for him after his eviction. Angel's siblings could not help very much: "I think everybody is struggling, they don't have a lot of income." He appreciated Sandra's help, but noted that they often "butted heads"; she disapproved of his drinking with friends and insisted it was time for Angel to mature and think about his son. Angel was convinced that his family believed he was "not going to do anything positive with his life."

These isolated young men had no kin who could link them to work when they struggled. They could not lean on their kin as Efrain, Leonardo, and so many others did. They all grew up in public housing, and their housing as young adults was precarious. With his $8 an hour job, Salvador paid for his own room and his food, even though he lived with his mother. This was a source of pride, but he would have had a much easier time if he had free housing, like many of the other young men in the study. Valentin was never sure when his friend was going to tell him to stop crashing on his couch. Angel had secured housing over the years with the help of a community organization, but in the follow-up study he was behind on rent and on the brink of eviction again. None of these young men had cars, and they had little, if any, money; confined to the neighborhoods, they were minimally exposed to the rest of Los Angeles.

Self-blamers longed for the moral support and encouragement that others in this study often took for granted. Salvador loved his mother and respected her for being "a strong woman," but lamented the minimal encouragement he received growing up. "All kids need that, they need some support. Instead of telling [you], 'Nah, you can't do that,' and having someone telling us no." He wished that his mother had said, "You could just try it, try it, you know. You are doing good," and felt that children should have "someone to inspire us, make us feel good." Salvador felt that his family had low expectations of him: "I mean, it's worser than being dumped, it's worser than getting cheated on, worse pain. People that are in your house, [when] your family thinks the worse of you, it's like a pain. It'll go away, but you'll still be scarred, it's like deep, deep inside."

Their earlier entanglements in conflicts or delinquent behavior—drug use, drug sales, or petty crime—continued to affect these young men and strain their relations with kin. Valentin learned from a young age that he was not a good role model for his younger cousins, nieces, or nephews and knew this was why he was shuffled from aunt to aunt. Eventually, Valentin learned to stay away. He opted not to live with family because he did not want to burden them further:

> I don't want to put all those pressures on other people, on my family. They got their own kids. They've got their own problems. They're not going to benefit. I'd rather struggle. I know if I really talked to my family, let them know what time it is [they would extend support] . . . but the thing is, they've done it so many times. I'm already older. They shouldn't be doing that for me. They shouldn't be doing that anymore. I'm supposed to be trying to do things by myself. I just don't want to be more weight to other people.

Valentin liked living out of state because his gang involvement had compromised the safety and well-being of his family: "There's no leverage over there, 'cause whatever happens, I did it to myself. Right here, I can't do anything because it will come right back to them." These young men's engagement in gangs or drug use often led them to isolate themselves from family, weakening their support further. Drug users isolated themselves with their addiction, often engaging in petty crime outside the neighborhood. Valentin's son was the only relationship he cultivated, but he said, "My son has a way better opportunity in life and chance without me, and he's better off with [his mother]. My life is over. No matter if I'm young. My life is over, straight up."

Not surprisingly, with such strained and broken ties, these young men felt alone. Valentin noted that he "had nothing to go home to" when he lived and worked in Arizona. It was out of state where he earned the most consistent money working, but he felt a void. He explained: "Even though I made all that money, I went to shows . . . I still came home empty-handed. There was nobody right there." Even though there were people who came over to hang out or party at his apartment, "smoking, doing whatever [drugs] . . . the next day you're gonna come home to yourself."

Angel felt a similar void in his life and said that he and his son needed a woman in his home. Though his mother was critical of his behavior, Angel appreciated her visits.

> When my mom comes around, the whole vibe changes. There's food, there's good food, and it smells good. I don't know if it's the woman's presence, I don't know what it is, but the whole energy in the house is different. When it's just me and my son, I don't know how to make it feel like that.

Besides the warmth his mother brought to his home, she also provided Angel with structure. "When we're alone, it's kinda freestyle here," he said. He tried to be "strict," setting rules and boundaries for his son, "but sometimes I get lost." Angel longed for a wife or girlfriend to make his home complete. Even Salvador, who lived with his mother, confessed: "I feel alone. I don't mention it to nobody. I keep everything to myself."

The fragmented support available to these young men had deep roots. Most had experienced multiple forms of violence growing up, and this increased their distrust of others, including their families and themselves. Another isolated young man was Eddy, Angelica's firstborn, who arrived with her as a single mother. Eddy witnessed many acts of violence in the housing projects and had many gang ties. But even though he never joined a gang, Angelica noted that he grew increasingly angry over time. He was not only aggressive but also depressed, sleeping long hours and locking himself in his room for days. Angelica traced his smoldering anger back to an incident of sexual abuse by a neighbor when he was a child. She knew too well that he would carry this pain for a lifetime—she also had been sexually abused growing up. Though Eddy was well connected in the neighborhood, he became acutely distrustful of those around him. He had been grazed by a bullet walking to school, and his friend was killed only a few months before I met him. The nineteen-year-old explained, "I don't got many friends. I'm not really close to people." Teachers at school, he felt, labeled him as a "troublemaker" and rarely paid attention to him. So he stopped attending Pueblo Viejo High when he was sixteen because he felt isolated and uncomfortable. He felt disconnected from everyone:

> I was not mad, but I was like, what am I doing here? I didn't have nobody around me, like man, I don't even [know] these people, so why am I going to waste my time and trying to do something that I'm not into it, so I just left [school]. Something was wrong. I wouldn't go to class, I would walk around, like, what am I doing here? I was not comfortable. I was not feeling it.

The continuation school he chose to attend was no better. There he got in fights and was "mazed" by police. Eddy claimed that he had not dropped out, but little by little he stopped attending school and was "mostly at home," where fights erupted with Angelica over his joblessness and lack of schooling. His stepfather Gilberto linked Eddy to a construction worker who needed help, but Eddy missed work often and lost the job. Eddy had no other kin ties to link him to work.

Salvador was also well networked in the neighborhood, having been in a tagging crew and linked to gang members, but he kept no one close. Growing up, he also experienced multiple forms of violence and reported having no real friends now. He said, "I don't really get attached to people. Maybe we'll talk for a while here and here, but then you do your thing, I'll do mine." He worried about people backstabbing him. "Like I said, I don't keep any fools close to me because if I am too nice to people and they try to get advantage of it." Like Eddy, Salvador never felt connected to anyone at school; he too bounced around from school to school, making unstable friendships.

Valentin was most distrustful of himself. He was afraid he would "snap one day" and hurt a loved one.

> I guess when someone has so much shit in their head, all it takes is one look and you snap. You know right from wrong, but at the moment, you're not gonna think about it and you're gonna do it. . . . I'm scared I might do something wrong, to the wrong person that has nothing to do with it or anybody.

To avoid such a tragedy, Valentin became reclusive. "I hold my ground. I stay quiet. Stay home, trying not to go out. People don't understand that." He explained why he isolated himself from others:

> I try to stay away from people. . . . I get drunk and then I wanna stab somebody with a bottle or I wanna just literally beat somebody. . . . I don't know

if I have a soul. I don't know if it's pain or it's anger—those two combined? I see fucking *Criminal Minds,*[31] and sometimes I say, "Is that me right there?" I feel like I might do something wrong—that's why I isolate. I just like to be by myself—isolated. . . . When everybody comes, I don't drink. I say no. But as soon as everybody leaves—boom. I'm drinking and smoking and shit, so that if whatever I do, if I hit a wall, whatever, it's just right there. . . . I'm a little guy, but I know that I could really hurt somebody.

Valentin, who was on general relief and still crashing on a sofa at the home of his ex-girlfriend's brother, declined help from those willing to give him clothes or money, saying, "If anybody asks, 'I've been good.'" He added, "If I show my pain, people will just use it against me, take advantage and shit." It was for this reason that he refused mental health services; he was afraid of a diagnosis that might label him further.

Kin could not help self-blamers as they wrestled with substance abuse and mental health issues; at times their closest kin, including their mothers, struggled with the same conditions. Community organizations were one of the few sources of support for these young men. The mentors and father-figures whom David and Benjamin found in community organizations had transformed their lives and opportunities. The same organization that helped Benjamin move away from gangs helped Angel as well. It linked Benjamin to work and tutoring and helped him return to school before he became a father. The priest at the organization extended similar support to Angel, if not more. He helped Angel get his first apartment with a friend, and years later the priest enrolled Angel in different substance abuse programs. Angel could not think of one time the priest turned him away: "That's the main thing, always being there, supportive, showing his love, treating you like a son." The priest continued to help with rent and provided Sandra with money to feed Angel's son when he was unemployed, then linked him to work when he was ready for it. Angel knew that he had to go back to "his positive friends" at the gang intervention program, but admitted that he was struggling with depression and anxious about keeping his job. His son was acting out in school, and Angel was missing work because he was often asked to come in. He juggled work and parenting on his own, confident in his love for his son but unsure of what he was doing. Angel was just trying to get by day to day.

Reconnecting with the support structure of the community organization remained Angel's best bet to turn his life around when I last saw him, yet leaving the neighborhood to do so was difficult. Self-blamers were the most entrenched in their neighborhood of all the study participants. In their mid to late twenties, they essentially never left the blocks where they grew up. Their immobility—without cars and with limited resources—shrank their social world to a handful of blocks and made it easier to fall back on neighborhood peer ties when life took a downturn. Angel began to "fuck up" after breaking up with his son's mother and haggling with the courts for custody of their son. It was then that he moved away from the organization that had helped him. Instead, he said, "I was chilling with the homies and shit . . . doing different drugs." "Hanging with the boys" always put Angel "in situations where he could be either in jail or in a really bad jam," but he found it hard to break from these ties: "Those are the only friends I have, well, not friends, but people that I can go hang out with." Reconnecting with these old ties had led Angel to get fired from his job at the community organization—the only employer he ever had—and then to be shot in the leg.

The Urban Paradox: Segregation and Toxic Meritocracy

Self-blamers were young men who experienced neglect at some point, multiple forms of violence, and isolation—all factors that profoundly affected their sense of well-being. Yet these young men who were highly confined to the neighborhood were also tormented by shame that was often self-defeating: they were well attuned to the moral context of the neighborhood and understood where they fell in relation to the moral boundaries in the community. Self-blamers internalized this moral order. As much as any of the young men in the study, they subscribed to a meritocratic ideology and an ideal of rugged individualism.

When I first met Valentin, he was twenty-two years old and a strong believer in America's opportunity structure:

> I think anybody can make it. If you messed up, that's why there is a GED—just go to college and work yourself out. That's it. There's always a second chance no matter what, but you got to look for it. Never give up, no matter how hard it is. No matter if it's impossible. Just never give up and just keep on walking.

He was confident then: "All I know is, if I put myself into it, I can do anything. . . . It's all on you." Valentin took great pride in his community college status—it gave him a sense of moral worth—and he looked down on his gang peers who had no interest in college: "Nah, they talk about stupid stuff, like robbing banks and shit like that, gangbanging, making money the easy way—through slanging, balling, and all that stuff." Most of his gang peers did not graduate from high school, and Valentin didn't think they "could make it" in college. He said, "I'm not trying to be conceited, but I'm a couple of steps ahead of the homies." His college campus job gave him bragging rights: "I work, I get paid. I get financial aid. So when I go to the 'hood, I smoke with [gang peers], and they are like, '*Damn,* this fool is going to school. I wish I could be like him. Go to school and get money.'" Though Valentin had respect for his drug-dealing friends, who he felt held "one of the hardest jobs I know," he looked down on those in his neighborhood "doing nothing, just bumming it."

Young men's strong adherence to meritocracy led most who had dropped out to re-enroll in school at some point. Nineteen-year-old Salvador needed a car, but "I want my education first," he said, "because I can get the car any other time. That's materialistic, but myself, I need to worry about myself first." Getting a high school diploma would have been a great accomplishment for Salvador, the first in his family to do so. Schooling allowed marginalized young men to redeem themselves in the eyes of kin and the community. Valentin took criminal justice courses at the community college, hoping to become a probation officer, which he saw as a path to redemption in the community. As a probation officer, he said,

> I can be like, "I used to gangbang. . . ." Just tell them my story, about my tattoos, messed-up record. "But look: I'm still right here doing right." I can be an example that people still come up no matter how fucked up their life is, no matter how many things you go through, like you can still make it, if you put your head into it.

For Salvador, Benjamin, and Valentin, holding a legal job while selling drugs offered moral worth in addition to money. Salvador did not feel bad about selling drugs: "My mentality was and still is, money is money, hustle for your money. No matter how you do it, it doesn't matter how it is, but it's money," he said. But when he didn't have a legal job or a school to go to, he felt like "a bum, low-life," and he had "really bad self-esteem." He said that, at such times, "I don't have a life. I don't go to school. I don't have a job. I don't have nothing. I have nobody around me." Salvador's favorite job was being a cook's assistant at a restaurant, but he lost it because he showed up late and hungover. He got a job at a grocery store but had to stop working when he got shot at a party by a bullet meant for someone else and consequently was unable to lift anything for a while. He then got a job at a warehouse—but soon started selling cocaine there; he lost that job too. When I met him, he claimed that he was no longer selling drugs because the risk of prison, he felt, had gotten too high. He blamed himself for his poor work record, but concluded that anyone who tries hard enough can get ahead: "The only person that can stop you is yourself."

Valentin also blamed himself. He lamented, "I had the chance to be a probation officer. I had the opportunities to do it, but I fucked it up. . . . I already had the little [internship] tag and everything. Next thing you know, I just got caught up and my whole dream just fuckin' popped." While Valentin could have applied for Social Security disability benefits and he was already on the county's general relief program, he refused to do so, insisting: "I don't want to be home fucking doing nothing and getting money. I want to do something. . . . I don't like to take advantage. That's why I don't like asking people for help." In his late twenties, after all he had gone through, Valentin felt that

> anything in life is possible to do when you try. . . . The doors are open for the dream, for the big mansion, to be a baller. The doors are open. It's just the person if, if they motivate themselves to become a better person, to get the car, the house, and be responsible. . . . The American Dream is always gonna be right here. . . . It's just what you do about it and how. . . . It's just, it's up to me.

Opportunities in the United States were there for the taking, he believed, if only he tried to take advantage of them.

In a neighborhood context that identified some as "hardworking" and others as "not hardworking," where a meritocratic ideology reigned, self-blamers were highly critical of their choices, dwelled on their deficiencies, and indicted themselves for not taking advantage of presumably existing opportunities. For young men who had made poor choices along the way that compromised their social mobility, this was especially easy to do. In this study, no one was as harsh on himself as Valentin. In the follow-up study, we caught up over lunch at a Mexican restaurant in a working-class neighborhood near where he was staying. Valentin seemed uncomfortable as we settled in. He had a shaved head and wore a white, well-ironed, long-sleeved button-up shirt. He pulled his sleeves down and his collar up, repeatedly. I realized that he was trying to cover up tattoos; running up his arm and into his chest, close to his neck, they associated him with his ex-gang. These were the markings that police honed in on to identify gang members in his neighborhood—the markings that led people in the community to fear or disdain young men like him. He said that he wished he could have them removed so that he could have a "new start" and could "be free." Even wearing long sleeves made him feel more positive about his future.

Once he was ostracized by the gang, Valentin was no longer involved in gang activity and avoided arrest, but he remained criminalized in his neighborhood. He believed that it was his tattoos that led to police harassment:

> When the cops stop me and they see me tatted up, "Hey, this fool right here." They punch in my name, nothing. Look at gang files, nothing. So . . . they give me a fucking ticket just because I am riding a bicycle and I was going the wrong way. I haven't gotten caught up. . . . I've been clean for three years, but no matter what, society's saying, "Oh, this fool's no good." . . . [The police] harass me—they want me to hit them and shit. But no matter what, each time I try to do good, there's always shit bringing me down. . . . That's why I can't function. Each time I try to do good, this shit just brings me down.

Valentin could not escape the stigma associated with his past gang life, and this weighed heavily on him. He felt that society had labeled him as a "drunkie, a druggie, or that fuckin' *cholo* that's no good."

Self-blamers were stigmatized in the community and found it hard to shake off the label of "criminal." Salvador tried to ignore the fact that community members saw him as a gang member, but recognized that he was always going to face discrimination: "It's stuck in their head, '[Those] fools that wears baggy pants, that wear shirts or whatever. They are *cholos*.' You know I am not going to change nobody minds." This labeling and stigma complicated their work search. Salvador felt dismissed on sight and was sure that potential employers threw his job application out as soon as he left. Valentin believed that he wouldn't feel discriminated against if only he didn't have tattoos.

Ultimately, self-blamers rationalized the discrimination as of their own making. Of police harassment, Valentin said, "I brought that upon myself. So like I said, it's not their fault. Come back to the same issue. It's my fault . . . I think of everything and everything just leads up; it's all my fault. It's all my fault." It pained Valentin to know he was doing nothing to get ahead. He said, "I'm just negative, you know? I don't try. It's nobody's fault. I know a lot of people, they get mad, they even give up on me 'cause I have so many doors open, but I don't do a damn thing about it . . . it's my fault. It's always been my fault." He repeated, "*Yo solo me estoy metiendo al hoyo, solo yo* [I'm putting myself in the hole, all me]."

Segregated in their urban immigrant neighborhood, these young men compared themselves to others in the neighborhood and drew similar moral boundaries, giving moral worth to "hard workers" and disdaining those "doing nothing." Undocumented, Salvador chastised the U.S.-born who had "lots of benefits" and didn't "take advantage of it," those who were "bumming it completely." He envisioned some of them as refusing to work. He tried not to get discouraged about his legal status, saying,

> I don't let it get in my way. There're thousands of people, millions, trillions, in the same situation that I am, and they are getting paid, they are making bank. They own their own house. They own their own cars and everything, so if they can do it, how come I can't? So [I'm] aiming, I am thinking high.

For Salvador, his undocumented status was not his biggest barrier or his master status, as Gonzalez suggests, but his criminal past was.[32] In these communities, help is extended to those who have moral worth; this includes the undocumented, but not those associated with criminality.

Insulated in their neighborhoods, self-blamers' point of reference was confined to their undocumented Latino context, one that reinforced the idea that opportunities abounded in the United States. Like resolute optimists, they were convinced that "doors are always open," and they blamed themselves for their joblessness and persistent difficulties. "I know I'm stupid," Valentin said. "I know what I got to do, but I'm not doing it." When he was offered a job, he heard in the back of his mind: "We didn't expect you to do nothing with your life! We expected you to be a loser." He said he sometimes wished that his ex-gang would just "shoot him already."

The Power and Deception of the American Dream

The American urban context is a place of paradox. Even as urban conditions and segregation deny urban residents opportunities and racialize them through its poverty concentration and criminalization, it also keeps the American Dream alive, lifting those who can fall back on a support network and punishing those who are on their own. The American Dream ethos minimizes the role of class and race and other forms of inequality in shaping life outcomes in the United States by privileging the role of the individual. Yet in a context of limited social mobility and rising inequality, those who can get by or get ahead rarely do it on their own.

Second-generation optimism is strongly informed by the immigrant narrative. Yet young Latino men in inner cities confront myriad challenges that impinge on this optimism as they seek social mobility. Those young men in the study who remained resolute optimists and the determined ones relied heavily on support from kin networks or institutional ties. Social support ties not only inspired and encouraged these young men during tough times but alleviated their hardship in concrete ways: by linking them to jobs, providing housing and child care, and subsidizing other costs of living. Social support was critical in the transition to adulthood for the young men in the study. It gave them hope and reinforced their resilience even as they were forced to come to terms with their constrained opportunities in a highly unequal society.

As discussed in chapters 5 and 6, segregation structured the social isolation of young men in this study. Here I have shown that it impacts their point of reference as they gauged America's opportunity structure. Isolated, urban residents draw internal comparisons that shape their sense of possibility, success, and moral worth. Their minimal cross-class and cross-racial interactions with the American middle class, specifically whites, minimize their sense of disparity and sustain abstract notions of meritocracy. Shielded in working-class networks in these neighborhoods, the second generation can remain hopeful as they cling to the promise of the American Dream. The presence of the undocumented population in Los Angeles has an additional impact: most residents of immigrant communities recognize their concrete advantage over their unauthorized coethnics. This increases the moral worth of the immigrant working poor in these communities, placing additional pressure on the second generation to adhere to principles of willingness to work and struggle to get ahead. This immigrant co-narrative corroborates meritocratic ideals and individualism as the impetus for success.

Study participants who could lean on support ties were empowered in the face of difficult odds by adhering to the belief that individual effort could surmount structural barriers. Those young men who had no support and were stuck, isolated, in their segregated neighborhoods were left with an unforgiving meritocratic ideology that led them to blame themselves for their limited social mobility.

Self-blamers are among the most vulnerable urban young adult men. With few, if any, support ties, they are isolated within these neighborhoods, as well as marginalized and criminalized; they carry the brunt of the social stigma linked to the urban context as strong moral boundaries are drawn against them. Being shunned in these morally contested communities debilitates their spirit as they are stigmatized not only within their communities but by society at large.

Like most myths, the American Dream ultimately serves to prop up the existing order. Those who stepped out of the segregated context slowly became attuned to this as their ideology and their sense of meritocracy, once well engrained, were shattered by exposure to more blatant racial discrimination and to stark class disparities. Most young men in the study remained segregated in their urban neighborhoods, however, and clung closely to the American Dream, keeping it alive in a context of rising inequality. Even in the face of racial and class disparities, urban young Latino men who are supported by kin and communities ties remain eager to pursue the American Dream.

CHAPTER 8

Conclusion

How the Inner City Shapes the Integration Process
of Second-Generation Latinos

C hildren of Latino immigrants are successfully integrating into American society—a society that is increasingly unequal and whose limited class mobility ensures that only a few who start at the bottom of the class ladder will reach the so-called American Dream. Many factors contribute to this stifling trend in American society, but one of the most consequential features of our society is our spatial arrangement: where you grow up continues to strongly determine how far you will get in life.[1] America's rising income and wealth inequality maps onto the American landscape, where communities are vastly distinct from one another in opportunities and resources. Spatial inequality reinforces existing disparities, particularly for racial and ethnic minorities, who are more likely to live in communities of concentrated poverty. The concentration of Latino immigrants and their children in some of America's most disadvantaged urban neighborhoods profoundly structures their integration into the United States. As children of low-skilled immigrants, the Latino second generation already faces difficult odds in their efforts to enter the American middle class, given their parents' limited human, financial, social, and cultural capital, and the inner city increases these difficulties. Most will remain within the ranks of the working poor and working class, despite their great optimism, dedication to hard work, belief in educational attainment, and determination to fare better than their parents.

The Integration of Latinos and the Role of American Cities

Immigration scholars debate whether the Mexican-origin group is experiencing "assimilation" or "racial exclusion."[2] This debate discusses the integration process of Latinos against either a white ethnic assimilation model or the experience of African Americans, but this black-white binary simply does not fit. The stories of my respondents point to clear obstacles in their structural assimilation, but few in their acculturation. The young men in this study were like many millennials in Los Angeles: they were juggling work and school and had high aspirations to fare better than their immigrant parents. They were driven by an immigrant narrative as much as by America's sense of individualism. Yet race *and* class mattered for this group. Latinos' concentration in poor, segregated neighborhoods sustains their racialization, as does the flow and rhetoric around Mexican (and Central American) immigration. In Los Angeles, the Mexican-origin group has received a constant flow of working poor and working-class migrants for over one hundred years, and children of post-1965 Mexican immigrants are embedded in this class-homogenous ethnic community. These factors have aligned to create what Vilma Ortiz describes as the "permanent working class."[3] Among participants in my study, social leverage ties expanded their opportunities, while lack of social capital locked the most vulnerable into these neighborhoods and set them on a path toward chronic poverty. More generally, urban neighborhood processes interact with the social capital of young Latino men and the broader economic context to reproduce their class status.

Fears that the second generation would experience "downward assimilation"—that they would move away from school and the labor market—proved baseless. Young men in this study were firmly attached to the labor market, and many pursued higher education; few were disconnected. High school noncompleters struggled more than others, but even these young men remained attached to work. In general, respondents did not move away from the immigrant ethic of hard work, as Herbert Gans predicted.[4] Most of these young men adhered to conventional norms and were optimistic that they would succeed, or at least determined to do so. As difficult as respondents' lives were at times, despair did not emerge as a dominant attribute—rather, struggle and perseverance did. Their orientations were modeled in the everyday life of immigrant families and sustained by supportive kin and community ties. As others have found, most respondents fared better than their immigrant parents, gaining significantly more years of schooling and often better-paying jobs that were less grueling than their parents' work.[5] Such progress motivated the young adult children of immigrants but was not enough to improve their life circumstances in a context of flat wages and exorbitant housing and living costs. Rather than "second-generation decline," most of these young men experienced class stagnation.

Scholars' concerns about downward assimilation may have been overblown, but segmented assimilation scholars rightly sounded the alarm about the second generation's difficulties in getting ahead after growing up in poor, segregated neighborhoods. For too long academics have emphasized the role of an oppositional culture in the inner city as the driver for poor life outcomes there, as reflected in the rhetoric of the policy debates touching on urban poverty. Yet urban scholars studying poor African American communities disprove the myth, and I found that the second-generation Latinos in my study did as well. I designed the study to test the argument that exposure to racial minorities in the inner city would result in a "reactive identity" or a negative type of acculturation.[6] The racial-ethnic composition of the young men's neighborhoods, however, did not factor into their stagnation. Both Central City and Pueblo Viejo had high rates of violence and social disorder driven by gang conflicts; both had punitive high schools that offered low-quality academic preparation; and both were heavily policed and could have benefited from more community youth programs. The fact that violence in Central City was at times viewed through a racial lens only "brightened" the racial boundaries there, making cross-racial acculturation contentious, but negative acculturation, reactive identity, and oppositional culture were absent.[7]

As I laid out in the previous chapters, it was the violence and social isolation experienced by young Latino men in Central City and Pueblo Viejo that constrained their social mobility. Segmented assimilation scholars have underestimated the impact that immigrants have on these poverty-entrenched neighborhoods and the resources they draw on to inhibit second-generation decline. As I have shown here, social support from kin ties and community institutions ensured that most of the young men in the study did not succumb to the risks in these neighborhoods. These social support ties allowed respondents to get by and remain optimistic about their future, even as they faced obstacles. The urban context shaped their acculturation process in surprising ways, and their social isolation only reinforced dominant ideologies. Despite their stagnation, most respondents remained strong believers in the American Dream.

How Urban Neighborhoods Matter

To my knowledge, this study is the first to examine how urban conditions factor into the integration process of second-generation Latino young adults. That growing up in America's poorest neighborhoods reproduces poverty or stifles social mobility is not new; in fact, this is a consistent finding across many studies.[8] What is less clear are the neighborhood mechanisms that produce such outcomes, and here I make several contributions to our understanding of these social processes.

Urban Violence

Few scholars have considered the challenge that violence presents for building community. In fact, urban violence strongly shaped the "context of reception" for Latino immigrants who settled in Los Angeles urban neighborhoods in the 1980s and early 1990s, and it profoundly affected the integration of their children into the United States. Immigrants in this study settled in Los Angeles as gang conflicts became lethal. Not surprisingly, urban violence emerged as the most salient feature of their neighborhoods. Parents fiercely guarded their children against the threat that violence posed to their children's well-being and future. With an influx of immigration, Pueblo Viejo and Central City were in transition, the kind of communities that scholars find have weak collective efficacy.[9] In fact, the immigrant parents I spoke to had initially turned inward, becoming reclusive, but with time most established social ties, including with community institutions. My finding that establishing such ties ameliorated the violence in immigrants' neighborhoods supports the theory that as immigrants settle in a poor context, violence declines.[10] As immigrants put down roots, they also drew strong moral boundaries against gang-affiliated and disconnected young men, giving moral worth to those who were associated with a strong work ethic, like the undocumented population. Far from a homogenous oppositional cultural context, as some depict, these boundaries created morally contested neighborhoods for the second generation to navigate. Building ties over time and reinforcing conventional norms revitalized Los Angeles neighborhoods, but drawing moral boundaries also unintentionally marginalized the most vulnerable. As Rios explains, the criminalization of inner-city young men derives from multiple institutions in these neighborhoods, including schools, community organizations, and even families.[11]

My findings extend a growing body of research that calls attention to the long reach of violence.[12] As studies increasingly show, exposure to violence is one of the most damaging features of American urban neighborhoods. Although the young men in this study entered adolescence as violence was declining across the United States, all experienced some level of it in their neighborhoods. In some cases, violence caused lasting physical damage. More often the damage was harder to perceive, emerging in episodes of anxiety, depression, and PTSD that carried over into their young adult years. I found that urban violence curtailed the educational attainment of some young men in the study.[13] Those most exposed to the neighborhood and its violence got "caught up" as they drew on gang and crew ties for protection, becoming entangled in obligations and acts of reciprocity that damaged their schooling. For the most entrenched in these neighborhoods, conflicts and violence carried over into their young adult years, increasing their odds of criminalization and incarceration and complicating their odds in the labor market. My findings extend the work of others who find that violence affects the sense of security and the mental health of residents and contributes to poor educational outcomes and lower incomes for these residents.[14] In short, exposure to urban violence dampened the social mobility of the young men in this study.

Social Isolation

Past research has focused on the urban young men most profoundly derailed by violence and crime. But America's persistent segregation by race and class punishes even those who skirt or manage urban risks successfully, those who are not "caught up" in those risks. Such punishment starts with the isolation of urban youth in highly inferior schools. In their seminal study, Telles and Ortiz argue that the limited educational attainment of Mexican Americans is the linchpin of their racial exclusion.[15] Today, Latino children are the most segregated in school, and they are concentrated in some of the least resourced and poorest-performing schools.[16] High-poverty schools leave academically underprepared students behind, making a college degree unobtainable for many.[17] As others find, second-generation

Latinos cannot bridge this structural gap and gain access to institutions of higher education without the help of "non-family" ties.[18] More specifically, they need the help of "institutional agents" or social leverage ties that exist outside the neighborhood and kin networks.[19] In my study a few found those resources, but most did not.

Segregation limited study participants' access to cross-class ties, which are critical for the upward mobility of the Latino second generation.[20] Immigration scholars have emphasized the lack of class diversity in the Mexican immigrant community, contrasting it with the higher diversity in the Asian immigrant community, without referencing how American segregation shapes Latinos' experience. Segregation structures the social networks available to the second generation, and as a result they have little contact with individuals and institutions that might enable them to establish a middle-class life.[21] The social isolation of inner-city young Latino men shapes their experience as they try to access and navigate institutions of higher education and the broader labor market.

The social isolation that I witnessed makes me less optimistic about the future prospects of the Latino second generation than Kasinitz and his colleagues, who see institutions of higher education as providing these young adults with "multiple chances" to get ahead.[22] In fact, some respondents with a college education remained socially isolated, such as Manuel, who in fact obtained an Ivy League degree. A broken system of higher education in the United States continues to disadvantage those who come from poor urban neighborhoods because such students are rarely fully integrated into these institutions and therefore do not reap their full benefits in the form of the social capital so vitally important in the labor market. Young men encountered unresponsive institutions to their plight as first-generation college students—regardless of the type of institution they navigated—from for-profit and community colleges to elite universities. In general, young men struggled academically and socially, finding it challenging to connect with others, establish support networks, or access mentors. It was often at these institutions that respondents first encountered various micro-aggressions directed at their race-ethnicity, class, and upbringing in a poor urban neighborhood. In the most elite institutions, "doubly disadvantaged" students like Manuel experience a profound sense of alienation as they become acutely aware of their poor background in the midst of America's affluent culture.[23]

My findings suggest that, as others find, a "college for all" model is not enough for this new generation if support systems are not embedded in these institutions.[24] Several respondents found themselves feeling lost in the community colleges or vocational programs in which they enrolled, struggling to transfer or graduate with diplomas and certificates to improve their job prospects. These institutional gaps handicapped my respondents, who relied on these institutions not only to build skills and earn credentials but to expand their networks and opportunities. Few found institutional agents for support, and the others fell back on their kin and neighborhood ties, who could only link them to lower-income jobs. This disconnect from the "cliques, clubs and institutions" of middle-class society reflected these young men's lack of structural assimilation.[25]

Neighborhood Effects Moderated by Social Capital

My diverse sample allowed me to further examine what drove the differing outcomes of young Latino men in spite of growing up in the same neighborhoods. As damaging as violence and social isolation could be, not all of these young men were similarly exposed to the neighborhood. Researchers now give ample attention to parental income in these neighborhoods as a key dimension of risk.[26] I found that what mattered, however, was social capital embedded in strong kin or institutional ties, which alleviated the impact of urban conditions. Social capital and neighborhood institutions were woven in and out of the lives of study participants and enabled some to circumvent the effects of violence and social isolation.

The social capital of the second generation originates with their immigrant parents. Some young men's parents were rich in social support, primarily through kin ties, and others found support through neighborhood institutions.[27] A few lacked any form of social capital at all. Studies that compare social capital across ethnic groups overlook this internal variation among Latinos. Parents from rural areas in Mexico had deeper migrant roots and more expansive kin networks in Los Angeles than urban migrants, and thus more social support. Some could lean heavily on kin ties, and those who could not turned to community institutions, like churches, community organizations, or schools. Several parents sought the help of priests as they folded their families, including their sons, into their churches, which served as buffers from the neighborhood. Some parents sought the support of other organizations that kept their sons busy, away from the street, and in a positive environment, such as sports leagues or after-school programs. In seeking help, these immigrants and their children became integrated into their communities as they volunteered at times and families aided one another along the way. With less exposure to the neighborhood and its violence, these young men skirted the conflicts and male peer dynamics that could prove so detrimental.

Neighborhood institutions that young men could access without their parents' prompting provided buffering as well. School magnet and busing programs provided young men with a buffer from neighborhood violence, giving them an alternative social context and leaving them with less time to spend in the streets. These programs, often embedded in urban schools, provided them with information and resources through college enrichment programs. Programs like Upward Bound and other college-prep programs gave respondents access to institutional agents who worked on their behalf to ensure their entry into the university—an important first step, despite the pitfalls presented by institutions of higher education. Institutional agents also played a key role in the life prospects of young men like Benjamin and David after they were incarcerated. Both had been highly exposed to the neighborhood in their youth, but mentors in community programs helped them turn their lives around. Both obtained their diplomas and were strongly attached to the labor market. Although respondents' social networks were primarily confined to kin and neighborhood ties, those who were *consistently* connected to programs or organizations in their neighborhood accessed valuable resources, including mentors and leverage ties, that lifted their social mobility and life prospects and often strengthened their sense of community.[28]

Two institutions had a damaging impact: the criminal justice system and the school-to-prison pipeline. As a growing body of research shows, heavy policing and surveillance in neighborhoods such as Central City and Pueblo Viejo increases the criminalization of young men and their incarceration rates. These law enforcement mechanisms seeped into schools, where zero-tolerance policies punished "troubled" youth and often propelled them into the criminal justice system. Expulsions and ticketing further disrupted their schooling as these young men were labeled and isolated in half-day continuation programs that only exposed them more to the neighborhood, reinforcing the effects of violence. Schools, then, could buffer a select few from the neighborhood through magnet and honors programs, but expose others through its punitive policies, increasing the vulnerability of already marginalized young men.[29]

The high incarceration rates of second-generation Latinos in both neighborhoods must be interpreted in light of the punitive shift in American society that coincided with their adolescence, not as a function of negative acculturation processes. Getting entangled with law enforcement made young men's social isolation worse as arrests, probation, and fees locked them into the neighborhood. In looking to law enforcement to manage their sons, often to keep them out of harm's way, some isolated immigrant parents only entangled them further. Being identified as a criminal made it harder for young men to get a job, especially for those with no support ties. Besides its effects on those with a criminal record, the heavy policing of these communities has other ramifications. Wacquant explains that the urban poor experience "territorial stigma": they are tainted by the reputation of their communities as violent and full of crime as they navigate out of their segregated contexts.[30] And as I have written elsewhere, young Latino men's criminalization in urban neighborhoods reinforces their racialization.[31]

The Valuable and Fragile Social Capital of the Latino Second Generation

In contrast to how some immigration scholars depict the social capital of low-skilled Latino immigrants, I find that kin and community ties are assets for the Latino second generation coming of age in an era of rising inequality. A number of studies suggest that a general depletion of social capital in the broader American context has left isolated Americans, particularly the poor and working class, feeling alone in their efforts to get ahead.[32] In an era of government retrenchment and a context of concentrated poverty, Latinos' kin and community ties are a valuable source of support for the second generation.

As others have noted, the segmented assimilation argument was much too pessimistic.[33] In the case of Mexican immigrants, scholars underestimated the value of kin ties and their links to institutions and how these could inhibit "downward assimilation." To be fair, segmented assimilation scholars emphasized that close ethnic ties could impede downward assimilation, and my findings support this. Yet these scholars framed ethnic social capital through the ethnic enclave model, which does not apply to a group with minimal class diversity. By considering social capital as only deriving from cross-class ethnic ties, these scholars missed a valuable form of social capital: the social support that derives from "bonding ties." In the face of rising inequality and a neoliberal context that encourages individuals to go it alone with dwindling government support structures, the second generation latches onto kin support structures to get by.

Social support was critical for the second generation. In most cases, kin ties linked respondents to jobs and mitigated the impact of a challenging economy, alleviating housing and child care costs. Similar dynamics, specifically the practice of helping relatives get hired, have been documented among the white working class.[34] Yet there is an important distinction between whites and the Mexican community in Los Angeles: the latter has a large undocumented population relegated to exploitative, low-paying jobs. When Latino fathers or uncles were connected to union jobs or were in the trades, the second generation benefited. But most immigrants did not hold such jobs; instead, they worked primarily as cooks, gardeners, maintenance workers, and so on. Still, the optimism and determination of their sons were rooted in the social support system established by these migrants, a system that allowed them to get by as they faced adversity. The resilience of the Latino second generation emerged from their low-skilled ethnic ties. Not only did kin ties offer tangible resources—links to jobs, housing, and financial support to help the second generation survive—but they sustained the second generation's conviction that they would get ahead, against the odds.

Of course, kin-based social capital is no panacea. Heavy reliance on kin can be taxing and strain relations over time. In a context of limited resources and poverty concentration, kin ties are fragile and support at times unreliable. As Cecilia Menjívar notes, social support depends on having access to kin ties and a flow of reciprocity among kin.[35] If such exchange falters, social capital withers. Exorbitant rental and housing costs and flat wages result in higher rates of intergenerational households in these families, and such living conditions can strain relations over time. Housing and economic conditions in Los Angeles led several family members in this study to move out of the county or out of state to places with a lower cost of living and lower housing costs. The intergenerational household experience in these communities strained resources, raising the question: for how long can families lean on one another?

In this book, I have called attention to a rarely discussed group, socially isolated Latino immigrants. These migrants' social isolation was often rooted in their migration. While some migrants established kin ties and community ties in Los Angeles, others remained socially isolated decades after their arrival. As parents, these socially isolated immigrants, most often women, struggled to raise their sons on their own, but found it harder to shield them from urban violence and later to help them navigate the labor market. It was their sons who were most at risk in these neighborhoods. These young men navigated the labor market with few, if any, resources and faced the greatest risk of chronic poverty.

The Enduring and Shifting Cultural Outlooks of Inner-City Young Men

Following the young men in my study over time allowed me to observe changes in their structural conditions. It also allowed me to see how their views about the American context and their chances of getting ahead either remained intact or shifted over time, particularly as the country came out of the Great Recession. The cultural outlooks of inner-city young men are often depicted as static and homogenous, yet my respondents varied in their outlooks in ways that reflected their social capital and degree of isolation in urban neighborhoods. Their views also shifted over the life course as they stepped out of the segregated environment.

Most young men were optimistic or determined to succeed in the United States. Researchers have attributed the optimism of the Latino second generation to their immigrant background, and indeed, the immigrant narrative emerged as a powerful tool that parents used to motivate their children.[36] This narrative hangs tightly together, coalescing around the experience of sacrifice and perseverance in the migrant journey, and it informs the decisions of children of low-skilled immigrants. The immigrant narrative drives young men to aspire against the odds and permeates the cultural fabric of the ethnic community. But this study gives attention to the obstacles encountered by second-generation Latinos in their transition to adulthood that challenge this optimism. The violence and social disorder in their neighborhoods, their difficulties with higher education, the modest wages they earn, and the high cost of living can chip away at their optimism.

The optimism I find is similar to what other immigration scholars find among second-generation Latinos.[37] Beyond optimism is a belief in the American opportunity structure, and much like other urban scholars, I find that it is strongest among the most isolated in poor neighborhoods.[38]

The American urban context is a place of paradox: it sustains the concept of the American Dream, while denying urban residents opportunities to attain it. The immigrant narrative reinforces this ideal, even as it interacts with race and class. Studies on children of Asian immigrants show that they too hold strongly to American meritocracy. The "model minority myth" reinforces this ideology, which second-generation Asians respond to differently depending on their class and ethnic community.[39] In short, adopting dominant ideologies while also sometimes resisting them is very much a part of the integration process and becoming American.

In this study, segregation informed Latinos' views. Most of the young men and their parents compared themselves to other Latinos in their neighborhoods, not white, wealthier Angelenos, in considering their life opportunities and resources. In Los Angeles urban neighborhoods, undocumented coethnics gave those with documentation a sense that they had wide-open opportunities. Insulated from blatant forms of prejudice in their neighborhoods, most immigrants and their children could imagine a brighter future. Their immigrant narrative of struggle and perseverance reinvigorated the concept of the American Dream, which was well and alive in these neighborhoods. Their insular communities served as their source of resilience, even as they lacked the connection to the mainstream institutions that sustained their exclusion.

Most young Latino men in the study adhered to meritocratic principles and the ideal of individualism, though young men's social capital and exposure outside the segregated context would shift this outlook. Adhering to meritocratic ideals kept them optimistic in the face of great adversity, so long as social support ties gave them some tools with which to meet that adversity. In the absence of social support, this same cultural logic debilitated young men's efforts as they blamed themselves for their limited progress.[40] The segregated urban context is not toxic because it sustains nonconventional norms, but rather because it sustains a dominant ideology that extols individualism for members of society who are in effect alone in that they lack the basic resource of a support network to help them keep going.

In this study, young Latino men who acknowledged class, race, and legal status as structural constraints in American society were exceptions. My findings on these upwardly mobile respondents resonate with what Anthony Jack found among the "doubly disadvantaged": "college is less about embracing new opportunities than it is about discovering new constraints."[41] These respondents formed a distinct understanding of the opportunities available to them. They were nonetheless determined to succeed against the odds, drawing their fervor not from mainstream ideologies but from within the Latino immigrant community, where they found inspiration and support in carving out their space in American society and taking on the Dream—not as a promise but as a feat.

America's Policy Landscape of Integration

The successful integration of Latinos into the United States rests on a host of national, local, and institutional policies that profoundly shape the lives of these new Americans. Too often policymakers frame the Latino experience and their successful integration within the confines of the immigration debate. While comprehensive immigration reform is greatly needed, a different kind of polarization has set in that threatens the successful integration of children of Latino immigrants today: Americans now increasingly live separate from one another along class lines, a pattern that reinforces racial segregation, denies equal opportunities, and excludes Latinos from reaping the full fruits of their hard work and effort. National efforts to alleviate rising inequality and correct for class and racial-ethnic segregation, however, promise to improve the social mobility opportunities for Latinos. Inevitably, any such efforts must address America's stagnant wages and housing crisis that are making the number of high poverty communities grow and making it hard for many Americans to be financially and socially secure. America's growing inequality has put a wedge across communities, where only some can prosper.

Policy efforts to alleviate poverty concentration and the social isolation of urban residents are critical. Efforts to deconcentrate the poor, that is, increase class and racial integration, could expand opportunities for children of immigrants. At the time of this writing, the issue of deconcentrating the poor was being revisited at the federal level through housing relocation programs. Studies on the Moving to Opportunity for Fair Housing experiment of the U.S. Department of Housing and Urban Development have found that relocating the poor to nonpoor neighborhoods improves their mental health and well-being, increases college attendance and earnings, and reduces single-parenthood rates for children who relocated before they turned thirteen.[42] This is promising, but relocation programs have limited reach, and subsidized housing programs remain abysmally underfunded. Most families in this study did not receive such government support. Many were not quite poor enough to qualify, and others were undocumented. Moreover, relocation programs are not a silver bullet. First, by their nature they depend on maintaining low-income people as a minority presence in wealthier neighborhoods, keeping the status quo of spatial inequality intact. And second, such programs can disrupt the social support ties that I find to be so vital; as studies have found, some recipients of relocation programs move back to their old neighborhoods in order to access the ties that made it possible for them get by.[43]

An alternative approach is to invest in urban communities, from strengthening social capital through community organizations to improving schools and police relations and connecting urban residents to better-resourced networks and opportunities. Policymakers should not ignore the resourcefulness of these communities, but they should also be aware that such heavy reliance on support ties simply to get by is problematic and symptomatic of unaffordable housing, flat wages, and expensive child care and higher education. The social support of Latino immigrant families is fragile in a context of poverty and has its limits. In this context, community institutions are critical to the integration process of immigrants and their children and require infusions of financial support to keep them running and meeting the demand in these communities. Investing in social capital mechanisms is especially important for the most vulnerable residents. The depletion of institutional support—from government aid to community programs—leaves these residents fending for themselves. As important as it is to provide these communities with more support, a special effort is needed to create opportunities for their residents to access "bridging ties," or cross-class ties, that can provide information, guidance, and local mentorship to lift their job prospects. In other words, these efforts should enhance the prospects of structural assimilation, facilitating links to institutions and institutional agents that can expand urban young men's networks and leverage ties.

It is important that young men live in safe communities. Immigrants in this study and their children witnessed significant shifts in American cities with the rise, peak, and fall of urban violence. Lower levels of violence have been a much welcome change across American cities, but the reduction has come on the heels of another colossal shift: dramatic increases in levels of mass incarceration, which derail the wellbeing and social mobility prospects of many young men of color.[44] In stark contrast to stories of police neglect in Pueblo Viejo and Central City when immigrants first arrived, the young men in this study experienced ample police surveillance

in their neighborhoods and schools. Efforts to scale back the heavy policing in these neighborhoods and reduce the number of arrests and tickets
that disproportionately affect these communities can only improve the
incorporation process of second-generation Latinos. The hurdles to getting
ahead after contact with the criminal justice system are multifaceted. For
the young men in this study, contact with law enforcement led to increased
surveillance and mounting fees, and the loss of a driver's license was devastating to their job prospects in Los Angeles—it functioned to further isolate
an already vulnerable group. As others have shown, this link to the criminal
justice system often starts in schools, and it is vital to reform punitive
school policies that criminalize youth.[45] Evidence suggests that school-based
restorative justice approaches may be a promising alternative.[46] Another is
to dismantle zero-tolerance policies and remove police from schools, particularly in light of the much lower rates of violence these communities
now experience.

Of course, segregated American urban schools have many troubling
issues, particularly in their role as the primary institution for integrating
the children of low-skilled immigrants. One hopeful example is found in
the minority of youth who are provided the resources to transition into
universities. Although their academic preparation often falls short, as students learn once they get to a university, magnet and honors programs that
cultivate a "college peer culture" and simultaneously create peer support
networks and link youths to various institutional agents are doing something right to at least advance students to college—more of this is needed
to reach a wider share of urban youth. The problem is that when the baton
is handed off to institutions of higher education, they fumble it.

In a context of high spatial inequality, the successful integration of children of Latino immigrants will require significant changes not only of
urban schools, but of America's struggling institutions of higher education
that have the highest college dropout rate of any industrialized nation.
These institutions represent the most viable means to expand opportunities
for social mobility of the most disadvantaged. In a "college for all" climate,
educators have focused on trying to graduate students from high school
and enroll them in college, and this has been a success. Less consideration is
given to what happens when these students enter institutions of higher education. Latino high school graduates now enroll in colleges at higher rates
than white high school graduates. Yet most of these college-going Latinos
fail to graduate with a degree.[47] And those who do graduate face difficulties

gaining access to highly coveted middle-class jobs. As I show, the damaging impact of Latinos' segregation extends beyond their poor academic preparation in urban schools, as these young men also find these institutions of higher education—from community colleges to elite universities—difficult to navigate, both logistically and socially. These institutions are tasked with preparing the new generation for a changing economy and labor market. This not only involves building the skills of first-generation college students but also providing professional development and cultivating networks that can link them to well-paying jobs.

Unfortunately, the young men in this study encountered various pitfalls navigating these institutions, regardless of type, whether a vocational program or an elite institution. Young men remained primarily focused on passing their courses and struggled to find institutional agents and connect with professional development opportunities. As experts point out, there is a critical need to revamp counseling programs in these institutions. For too many students from poor urban neighborhoods, surviving the courses, culture, and overall climate seems nearly impossible. Universities and college campuses must make genuine efforts to address campus-climate issues that make these spaces at times unwelcoming for urban students, who experience microaggressions rooted in the ill perceptions of their segregated, poor neighborhoods. Moreover, programs with mentorship opportunities like internships help expand social networks. Even though elite universities have high graduation rates—about 90 percent—Manuel's story reveals that "doubly disadvantaged" young men at prestigious universities are not necessarily fully integrated, socially or institutionally.

College degrees and certificates yield the highest returns on schooling. Yet college, without institutional agents to guide urban youth, sets many up for failure. Those who do not complete their degree or who do not build networks may be worse off for entering college, given the burden of student loans, especially those who attend for-profit institutions. The "college for all" mentality aids for-profit institutions in exploiting disadvantaged students by obscuring the fact that the four-year college track and graduate school on average yield the highest returns.[48] Institutional efforts to open up paths of social mobility must be multipronged and cut across these institutions; these must include efforts to expand and strengthen existing programs that build the social capital of first-generation college students, helping them not just get through college but land good jobs. Gaining entry into institutions of higher education alone does not necessarily result in social leverage ties as young men in this study experienced various forms of exclusion in these institutions. The social mobility prospects of second-generation Latinos could be altered only when accompanied by meaningful *social integration* aimed at enhancing the social capital of this group. Absent these support systems, we will continue to see high college noncompletion rates and a "college-for-all" mentality will continue to fuel for-profit institutions that exploit the dreams and disadvantage of urban youth.

Institutions of higher education might explore place-based initiatives when trying to provide support for poor and first-generation college students. Some existing programs serve only the most disadvantaged students who fall under the poverty line, missing the "near poor" and working-class students who are also socially isolated, having grown up in some of the most violent neighborhoods and with the worst academic preparation.[49] Institutions of higher education must take seriously the drastic skewing of the playing field by America's spatial inequality and provide guidance and mentoring opportunities for students who come from the poorest neighborhoods and attended the most disadvantaged schools.

The successful integration of Latino immigrants and their children will require taking into account that America provides distinct geographies of opportunities. This requires accounting for how their racial segregation reflects Latinos' experience with racialization and exclusion. By the end of this study, Mexican migration had stopped growing, in response to not only economic conditions in the United States with its dwindling opportunities, but also to population changes in Mexico itself.[50] Yet Mexican-origin migrants, like other Latino migrants, were experiencing an assault on their communities—specifically on their families. Not only has the United States become hostile to undocumented migrants on an unprecedented scale, but it has specifically trampled on kin ties. The new direction in immigration policy under the Trump administration is not just harsh but inhumane, as it strips away from migrants the strong support system that allowed most of them to get by in the United States. At the time of this writing, there were millions of children of immigrants—many of them young adults—in mixed-status families in which the undocumented status of some members weighed on the prospects of the entire family, with lasting impacts over time.[51] Family reunification policies have come under scrutiny, children are being separated from Central American asylum-seekers, and the president expressed an intention to deny citizenship to the children of these immigrants. A more humane immigration system is needed for the healthy integration of all immigrants and their children, one that does not close doors but instead recognizes the value of keeping families together and creating opportunities for advancement.[52]

The Future of the Latino Second Generation

Even as Mexican immigration has slowed, the Latino population continues to grow. Inner-city Latino millennials are knocking on America's door, waiting to fulfill its promise. Children of immigrants are a growing and significant share of American society, such that their welfare will reflect the well-being of America as a whole. The story of inner-city second-generation Latinos affirms that the United States is structured in a way that limits successful integration for this group. The nation's persistent racial and ethnic segregation and poverty concentration inhibit the social mobility prospects of this new generation, challenging its ability to achieve the American Dream, even while most wholeheartedly believe and remain committed to this ideal. The American Dream thrives in the Latino immigrant inner city.

Latinos are now the largest minority group in the United States, and we are only beginning to learn how features of our current economy and its institutions are shaping the integration process of this group. Much of what we know about the urban context and its impact on social mobility focuses on the experience of poor majority-black neighborhoods where a substantial portion of families have lived in poverty-stricken conditions for generations.[53] *Barrios* have been a persistent feature of the U.S. landscape—and a testament to the challenge that Latinos face as they try to integrate. Mexican-origin people are concentrated in poor urban neighborhoods not just because of an influx of recent immigrants; as I found, both violence and isolation in the American urban context sustain intergenerational poverty and the class reproduction of the group. There is evidence that, as Latinos experience upward mobility, they become more spatially integrated with white, middle-class Americans.[54] Yet this has been slow to happen, as few Latinos rise. America's residential arrangements, characterized by persistent class and racial-ethnic segregation, stall Latino social mobility. Today poverty concentration is not just a feature of

American cities; in fact, poverty has moved into American suburbs, where many Latino families settle in large numbers, hoping to escape the violence and social disorder of the inner city and fulfill the American promise of a better life.

During the study, profound changes took place in the East and South Central areas of Los Angeles, including the two neighborhoods in this study. The decline of violence has improved the quality of life considerably. But the problem of crowded housing has intensified, and long-term immigrants now increasingly live in multigenerational households. Today several of the young men in this study are raising their children—the third generation—in these same neighborhoods. Their children are less exposed to violence, but they experience a greater presence of police. The threat of deportation continues to loom over many families in these communities. Respondents entered adulthood in the highly contentious Trump political era, when racist language is now used more openly. I suspect that this new context has awakened more of the young men in my study to these features of American society, shifting once resolutely optimistic young men into the camp of determined Latinos.

Gentrification will likewise have an impact on the group I studied, as well as on subsequent generations. By the end of the study in 2012 and 2013, Los Angeles, like many cities throughout the country, was experiencing an influx of affluent groups into its downtown, putting pressure on both Central City and Pueblo Viejo as developers came in and housing costs soared. Many Latino families left Los Angeles for its suburbs, and poverty followed them there; some moved out of the state, seeking a lower cost of living. Employment rates improved from the years of the economic downturn, but wages did not rise for the millennials. By the end of the study, Los Angeles was facing a housing crisis as rents and home prices soared out of reach for most workers and homelessness skyrocketed and spread throughout southern California. Isolated young men like those in this study are the most vulnerable in this era of neoliberalism.[55] In this political context, individuals are encouraged to go it alone, many resist "handouts" or government aid out of pride or shame, and the social safety net that could help them get by is rapidly disappearing. As such, the future of "self-blamers" seems highly uncertain. Valentin and Angel had precarious housing arrangements, and both struggled to provide for their sons. Salvador wrestled with his drug-dealing past and working-man identity, while Eddy was detached from school and work altogether. Ismael was already in prison, and he would be highly vulnerable to recidivism upon leaving. These young men faced the greatest odds of remaining in chronic poverty.

At the same time, high school noncompletion rates dropped to their lowest levels for Latinos, and their college enrollment rates soared. The young men in this study came of age in Los Angeles during its worst urban conditions. In their young adulthood, they faced the worst recession since the Great Depression and all-time high levels of inequality. Yet they remained hopeful and determined to succeed. *La lucha*—the struggle—continues.

METHODOLOGICAL NOTES

....

In what follows, I describe how I carried out this study of the lives of forty-two young men and their parents, across two neighborhoods and over time. The first phase took place when I was a graduate student, the second after I became an assistant professor. I describe how I designed the study, discuss the role of theory, and detail the practical and ethical considerations I wrestled with during the research. Longitudinal qualitative studies are not common, and while the scholars who study the children of immigrants are fairly balanced between males and females, the urban scholarship on inner-city young men is primarily conducted by males. I am a woman of color who identifies as Latina/Mexican/Chicana and comes from a working-class background. My particular perspective on the subject, though no better or more complete than other perspectives, is rare in the literature.

Positionality

There are strengths and weaknesses to being an "insider" or "outsider" researcher—and in this study I was both. I am a child of Mexican immigrants, born and raised in a Los Angeles neighborhood not too far, or too different, from those that I studied. When I returned to Los Angeles to do my fieldwork, I moved back in with my parents. When I timed it right, both neighborhoods in my study were a fifteen-minute drive—in opposite directions. I was very much at home.

As an insider researcher, I was comfortable in both neighborhoods and attuned to the social dynamics of the families and the rhythm of life there. I spent my childhood living next door to my grandparents and extended family in a working-class Mexican neighborhood in the L.A. Harbor area, near the port, surrounded by oil refineries and passing semi-trailer trucks.

There our family of five shared a one-bedroom rental. When I was ten years old, my parents bought a two-bedroom home in a neighborhood much like Central City, a black community becoming Latino. My peers in middle and high school were black and Latinx, and I was comfortable in that demographic mix. Our high school was ranked in the bottom tenth percentile in academic performance in the state. Metal detectors and security guards welcomed us every morning as we entered school. The 1992 Los Angeles riots had burned down local businesses, and our neighborhood was hard-struck by rising violence. It was sometime in high school that I came to realize that I lived in a special kind of place, one that often made the six o'clock news.

I share a similar neighborhood background with my study participants, but because I am female, I did not experience my neighborhood the way the young men in the study did. Growing up, I had male friends who got beat up walking to and from school. This happened to girls too, but not as often; it was usually catcalls that made our walks uneasy. There were many gangs and crews, but I was on the margin of these groups. I recall resorting to the help of some close friends in a crew once, when some boys began to harass me sexually in health class; the crew, who had built a reputation, made one visit to the class, warned the boys to leave me alone, and the problem ended. My friends from the crew fought regularly and described themselves as my protectors—not that I had any conflicts. I was invited to parties, but as a "school girl" who was heavily involved in extracurricular activities, I remained an outsider in their social world. I had none of this in mind going into the study. I had grown up earlier, in a different time, and theories about these neighborhoods now swirled in my mind. Going in, I knew I had much to learn from my male respondents—not only how they navigated their surroundings, but how they made decisions and envisioned their futures. My young adult years were spent on a college campus, but most of my study participants remained in the neighborhood as young adults. They were aware of my ignorance and kindly walked me through their daily routines, social worlds, thoughts, and everyday decisions as young men.

It is important that researchers account for their background, as it can create blind spots. It's telling, for instance, that I began my field research *not* anticipating violence. My parents' house sits on a corner, surrounded by apartment buildings. When they bought it, they did not know that it sat in the middle of a gang turf war. When I was growing up, there were many drive-by shootings near our home, several neighbors were shot and killed, and gang members frequently tagged the outside of our house, in huge letters. I moved out of our corner house to go to college in 1996, at the peak of the violence in Los Angeles, and I recall lying on my bed in my dorm feeling very lucky to be one of the few from my high school to be at a university. At the same time, I felt profoundly guilty. I was safe in a quiet, pristine suburban town while my family remained in the corner house. Who would yank my younger sisters off their beds to the floor when the back-and-forth shooting began? During my freshman year in college, our drug-dealing neighbor's boyfriend got shot in her driveway, a few feet away from where my sisters slept in the room we once shared. The later decline of violence made it easier to shove these memories deep down. I did not consciously go into my research expecting to find that violence would have an enormous impact on my respondents; only as it became apparent in my data did I begin to recognize its profound influence. I realized that I had not thought carefully about violence and had taken it for granted. Our lived experience informs how we approach our research, but not always in the expected ways.

I do not believe that occupying either position—being an insider or an outsider—should deter researchers from engaging with particular questions, but it is important to account for our positionality. It is important to recognize that respondents read us just as much as we read them, and who we are to them matters: it can open channels of communication or make it harder to build trust and rapport. My sense is that respondents opened up as much as they did—and more than I expected—because I am female; I was also nonthreatening because I was young and a student. The few who had heard of Harvard, where I was doing my graduate work, considered that a reason to respect my study. Most just understood that I had been in college for a long time, I was getting another degree, and I was from a nearby neighborhood.

Admittedly, I began my research a bit frustrated, feeling like the academic scholarship had given me an incomplete, at times distorted, interpretation of life in these neighborhoods. I was disturbed that so much scholarly and policy debate about urban neighborhoods concentrated on the culture of their residents. Study after study focused on crime and social disorder, painting a Hollywood picture of a toxic, homogenous ghetto that felt so far from the communities I knew. In addition to gang violence, my community also had thriving churches and community members trying hard to improve our struggling schools and our city. We had school walkouts to protest anti-immigration laws and demonstrated against police abuse and gun violence. My community, like others, was troubled and neglected, but also resilient and at times empowered.

I believe that no research is objective. Researchers ask questions, design studies, collect data, and then analyze their findings through their own lens. I once heard that people like me should not study our communities because we are too close to them. I'm thankful I did not pay much attention to this advice. Meanwhile, I hope that the ranks of scholars with backgrounds like mine will grow; we need these perspectives to fill holes, inform, complicate, and expand the conversation.

Choosing the Two Neighborhoods

I identified the two neighborhoods using census data. As tables A.1 and A.2 show, they were strikingly similar in disadvantage. In 2000, 37 percent of residents were living below the poverty line in both neighborhoods; ten years later, the share was roughly 32 percent in both neighborhoods. In California and Los Angeles, African Americans have a higher SES than Latinos, owing to the presence of a black middle class and a large undocumented Latino population. Yet in Central City, African Americans were more disadvantaged than Latinos on several measures, including higher rates of unemployment and single-parent homes and overall less income. These black residents were "the truly disadvantaged," to use the term coined by Wilson.[1]

The choice of the neighborhoods was theoretically driven. I chose two of the most disadvantaged neighborhoods in Los Angeles as the most consistent neighborhood predictor associated with various poor life outcomes is poverty. In the literature, neighborhoods of concentrated poverty are those where more than 30 percent of residents live below the poverty line; communities of extreme poverty are those with more than 40 percent of residents living in poverty. The segmented assimilation framework, which continues to dominate the study of the incorporation process of the children of immigrants, claims that exposure to native-born racial minorities in these high-to-extreme poverty neighborhoods drives negative acculturation processes that result in poor outcomes for the second generation.[2] Based on these different theoretical strands, I did my research on young men in two similarly high-poverty contexts that differed in their racial-ethnic composition. There are no comparisons across the two neighborhoods because

I found no difference in the processes shaping young men's lives; poverty concentration played a strong role; more specifically, what mattered was violence and social isolation.

Per the segmented assimilation framework, the ideal study would have compared the children of Mexican immigrants who grew up in an immigrant context, like Pueblo Viejo, with those who grew up in a similarly poor, predominantly Chicano or third-plus-generation Latinx demographic, who are presumed to subscribe to a "reactive identity." The census does not distinguish residents by generational status and national origin, however, making it hard to identify this group spatially. From what I could ascertain, this group was spread throughout the region, and any clustering was found outside the inner city. Moreover, immigrants and their children greatly outnumbered third-plus-generation Latinos in Los Angeles, begging an alternative question: how do immigrants affect native-born Latinos? To address these demographic and logistical issues, I opted to focus on Central City, which had a large poor black population, a community some scholars have long characterized—and many disputed—as sustaining an "underclass" or "oppositional" culture.

I gave both neighborhoods pseudonyms in an attempt to preserve the anonymity of my study participants, who were very generous with personal information, and most of whom continued to live in these two neighborhoods in 2012–2013 and may still. I also do not provide the names of neighborhood institutions in the two communities, although their highly valuable work should be recognized.

Selecting the Sample:
A Multiple Case Study of Young Adult Latinos

Whereas my two neighborhoods were theoretically selected, I selected the sample along diverse educational categories. I had a purposeful sample that included high school noncompleters, college-going youth, and those in between—high school graduates—from the same neighborhoods. One purpose was to not focus *only* on school noncompleters and those involved with crime—a population overrepresented in urban scholarship and one to which I knew the majority of the young men did not belong. I also wanted to capture young men on seemingly different social mobility trajectories, theorizing that if neighborhoods mattered, their effects would cut across these types.

Coming up with the right number of cases is tricky; in the end, I decided on forty-two. Several well-known ethnographies are based on a small number of participants, sometimes only five to ten people, but my study was different in several ways. I wanted to compare a range of young men *within* each neighborhood and similar young men *across* neighborhoods. I wanted not only to account for internal diversity but to ascertain whether respondents faced similar or different circumstances across neighborhoods. Thus, I needed to select enough types of young men that cut across and within these neighborhoods. I figured that I needed half of my cases from each neighborhood—twenty-one in each. I then sliced them across the three educational types in each neighborhood, ending up with fourteen in each educational category, half each from each neighborhood. I felt that this number of cases would give me enough depth across the neighborhoods and within educational categories. I intended to study these forty-two young men and their parents in-depth for a year.

To select respondents beginning their transition to adulthood, I determined that they would be ages seventeen to twenty-three. At the time, most studies on the children of immigrants and on neighborhood effects focused on youth. But I was interested in social mobility trajectories beyond adolescence. I wanted to understand just how far out in the young adult years the neighborhood mattered, and how. I found working with this age group rewarding; the older the young men were, the more thoughtful they were in their responses and the richer the data I collected.

Leaving young women out of the study was not a decision I made lightly. With more time and resources, it would have been great to include female participants, as I am aware that their experience in these neighborhoods and as children of immigrants differs from that of their male counterparts. Yet adding another source of difference would have made the study even more complicated. Diving deep into the lives of forty-two respondents and their immigrant parents was a challenging and enormously rewarding task; doubling the sample would have made it impossible. In light of research showing that young Latino men were having a more difficult time in school, in both inner-city neighborhoods and the labor market, I opted to focus on them.

Finding the Sample, Observing, and Interviewing

Having decided on my two neighborhoods and envisioned my purposeful sample, I set out to find my study participants: each would be male, a child of Mexican immigrants, between the ages of seventeen and twenty-three, and on one of the three educational paths. I began by tapping into my personal networks—ties who helped me link to people who lived and worked in both neighborhoods. Professors I knew who worked with these communities and old neighborhood friends linked me to teachers in schools, academic counselors, staff in community organizations, and families they knew. These new community contacts then helped me find young men who fit my age and education criteria. I also knocked on many doors on my own, meeting local priests who linked me to youth groups and staff members at various community organizations, from after-school programs to programs for ex-convicts. I visited high school classrooms and invited seniors to participate. I visited continuation schools, nearby community colleges, and work agencies in the two neighborhoods. Some of the people I met there linked me to young men from the community who had gone off to college and were living elsewhere. I was concerned that by finding my sample primarily through neighborhood institutions, I would miss the most vulnerable young men, the disconnected, but community members helped here as well. Knowing that I was looking for such young men, they pointed me in promising directions. For instance, a woman volunteer at one organization said, "Oh, I know a lady who lives down the street and has three sons. None of them have graduated from school." In following these threads, it was important that people in the community vouched for me.

When I gave my pitch about the study to these young men in group settings or one-on-one meetings, I asked to meet with them a total of three times over the span of a year and to interview one of their parents or guardians. I explained that I would compensate them for their time by paying them $10 for each visit. In the end, half of them declined the money. The vast majority of interviews took place in local burger joints or *tacquerias,* parks, or meeting rooms in community organizations or churches. Only on a few occasions did I interview young men at home, and these interviews took place outside, out of their parents' earshot.

I met many people while doing research, particularly as I moved in and out of various neighborhood institutions, negotiating access to community members and spaces to do the interviews. This process gave me a good window onto life in these communities and the kind of resources that were accessible to young men and their parents. In general, the community was supportive of my study and helped me along the way.

I included high school seniors on purpose. Not only were they beginning their young adult years, but I could capture more directly a slice of the urban school experience through these cases. School administrators gave me access to high schools and continuation schools, where I conducted observations and even held interviews during students' service period (a period dedicated to assisting staff at school). Given overcrowded school conditions, I interviewed a few respondents in a near-closet where one school kept a copier and there was just enough room for two chairs; it was a very uncomfortable place, but it was private. I got to know school security personnel, who gave me access as arranged, though on one occasion one guard tried to rush me into a class, yelling at me as though I were one of the students. Most staff did not know who I was or why I was there, and many commented that I looked young for my age; I seemed to blend in with the crowd of students. Some teachers slammed the door in my face when I tried to request time in their classroom to make an announcement. One loudly blurted out, "You don't want to talk to any of *these* students, they're all the knuckleheads!" Not least because of such interactions, respondents did not seem to associate me with school administrators or staff members, and I believe this perception made them more comfortable sharing their schooling experience with me.

Unlike many urban ethnographers, I did not hang out with the young men on street corners to see and learn how they navigated their environment. I recorded my field observations, but my primary method was the interview. The bulk of my data come from sitting down with respondents for several hours on multiple occasions, asking questions, and listening. In 2007, I was juggling many interviews with the young men and their parents across two neighborhoods. At each of the three interviews with the young men, I would dive into different topics: neighborhood experiences, their identity, their social relations, their thoughts about school and work. For two-thirds of the young men, I also interviewed at least one parent at least once. I was able to meet with a few of the young men more than three times. Each interview lasted two hours on average, but sometimes I spent half the day with the respondent. The scheduling was hectic at times. Doing three interviews back to back made for a long and exhausting day, so I typically did two a day. I tried to schedule interviews in only one neighborhood on a given day, but respondents' availability sometimes required traveling between them. That year, I carried out about 160 interviews total, having met with study participants multiple times.

Given my focus on interviewing, my field notes captured public spaces and interactions with community members working with my population of interest in the various institutions I approached for help. Once I had selected the study participants, my field notes focused on their surroundings, such as family members and friends I would meet, or respondents' social interactions in the community. As part of the study, I asked the young men to show me around their neighborhood on foot or by car; since we were in Los Angeles—and the inner city—most got into my car and navigated as they told me about their neighborhood, my audio recorder running as I drove. From the safety of the car, the young men pointed out long-established gang turfs and their boundaries, good food joints, places where residents engaged in drug use, places where fights often broke out, places where families ran everyday errands, places to avoid, places that were safe, and places where prostitutes walked the street late at night. Throughout the time I spent with these young men I bore witness to much of this and the constant presence of police in the neighborhood. These drives allowed me to understand not only the context in which these young men lived but the meaning they derived from their surroundings.

An Imperfect Sample

I took many steps and spoke to many people to find and identify each case in this study. When I finally sat down to interview the young men, with a signed consent form in hand, some revealed, quite casually during our first interview, that they did not exactly fit my criteria of U.S.-born children of Mexican immigrants—the second generation. With respect to nativity, I decided to adjust my parameters to include young men who were foreign-born, so long as they had arrived in the United States before the age of five; my sample thus included five who remained unauthorized even at the end of the study. Most had obtained their legal residency through family immigration policies or the 1986 IRCA legislation, and I ultimately found that including undocumented participants added to the study. In fact, this 1.5 generation identified as second-generation.

I also adjusted my parameters with respect to the original nationality of the young men's parents. It was quite amusing when the five interviewees from Central America reacted to my question about what part of Mexico their parents were from. These young men had volunteered for the study with a loose conception of the "Mexican" label. All noted that they were frequently taken for Mexican and referred to as such; they figured I was using "Latino" and "Mexican" interchangeably. Once I had them there in front me, ready to go, having answered some questions, I decided I might as well continue. The reality was that in Los Angeles, the Central American community has grown significantly and lives side by side with Mexicans, experiencing urban life similarly. As table A.2 shows, 16 percent of Pueblo Viejo residents were non-Mexican Latinos in 2000. This figure did not change much in ten years, and Pueblo Viejo remained primarily Mexican. Yet Central City was different. There 20 percent of residents were non-Mexican Latinos, and this figure increased to almost one-quarter of all residents by 2010. Most of these Latinos were Central American, primarily Salvadoran. I did not account for the distinct migratory experience of these five respondents, and that is a shortcoming of my study. The experiences of these Central American young men and their immigrant parents echoed the experiences of others in the study, but readers should recognize that the Central American incorporation process differs from the Mexican case, given their distinct migration history. Menjívar has pointed out in her work on Salvadoran immigrants in San Francisco that their social networks differ from those of Mexicans—being more fractured—and this may have significant implications for the second generation.[3]

Some young men turned me down when I asked them to participate, but this was rare. Most seemed to think that they would enjoy being part of the project and to like the idea of being of help to me. Some were disappointed to learn that I could not reveal their real names; their hope was that their own story would make it out into the world someday.

In the end, I reached my goal of identifying forty-two young men for the study, having expanded my categories as noted. Four of these young men became hard to contact after they committed to participate in our initial interview and ultimately dropped out of the study after some back-and-forth phone calls—including one respondent I dropped from the study after he made me feel unsafe at our first interview. I learned basic information about them and explored some themes of the study, but the bulk of the in-depth data in this book come from the thirty-eight study participants I spent hours and days getting to know over time. I did reach saturation: by the time I was interviewing my last respondents, I was learning significantly less.

A Multigenerational Study: Including Immigrant Parents

My initial thinking about including immigrant parents in the study was that they would provide me with the family's immigrant story, accounts of their initial adaptations to American life, and descriptions of how they managed the acculturation processes for their children. As it turned out, I learned much more than that from parents. I uncovered variation across immigrants rarely discussed in the literature; some of these parents emerged as much more vulnerable than others in these environments. The literature did not point to how much kin-based social support mattered, or the severe isolation of some immigrants. The role of kin networks became more relevant in the follow-up study when it became clear that most of the young men continued to live in intergenerational households and to rely extensively on kin ties. The follow-up study gave me a more extended view of these immigrant parents' incorporation into the United States, one that included their young adult children. This gave me insight into how these long-term immigrants were adapting to changing social and economic conditions in the country that were not only making it hard for them to get by but also making it hard for their children.

Most of the young men linked me to their immigrant parents and brokered my initial interaction, at times just by telling them that I, a student researcher, wanted to talk to them. Most parents were initially suspicious, but I clarified in person or over the phone, in Spanish, who I was and what I was doing in the study and why. It helped that I was a student. Some expressed pride in my university efforts as a Latina trying to get her degree; by contrast, others were simply not interested in talking to me at all. In some cases, it was unclear whether the young men had even tried to link me to their parents. Not surprisingly, the harder-to-access parents were those whose sons were having a harder time in school or the labor market. I eventually learned about these parents through their sons.

The parents who spoke to me were generous with their time and kindly opened their homes. On several occasions, I went home with fruits and vegetables from their gardens, and many of them said blessings over me. Like the young men, half of these parents declined the payment I offered, though all accepted the meals we shared as I interviewed them and the car rides. Some asked me for college information, which I gladly provided.

The parent interviews helped me triangulate the data with the young men's interviews and my ethnographic observations. Parents provided a different perspective on the neighborhood that provided a cultural layer that would emerge in the young men's decisions and orientations. Coupling their interviews with those of the young men provided a more comprehensive understanding of their communities and family life. The information I collected from the parents and young men usually coincided, confirming what they shared. In a few cases, I received conflicting information. Most often it was the parents who skirted around sensitive topics, omitting details that the young men openly volunteered. I respected these boundaries. At times parents volunteered information that the young men did not. In the end, most of these contradictions were irrelevant; what mattered was how immigrants and their sons were making sense of their circumstances.

The Longitudinal Study: Following over Time

I did not intend to return to the field and expand this into a longitudinal study, but it made sense when I started to craft the book proposal. The Great Recession set in a year after I finished the field research, and I felt that I could not write a book about these young men coming of age without accounting for the significant shifts taking place in the U.S. economy and housing market. By the time I secured funding for the follow-up study, I was an assistant professor and mother of two very young children, both under the age of three. I had limited time and funds, so I followed up with half of the original forty-two cases, making sure that these once again fell into the educational categories I created years back, and that approximately half came from each neighborhood.

This time around, I did not have to do the legwork I had done years earlier to get into these communities; I simply had to find my respondents again. Most of the telephone numbers I had used in 2007 were still effective. To find the remaining interviewees I reached out to my original contacts, the individuals who had initially linked me to these cases. This proved fruitful as well. Only one young man I contacted by these means declined to participate again, stating that he had no time, but I was able to find twenty-one participants as I had envisioned. This time I met with them only once to catch up on their lives and learn how they were navigating school and work and how the neighborhood had changed, if at all. I also wanted to mine their views about their future. I interviewed their parents again as well.

This time I interviewed most respondents in their home, but I also met them in local coffee shops or eateries. As working young adults, some with young families, they were more pressed for time than they had been in their early twenties. This time around most respondents took the compensation I offered, $30. That I was no longer a student may have made it more comfortable to accept the money. My new status as a mother mattered just as much as my new status as a professor; I had a new layer of commonality with parents, particularly the women, and they applauded my new job. The young men also gave me a new level of respect as a mother and a professor. Overall, respondents were just as forthcoming about their everyday struggles as they had been in the first wave. The story of their neighborhood, while still a part of them, had faded into the background as they struggled on a daily basis with their experiences in institutions of higher education or work. The interviews took a turn toward more adult matters: college and building skill sets, work, responsibilities, juggling family life, and commentaries on the economy, housing, and making ends meet more generally.

I found enormous value in the follow-up study, as it clarified how the trajectories of these young men merged into a shared working-class experience. Following respondents over time allowed me to see how trajectories that seem so certain can unravel or shift; life has many twists and turns. This highlights the problem with making projections from data focused on one point in time. Cultural outlooks are a case in point, as these are fluid, changing not only by context but over time as well.

Tricky Situations and Ethical Dilemmas

Qualitative research requires that we interact with other human beings face to face, often for an extended period of time, in unequal power relations. This will undoubtedly present ethical dilemmas. Is it bribery to pay respondents? Is the payment enough or too little? Could I do something for the community instead? What would be appropriate? Or would it be intervening in the study? How do I handle it when respondents cross boundaries or I feel unsafe? Can I actually do justice to these individuals' stories? What do I do if I witness or learn about criminal behavior or abuse?

It is important to manage expectations when one is out in the field. Respondents knew that I was there to learn from them and advance my studies, and that I hoped something good might come out of our interactions—and perhaps one day I would write a book about their lives. I never promised that my work would result in any kind of change, neither in their personal life nor their community. As someone with a privileged background—I was a graduate student and then a professor by the time of the follow-up study—I was looked to for help and guidance.

Parents more often than respondents sought my guidance in relation to college. I offered what I could, though I often felt that it was not enough; most of their sons were not following a four-year university path, and I knew little about community or junior college. Once I became a professor, some respondents got the impression that maybe I could pull strings in my institution to get them in. I was sorry to disappoint them.

There were times when I felt compelled to offer help only to learn that it was unwanted. Given what some respondents shared, I felt that they could benefit from mental health services, but not everyone had insurance that would cover such help, or thought it was necessary. I suggested a few programs and some respondents took telephone numbers, but most did not. They considered these psychic wounds a thing of the past, stated that they had no time for therapeutic programs, or openly voiced distrust. Graduate school had not prepared me to deal with people's serious mental health issues and psychological pain. At times, I was left psychologically drained—mentally and emotionally spent. It was hard not to feel their pain, and at moments I questioned my professionalism when I struggled to hold tears back. I have now concluded that we are not robots and expressing empathy is okay.

Luckily, most interviews were not so heavy, and what I had to guard against instead was letting the interview go off in some random direction. Several respondents were quite engaging and funny, raising the risk that our conversations could easily lose focus on the study. Being on the younger side when I began the study allowed me to connect with the young men more easily, but being almost an age peer also raised this risk of losing focus. During these moments, I would yank my interview guide out of my bag as a signal that we needed to get back on track. After the study ended, months or years later, a few respondents sought me out and requested my friendship on Facebook. By not accepting their friend request, I felt that I was betraying the trust they granted me, but this was a boundary I knew I had to maintain. I handled the situation by pinning it on institutional rules: "I'm sorry, I'm not allowed to be friends per university rules." I did message a few respondents, emailing them articles that I had published using the data. I also responded to those who emailed me with questions, maintaining amicable ties.

Managing certain boundaries in the field can be tricky at times. In the first wave, I learned to wear my engagement ring to preempt unwelcome flirting. Inevitably, I believe, some people will be confused by the focused listening required in an interview. Some simply chose to disrespect established boundaries.

With respect to criminality, I secured a "Certificate of Confidentiality" through the National Institutes of Health. This protected my respondents in case of a subpoena: the data I collected could not be used against them. I learned about some criminal actions but did not witness any. On one occasion, a respondent jumped into my car with a lit marijuana joint, leaving me unsure what to do, not least because having him in my car with the drugs left me open to arrest at the time. I let him stay in the car, and we drove to his place, where we sat outside talking. Another time a respondent was high on another substance and I opted to reschedule.

Some may wonder about safety in these neighborhoods. While violence has declined significantly from the peak years of violence, these communities, among the most disadvantaged in Los Angeles, continue to struggle with the problem of urban violence. Given the concentration of violence around the housing projects and certain apartment complexes, I opted out of interviewing there late in the evening. I did witness several police chases, helicopter runs, police with guns drawn, pocket-checks, and other forms of assault. As I did growing up, I drew on my common sense and stayed away. Yet during most of my visits, these communities were peaceful, and the busy streets were crowded.

Only on two occasions did I feel unsafe. One respondent, an active gang member, requested that we speak somewhere in private, and I drove to a lonely street on the outskirts of Pueblo Viejo. He was not only distrustful of me but carried anger—at something—and seemed paranoid. In that lonely street, this disturbed young man began to interrogate me somewhat aggressively; with no one in sight, a chill went up my spine. I carefully stepped back from the situation, downplaying the conversation and let him know it was okay if he did not participate (as he had committed to doing) if he felt uncomfortable. I dropped him off at home and concluded that for my own safety it was best not to interview him again.

The other time I felt unsafe was during an interview visit in the housing projects in Central City. Rufina, the only mother I spoke with whose personality I found abrasive, held open the door to her home while cursing loudly at a neighbor next door—about two feet away—who made the mistake of staring at us as I walked in. Clearly there was history between the two, and for a minute I thought I would end up in the middle of a fight between them. Closing the door, Rufina reminded me that one had to be tough in the projects or "they'll trample all over you." In the middle of our interview, her eldest son, a tall and muscular man in his early thirties and recently released from prison, came home, and he was not pleased to witness his mother answering a whole host of questions from a stranger. Rufina exerted control of her home, we continued the interview, and her son left the room, but as she stood at their doorway watching to see that I got safely to my car, parked across the street, he towered behind her, making sure I could see his expression, which let me know not to come back. Years later I would talk to Rufina again.

Interviewing and Analyzing

There is a distinct kind of data that one collects with observation that interviews cannot capture; the opposite is also true. I believe that my reliance on interviews, as well as my being female, led me to gather much more personal information than I anticipated. I loosely followed a semi-structured interview guide in each interview. Questions were organized around themes that the literature indicated might be relevant: the neighborhood context, social ties in and out of the neighborhood, identity and acculturation, and so on. Each young man provided a sociogram of his peer ties, which allowed me to visualize his networks and see how its organizational structure worked; I would use this tool as he discussed his social world. Caught up as I was in competing theoretical arguments, I had not foreseen that respondents would open up about other matters, unprompted.

I was unprepared to hear about various forms of abuse and trauma, stress, depression, anxiety, and even PTSD; all this is well represented in public health research on disadvantaged contexts, but such mental health issues were not the focus of my study. An interviewer needs to be a focused and empathetic listener. My interviews with these young men struck an interesting balance of them "schooling me" on what they felt I did not understand about being a Latino male in the inner city, on the one hand, while also serving as an opportunity for them to air matters weighing heavily on them, on the other. Something similar took place with their parents. Matters of trauma and mental health were tightly interwoven with each family's migrant history and lived experience in the United States. What they shared gave depth to how I came to understand the impact of urban violence and social isolation on urban residents. These deeper layers are harder to uncover through observation alone and are revealed only when people open up and share their stories.

Interviewing takes a psychological toll on interviewers, particularly when painful matters emerge. Self-care is important, as the stories we hear can not only pull on our heart strings and sensibilities but continue to haunt us years later. Establishing trust and rapport is not always easy, but it is key to collecting "rich" data and getting closer to unpacking the multiple layers in people's lives. Such trust also comes with a huge sense of responsibility.

During my fieldwork, I often felt conflicted when participants thanked me for listening, as many did. For some respondents—typically those who were rarely heard—this listening exercise, even when I offered nothing but an empathetic nod, could be therapeutic. I felt uncomfortable at times knowing that I was listening to collect data. In the end, I made peace with my identity primarily as a researcher, but also aware that I had served as a needed outlet.

In the end, I got to know the respondents well and collected an overwhelming amount of data. I was fortunate to receive financial support to help transcribe the 160 or so interviews I had collected, though I transcribed many of these myself. I entered the interview transcripts into a data management program, Atlas-ti, that allowed me to organize and sort through the data. Analyzing qualitative data, particularly with a longitudinal component, is complicated by the nonlinear stories and the contradictions or puzzles one has to sort out. In the first wave, I carefully read through my data innumerable times and coded these—that is, I looked for the emergent themes that I would carefully analyze across young men and neighborhoods.

Years later, I would receive financial support to conduct my follow-up study. Again, I did the interviews on my own, but this time I hired students to transcribe the Spanish and English interviews. I coded my data again, building from my existing coding scheme. Yet with the book in mind, and now with longitudinal data, I took a different approach to my analysis: I hired research assistants to help me produce case reports on each young man and his parents. These case reports allowed me to dive deeply into each case, explore the unfolding of prominent themes for each young man— neighborhoods, social relations, identity, outlooks on getting ahead—and capture how they changed over time. I then compared these themes across cases to discern similarities and distinctions among the young men.

It is my hope that I have done justice to the stories shared by those in my study. Writing this book took much longer than I had hoped, but I finally finished it thanks to the many people who helped me along the way. Graduate school was hard for me. Of all my cases, I identified the most with Manuel—we shared the unique experience of navigating an Ivy League university coming from similar urban neighborhoods; I understand well his sense of alienation. Had it not been for my parents and community, as well as caring mentors and good friends, I would have left graduate school. I share this as part of my reality in carrying out this study; I am in the end a first-generation and nontraditional scholar. I wrote this book while raising my two daughters on my own and trying to get tenure. While challenging, this entire project has been cathartic. It took me home, grounding me in more ways than one, reminding me why I left my community in the first place, why I so often return home, and why I keep going.

Socioeconomic Characteristics
of the Neighborhoods

I drew on the 2000 census to select the two neighborhoods along the dimensions of socioeconomic conditions and racial and ethnic composition. I used zip code–level data that encompassed several census tracts and a local high school. Respondents' understanding of neighborhood boundaries aligned with the zip code, though not perfectly. While these neighborhoods had experienced some change by the time of the follow-up study, they remained among the most disadvantaged in Los Angeles.

The Racial and Ethnic Composition
of the Two Neighborhoods

Almost half of the population of Los Angeles County was Latino in 2000 and 2010. The racial and ethnic composition of Pueblo Viejo, a predominantly Mexican-origin community, remained stable between 2000 and 2010. Central City experienced demographic shift as the Latino population increased 9 percent and the non-Latino black population decreased by the same percentage. In Central City, Latinos were Mexican and Central American, and both groups increased in numbers in the neighborhood during the study. With these shifts in Central City, a neighborhood that was black-Latino at the beginning of the study was one in which Latinos outnumbered blacks by the follow-up study.

Table A.1 *Socioeconomic Characteristics of the Two Neighborhoods and Los Angeles County, 2000 and 2010*

	FEMALE-HEADED HOUSEHOLD	MALES AGE SIXTEEN OR OLDER NOT IN THE LABOR FORCE*	MALES AGE SIXTEEN OR OLDER, UNEMPLOYMENT*	MEDIAN HOUSEHOLD INCOME*	INDIVIDUALS BELOW THE POVERTY LEVEL*
LOS ANGELES COUNTY					
2000	0.21	0.32	0.08	$42,189	0.18
Latinos	0.22	0.32	0.09	33,820	0.24
African Americans	0.47	0.40	0.16	31,905	0.24
2010	0.15	0.27	0.07	56,266	0.16
Latinos	0.20	0.23	0.08	45,706	0.21
African Americans	0.29	0.38	0.10	42,255	0.21
PUEBLO VIEJO					
2000	0.30	0.43	0.12	22,429	0.37
Latinos	0.30	0.41	0.11	22,942	0.37
2010	0.25	0.30	0.09	29,524	0.33
Latinos	0.27	0.28	0.10	30,710	0.33
CENTRAL CITY					
2000	0.40	0.41	0.14	22,091	0.37
Latinos	0.22	0.32	0.11	26,031	0.37
African Americans	0.57	0.53	0.19	19,065	0.38
2010	0.31	0.32	0.09	29,459	0.32
Latinos	0.24	0.20	0.07	34,288	0.33
African Americans	0.37	0.51	0.11	25,185	0.31

Source: 2000 and 2010 U.S. Census data.
*2011 five-year American Community Survey.

Table A.2 *Racial-Ethnic Composition of the Two Neighborhoods and Los Angeles County, 2000 and 2010*

	LATINO	MEXICAN-ORIGIN	OTHER LATINOS	NON-LATINO WHITE	AFRICAN AMERICAN	OTHER
2000						
Los Angeles County	0.45	0.32	0.13	0.31	0.09	0.15
Pueblo Viejo	0.92	0.76	0.16	0.02	0.02	0.04
Central City	0.52	0.32	0.20	0.01	0.45	0.01
2010						
Los Angeles County	0.48	0.36	0.12	0.28	0.08	0.16
Pueblo Viejo	0.92	0.78	0.14	0.02	0.01	0.05
Central City	0.61	0.37	0.24	0.01	0.37	0.02

Source: 2000 and 2010 U.S. Census data.

Longitudinal Cases

First and Second Waves

Angel, twenty-seven, unemployed. *Self-blamer.* The ex-gang member earned his GED with the help of a community organization. He struggled in the labor market, being undocumented. Angel had full custody of his son, but struggled to parent; he had a drinking problem, attended rehab, and was evicted. He lived on his own with his son and received support from his mother Sandra at times, but he was socially isolated otherwise.

Benjamin, twenty-eight, case manager at a nonprofit organization on skid row. *Resolute optimist.* The ex-gang member earned his GED in his early twenties and turned his life around with the support of his mother Rosita (an urban migrant) and a priest who linked him to a nonprofit organization that helped ex-gang members. He grew up in a family of twelve and was undocumented into his midtwenties. The single father earned $19 an hour, shared custody of his son, and lived on the outskirts of Pueblo Viejo.

Cristian, twenty-three, working for ICE. *Resolute optimist.* A graduate of a California State University, Cristian was juggling four internships, earning $15 an hour. He attended a local Catholic high school. His mother Josefina (a rural migrant from Guatemala) and stepfather divorced during the study, and he lived with his mother in the Central City area. He was single, had no children, and had applied to work for the U.S. Marshals.

David, twenty-four, unemployed. *Resolute optimist.* David, a recovered drug addict, sought guidance and mentorship from a boys' and girls' club in Pueblo Viejo. His mother and sisters were in and out of jail because of their drug addiction. With the help of close mentors, David turned his life around, received a GED, and trained at a firefighting academy for "at-risk" youth. He was determined to succeed. He was single and had no children.

Efrain, twenty-seven, unemployed. *Resolute optimist.* The school non-completer tried to earn a GED as a young adult but stopped after being caught up in a shooting outside adult school. The father of three lived with his undocumented wife at his in-laws' in Central City, blocks away from his parents, Dario and Ester (rural migrants). He quit his job at a hotel after three years and was interviewing for a similar position earning a bit more, $12 an hour. He was sure that he would be hired.

Federico, twenty-three, college graduate. *Determined.* Federico was bused out of the neighborhood to an affluent high school and enrolled in a private university in Los Angeles. The college graduate, who was undocumented, struggled to find a job. After the study, I learned that he became a DACA recipient, at age twenty-five, and enrolled in graduate school at a University of California campus. He was single, with no children, and lived with his parents Octavio and Pricila (urban migrants) in Central City, where they owned a home.

Fernando, twenty-seven, air conditioning company employee, college noncompleter. *Determined.* Fernando earned $20 an hour at the air conditioning company. Soon to marry, he felt pressure to return to college and earn an engineering degree; he was only a few courses shy of graduating. He continued to live in Pueblo Viejo with his parents Fidel and Mariana (urban migrants) in the apartment where he was raised. He had the most highly educated family: all of his siblings and his mother earned a college degree.

Genaro, twenty-five, hotel representative. *Resolute optimist.* The school noncompleter was unemployed for over a year during the recession before securing a hotel job at $17 an hour. Single, with no children, he lived with his parents Esperanza and José (rural migrants), who became homeowners after their housing project was demolished.

Gonzalo, twenty-four, aspiring real estate and insurance agent. *Resolute optimist.* The high school graduate, uninterested in college, hoped to make it big one day selling life insurance. He worked on commission, shadowing a Latino insurance agent whom he saw as successful. Gonzalo was single, had no children, and continued to live with his parents Rodolfo and Irene (rural migrants), who were homeowners in Pueblo Viejo.

Ismael, twenty-five, incarcerated. *Self-blamer.* Ismael was schizophrenic and a drug addict. He was arrested for drug use, theft and probation violations multiple times in his adolescence, and he had spent most of his young adult life incarcerated, having never worked. Ismael did not complete school. When out of jail, he lived with his mother Rufina and two siblings in the Central City housing projects. Rufina was the most socially isolated immigrant in the study.

Jaime, twenty-three, factory worker. *Resolute optimist.* Strongly attached to his crew, Jaime was expelled many times from school and never completed it. He was arrested several times for tagging and was on probation during the study. He lived briefly with his girlfriend, had no children, and was back home living with his parents Raymundo and Leticia (rural migrants), who were homeowners in Central City.

Jesús, twenty-three, community college student. *Determined.* Jesús struggled to get through college, uncertain what to pursue. He lived with his parents Katia and Hector (urban migrants) and received guidance from his undocumented aunt Sonia. She helped Jesús land a part-time job earning $10.75 an hour as a teacher's assistant at a local school. He was single and had no children.

Leo, twenty-five, school police officer. *Resolute optimist.* Leo was raised with two sets of twin brothers by his single mother Jovita in Pueblo Viejo. His father Luis (an urban migrant) was mostly absent. Jovita kept the boys active in sports, where they found community. Leo briefly attended community college but found his calling in law enforcement and now earned $54,000 a year. He lived with Jovita and his brothers, who together bought a home in a lower-middle-class neighborhood in Los Angeles.

Leonardo, twenty-six, part-time banker and insurance agent. *Determined.* The California State University graduate juggled his two jobs, earning $16 an hour. He had no children, occasionally traveled with his girlfriend, and lived with his parents Jesusita and Damian (urban migrants) in their Central City home. The family was well integrated into the community and ran a soccer league for many years. Leonardo was acquiring licenses to advance as an insurance agent and hoped to serve the Latino community in this capacity.

Manuel, twenty-seven, unemployed. *Determined.* The Ivy League graduate struggled in the labor market and was often unemployed. He left a master's program in literature at a CSU to pursue a real estate license. Divorced, he had full custody of his son, and they lived with his mother and sister in Central City. The most he had earned was $15 an hour.

Noel, twenty-four, construction worker. *Resolute optimist.* Noel struggled to get through high school but managed to graduate. He had no intention of pursuing higher education and was committed to blue-collar work. He became a full-time construction worker and lived with his parents Adriana and Vidal. His father helped Noel get into his union, and he earned $30 an hour. He was soon to marry and move out on his own.

Osvaldo, twenty-seven, animal control specialist. *Determined.* Osvaldo, a father of two, was married and earned about $70,000 annually working as an animal control specialist in a nearby county. He purchased a two-apartment duplex across the street from where his mother Rosa and his stepfather lived in Central City. Osvaldo earned an associate's degree and transferred to a California State University, but dropped out after two academic quarters when he was offered the county job.

Pedro, twenty-seven, electrician. *Resolute optimist.* Pedro left high school and earned a GED, worked at LAX for several years, and obtained an electrician's license through a for-profit college. He worked at a pharmaceutical company, earning $75,000 annually, and purchased a home in Central City that he rented out. He lived in an apartment with his girlfriend and her son in Central City. Pedro's mother and two brothers continued to live in the housing projects where he grew up.

Raul, twenty-six, Social Security office employee. *Determined.* Raul grew up in Pueblo Viejo with his single mother Dolores (a rural migrant), who eventually coupled with Ignacio. Raul graduated from a branch of the University of California. It took him three years to land his government job, in which he earned $50,000 annually and had opportunities for advancement. He had no children and lived with his girlfriend, a graduate student, and another couple in a middle-class, mixed-race community.

Rigo, twenty-three, LAX worker. *Resolute optimist.* Rigo, single and without children, lived on his own in a lower-middle-class city outside of L.A. County and had a two-hour commute to work. He graduated from high school and moved up at the Los Angeles airport, where he earned $54,000 annually. His father had been deported, and his mother Rocio (a rural migrant) eventually moved back to Mexico.

Valentin, twenty-seven, unemployed, on general relief. *Self-blamer.* Valentin grew up with relatives as a foster child and was living with his girlfriend by age eighteen. The ex-gang member earned his high school diploma in juvenile hall and enrolled in community college, but he was arrested during the study. Valentin struggled in the labor market and got on general relief after gang members broke his leg and he had to be hospitalized. He was single by the end of the study, and his ex-girlfriend had full custody of their son, whom he saw on and off.

First Wave Only

Alex, nineteen, unemployed. *Self-blamer.* Alex was raised by his immigrant grandparents, Timoteo and Estela (rural migrants). His father was deported, and his mother lived separately. He graduated from high school despite being illiterate and struggled to find work.

Alfredo, eighteen, community college student. *Determined.* Alfredo was an honors student who enrolled in community college instead of college because he lacked documentation. He was single, had no children, and lived in Central City with his parents Jorge and Martha (urban migrants), who had kept him and his brothers active in sports during their adolescence.

Bernardo, twenty-one, community college student. *Determined.* Bernardo got into several top universities after high school but was forced to attend community college because he was undocumented. He was authorized as a legal resident shortly after graduating but remained in community college and worked at a coffee shop. He was single, without children, and lived with his parents Flora and Marcos (urban migrants) and two younger siblings in Central City.

Cristobal, eighteen, senior accepted to a University of California campus. *Resolute optimist.* Cristobal was single, had no children, and lived with his parents Humberto and Alicia (rural migrants) and his siblings in Central City. They lived in an apartment building owned by his uncle Ramon and managed by his father.

Eddy, eighteen, unemployed. *Resolute optimist.* Eddy was disconnected from school and work. He never finished high school and lived with his mother Angelica and stepfather Gilberto (rural migrants). During the study, the family was evicted from the housing projects in Pueblo Viejo when his teenage brother was arrested.

Enrique, twenty, college student. *Resolute optimist.* Enrique was a full-time student at a California State University and worked part-time at a department store. He lived in Pueblo Viejo with his parents (rural migrants), who were retired. They kept a close watch on Enrique, installing a GPS system to track his whereabouts.

Ezequiel, nineteen, factory worker. *Resolute optimist.* This ex-crew member with strong gang ties stopped attending continuation school to work full-time earning minimum wage. He had no children and lived with his parents (rural migrants) in Central City.

Joaquin, eighteen, high school senior. *Resolute optimist.* Joaquin worked closely with his father in high school and was on track to graduate. He evaded gangs in the neighborhood and planned to work after graduating. He had no children and lived with parents (rural migrants) in Pueblo Viejo.

Julian, nineteen, school noncompleter. *Self-blamer.* This young man was an active gang member and highly suspicious of my motives. He emphasized his gang affiliation and was defensive about his school and work decisions. He was the only young man with whom I felt unsafe. He left the study early on.

Mario, seventeen, high school graduate. *Resolute optimist.* Mario intended to pursue vocational training as an electrician, following in the footsteps of his male relatives. He had no children and lived with his parents Claudia and Lucio (urban migrants) and other relatives in Pueblo Viejo.

Mauricio, eighteen, high school graduate. *Resolute optimist.* Mauricio lived with his parents Ramiro and Mina (urban migrants) in a crowded three-bedroom apartment with a total of twelve relatives. In high school, he worked with his father filming weddings and *quinceañeras*. He had no children and was enrolled in community college.

Nestor, nineteen, community college student. *Resolute optimist.* Nestor was a full-time community college student and was unemployed. He lived with his parents (rural migrants from El Salvador) in Pueblo Viejo with his little sister, whom he often babysat. His parents juggled several jobs to make ends meet.

Omar, eighteen, senior. *Resolute optimist.* This high school senior lived in Pueblo Viejo with his two parents (rural migrants). He was scheduled to graduate and planned to attend community college and to work. Unable to commit to the interviews, he dropped out of the study.

Ruben, eighteen, continuation school. *Resolute optimist.* Ruben, a crew member, had been kicked out of Pueblo Viejo High and enrolled in a continuation school, hoping to earn a diploma. Shortly after we met, he stopped attending school, and I lost contact with him. He dropped out of the study.

Salvador, twenty-one, factory worker. *Resolute optimist.* This school noncompleter was undocumented and earned minimum wage. He was raised by his mother Maritza (an urban migrant) who lost custody of her children at some point. Salvador spent a few years in foster care, and the family had a history of abuse. He was a recovering drug user, was incarcerated several times, and spent months homeless. He grew up in Pueblo Viejo but lived in Central City in his young adult years. His family was evicted from the housing projects after his last arrest. He had no children.

Sergio, eighteen, senior in high school, enrolled in military. *Resolute optimist.* Sergio was on his way to boot camp after he graduated from high school. He had no children and lived in Central City with his parents Isela and Carlos (rural migrants). He was strongly connected to the gang in his gang complex and saw the military as a way out of the neighborhood dynamics and a way to get ahead.

Simon, twenty-one, community college student. *Self-blamer.* Simon, once a magnet student, was a part-time community college student who also worked at sports venues, earning $10 an hour. He lived with his Salvadoran parents (rural migrants), his mother Brisa and his father, who was mostly absent and contributed minimally. He had no children and blamed himself for not advancing in college as most of his peers were doing.

Tomas, eighteen, community college student. *Resolute optimist.* This student was thinking of leaving college to enroll at an art school to pursue his passion. He had been bused out of Central City and was connected to the community through a youth group at church. He worked a few hours as a mail courier and lived with his parents (urban migrants) in Central City.

Ulises, eighteen, high school graduate, unemployed. *Resolute optimist.* Ulises lived with his parents Ernesto and Patricia (rural migrants) in the backhouse of the home of his sister and brother-in-law in Pueblo Viejo.

Wilmer, twenty, high school graduate. *Resolute optimist.* A Salvadoran American, Wilmer graduated from Central City High. He worked part-time and was enrolled in community college. I had a hard time scheduling him, and he eventually dropped out of the study.

Zacarias (Zach), eighteen, senior, accepted to a University of California campus. *Resolute optimist.* Zach lived with his parents Agustina and Ricardo and was close to his large extended family. His parents were trying to sell their home during the study but after the onset of the Great Recession were unable to do so.

NOTES

....

Chapter 1: Introduction: The Inner City and Second-Generation Latinos

1. There were 55.3 million Latinos in the United States in 2014, comprising 17.3 percent of the total U.S. population. In 2014, 35 percent of Latinos were foreign-born, and 65 percent were U.S.-born. Half of all Latinos born in the United States are children of immigrants (Patten 2016). Youth and young adults from immigrant families today represent one in four people in the United States between the ages of sixteen and twenty-six—up from one in five just fifteen years ago. Half of these 11.3 million young adults are children of Latino/a immigrants (Batalova and Fix 2011).

2. I use "Latino/a" when discussing the immigrant population, a common usage of this term in the immigrant community. Cognizant of more inclusive and shifting identities in the United States, I use "Latinx" when discussing the community of the children of immigrants.

3. Wilkes and Iceland 2004.

4. Pew Research Center 2011. While Latinos in general were more negatively hurt by the recession relative to whites and Asians, U.S.-born Latinos had a more difficult time recovering from the recession relative to the immigrant Latino population who is increasingly older and comprised of long-term immigrants (Pew Research Center 2019).

5. Millennials are the generation born between 1981 and 1996. One-quarter of U.S. millennials are either immigrants or children of immigrants, and approximately 60 percent of Latinos in the United States are millennials or younger (Patten 2016).

6. Anderson 1999; De la Roca, Ellen, and Steil 2018; Massey and Denton 1993; Rios 2011; Vigil 1988; Wilson 1987, 1996.

7. Brooks-Gunn, Duncan, and Aber 1997; Kawachi and Berkman 2003; Roux and Mair 2010.

8. Sampson, Morenoff, and Gannon-Rowley 2002.

9. Ainsworth 2002; Card and Rothstein 2007; Clark 1992; Crane 1991; Crowder and South 2003; Ensminger, Lamkin, and Jacobson 1996; Harding 2003; Pong and Hao 2007.

10. Chetty, Hendren, and Katz 2016; Sharkey and Torrats-Espinosa 2017; Valencia, Menchaca, and Donato 2002.

11. Camarillo 1979; Fox and Guglielmo 2012; Jones-Correa 2000; Katznelson 2005; Massey and Denton 1993; Ming 1949.

12. Chetty et al. 2014.

13. Pew Research Center 2015, 2016a.

14. Kneebone and Homes 2016; Kneebone, Nadeau, and Berube 2011.

15. Chetty et al. 2014; Chetty and Hendren 2015a, 2015b; Chetty, Hendren, and Katz 2016; Sampson 2012.

16. Fuller et al. 2019; Orfield and Lee 2007; Orfield et al. 2016.

17. Owens, Reardon, and Jencks 2016; Reardon and Bischoff 2011; Reardon 2011; Reardon and Owens 2014.

18. Scholars find that neighborhood contextual factors and school institutional factors explain the poor educational outcomes of urban youth. Increasingly, studies isolate or disentangle neighborhood from school effects (Ainsworth 2002; Briggs, Popkin, and Goering 2010; Cook et al. 2002; Owens 2010; Pong and Hao 2007; Rendón 2013; Sanbonmatsu et al. 2006), trying to ascertain how schools moderate or mediate neighborhood effects (Arum 2000; Goldsmith 2009; Johnson 2012; Sykes and Musterd 2011) or produce feedbacks into neighborhoods whereby contextual effects may offset each other or exacerbate conditions (Mateu-Gelabert and Lune 2003).

19. Rios 2011; Noguera 2003.

20. Sampson, Morenoff, and Gannon-Rowley 2002; Small and Feldman 2012.

21. Crowder and South 2003; Sharkey 2013; Wodtke, Harding, and Elwert 2011.

22. Moore and Pinderhughes 1993.

23. Bean, Brown, and Bachmeier 2015.

24. Ainsworth 2002; Crane 1991; Patterson 2015; Small, Harding, and Lamont 2010; Vigil 1988. In his research on Mexican American gangs, Diego James Vigil (1988) identifies socialization and "neighborhood acculturation" processes as significant in the proliferation of gangs in Los Angeles in the 1980s and 1990s.

25. Wilson 1987, 1996; Massey and Denton 1993.

26. Anderson 1999; Bourgois 2003; Contreras 2013; Venkatesh 2008; Vigil 1988.

27. Portes and Zhou 1993; Portes and Rumbaut 2001.

28. Segmented assimilation remains the dominant theoretical framework put forward to understand the divergent integration pathways of children of immigrants. The three segments are (1) acculturation into the American mainstream and entry into the middle class; (2) structural assimilation into the American middle class by turning inwards and relying on ethnic ties and ethnic enclave; and (3) downward assimilation into chronic poverty in the absence of strong ethnic ties.

29. Not all scholars believe that segmented assimilation occurs, and many question the notion of downward assimilation as applied to the Mexican-origin group as too pessimistic. Richard Alba and Victor Nee (2003) argue that today's immigrants and their children, Mexicans included, are likely to integrate into the American mainstream, as earlier generations of immigrants were able to do. These and other scholars acknowledge that Mexicans' progress has been slower than the progress achieved by Southern, Central, and Eastern European immigrants (Bean and Stevens 2003; Farley and Alba 2002; Perlmann 2005; Smith 2003). Some describe this as "delayed assimilation" (Brown

2007), while others adopt Gans's (1992b, 44) concept of "bumpy" assimilation, where the bumps are described as the "various adaptations to changing circumstances—and with the line having no predictable end."

30. Kahn 1987; Kasinitz et al. 2008.

31. Zhou 1997. As William Haller, Alejandro Portes, and Scott Lynch (2011, 737) explain, it is in the "worse sections of the city" that the second generation is exposed to "the proliferation of gangs and the drug trade that provide an alternative path to staying in school and completing an education."

32. Portes and Rumbaut 2001, 59.

33. See also Lopez and Stanton-Salazar 2001.

34. Gans 1992a, 173–74.

35. Rumbaut 1997.

36. Portes and Zhou 1993; Zhou and Bankston 1998.

37. The mode of incorporation refers to "the complex formed by the policies of the host government; the values and prejudice of the receiving of society; and the characteristics of the co-ethnic community" (Portes and Zhou 1993).

38. Rendón 2015.

39. Ortiz 1996.

40. Alba, Kasinitz, and Waters 2011; Kao and Tienda 1995; Lee and Zhou 2014; Portes, Fernández-Kelly, and Haller 2005; Suárez-Orozco and Suárez-Orozco 1995. Immigration scholars have come across a paradox: low-achieving children of immigrants are more optimistic than the high-achieving. Specifically, children of Asian immigrants often hold pessimistic views about their chances to succeed in the United States, while Latinx of more modest backgrounds look forward to promising futures. Vivian Louie (2006) attributes this paradox to the greater transnational experience of the Latinx community, stating that Asians reference the stringent U.S. "model minority" ideal in formulating their idea of success. Jennifer Lee and Min Zhou (2014) find that Asians adhere to a narrow "success frame," as measured by academic achievement and degrees, while an acceptable "success frame" for the Mexican-origin group includes graduating from high school, receiving some college education, and/or attaining a stable, blue-collar job. They explain that Mexicans take their low-skilled parents' starting point into consideration when calibrating their understanding of success.

41. Smith 2006.

42. Portes, Fernández-Kelly, and Haller 2005.

43. Alba, Kasinitz, and Waters 2011.

44. Kasinitz et al. 2008.

45. Lee and Zhou 2014, 2015; Smith 2003; Tran and Valdez 2017.

46. Lee and Zhou (2015) explain that most children of immigrants who acquire high levels of human capital—many of Asian descent—start off with high-skilled immigrant parents. Given Mexican immigrants' very low levels of human capital, their children make large gains even when they earn minimal schooling by U.S. standards.

47. Smith 2006.

48. Fry and Taylor 2013; Pew Research Center 2016b.

49. Cross-sectional studies find that third-generation Mexican Americans do not differ very much from, or are worse off than, their second-generation counterparts in terms

of education and income (Chapas 1988; Farley and Alba 2002; Livingston and Kahn 2002; Perlmann 2005; Perlmann and Waldinger 1997; Smith 2003; Tran and Valdez 2017; Wojtkiewicz and Donato 1995). Similarly, Edward Telles and Vilma Ortiz (2008) find minimal advancement in socioeconomic status (SES) between the second and third generations in their longitudinal study.

50. Telles and Ortiz 2008.

51. Portes and Böröcz 1989; Portes and Rumbaut 2001.

52. Portes and Rumbaut 2001, 49.

53. While only five young men in this study remained undocumented by the end of the study, some of their parents remained so, while others had siblings, partners, or in-laws who were undocumented. Some of the one-quarter of the young men who were in mixed-status families by the end of the study had coupled with an undocumented partner over the course of the study.

54. Martha Menchaca (2001) documents how the U.S. legal system historically has distinguished the Mexican population as a race. In 1848, the United States and Mexico signed the Treaty of Guadalupe Hidalgo ending the Mexican-American War. This treaty declared that Mexicans who lived within the newly annexed territory of the Southwest would be "incorporated into the Union of the United States" with the "enjoyment of all the rights of citizens" (Menchaca 2001, 215). Menchaca explains that, a year later, "the U.S. violated the treaty with respect to the citizenship articles and refused to extend Mexicans full political rights on the basis that the majority population was not White" (217). The United States subsequently began the "process of racializing the Mexican population and ascribing them different legal rights on the basis of race" (217). Menchaca defines "the process of racialization as the use of the legal system to confer privilege upon Whites and to discriminate against people of color. Under this legal process Mexicans who were White were accorded the full legal rights of United States citizens, while most mestizos, Christianized Indians and afromestizos were accorded inferior legal rights" (215). Other scholarship on violence and the exclusion of Mexican Americans as a racial group include Escobar 1999; Fox 2012; Gómez 2018; López 2009; Molina 2006, 2014.

55. Donato and Hanson 2012; Fox and Gugliemo 2012; Fox 2012; Gonzales 2013; Jones-Correa 2000; Menchaca and Valencia 1990.

56. Vigil 1988.

57. Rugh 2014; Rugh and Massey 2010; Turner et al. 2013.

58. Rendón, Aldana, and Hom 2018; Rios 2011.

59. Chetty et al. 2014.

60. Jack 2019; Rosenbaum, Ahearn, and Rosenbaum 2017.

61. Symonds, Schwartz, and Ferguson 2011.

62. U.S. Census Bureau, American Community Survey data from 2009–2013.

63. Chen 2015; Mazelis 2017; Putnam 2016; Silva 2013.

64. Lardier et al. 2019; MacLeod 1995; Young 2004. Scholars also identify the pervasiveness of this American Dream ideology among second-generation Asians. Louie (2004) discusses these views among children of Chinese immigrants. Others discuss this ideology with Koreans (Lee 2004) and other Asian groups (Lee and Zhou 2014) in relation to the "model minority myth."

65. Lopez, Morin, and Krogstad 2016.

66. The minimum wage in Los Angeles in 2012 was $8 an hour. By 2015, the city had voted to increase its minimum wage to $15 an hour, effective in 2020. Los Angeles County and then California followed suit in 2016.

67. Chen 2015; Putnam 2016; Silva 2013.

68. Putnam 2016; Mazelis 2017; McPherson, Smith-Lovin, and Brashears 2006; Silva 2013.

69. Researchers continue to examine issues of neighborhood selection (Sampson and Sharkey 2008; Sharkey 2012; Sharkey and Elwert 2011), but a significant body of literature finds that neighborhoods have an independent impact on life outcomes above and beyond individual characteristics (Brooks-Gunn et al. 1993; Brooks-Gunn, Duncan, and Aber 1997; Burdick-Will et al. 2011; Chetty and Hendren 2015a, 2015b; Kawachi and Berkman 2003; Leventhal and Brooks-Gunn 2000; Sampson, Morenoff, and Gannon-Rowley 2002; Sampson and Sharkey 2008; Sharkey 2012; Sharkey and Elwert 2011).

70. Wilson 1996, 51–52.

71. Massey and Denton 1993, 137. Despite these structural differences between Latino and black neighborhoods in Chicago at the time, segmented scholars suggested that Latinos would nonetheless experience poor outcomes and used the "underclass" concept to describe downward assimilation.

72. See Chapa 1988; Dohan 2003; Moore 1989; Moore and Pinderhughes 1993; Velez-Ibanez 1993. Others have extended these arguments to counter the idea of segmented assimilation. Joel Perlmann (2005, 124) points out that despite having the highest high school dropout rates and lagging relative to whites in terms of education and income, second-generation Mexican Americans do not have comparable rates of incarceration and detachment from the labor market as blacks.

73. Wilkes and Iceland 2004.

74. Massey 1996.

75. Dwyer 2007; Massey and Fischer 2003; Reardon and Bischoff 2011.

76. Cooley-Quille et al. 2001; Goldman et al. 2011; Thompson and Massat 2005.

77. Burdick-Will 2016, 2018; Harding 2009a; Harding et al. 2011; Macmillan and Hagan 2004; Schwartz and Hopmeyer Gorman 2003; Sharkey 2010.

78. On schools, see Anderson 1999; Bowen and Van Dorn 2002; Mateu-Gelabert and Lune 2003, 2007; Peguero, Connell, and Hong 2018; on learning impairment, see Burdick-Will 2016, 2018; Burdick-Will et al. 2011; Schwartz and Hopmeyer Gorman 2003; Sharkey 2010.

79. Anderson 1999; Burdick-Will 2018; Harding 2009b; Rendón 2014.

80. Wilson 1987, 60.

81. Since Wilson wrote *The Truly Disadvantaged* (1987) and *When Work Disappears* (1996), scholars have complicated how we understand the social isolation of poor blacks by finding greater overlap with the black middle class (Pattillo 2013) and highlighting how trust factors into the mobilization of social networks (Smith 2007).

82. Massey and Denton 1993.

83. But see De la Roca, Ellen, and Steil 2018.

84. Krivo et al. 2013.

85. Britton and Goldsmith 2013; Fernandez and Harris 1992; Krivo et al. 2013. Marcus Britton and Pat Goldsmith (2013) find minimal change in young Latino adults' exposure to whites relative to their exposure to whites in their youth, indicating pervasive segregation over time.
86. Gordon 1964.
87. Briggs 1998.
88. Lardier et al. 2019; MacLeod 1995; Young 2004.
89. Wacquant 2007; Anderson 2012.
90. Rendón, Aldana, and Hom 2018.
91. Kozol 2012; Noguera 2003; Valenzuela 2010. On the select few, see Conchas 2001; Louie 2012.
92. Devine 1996; Hirschfield 2008; Hirschfield and Celinska 2011; Peguero and Shekarkhar 2011; Peguero et. al 2015; Rios 2011.
93. DeLuca, Clampet-Lundquist, and Edin 2016; Flores 2013; Furstenberg et al. 1999. On children of immigrants, see Louie 2012; Suárez-Orozco, Suárez-Orozco, and Todorova 2008.
94. Portes and Zhou 1993; Portes and Rumbaut 2001.
95. Portes, Fernández-Kelly, and Haller (2005) explain that "parental controls can wane fast when confronted with the sustained challenges of deviant lifestyles." They note that, "for isolated families, the situation can easily devolve into a pattern of parental powerlessness, early abandonment of school by children, and involvement in gangs and drugs. Alternatively, when parental expectations are reinforced by others in the community, the probability of successful adaptation increases." These scholars examine social capital at the community level and suggest that cohesion is beneficial irrespective of the class composition of these communities.
96. Portes, Fernández-Kelly, and Haller 2005, 1013.
97. Zhou and Bankston (2006, 119) explain: "The bifurcation, as we called it, resulted from the fact that the youth were subject to two opposing sets of contextual influences. On the one hand, the ethnic community was tightly knitted and encouraged behaviors such as respect for elders, diligence in work, and strive for upward social mobility into mainstream American society. The local American community, on the other hand, was socially marginalized and economically impoverished, where young people reacted to structural disadvantages by erecting oppositional subcultures to reject normative means to social mobility." They add: "As predicted by the segmented assimilation theory, we found that Vietnamese youth with close connections to their ethnic community through their families were likely to concentrate on upward social mobility through education and that they were able to do so because of the support, control, and direction that they received from their ethnic community." Yet ten years later, Zhou and Bankston returned to this community to discover that Vietnamese youth of the first and second generations were less bifurcated between "valedictorians" and "delinquents," and that the latter group was growing in size. Their finding that greater generation gaps and ethnic ties were now less effective called into question how durable ethnic cohesion is under conditions of urban poverty and if "bounded solidarity" is actually a source of protection.

98. Waters et al. 2010, 1189.

99. Lee and Zhou 2015; Louie 2012.

100. Lee and Zhou 2015.

101. Examining networks at the individual level to understand the impact of social capital on social mobility patterns extends the work of James Coleman (1988). Coleman examined social capital at the individual level to make sense of educational achievement, noting that family cohesion and family connections to one another create a closed network that reinforces academic expectations. Barry Wellman and Scot Wortley (1990) identified social support from kin and neighbors as an important source of "community ties," finding these to be the most sought-out relations. More recently, immigration scholars have observed this as well. Filiz Garip (2017) has identified the increasing importance of kin ties—as opposed to ethnic ties—in the 1980s and 1990s for Mexican migration. Health researchers are also finding that individual-level connections are more important than community-level cohesion in explaining the Latino health paradox (see Mulvaney-Day, Alegria, and Sribney 2007).

102. Briggs 1998, 178. See also Dominguez and Watkins 2003; Mazelis 2017; Menjívar 2000; Stack 1974; Verdery and Campbell 2019; Wellman and Wortley 1990.

103. Smith 2000.

104. Stack 1974; Menjívar 2000.

105. Some studies find that the poor and racial and ethnic minorities report less social support relative to the middle class or whites. Yet the only study to draw on national data over time (Verdery and Campbell 2019) to look at access to social support ties across various groups finds convergence over time (1990 to 2011) between whites, blacks, and Hispanics in reported access to family support. Lower-income groups are still more likely to rely on family, while higher-SES groups report additional support from friends as well.

106. Mazelis 2017.

107. Lee and Zhou 2015; Waters et al. 2010.

108. Gordon 1964.

109. Louie 2012; Suárez-Orozco, Suárez-Orozco, and Todorova 2008.

110. Louie 2012.

111. Stanton-Salazar 2011, 1066.

112. Blanchard and Muller 2015; Stanton-Salazar 2001, 2011; Valenzuela 2010.

113. Suárez-Orozco, Suárez-Orozco, and Todorova 2008; Zhou and Bankston 2006.

114. Moore and Vigil 1987; Vigil 1988.

115. Briggs, Popkin, and Goering 2010; Curley 2009; Dominguez and Watkins 2003; Menjívar 2000.

116. Chen 2015.

117. Lewis 1961, 1966; Moynihan, Rainwater, and Yancey 1967; Rainwater 1970.

118. Anderson 1999; Harding 2010; Newman 2009; Sullivan 1989.

119. Patterson 2015.

120. DeLuca, Clampet-Lundquist, and Edin 2016; Lardier et al. 2019; MacLeod 1995; Young 2004.

121. Lee 2004; Louie 2012.

122. Darity 2011; Small, Harding, and Lamont 2010; Small and Newman 2001.

123. Small, Harding, and Lamont 2010. See also Anderson 1999; Estrada and Hondagneu-Sotelo 2011; Lamont 2002; Sherman 2006.

124. Small, Harding, and Lamont 2010, 11; see also Goffman 1974.

125. Small, Harding, and Lamont 2010, 14.

126. Mexicans are the largest immigrant group in Los Angeles, at 41 percent of the foreign-born population. There are of course multiple generations of Mexican Americans in the city as well.

127. Johnson and Sanchez 2019. Over half (52 percent) of California's immigrants are naturalized U.S. citizens, and over a third (34 percent) have some other legal status (including green cards and visas). According to the Center for Migration Studies (2016), about 14 percent of immigrants in California are undocumented.

128. 2018 U.S. Census QuickFacts estimates draw on U.S. Census Bureau, American Community Survey (ACS), 5-Year Estimates. 2013–2017: https://www.census.gov/quickfacts/fact/table/losangelescountycalifornia/PST045218.

129. Frey 2018. In Los Angeles, Hispanics compose nearly half of the Millennial population, with Asians making up 15 percent and blacks only 7 percent. See also Pastor et al. 2012.

130. Hayes and Hill 2017.

131. I challenge this argument in other work; see Rendón 2015.

132. See Alba, Logan, and Stults 2000; Brown 2007; Jargowsky 2003; Logan, Stults, and Farley 2004; Wilkes and Iceland 2004. Several studies have found that whereas all other groups, including blacks, experienced a slight decrease in segregation throughout the 1990s, Latinos experienced increased levels of segregation (Alba and Denton 2004). In fact, studies throughout the 1980s consistently showed that Latinos never experienced hypersegregation. But then, as Rima Wilkes and John Iceland (2004) found, hypersegregation affected the community for the first time in the 1990s: in New York City, where Puerto Ricans have concentrated historically, and in Los Angeles, one of the two cities where Mexicans have experienced high levels of segregation since the 1980s. Prior to the 1990s, according to these researchers, Mexican poor urban neighborhoods had been moderately segregated, but levels of segregation for Mexicans climbed in Los Angeles with the rapid influx of immigrants in the 1990s.

133. All SES indicators show an improvement in the two neighborhoods in this study between 2000 and 2010. For example, in 2000 these communities had above-average rates of male unemployment—12 percent in Pueblo Viejo and 14 percent in Central City—compared to 8 percent in Los Angeles. These figures had dropped by 2010 to 9.5 percent in Pueblo Viejo and 9 percent in Central City (compared to 7 percent in Los Angeles). See table A.2 for a comparison of the percentage of female-headed households and the percentage of males not in the labor force in the two neighborhoods and Los Angeles County.

134. Other studies that examine black-Latino relations find the same; see Telles, Sawyer, and Rivera-Salgado 2011.

135. Gonzales 2011.

136. Gonzales 2011.

137. DACA, which went into effect in August 2012, provided a temporary reprieve from deportation and legal access to work permits to undocumented young adults who

came to the United States before the age of sixteen, were under thirty-one, and had
been in the country continuously for the past five years.

138. See the methodological notes for more detail on my process.

Chapter 2: The Contested Immigrant City:
Navigating Violence, Family, and Work

1. Sharkey 2018a; Vigil 2002.
2. Wilson 1987; Massey and Denton 1993.
3. Gans 1992a, 1992b; Portes and Zhou 1993.
4. Wilson 1987.
5. Moore and Vigil 1987; Vigil 1988. Latino gang experts, Moore and Vigil (1993) have
long observed that an influx of immigrants into well-established poor Mexican communities slows the process of gang formation. They explain that immigrants "may be
poor, and poverty may have become more concentrated, but they are conventional
families with high family solidarity, and they tend to reenergize the social controls in
the neighborhood" (46).
6. Sampson 2008.
7. Lee and Martinez 2009; Martinez 2002; Martinez and Valenzuela 2006; Ousey and
Kubrin 2018; Reid et al. 2005; Sampson 2008.
8. Vigil 2002.
9. See Sampson, Raudenbush, and Earls 1997.
10. Many of the men in this study, like Carlos, were "risk diversifiers" who arrived in the
1970s to mid-1980s at a young age, following older kin, typically fathers; they would
send remittances to Mexico before their wives joined them. These migrants traveled
back and forth easily between the United States and Mexico, many as legal migrants
(Garip 2012).
11. *Zonas calientes,* which translates as "hot areas," is a figure of speech referring to an active
area of acute violence and crime.
12. Sampson and Raudenbush (2004) find that the racial and class composition of neighborhoods often influences the perception of social disorder, with higher numbers
of nonwhites in a neighborhood, particularly blacks, increasing the perception of
crime in an area. This perception of race and crime was especially acute for Latinos
in their research, many of whom were immigrants and recent arrivals (Sampson and
Raudenbush 2005).
13. Studies show that most urban violence is intraracial, not across racial groups. Hipp,
Tita, and Boggess 2009; Martinez 2016; Martinez and Rios 2011.
14. Research has long supported the interpretation that poor, Latino neighborhoods are
working poor or working class (Ortiz 1996). Mexicans and African Americans have
similar poverty rates, but greater joblessness among African Americans is believed
to affect the social organization of their communities. In a study of Chicago neighborhoods from 1970 to 1990, Jeffrey Morenoff and Marta Tienda (1997) found that
working-class neighborhoods, while declining in number, were strongly populated
by Latinos. The neighborhoods that they labeled as "underclass"—those with a high

"rate of poverty, unemployment, public assistance, and female-headed families"—were "racially homogenous, averaging 90 percent Black." Roger Waldinger and Cynthia Feliciano (2004) find that, unlike for blacks, who experience higher rates of joblessness and lower income in the central city, living in the central city is associated with higher levels employment and higher wages for the Mexican second generation. See also Moore 1989; Moore and Pinderhughes 1993 on this debate. Also, scholars have moved away from the "underclass" term to describe conditions in poor black neighborhoods.

15. See Solis and Galvin 2012.

16. Note that the same established migrant networks that facilitate access to low-skilled jobs for the Mexican-origin group also keep them confined to the lowest-tier jobs in American society (Rosales 2014; Smith 2000).

17. See also Dohan 2003; Van Hook and Bean 2009.

18. Mario Small, David Harding, and Michèle Lamont (2010) explain: "These symbolic boundaries constitute a system of classification that defines a hierarchy of group and the similarities and differences between them. They typically imply and justify a hierarchy of moral worth across individuals and groups" (17). A growing body of literature shows how these moral boundaries unfold in central cities. Scholars find that in poor black communities urban residents draw moral distinctions between residents, characterizing them as "decent" versus "street," and "dirty" versus "clean" (Anderson 1999; Goffman 2014). Researchers find that to perform low-status jobs with dignity, lower-status workers draw moral boundaries (Lamont 2002; Sherman 2006). Research shows that *jornaleros,* day laborers, draw moral boundaries against others—low-income whites (Hallet 2012), Americans generally (Trujillo-Pagan 2012), even other *jornaleros* (Purser 2009)—by emphasizing their superior work ethic, sense of responsibility, and sacrifice; making these distinctions counters the stigma associated with their exploitation. Similarly, Emir Estrada and Pierrette Hondagneu-Sotelo (2011) find that Latino youth in Los Angeles who work as street vendors counter stigma attached to their labor by devising new narratives of "intersectional dignity" that are affirming, restored identities. They find these youth gained a sense of dignity and moral worth by positioning themselves against gangsters and *fresitas* (privileged or spoiled youth).

19. Few studies have examined how long-term immigrants in the United States make sense of their meager wages or exploitative work conditions. In general, researchers find that immigrants have a more positive orientation about work in the United States compared to U.S.-born Latinos. In his study comparing a Mexican immigrant and Mexican American neighborhood, Daniel Dohan (2003) found that transnational ties gave distinct meaning to low-wage jobs. Recent immigrants, he wrote, "saw low wages as relative valuable, believed they would work in low-wage jobs for only a limited period of time before returning to Mexico and took their tenure in low-jobs as indicative of upward economic mobility" (13). The immigrants in my study were not recent immigrants, and they were willing to discuss their exploitation and limited social mobility.

20. See table A.1 in the appendix.

21. The greater visibility of young black men in public spaces such as parks or street corners was mentioned by some interviewees and observed during the study. Such visibility is well documented in communities with high rates of joblessness (Anderson 1999;

Wilson 1996). Immigrants' strong moral boundaries against black youth also align with research showing that the presence of blacks in neighborhoods increases the perception of crime there (Sampson and Raudenbush 2004, 2005).

22. Krogstad and Fry 2015; Rendón 2013; Tran and Valdez 2017.
23. Waldinger and Feliciano 2004.
24. Van Hook and Bean 2009.
25. Sharkey 2018a.
26. Wilson 1987, 1996.
27. Royster 2003; Smith 2000, 2007.

Chapter 3: Same Landing, Unequal Starts: The Varying Social Capital of Mexican Immigrants

1. Sampson, Raudenbush, and Earls 1997.
2. Portes and Zhou 1993.
3. Vigil 1988, 2002.
4. Briggs 1998.
5. Familism, understood as family solidarity and mutual support and reflecting the great value attached to the family over individual interest, was strongly prevalent in the families in this study (Baca Zinn 1975, 1977, 1982; Keefe 1979, 1980; Sabogal et al. 1987; Segura and Pierce 1993).
6. Coleman 1988.
7. Vigil 1988, 2017.
8. Garip 2017, 87.
9. Garip (2017) shows how Mexican immigrants vary in their networks over time. Most scholarship that examines Mexican migrants' social support ties has mixed findings because it does not look at these variations. The finding by Edna Viruell-Fuentes and her colleagues (2013) that immigrants have fewer networks than U.S.-born Latinos makes sense considering that networks develop over time.
10. Dominguez and Watkins 2003; Mazelis 2017; Menjívar 2000; Portes and Sensenbrener 1993.
11. To my knowledge, no study has examined the extent to which kin ties continue to aid immigrants over time and across generations.
12. Garip (2017) describes four migrant types that changed the character of Mexican migration to the United States from 1965 to 2010: (1) 70 percent of first-time migrants in the 1965–1970s era were "circular migrants," typically married men who were household heads, came from rural central-western Mexico with little education, worked mostly in agriculture in Mexico and the United States, and took multiple trips of short duration; (2) between 1980 and 1990, "crisis migrants" were the most dominant group (50 percent); typically these were young men who had migrant ties, were from families with small plots of land or property, and migrated following the economic crises in Mexico; Garip's explanation that crisis migrants were more likely to rely on "strong ties" as opposed to "weak ties" is borne out in her data: "A significantly larger share of crisis migrants (77%) have household members who have already migrated to the

United States, compared to circular migrants. . . . [This] suggests . . . [that] migrants increasingly draw on the experience of immediate family members rather than more distant relations in the extended family or community" (88); (3) between 1987 and 1990, following passage of the Immigration Reform and Control Act (IRCA) of 1986, one-third of migrants were "family migrants," mostly women but also children and other relatives with kin ties in the United States who migrated to reunify with family, often with legal documentation; (4) beginning in the 1990s, "urban migrants" became the most dominant group; making up 70 percent of all first-time migrants by 2010, these migrants came from nontraditional sending areas (often border communities or central-south or southeastern regions), were more educated, earned significantly more than other migrants, and made fewer trips to Mexico. Both crisis and family migrants relied extensively on family ties to facilitate their migration to the United States, in contrast to circular migrants, who could rely on broader ethnic, village ties, and to recent urban migrants, who have less developed migrant networks and increasingly rely on "network externalities"—that is, smugglers and so on (see Hernández-León 2008). See also Massey and Espinoza 1997.

13. Donato 2010; Hondagneu-Sotelo 1994.

14. Jorge Durand and Douglas Massey (2003) call this "the historical region"; it encompasses the states of Durango, Zacatecas, San Luis Potosí, Aguascalientes, Guanajuato, Jalisco, Nayarit, Colima, and Michoacán. According to these scholars, from the 1920s until recently at least 50 percent of the total outflow to the United States originated in this region. The share peaked between 60 and 70 percent during the 1970s, however; since then, it has declined steadily, reaching levels just below 50 percent early in the new century (Durand and Massey 2003) and, more recently, just below 40 percent.

15. Given the length of Mexican migration to the United States, scholars have identified distinct eras. Massey describes these as the "classical era" (1890–1920s), the "bracero era" (1942–1964), the "undocumented era" (1965–1985), and the "urban era" (post-1985). See also Durand, Massey, and Zenteno 2001; Fernandez and Gonzalez 2012; Riosmena and Massey 2012.

16. By the late 1950s, a massive circular flow of Mexican migrants had become deeply embedded in employer practices and migrant expectations and was sustained by well-developed and widely accessible migrant networks (Massey, Durand, and Malone 2002). As a result, when avenues for legal entry were suddenly curtailed after 1965, the migratory flows did not disappear but simply continued without authorization or documents.

17. Established in 1942, the bracero program was a binational treaty that arranged for the "temporary importation" of contract workers into the United States for short-term periods of farm labor. Under the treaty, Mexicans such as Esperanza's father were granted renewable six-month visas to work for approved agricultural growers, located mostly in the southwestern United States. Roughly 500,000 temporary guest workers entered the United States annually from 1942 to 1964. These migrants were part of what Garip (2017) describes as "circular migrants."

18. Durand, Massey, and Zenteno (2001) write: "In one form or another, this 'temporary' wartime measure was extended annually until 1964 (Calavita 1992). Over the course

of the program's twenty-two years, more than 4.6 million Mexican workers were imported into the United States (Cornelius 1978). By the 1960s, however, the bracero program had come to be seen as an exploitive labor regime on a par with Southern sharecropping, and in 1964 Congress voted to terminate it (Calavita 1992; Massey, Durand, and Malone 2002). With changes in immigration reform that same year, Mexico went from annual access to around 450,000 guest worker visas and a theoretically unlimited number of resident visas in the United States (in practice averaging around 50,000 per year) to a new situation in which there were no guestworker visas and just 20,000 resident visas annually" (see also Durand and Massey 2003; Massey 2007).

19. Massey (1990) applied the term "cumulative causation" to describe the self-feeding character of migration. The theory posits that each act of migration leads to a series of changes in the origin community, and these changes make future migration more likely. For example, with each new migrant, the social networks that connect individuals in the origin country to migrants in the destination country expand. More individuals can rely on these networks to migrate; with more migrants, the networks expand even more. Through this feedback loop, migration flows become self-sustaining, and eventually they are decoupled from the economic or political conditions that initiated them in the first place.

20. According to Massey, Durand, and Malone (2003), from 1965 to 1985, about 5.7 million Mexican migrants entered the country, 80 percent of them undocumented. In this study, only seven immigrant parents who migrated prior to 1986 arrived authorized in Los Angeles.

21. As during the bracero era, the undocumented flow after 1965 was overwhelmingly circular, with 85 percent of undocumented entries being offset by departures (Massey and Singer 1995). For this reason, the undocumented population grew slowly and had increased to just 3.2 million by 1986, when Congress passed the IRCA legislation.

22. Garip 2017.

23. Several scholars have documented the historical presence of Mexican female immigrants in the United States throughout the twentieth century. See Curran et al. 2006; Hondagneu-Sotelo 2003; Kanaiaupuni 2000; Ruiz 1998.

24. The IRCA legislation greatly expanded the resources, personnel, and power of the U.S. Border Patrol, criminalized the hiring of undocumented migrants, and generally militarized the Mexico-U.S. border. See Andreas 1998; Dunn 1996; Fragomen 1997; Massey, Durand, and Malone 2002; Singer and Massey 1998.

25. Esperanza's father was not a naturalized citizen but was still able to help her get her "green card," or legal residency.

26. Portes and Zhou 1993; Portes and Rumbaut 2001.

27. Instituto National de Estadisticas y Geografia, https://www.inegi.org.mx/ (accessed August 9, 2019).

28. Hernández-León 2008.

29. Hernández-León 2008.

30. Cornelius 1992.

31. Hernández-León 2008.

32. Garip 2017. Durand, Massey, and Zenteno (2001) find that the growing representation of urban migrants partly stemmed from Mexico's urbanization since the 1950s. Although the majority of migrants no longer come from rural areas, rural migrants are still overrepresented in the migrant flow. Although only 22 percent of the Mexican population lives in rural localities, 40 percent of migrants come from rural places (see Hernández-León 2008; Marcelli and Cornelius 2001; Smith 2006).

33. Hernández-León (2008) finds that the west-central region of Mexico, the historical migrant-sending region, is always overrepresented in streams to traditional destinations. Yet this region represents only 30, 27, and 13 percent of migrants going to the U.S. Southeast, South, and Northeast. The striking underrepresentation of the historical region in flows to the Northeast—and to a lesser extent, the South and Southeast—suggests that old networks from central-western Mexico do not operate in the same way to guide migrants to new destinations as they do in channeling migrants to communities in traditional and reemerging gateways (see also Smith 2006; Zuniga and Hernández-León 2001).

34. The combination of continued in-migration and declining out-migration sharply increased the net rate of the undocumented population in the 1980s and 1990s. Numerous studies find that the rate of growth slowed and ultimately came to a halt in 2008, when the undocumented population peaked at around 12 million (Wasem 2012; Warren and Warren 2013). Since then, the number of undocumented residents has fallen, hovering around 11 million. The Mexican-origin group has historically been the majority of the undocumented population, but is now roughly half (Krogstad, Passel, and Cohn 2017).

35. Between 1986 and 2000, the number of Border Patrol officers nearly tripled and the agency's budget grew by a factor of seven (Massey, Durand, and Malone 2002). The United States thus spent $35 billion on border enforcement between 1970 and 2010. After the creation of the Department of Homeland Security in 2003, the budget of U.S. Customs and Border Protection (CBP) more than doubled, from $5.9 billion to $13.2 billion by 2016. During that period, the number of Border Patrol agents doubled, to 49,000. On top of that, U.S. Immigration and Customs Enforcement (ICE) spending grew 85 percent, from $3.3 billion since its inception to $6.1 billion by 2016. See the American Immigration Council (2007) report on the cost of immigration enforcement and security.

36. As border enforcement accelerated, the rate of cross-border circulation steadily fell (Massey, Durand, and Malone 2002). The resulting drop in return migration has had what has been called a "caging effect": a hardened border functions to "cage in" migrants north of the border (Rosenblum 2012).

37. Garip 2017.

38. Flores-Yeffal 2013; Garip 2017.

39. Hernández-León 2008. In her research on rural and urban migrants from Guanajuato, Mexico, Nadia Flores-Yeffal (2013) finds that urban migrants are at a great disadvantage relative to the rural migrants who draw on well-established kin and nonkin ties, or "migrant-trust networks," to help them settle and find jobs in the United States upon their arrival. Although some urban migrants gain access to migrant-trust networks through rural ties, others are "orphaned urban migrants" who function outside these structures. Flores-Yeffal discusses the great challenges that these urban migrants face

in the United States upon their arrival and notes their implications for the second generation, but such analysis is not part of her study. Similarly, Garip (2017) explains, "The social facilitation and normative influence mechanism are unlikely to work as well for urban migrants as they did for the other three migrant groups," noting that these migrants originate from regions with historically low levels of migration and live in large urban communities with weaker migration norms (147–48).

40. Flores-Yeffal (2013) argues that "clique-like network structures" (like a church) provide urban migrants with a "migrant-trust network" effect.

41. Migration is often proscribed by gender socialization, expectations, and concerns about risks. Sara Curran and Estela Rivero-Fuentes (2003) write, "Because of a culture of 'domesticity' . . . women are perceived to face greater risks and are subjected to greater control over their movements, especially when they [immigrate] on their own. As a result, women face different barriers to U.S. migration than men do and must rely on different sources of support for getting to the United States. . . . Young single women have had an important presence in migratory movements within Mexico since the 1940s. Although they did not constitute the majority of internal migrants until 1980, they dominated the migration flows to metropolitan areas, where they worked as domestics and in the service sector" (292).

42. The processes, motivations, and social norms governing men's and women's movements and how they settle in the receiving society are different (Curran and Saguy 2001; Hondagneu-Sotelo 1994; Pedraza 1991; Pessar 1999a, 1999b). Hence, the importance of networks may vary for men and women migrants and the potential for help is not the same (Cerrutti and Massey 2001; Donato 1993; Hondagneu-Sotelo 1992, 1994; Menjívar 2000).

43. Researchers find that the nature of the work that Mexican females find, such as being domestics or nannies, limits the kinds of networks they develop (Hondagneu-Sotelo 1994; Garip 2017).

44. See Kanaiaupuni 2000.

45. Hondagneu-Sotelo 1994.

46. Taggers are typically not in neighborhood gangs but are part of "tagging crews," a group of primarily young men who do graffiti, often vandalizing property. I elaborate on the distinction between gang members and taggers in the following chapter.

47. Treviño 2006.

48. Portes and Zhou 1993; Portes and Rumbaut 2001.

49. Recent research calls attention to the diversity within the Mexican migrant group (Alba, Jimenez, and Marrow 2014) but has not specifically addressed the impact of this diversity on social capital. To date, Garip (2017) provides the most comprehensive examination of the diversity within the Mexican immigrant flow.

50. Garip 2017.

Chapter 4: Caught Up and Skirting Risk: Young Latino Men in the Inner City

1. Horowitz 1983; Vigil 1988, 2017.

2. Papachristos, Hureau, and Braga 2013; Papachristos 2009.

3. On academic performance, see Burdick-Will 2016, 2018; Burdick-Will et al. 2011. On school noncompletion, see Harding 2009a; Rendón 2014. On lower incomes, see Sharkey and Torrats-Espinosa 2017.

4. Portes and Zhou 1993.

5. Harding 2009b; Rendón 2014; Chan Tack and Small 2017.

6. Vigil 1988.

7. Contreras 2018; Rendón 2014.

8. Swidler 1986.

9. See Alsybar 2007; Lopez et al. 2006.

10. The segmented assimilation framework suggests that the Latino second generation in high-poverty neighborhoods will socialize with and acculturate to the presumed oppositional orientation of native-born racial minorities. Yet with urban conditions that strained race relations between Latinos and blacks, race informed how violence was experienced and understood in Central City, making socialization and acculturation challenging. As I have written elsewhere, as newcomers to the predominantly black neighborhood, the Latino second generation experienced Central City as a contested space and violence, though circumscribed by gang affiliation, as racially charged (Rendón 2015).

11. Vigil 1988.

12. Portes 1998; Portes and Landolt 1996.

13. The cross-racial tension that peaked that year in some Los Angeles city schools got the attention of local media, who minimized the underlying role of local gang conflicts and played up the role of race.

14. Coleman 1988, S102; Portes 1998; Portes and Landolt 1996.

15. Portes 1998, 15.

16. For the many studies that challenge claims that racial minorities do not subscribe to an achievement ideology owing to racial discrimination and their perception of blocked opportunities (see, for example, Fordham and Ogbu 1986), finding instead that urban youth subscribe to dominant and nondominant cultural outlooks regarding education, see Ainsworth-Darnell and Downey 1998; Carter 2005; Cook and Ludwig 1998; Downey, Ainsworth, and Qian 2009; Harding 2010; Harris 2011; Solorzano 1992; Tyson, Darity, and Castellino 2005; Warikoo 2011. In fact, several scholars find that black youth are more likely than whites to embrace meritocracy (Mickelson 1990).

17. Neighborhood effects research often excludes the independent impacts of schools. However, schools may shape life outcomes more than neighborhoods, given that youth spend more time in schools than in neighborhoods. For instance, youth may be exposed to role models or gain access to social capital in school, and they may also be exposed to negative peer ties there. Curriculum or school quality measures may also reflect the influence on these outcomes of school contexts. Moreover, schools exacerbate inequities across neighborhoods, as better-resourced parents often select into higher-quality schools for their children, leaving behind the most disadvantaged in traditional neighborhood public schools. For instance, it could be that the social capital or negative acculturation believed to contribute to poor outcomes in

disadvantaged contexts are not transmitted via the neighborhood, but in the school context instead. Thus, even though I focus on neighborhoods, I do not dismiss the impact of schools on the outcomes of these young men. See Mateu-Gelabert and Lune (2003) for how neighborhood violence and school conflicts reinforce one another.

18. Gregory, Skiba, and Noguera 2010; Rumberger 2011; Rumberger and Losen 2016.

19. Continuation schools are alternative schools attended by students who are behind on academic credits, often have been expelled or suspended, and have high rates of high school noncompletion. Typically, students attend for a shorter period of time daily, such as a half-day. Some students at continuation schools obtain a GED instead of a high school diploma, though a diploma can also be obtained.

20. Rios 2011.

21. "Wetback" is a common racial slur for Mexican-origin people that refers to the undocumented immigrants who cross the U.S.-Mexico border via land and "wet their back" crossing the river that runs along the border. *Mojado* (wet person) is the Spanish version of this term.

22. See Elliott et al. 2006; Furstenberg et al. 1999; Small and Feldman 2012; Wodtke, Harding, and Elwert 2011.

23. Without disputing studies suggesting that a sense of self-efficacy has an impact on inner-city young men's chances of achieving social mobility (Sharkey 2006; Wolkow and Ferguson 2001), I found that exposure to violence in their neighborhoods seemed to have a far more reliable impact on young men's risk of school noncompletion.

24. See Burton and Jarret 2000; Elliott et al. 2006; Furstenberg 2000.

25. Lareau 2003.

26. Most parents in this study were unaware of busing programs and therefore could not exercise the option to petition to have their children enrolled in them. Those who learned about the program did so either through a teacher who identified their son as a good candidate or through their personal network, such as kin or neighbors. Parents stated that they bused their children to receive a better education, but their assessment of a "good" school typically centered on issues of social disruption and violence.

27. Furstenberg et al. 1999; Vigil 1988, 2017.

28. Studies show that fathers today spend more time with their children than years past, particularly spending time playing or are more likely to take their children to after-school programs, alleviating this responsibility once relegated to women. Yet there has been minimal progress in other areas. For example, even when both parents work similar hours, men do not necessarily take on more household responsibilities than their wives, women are also more likely to multitask than men and spend less time relaxing. See Pew Research Center 2013; Musick, Meier, and Flood 2016.

29. Studies show that victims of violence and violence perpetrators are more likely to have histories of "co-occurrence violence": violence in the home, among peers, and in the community. See Margolin et al. 2009; Aisenberg and Herrenkohl 2008; Buka et al. 2001.

30. Portes and Zhou 1993; Portes and Rumbaut 2001.

31. See Papachristos, Hureau, and Braga 2013; Papachristos 2009.

Chapter 5: Collapsing into the Working Class: Social Support, Segregation, and Class Convergence

1. Krogstad and Fry 2015; Rendón 2013; Tran and Valdez 2017; Waldinger and Feliciano 2004.

2. In Mexico, the colloquial and slang word *palancas* can also have the negative connotation of not just having social connections but engaging in nepotism. Osvaldo used this term only in the former sense—as synonymous with having social leverage ties—and I use it in this same sense throughout the chapter.

3. Portes and Zhou 1993; Portes and Rumbaut 2001.

4. Rendón 2013; Tran and Valdez 2017.

5. Waldinger and Feliciano 2004.

6. Lee and Zhou 2014; Telles and Ortiz 2008; Tran and Valdez 2017.

7. In early work, I discussed how urban conditions, primarily violence, "brightened" rather than "blurred" boundaries between African Americans and Latinos in Central City, challenging the idea that the second generation would acculturate across race (Rendón 2015). In his study, Robert C. Smith (2014) found that Mexican youth who identified closely with blacks, rather than experiencing "decline," adopted a black culture of mobility that helped them get ahead.

8. Kasinitz and his colleagues (2008) find that second-generation Latinos in New York fare better than native-born racial minorities (African Americans and Puerto Ricans) in that they move away from ethnic enclaves, find mainstream work, and enroll in institutions of higher education (see also Rendón 2013; Smith 2006; Stepick and Stepick 2010; Tran and Valdez 2017).

9. Earning $15 an hour is roughly $32,000 annually if working full-time. However, some young men worked only part-time as students, earning significantly less in the year. The median income in Los Angeles was $56,266 in 2010. It was $30,710 for Latinos in Pueblo Viejo and $34,288 for Latinos in Central City (see table A.1).

10. Telles and Ortiz 2008, 274.

11. Chetty et al. 2014; Chetty and Hendren 2015a, 2015b; Chetty, Hendren, and Katz 2016; Sampson 2012; Sharkey 2008.

12. Lee and Zhou 2015.

13. Lee and Zhou 2015: Louie 2012; Waters et al. 2010.

14. Louie 2012 ("non-family" ties); Stanton-Salazar 2011 ("institutional agents").

15. Ortiz 1996. In California, Latinos are overrepresented among the working poor, averaging 56 percent versus 36 percent of all working adults from 2014 to 2016. See also Waldinger, Lim, and Cort 2007.

16. See Rendón, Aldana, and Hom 2018.

17. Orfield and Lee 2007; Orfield et al. 2016.

18. Krivo et al. 2013.

19. Wacquant 2007; Yosso et al. 2009.

20. Gordon 1964.

21. Studies on young adult children of Mexican immigrants in the American South find that they are experiencing upward mobility as measured by occupational positions and

income (Hernández-León and Morando Lakhani 2013; Morando 2013. The same can be said about most second-generation young men in this study. Yet the higher cost of living in Los Angeles made their gains almost insignificant, and they continued to depend on the support of kin ties. For those whose parents had purchased homes in a very different market, the high cost of housing actually wiped out any advantage of a few extra dollars an hour in their earnings.

22. Like many Millennials, the majority of young men in this study were postponing marriage and starting a family. The seven who became parents struggled to be independent. Young people typically lived with their parents even after having children; eleven of the immigrant families were three-generation households owing to the presence of the children of the study participants or their siblings. Some study participants had older siblings who had moved out of Los Angeles or out of state, where housing was more affordable, but the Great Recession brought some of them back home.

23. Kasinitz et al. 2008; Louie 2012. The parallels are similar to the position of working-class Koreans in New York, in that they are not as nested in an ethnic enclave as the Chinese. See Lee 2004.

24. See Rosales 2014; Smith 2000.

25. Thirty-two of the young men in this study (75 percent) found a job via kin tie or neighbor tie at some point. Only eight out of forty-two young men obtained a job outside the kin and neighborhood network.

26. While the middle category represents the most dominant path in general, only one-third of the young men in this study fell into this category as I sampled along educational trajectories within the neighborhood to account for diversity and to account for whether and how the neighborhood mattered across groups.

27. Sherman (2006) calls this "moral capital."

28. The immigrant homeowners in this study were able to purchase homes in Los Angeles before home prices skyrocketed. Although the second generation often earned a bit more than their parents, it was not enough to purchase a home in today's much more expensive housing market.

29. Rosenbaum, Ahearn, and Rosenbaum 2017; Symonds, Schwartz, and Ferguson 2011.

30. Parents with low human capital have fewer resources to guide their children academically than those with greater educational attainment. Typically these parents also lack financial resources to pay for tutoring if their children need it. For immigrants, class disadvantages are amplified by language and cultural barriers. These parents are much less familiar with navigating the American educational system than their economic peers in other communities.

31. Rosenbaum, Ahearn, and Rosenbaum 2017; Symonds, Schwartz, and Ferguson 2011.

32. Campaign for College Opportunity 2017; Rosenbaum, Ahearn, and Rosenbaum 2017; Symonds, Schwartz, and Ferguson 2011.

33. Campaign for College Opportunity 2017; Community College Research Center 2017; Long and Kurlaender 2009.

34. Rosenbaum 2001.

35. Symonds, Schwartz, and Ferguson 2011.

36. Deming, Goldin, and Katz 2013; Gelbgiser 2018; Lynch, Engle, and Cruz 2010; Ma and Baum 2016.
37. Stanton-Salazar 2011.
38. Stanton-Salazar 2011, 1086.
39. I linked Jesús to those in the university who could guide him with the application and financial aid processes. He erroneously believed that I had influence over the application process.
40. For other work on this population, see Gandara 1995; Louie 2012; Smith 2008.
41. Conchas 2001; Gibson, Gandara, and Koyama 2004.
42. "Such support includes the cultural transmission of distinct *discourses,* access to key funds of knowledge, academic support, advice, and guidance, and forms of modeling and training designed to promote effective communication and relational competencies enabling effective help seeking and the reciprocal exchange with different adult and peer networks" (Stanton-Salazar 2011, 1070).
43. Studies find that social support mechanisms, including kin ties, are important for the college success of Latinx students (see Crockett et al. 2007; Valenzuela and Dornbusch 1994).
44. Jack 2019.
45. Lee and Chin 2015.
46. Class reproduction in American society is irrefutable. In fact, studies indicate that social mobility in the United States has slowed down with rising inequality. The middle and upper classes pass on privilege to their children through their resources, including better neighborhoods, better schools, and a wealth of extracurricular activities that secure their children's place in the social ladder. These strategies and opportunities put the poor and working class at a great disadvantage.
47. Louie 2012.
48. Rendón 2013; Tran and Valdez 2017; Waldinger and Feliciano 2004.
49. Menjívar 2000.
50. Bean, Brown, and Bachmeier 2015. See also Enriquez 2015.
51. Wilson 1987.
52. Ortiz 1996.

Chapter 6: Getting Ahead or Falling Behind: The Impact of Social Leverage Ties and Social Isolation

1. Briggs 1998.
2. Stanton-Salazar 2011.
3. Gordon 1964.
4. Cristian obtained his job with ICE in 2012, during the Obama administration.
5. By 2010, the median household income in Los Angeles County was $56,266, and the median income for Latinos was $45,706. Benjamin was doing better than most of his Latino coethnics in Pueblo Viejo, where he continued to live: the median income there was $30,710. See the appendix for the socioeconomic characteristics of the neighborhoods.

6. Blanchard and Muller 2015; Stanton-Salazar 2011; Valenzuela 2010.
7. Chen 2015.
8. The first onset of a schizophrenic episode can occur in the teenage years. With medication, this condition can be controlled, but episodes can recur.
9. Scholars find that young men engaged in violence were often victims of multiple forms of violence growing up (Buka et al. 2001; Margolin et al. 2009; Rich and Grey 2005).

Chapter 7: Making Sense of Getting Ahead:
The Enduring and Shifting Cultural Outlooks of Young Latino Men

1. Latinos lost footing on their ascent into the middle class during the recession because they were especially hard hit when they disproportionately lost their homes, including families in this study (Kochhar, Fry, and Taylor 2011).
2. Lewis 1961, 1966; Rainwater 1970.
3. Portes and Zhou 1993; Zhou 1997.
4. DeLuca, Clampet-Lundquist, and Edin 2016; Hochschild 1995; Lardier et al. 2019; MacLeod 1995; Young 2004.
5. Lardier et al. 2019; MacLeod 1995; Young 2004.
6. In their longitudinal study comparing generations of Mexican Americans, Telles and Ortiz (2008) note the exceptional optimism of the second generation compared to later generations.
7. Darity 2011; Small, Harding, and Lamont 2010; Small and Newman 2001.
8. Anderson 1999; Carter 2005; Harding 2010; Newman 2009.
9. Huntington 2004.
10. Brown 2007.
11. Small, Harding, and Lamont 2010.
12. Fordham and Ogbu 1986.
13. Ainsworth-Darnell and Downey 1998; Carter 2005; Cook and Ludwig 1998; Downey, Ainsworth, and Qian 2009; Harding 2010; Harris 2011; Solorzano 1992; Tyson, Darity, and Castellino 2005; Warikoo 2011.
14. Other researchers have called young people who persevere despite difficult odds "resilient" or "gritty." I depart from these terms, which emphasize individual tendencies, to account for how differential exposure to varying contexts or resources affects frames.
15. Lee and Zhou (2015) find that their greater years of schooling relative to their immigrant parents' education gives the Latino second generation a sense of "success." In particular, they find that, relative to children of Chinese and Vietnamese immigrants, who adopt a narrow frame of success—defined as becoming a doctor, engineer, or lawyer—children of Mexican immigrants may perceive graduating from high school and finding a job or pursuing a college education in any area as success.
16. Future studies should examine how gender or masculinity informs cultural outlooks for this group. Although female kin figured prominently in young men's social capital, fathers and father-figures played a unique role in the minds of the young men. Despite being among the lowest-paid workers in the United States, these immigrant

men inspired second-generation males and offered them valuable resources, including blue-collar skills and links to working-class jobs. This helps explain why these second-generation males did not necessarily shun or refuse "immigrant jobs," as some would have predicted (Gans 1992a); instead, they approached these jobs as stepping-stones in their journey toward upward mobility. Importantly, most respondents framed success within the realm of the working class, where they perceived opportunities for advancement (Lee and Zhou 2014).

17. In this study, seven out of forty-two of the young men were fathers when I last met with them.

18. Hochschild 1995; Lardier et al. 2019; MacLeod 1995; Young 2004.

19. In other work, I show how inner-city Latinos obscure the role of race in their criminalization (Rendón, Aldana, and Hom 2018).

20. Rendón, Aldana, and Hom 2018.

21. O'Conner 1999.

22. Undocumented young men in this study also underwent this cognitive shift. They were forced to deal with the consequences of their unauthorized status but nonetheless identified with the other U.S.-born children of immigrants in this study in rejecting the exploitative working conditions experienced by undocumented immigrant men who did not arrive in the United States as children.

23. Rendón, Aldana, and Hom 2018.

24. Manuel was in college between 2001 and 2005, before the shift away from television and toward streaming services like Netflix.

25. Jack 2019.

26. Wage theft is common among undocumented workers (Fussell 2011).

27. Wacquant 2007.

28. Anderson 2012.

29. Gonzales 2011.

30. Manuel was born in Mexico and arrived in Los Angeles before the age of five. Like the rest of his siblings, he would acquire legal residency by the time he graduated from high school.

31. A crime drama television series.

32. Gonzalez 2011. See also Enriquez 2017.

Chapter 8: Conclusion: How the Inner City
Shapes the Integration Process
of Second-Generation Latinos

1. Chetty et al. 2014; Chetty and Hendren 2015a, 2015b; Chetty, Hendren, and Katz 2016; Sampson 2012; Sharkey 2008, 2013.

2. Alba and Nee 2003; Telles and Ortiz 2008. See also Bean and Stevens 2003; Brown 2007; Farley and Alba 2002; Perlmann 2005; Smith 2003; Waldinger, Lim, and Cort 2007.

3. Ortiz 1996.

4. Gans 1992a.

5. Kasinitz et al. 2008; Lee and Zhou 2015.

6. Portes and Zhou 1993.

7. Rendón 2015.

8. Chetty et al. 2014; Chetty and Hendren 2015a, 2015b; Chetty, Hendren, and Katz 2016; Sampson 2012.

9. Sampson, Raudenbush, and Earls 1997.

10. Lee and Martinez 2009; Martinez and Valenzuela 2006; Ousey and Kubrin 2018; Reid et al. 2005; Sampson 2008.

11. Rios 2011.

12. Sharkey 2018b.

13. Burdick-Will 2018; Harding 2009a; Rendón 2014.

14. Burdick-Will 2016, 2018; Burdick-Will et al. 2011; Harding 2009a; Rendón 2014; Sharkey and Torrats-Espinosa 2017.

15. Telles and Ortiz 2008.

16. Orfield and Lee 2007; Orfield et al. 2016.

17. Reardon 2011; Reardon and Owens 2014.

18. Louie 2012.

19. Stanton-Salazar 2001 ("institutional agents"); Briggs 1998 (outside social leverage ties).

20. Louie 2012; Lee and Zhou 2015; Waters et al. 2010.

21. Wilson 1987.

22. Kasinitz et al. 2008.

23. Jack 2019.

24. Rosenbaum, Ahearn, and Rosenbaum 2017; Symonds, Schwartz, and Ferguson 2011.

25. Gordon 1964.

26. Wodtke, Elwert, and Harding 2016.

27. Bostean et al. 2018.

28. Gibson, Gandara, and Koyama 2004; Grossman and Rhodes 2002; Louie 2012; Roffman, Suárez-Orozco, and Rhodes 2003.

29. Rios 2011; Skiba and Knesting 2001.

30. Wacquant 2007.

31. Rendón, Aldana, and Hom 2018.

32. Chen 2015; Mazelis 2017; Putnam 2016; Silva 2013.

33. Alba and Nee 2003; Alba, Kasinitz, and Waters 2011; Bean and Stevens 2003; Farley and Alba 2002; Kasinitz et al. 2008; Perlmann 2005; Smith 2003.

34. Royster 2003.

35. Menjívar 2000.

36. Alba, Kasinitz, and Waters 2011; Kao and Tienda 1995; Lee and Zhou 2014; Portes, Fernández-Kelly, and Haller 2005; Smith 2003.

37. Kasinitz et al. 2008; Lee and Zhou 2015; Louie 2006, 2012; Suárez-Orozco, Suárez-Orozco, and Todorova 2008.

38. Hochschild 1995; Lardier et al. 2019; MacLeod 1995; Young 2004.

39. Lee 2004 (according to class); Louie 2006 (according to ethnic community).

40. See also Lardier et al. 2019; MacLeod 1995; Shildrick and MacDonald 2013; Young 2004.

41. Jack 2019, 44.

42. Ludwig et al. 2013 (on improvements to mental health and well-being); Chetty, Hendren, and Katz 2016 (on reduced single-parenthood rates).

43. Briggs, Popkin, and Goering 2010; Clampet-Lundquist 2010.

44. Sharkey 2018a.

45. Rios 2011.

46. González 2012.

47. Fry and Taylor 2013.

48. Hout 2012.

49. Newman and Chen 2007. See Cashin 2014.

50. Warren 2016.

51. Bean, Brown, and Bachmeier 2015. Enriquez 2015.

52. At the time of this writing, the Trump administration is responding to the outrage caused by the president's "zero-tolerance" immigration policy of separating families at the border. These children will carry the trauma inflicted on them throughout their lives, and some may never be reunited with their parents. Aside from its inhumanity, the policy essentially destroys one of the few assets that immigrants bring to survive in this country—their loved ones. Rather than provide government support to help asylum-seekers from Central America or to process the millions of undocumented immigrants already in the country, the government has set out to separate these families. Immigrants exert themselves in the United States, in some of the toughest conditions, for the sake of their children. In turn, many of their children go forward hoping to find a way to repay their immigrant parents for their sacrifice.

53. Sharkey 2013.

54. Brown 2006, 2007.

55. Chen 2015; Mazelis 2017; Putnam 2016; Silva 2013.

Methodological Notes

1. Wilson 1987.

2. Portes and Zhou 1993; Zhou 1997.

3. Menjívar 2000.

REFERENCES

....

Ainsworth, James W. 2002. "Why Does It Take a Village? The Mediation of Neighborhood Effects on Educational Achievement." *Social Forces* 81(1): 117–52.

Ainsworth-Darnell, James W., and Douglas B. Downey. 1998. "Assessing the Oppositional Culture Explanation for Racial/Ethnic Differences in School Performance." *American Sociological Review* 63(4): 536–53.

Aisenberg, Eugene, and Todd Herrenkohl. 2008. "Community Violence in Context: Risk and Resilience in Children and Families." *Journal of Interpersonal Violence* 23(3): 296–315.

Alba, Richard, and Nancy Denton. 2004. "Old and New Landscapes of Diversity: The Residential Patterns of Immigrant Minorities." In *Not Just Black and White: Historical and Contemporary Perspectives on Immigration, Race, and Ethnicity in the United States*, edited by Nancy Foner and George M. Frederickson. New York: Russell Sage Foundation.

Alba, Richard, Tomás R. Jiménez, and Helen B. Marrow. 2014. "Mexican Americans as a Paradigm for Contemporary Intra-group Heterogeneity." *Ethnic and Racial Studies* 37(3): 446–66.

Alba, Richard, Philip Kasinitz, and Mary Waters. 2011. "The Kids Are (Mostly) Alright: Second-Generation Assimilation: Comments on Haller, Portes, and Lynch." *Social Forces* 89(3): 763–73.

Alba, Richard D., John R. Logan, and Brian J. Stults. 2000. "The Changing Neighborhood Contexts of the Immigrant Metropolis." *Social Forces* 79(2): 587–621.

Alba, Richard D., and Victor Nee. 2003. *Remaking the American Mainstream: Assimilation and Contemporary Immigration*. Cambridge, Mass: Harvard University Press.

Alsybar, Bangele Deguzman. 2007. "Youth Groups and Youth Savers: Gangs, Crews, and the Rise of Filipino American Youth Culture in Los Angeles." PhD diss., University of California at Los Angeles, Anthropology Department.

American Immigration Council. 2017. "Fact Sheet: The Cost of Immigration Enforcement and Border Security." May 17. https://www.americanimmigrationcouncil.org/research/the-cost-of-immigration-enforcement-and-border-security.

Anderson, Elijah. 1999. *Code of the Street: Decency, Violence, and the Moral Life of the Inner City.* New York: W. W. Norton & Co.

———. 2012. "The Iconic Ghetto." *Annals of the American Academy of Political and Social Science* 642(1): 8–24.

Andreas, Peter. 1998. "Escalation of U.S. Immigration Control in the Post-NAFTA Era." *Political Science Quarterly* 113(4): 591–615.

Arum, R. 2000. "Schools and Communities: Ecological and Institutional Dimensions." *Annual Review of Sociology* 26: 395–418.

Baca Zinn, Maxine. 1975. "Political Familism: Toward Sex Role Equality in Chicano Families." *Aztlan* 6(1): 13–26.

———. 1977. "Urban Kinship and Midwest Chicano Families: Review and Reformulation." Paper presented at the annual meeting of the Western Social Science Association, Denver, Colo.

———.1982. "Familism among Chicanos: A Theoretical Review." *Humboldt Journal of Social Relations* 10(1): 224–38.

Batalova, Jeanne, and Michael Fix. 2011. "Up for Grabs: The Gains and Prospects of First- and Second-Generation Young Adults." Migration Policy Institute, November.

Bean, Frank D., Susan K. Brown, and James D. Bachmeier. 2015. *Parents without Papers: The Progress and Pitfalls of Mexican American Integration.* New York: Russell Sage Foundation.

Bean, Frank, and Gillian Stevens. 2003. *America's Newcomers and the Dynamics of Diversity.* New York: Russell Sage Foundation.

Blanchard, Sarah, and Chandra Muller. 2015. "Gatekeepers of the American Dream: How Teachers' Perceptions Shape the Academic Outcomes of Immigrant and Language-Minority Students." *Social Science Research* 51: 262–75.

Bostean, Georgiana, Flavia Cristina Drummond Andrade, and Edna A. Viruell-Fuentes. 2018. "Neighborhood Stressors and Psychological Distress among U.S. Latinos: Measuring the Protective Effects of Social Support from Family and Friends." *Stress and Health* (October 14). DOI: 10.1002/smi.2843.

Bourgois, Philippe. 2003. *In Search of Respect: Selling Crack in El Barrio.* New York: Cambridge University Press.

Bowen, Gary L., and Richard A. Van Dorn. 2002. "Community Violent Crime Rates and School Danger." *Children and Schools* 24(2): 90–104.

Briggs, Xavier de Souza. 1998. "Brown Kids in White Suburbs: Housing Mobility and the Many Faces of Social Capital." *Housing Policy Debate* 9(1): 177–221.

Briggs, Xavier de Souza, Susan J. Popkin, and John Goering. 2010. *Moving to Opportunity: The Story of an American Experiment to Fight Ghetto Poverty.* New York: Oxford University Press.

Britton, Marcus L., and Pat Rubio Goldsmith. 2013. "Keeping People in Their Place? Young-Adult Mobility and Persistence of Residential Segregation in U.S. Metropolitan Areas." *Urban Studies* 50(14): 2886–2903.

Brooks-Gunn, Jeanne, Greg Duncan, and J. Lawrence Aber. 1997. *Neighborhood Poverty: Context and Consequences for Children.* New York: Russell Sage Foundation.

Brooks-Gunn, Jeanne, Greg J. Duncan, Pamela Kato Klebanov, and Naomi Sealand. 1993. "Do Neighborhoods Influence Child and Adolescent Development?" *American Journal of Sociology* 99(2): 353–95.

Brown, Susan K. 2006. "Structural Assimilation Revisited: Mexican-Origin Nativity and Cross-Ethnic Primary Ties." *Social Forces* 85(1): 75–92.

———. 2007. "Delayed Spatial Assimilation: Multigenerational Incorporation of the Mexican-Origin Population in Los Angeles." *City and Community* 6(3): 193–209.

Buka, Stephen L., Theresa L. Stichick, Isolde Birdthistle, and Felton J. Earls. 2001. "Youth Exposure to Violence: Prevalence, Risks, and Consequences." *American Journal of Orthopsychiatry* 71(3): 298–310.

Burdick-Will, Julia. 2016. "Neighborhood Violent Crime and Academic Growth in Chicago: Lasting Effects of Early Exposure." *Social Forces* 95(1): 133–58.

———. 2018. "Neighborhood Violence, Peer Effects, and Academic Achievement in Chicago." *Sociology of Education* 91(3): 205–23.

Burdick-Will, Julia, Jens Ludwig, Stephen W. Raudenbush, Robert J. Sampson, Lisa Sunbonmatsu, and Patrick Sharkey. 2011. "Converging Evidence for Neighborhood Effects on Children's Test Scores: An Experimental, Quasi-Experimental, and Observational Comparison." In *Opportunity? Rising Inequality, Schools, and Children's Life Chances*, edited by Greg J. Duncan and Richard J. Murnane. New York: Russell Sage Foundation.

Burton, Linda M., and Robin L. Jarrett. 2000. "In the Mix, Yet on the Margins: The Place of Families in Urban Neighborhood and Child Development Research." *Journal of Marriage and the Family* 62(4): 1114–35.

Calavita, Kitty. 1992. *Inside the State: The Bracero Program, Immigration, and the INS*. New London: Routledge.

Camarillo, Albert. 1979. *Chicanos in a Changing Society: From Mexican Pueblos to American Barrios in Santa Barbara and Southern California, 1848–1930*. Dallas: Southern Methodist University Press.

Campaign for College Opportunity. 2017. "The Transfer Maze: The High Cost to Students and the State of California." September. https://collegecampaign.org/portfolio/september-2017-transfer-maze/.

Card, David, and Jesse Rothstein. 2007. "Racial Segregation and the Black-White Test Score Gap." *Journal of Public Economics* 91(11/12): 2158–84.

Carter, Prudence L. 2005. *Keepin' It Real: School Success beyond Black and White*. New York: Oxford University Press.

Cashin, Sheryll. 2014. Place, Not Race: A New Vision of Opportunity in America. Boston: Beacon Press.

Center for Migration Studies. 2016. "State-Level Unauthorized Population and Eligible-to-Naturalize Estimates." New York: Center for Migration Studies.

Cerrutti, Marcela, and Douglas S. Massey. 2001. "On the Auspices of Female Migration from Mexico to the United States." *Demography* 38(2): 187–200.

Chan Tack, Anjanette M., and Mario L. Small. 2017. "Making Friends in Violent Neighborhoods: Strategies among Elementary School Children." *Sociological Science* 4: 224–48.

Chapa, Jorge. 1988. "The Question of Mexican American Assimilation: Socioeconomic Parity or Underclass Formation?" Public Affairs Comment. Lyndon B. Johnson School of Public Affairs, University of Texas–Austin (Fall).

Chen, Victor Tan. 2015. *Cut Loose: Jobless and Hopeless in an Unfair Economy*. Berkeley: University of California Press.

Chetty, Raj, and Nathaniel Hendren. 2015a. "The Impacts of Neighborhoods on Inter-generational Mobility: Childhood Exposure Effects." *Quarterly Journal of Economics* 133(3): 1107–62.

———. 2015b. "The Impacts of Neighborhoods on Intergenerational Mobility: County-Level Estimates." *Quarterly Journal of Economics* 133(3): 1163–28.

Chetty, Raj, Nathaniel Hendren, and Lawrence Katz. 2016. "The Effects of Exposure to Better Neighborhoods on Children: New Evidence from the Moving to Opportunity Experiment." *American Economic Review* 106(4): 855–902.

Chetty, Raj, Nathaniel Hendren, Patrick Kline, Emmanuel Saez, and Nicholas Turner. 2014. "Is the United States Still a Land of Opportunity? Recent Trends in Intergenerational Mobility." *American Economic Review* 104(5): 141–47.

Clampet-Lundquist, Susan. 2010. "'Everyone Had Your Back': Social Ties, Perceived Safety, and Public Housing Relocation." *City and Community* 9(1): 87–108.

Clark, Rebecca L. 1992. *Neighborhood Effects on Dropping Out of School among Teenage Boys.* Washington, D.C.: Urban Institute.

Coleman, James S. 1988. "Social Capital in the Creation of Human Capital." *American Journal of Sociology* 94: S95–S120.

Community College Research Center. 2017. "Is It Really Cheaper to Start at a Community College? The Consequences of Inefficient Transfer for Community College Students Seeking Bachelor's Degrees." Teachers College, Columbia University.

Conchas, Gilberto. 2001. "Structuring Failure and Success: Understanding the Variability in Latino School Engagement." *Harvard Educational Review* 71(3): 475–505.

Contreras, Randol. 2013. *The Stickup Kids: Race, Drugs, Violence, and the American Dream.* Berkeley: University of California Press.

———. 2018. "From Nowhere: Space, Race, and Time in How Young Minority Men Understand Encounters with Gangs." *Qualitative Sociology* 41(2): 263–80.

Cook, Philip J., and Jens Ludwig. 1998. "The Burden of 'Acting White': Do Black Adolescents Disparage Academic Achievement?" In *The Black-White Test Score Gap,* edited by Christopher Jencks and Meredith Phillips. Washington, D.C.: Brookings Institution Press.

Cook, Thomas D., Melissa R. Herman, Meredith Phillips, and Richard A. Settersten. 2002. "Some Ways in Which Neighborhoods, Nuclear Families, Friendship Groups, and Schools Jointly Affect Changes in Early Adolescent Development." *Child Development* 73(4): 1283–1309.

Cooley-Quille, Michele, Rhonda C. Boyd, Erika Frantz, and James Walsh. 2001. "Emotional and Behavioral Impact of Exposure to Community Violence in Inner-City Adolescents." *Journal of Clinical Child Psychology* 30(2): 199–206.

Cornelius, Wayne A. 1978. *Mexican Migration to the United States: Causes, Consequences, and U.S. Responses.* Cambridge, Mass.: Center for International Studies, Massachusetts Institute of Technology.

———. 1992. "From Sojourners to Settlers: The Changing Profile of Mexican Immigration to the United States." In *U.S.-Mexico Relations: Labor Market Inter-dependence,* edited by Jorge A. Bustamante, Clark W. Reynolds, and Rauil Hinojosa-Ojeda. Stanford, Calif.: Stanford University Press.

Crane, Jonathan. 1991. "The Epidemic Theory of Ghettos and Neighborhood Effects on Dropping Out and Teenage Childbearing." *American Journal of Sociology* 96: 1226–59.

Crockett, Lisa J., Maria I. Iturbide, Rosalie A. Torres Stone, Meredith McGinley, Marcela Raffaelli, and Gustavo Carlo. 2007. "Acculturative Stress, Social Support, and Coping: Relations to Psychological Adjustment among Mexican American College Students." *Cultural Diversity and Ethnic Minority Psychology* 4: 347.

Crowder, Kyle, and Scott J. South. 2003. "Neighborhood Distress and School Dropout: The Variable Significance of Community Context." *Social Science Research* 32(4): 659–98.

Curley, Alexandra M. 2009. "Draining or Gaining? The Social Networks of Public Housing Movers in Boston." *Journal of Social and Personal Relationships* 26(2–3): 227–47.

Curran, Sara R., and Estela Rivero-Fuentes. 2003. "Engendering Migrant Networks: The Case of Mexican Migration." *Demography* 40(2): 289–307.

Curran, Sara R., and Abigail C. Saguy. 2001. "Migration and Cultural Change: A Role for Gender and Social Networks." *Journal of International Women's Studies* 2(3): 54–77.

Curran, Sara R., Steven Shafer, Katharine M. Donato, and Filiz Garip. 2006. "Mapping Gender and Migration in Sociological Scholarship: Is It Segregation or Integration?" *International Migration Review* 40(1): 199–223.

Darity, William. 2011. "Revisiting the Debate on Race and Culture: The New (Incorrect) Harvard/Washington Consensus." *Du Bois Review: Social Science Research on Race* 8(2): 467–76.

De la Roca, Jorge, Ingrid Gould Ellen, and Justin Steil. 2018. "Does Segregation Matter for Latinos?" *Journal of Housing Economics* 40(1): 129–41.

DeLuca, Stefanie, Susan Clampet-Lundquist, and Kathryn Edin. 2016. *Coming of Age in the Other America.* New York: Russell Sage Foundation.

Deming, David, Claudia Goldin, and Lawrence Katz. 2013. "For-Profit Colleges." *The Future of Children* 23(1): 137–63.

Devine, John. 1996. *Maximum Security: The Culture of Violence in Inner-City Schools.* Chicago: University of Chicago Press.

Dohan, Daniel. 2003. *The Price of Poverty: Money, Work, and Culture in the Mexican American Barrio.* Berkeley: University of California Press.

Dominguez, Silvia, and Celeste Watkins. 2003. "Creating Networks for Survival and Mobility: Social Capital among African-American and Latin-American Low-Income Mothers." *Social Problems* 50(1): 111–35.

Donato, Katherine M. 1993. "Current Trends and Patterns of Female Migration: Evidence from Mexico." *International Migration Review* 27(4): 748–71.

———. 2010. "U.S. Migration from Latin America: Gendered Patterns and Shifts." *Annals of the American Academy of Political and Social Science* 630: 78–92.

Donato, Rubén, and Jarrod Hanson. 2012. "Legally White, Socially 'Mexican': The Politics of De Jure and De Facto School Segregation in the American Southwest." *Harvard Educational Review* 82(2): 202–25.

Downey, Douglas B., James W. Ainsworth, and Zhenchao Qian. 2009. "Rethinking the Attitude-Achievement Paradox among Blacks." *Sociology of Education* 82: 1–19, 19.

Dunn, Timothy J. 1996. *The Militarization of the U.S.-Mexico Border, 1978–1992: Low-Intensity Conflict Doctrine Comes Home*. Austin: CMAS Books, University of Texas.

Durand, Jorge, and Douglas S. Massey. 2003. *Clandestinos: Migración México-Estados Unidos en los albores del siglo XXI*. México: UAZ/Miguel Ángel Porrúa.

Durand, Jorge, Douglas S. Massey, and Rene M. Zenteno. 2001. "Mexican Immigration to the United States: Continuities and Changes." *Latin American Research Review* 36(1): 107–27.

Dwyer, Rachel E. 2007. "Expanding Homes and Increasing Inequalities: U.S. Housing Development and the Residential Segregation of the Affluent." *Social Problems* 54: 23–46.

Elliott, Delbert, Scott Menard, Bruce Rankin, Amanda Elliott, William Julius Wilson, and David Huizinga. 2006. *Good Kids from Bad Neighborhoods: Successful Development in Social Context*. New York: Cambridge University Press.

Enriquez, Laura E. 2015. "Multigenerational Punishment: Shared Experiences of Undocumented Immigration Status within Mixed-Status Families." *Journal of Marriage and Family* 77(4): 939–53.

———. 2017. "A 'Master Status' or the 'Final Straw'? Assessing the Role of Immigration Status in Latino Undocumented Youths' Pathways out of School." *Journal of Ethnic and Migration Studies* 43(9): 1526–43.

Ensminger, Margaret E., Rebecca P. Lamkin, and Nora Jacobson. 1996. "School Leaving: A Longitudinal Perspective Including Neighborhood Effects." *Child Development* 67(5): 2400–2416.

Escobar, Edward J. 1999. *Race, Police, and the Making of a Political Identity: Mexican Americans and the Los Angeles Police Department, 1900–1945*, vol. 7. Berkeley: University of California Press.

Estrada, Emir, and Pierrette Hondagneu-Sotelo. 2011. "Intersectional Dignities: Latino Immigrant Street Vendor Youth in Los Angeles." *Journal of Contemporary Ethnography*. DOI: 10.1177/0891241610387926.

Farley, Reynolds, and Richard Alba. 2002. "The New Second Generation in the United States." *International Migration Review* 36(3): 669–701.

Fernandez, Raul E., and Gilbert G. Gonzalez. 2012. *A Century of Chicano History: Empire, Nations and Migration*. London: Routledge.

Fernandez, Roberto, and David Harris. 1992. "Social Isolation and the Underclass." In *Drugs, Crime, and Social Isolation: Barriers to Urban Opportunity*, edited by George E. Peterson and Adele Harrell. Washington, D.C.: Urban Institute.

Flores, Edward Orosco. 2013. *God's Gangs: Barrio Ministry, Masculinity, and Gang Recovery*. New York: New York University Press.

Flores-Yeffal, Nadia Yamel. 2013. *Migration-Trust Networks: Social Cohesion in Mexican U.S.-Bound Emigration*. College Station: Texas A&M University Press.

Fordham, Signithia, and John U. Ogbu. 1986. "Black Students' School Success: Coping with the 'Burden of "Acting White"'." *Urban Review* 18(3): 176–206.

Fox, Cybelle. 2012. *Three Worlds of Relief: Race, Immigration, and the American Welfare State from the Progressive Era to the New Deal*. Princeton, N.J.: Princeton University Press.

Fox, Cybelle, and Thomas A. Guglielmo. 2012. "Defining America's Racial Boundaries: Blacks, Mexicans, and European Immigrants, 1890–1945." *American Journal of Sociology* 118(2): 327–79.

Fragomen, Austin T.1997. "The Illegal Immigration Reform and Immigrant Responsibility Act of 1996: An Overview." *International Migration Review* 31(2): 438–60.

Frey, William H. 2018. "The Millennial Generation: A Demographic Bridge to America's Diverse Future." In *Metropolitan Policy Program*. Washington, D.C.: Brookings Institution.

Fry, Richard, and Paul Taylor. 2013. "Hispanic High School Graduates Pass Whites in Rate of College Enrollment: High School Drop-Out Rate at Record Low." Pew Research Center, May 9. https://www.pewhispanic.org/2013/05/09/hispanic-high-school-graduates-pass-whites-in-rate-of-college-enrollment/.

Fuller, Bruce, Yoonjeon Kim, Claudia Galindo, Shruti Bathia, Margaret Bridges, Greg J. Duncan, and Isabel García Valdivia. 2019. "Worsening School Segregation for Latino Children?" *Educational Researcher*. Published online July 29, 2019.

Furstenberg, Frank F. 2000. "The Sociology of Adolescence and Youth in the 1990s: A Critical Commentary." *Journal of Marriage and the Family* 62(4): 896–910.

Furstenberg, Frank F., Thomas D. Cook, Jacquelynne Eccles, Glen H. Elder, and Arnold Sameroff. 1999. *Managing to Make It: Urban Families and Adolescent Success.* Chicago: University of Chicago Press.

Fussell, Elizabeth. 2011. "The Deportation Threat Dynamic and Victimization of Latino Migrants: Wage Theft and Robbery." *Sociological Quarterly* 52(4): 593–615.

Gandara, Patricia. 1995. *Over the Ivy Walls: The Educational Mobility of Low-Income Chicanos.* Albany: State University of New York Press.

Gans, Herbert J. 1992a. "Second-Generation Decline: Scenarios for the Economic and Ethnic Futures of the Post-1965 American Immigrants." *Ethnic and Racial Studies* 15(2): 173–92.

———. 1992b. "Comment: Ethnic Invention and Acculturation: A Bumpy-Line Approach." *Journal of American Ethnic History* 11(1): 42–52.

Garip, Filiz. 2012. "Discovering Diverse Mechanisms of Migration: The Mexico-U.S. Stream 1970–2000." *Population and Development Review* 38(3): 393–433.

———. 2017. *On the Move: Changing Mechanism of Mexico-U.S. Migration.* Princeton, N.J.: Princeton University Press.

Gelbgiser, Dafna. 2018. "College for All, Degrees for Few: For-Profit Colleges and Socioeconomic Differences in Degree Attainment." *Social Forces* 96(4): 1785–1824.

Gibson, Margaret A., Patricia C. Gandara, and Jill Peterson Koyama, eds. 2004. *School Connections: U.S. Mexican Youth, Peers, and School Achievement.* New York: Teachers College Press.

Goffman, Alice. 2014. *On the Run: Fugitive Life in an American City.* Chicago: University of Chicago Press.

Goffman, Erving. 1974. *Frame Analysis: An Essay on the Organization of Experience.* Cambridge, Mass.: Harvard University Press.

Goldmann, Emily, Allison Aiello, Monica Uddin, Jorge Delva, Karestan Koenen, Larry M. Gant, and Sandro Galea. 2011. "Pervasive Exposure to Violence and Posttraumatic

Stress Disorder in a Predominantly African American Urban Community: The Detroit Neighborhood Health Study." *Journal of Traumatic Stress* 24(6): 747–51.

Goldsmith, Pat Rubio. 2009. "Schools or Neighborhoods or Both? Race and Ethnic Segregation and Educational Attainment." *Social Forces* 87(4): 1913–41.

Gómez, Laura E. 2018. *Manifest Destinies: The Making of the Mexican American Race.* New York: New York University Press.

Gonzales, Roberto G. 2011. "Learning to Be Illegal: Undocumented Youth and Shifting Legal Contexts in the Transition to Adulthood." *American Sociological Review* 76(4): 602–19.

Gonzalez, Gilbert G. 2013. *Chicano Education in the Era of Segregation.* Denton: University of North Texas Press.

González, Thalia. 2012. "Keeping Kids in Schools: Restorative Justice, Punitive Discipline, and the School to Prison Pipeline." *Journal of Law and Education* 41: 281.

Gordon, Milton Myron. 1964. *Assimilation in American Life: The Role of Race, Religion, and National Origins.* New York: Oxford University Press.

Gregory, Anne, Russell J. Skiba, and Pedro A. Noguera. 2010. "The Achievement Gap and the Discipline Gap: Two Sides of the Same Coin?" *Educational Researcher* 39(1): 59–68.

Grossman, Jean B., and Jean E. Rhodes. 2002. "The Test of Time: Predictors and Effects of Duration in Youth Mentorship Relationships." *American Journal of Community Psychology* 30(2): 199–219.

Haller, William, Alejandro Portes, and Scott M. Lynch. 2011. "Dreams Fulfilled, Dreams Shattered: Determinants of Segmented Assimilation in the Second Generation." *Social Forces* 89(3): 733–62.

Hallet, Miranda Cady. 2012. "Better than White Trash: Work Ethic, Latindad, and Whiteness in Rural Arkansas." *Latino Studies Journal* 10(1/2): 81–106.

Harding, David J. 2003. "Counterfactual Models of Neighborhood Effects: The Effect of Neighborhood Poverty on Dropping Out and Teenage Pregnancy." *American Journal of Sociology* 109(3): 676–719.

———. 2009a. "Collateral Consequences of Violence in Disadvantaged Neighborhoods." *Social Forces* 88(2): 757–84.

———. 2009b. "Violence, Older Peers, and the Socialization of Adolescent Boys in Disadvantaged Neighborhoods." *American Sociological Review* 74(3): 445–64.

———. 2010. *Living the Drama: Community, Conflict, and Culture among Inner-City Boys.* Chicago: University of Chicago Press.

Harding, David J., Lisa Gennetian, Christopher Winship, Lisa Sunbonmatsu, and Jeffrey R. Kling. 2011. "Unpacking Neighborhood Influence on Education Outcomes: Setting the Stage for Future Research." In *Whither Opportunity? Rising Inequality, Schools, and Children's Life Chances*, edited by Greg J. Duncan and Richard J. Murnane. New York: Russell Sage Foundation.

Harris, Angel L. 2011. *Kids Don't Want to Fail: Oppositional Culture and the Black-White Achievement Gap.* Cambridge, Mass.: Harvard University Press.

Hayes, Joseph, and Laura Hill. 2017. "Undocumented Immigrants in California." Public Policy Institute of California, March. https://www.ppic.org/content/pubs/jtf/JTF_UndocumentedImmigrantsJTF.pdf.

Hernández-León, Rubén. 2008. *Metropolitan Migrants: The Migration of Urban Mexicans to the United States*. Berkeley: University of California Press.

Hernández-León, Rubén, and Sarah Morando Lakhani. 2013. "Gender, Bilingualism, and the Early Occupational Careers of Second-Generation Mexicans in the South." *Social Forces* 92(1): 59–80.

Hipp, John R., George E. Tita, and Lyndsay N. Boggess. 2009. "Intergroup and Intragroup Violence: Is Violent Crime an Expression of Group Conflict or Social Disorganization?" *Criminology* 47(2): 521–64.

Hirschfield, Paul J. 2008. "Preparing for Prison? The Criminalization of School Discipline in the USA." *Theoretical Criminology* 12(1): 79–101.

Hirschfield, Paul J., and Katarzyna Celinska. 2011. "Beyond Fear: Sociological Perspectives on the Criminalization of School Discipline." *Sociology Compass* 5(1): 1–12.

Hochschild, Jennifer L. 1995. *Facing Up to the American Dream: Race, Class, and the Soul of the Nation*. Princeton, N.J.: Princeton University Press.

Hondagneu-Sotelo, Pierrette. 1992. "Overcoming Patriarchal Constraints: The Reconstruction of Gender Relations among Mexican Immigrant Women and Men." *Gender and Society* 6(3): 393–415.

———. 1994. *Gendered Transitions: Mexican Experiences of Immigration*. Berkeley: University of California Press.

———. 2003. *Gender and U.S. Immigration: Contemporary Trends*. Berkeley: University of California Press.

Horowitz, Ruth. 1983. *Honor and the American Dream: Culture and Identity in a Chicano Community*. New Brunswick, N.J.: Rutgers University Press.

Hout, Michael. 2012. "Social and Economic Returns to College Education in the United States." *Annual Review of Sociology* 38: 379–400.

Huntington, Samuel P. 2004. "The Hispanic Challenge." *Foreign Policy* (March/April): 30–45.

Jack, Anthony Abraham. 2019. *The Privileged Poor: How Elite Colleges Are Failing Disadvantaged Students*. Cambridge, Mass.: Harvard University Press.

Jargowsky, Paul A. 2003. *Stunning Progress, Hidden Problems: The Dramatic Decline of Concentrated Poverty in the 1990s*. Washington, D.C.: Brookings Institution.

Johnson, Hans, and Sergio Sanchez. 2019. "Immigrants in California Just the Facts." Public Policy Institute of California, May. https://www.ppic.org/wp-content/uploads/jtf-immigrants-in-california.pdf.

Johnson, Ottis. 2012. "A Systematic Review of Neighborhood and Institutional Relationships Related to Education." *Education and Urban Society* 44(4): 471–511.

Jones-Correa, Michael. 2000. "The Origins and Diffusion of Racial Restrictive Covenants." *Political Science Quarterly* 115(4): 541–68.

Kahn, Bonnie M. 1987. *Cosmopolitan Culture: The Gilt-Edged Dream of a Tolerant City*. New York: Atheneum.

Kanaiaupuni, Shawn Malia. 2000. "Reframing the Migration Question: An Analysis of Men, Women, and Gender in Mexico." *Social Forces* 78(4): 1311–47.

Kao, Grace, and Marta Tienda. 1995. "Optimism and Achievement: The Educational Performance of Immigrant Youth." *Social Science Quarterly* 76(1): 1–19.

Kasinitz, Philip, John H. Mollenkopf, Mary C. Waters, and Jennifer Holdaway. 2008. *Inheriting the City: The Children of Immigrants Come of Age.* Cambridge, Mass., and New York: Harvard University Press and Russell Sage Foundation.

Katznelson, Ira. 2005. *When Affirmative Action Was White: An Untold History of Racial Inequality in Twentieth-Century America.* New York: W. W. Norton & Co.

Kawachi, Ichiro, and Lisa F. Berkman. 2003. *Neighborhoods and Health.* New York: Oxford University Press.

Keefe, Susan Emley. 1979. "Urbanization, Acculturation, and Extended Family Ties: Mexican Americans in Cities." *American Ethnologist* 6(2): 349–65.

———. 1980. "Acculturation and the Extended Family among Urban Mexican Americans." In *Acculturation: Theory, Models, and Some New Findings,* edited by Amado M. Padilla. Boulder, Colo.: Westview Press.

Kneebone, Elizabeth, and Natalie Holmes. 2016. *U.S. Concentrated Poverty in the Wake of the Great Recession.* Washington, D.C.: Brookings Institution.

Kneebone, Elizabeth, Carey Nadeau, and Alan Berube. 2011. "The Re-emergence of Concentrated Poverty: Metropolitan Trends in the 2000s." In *Metropolitan Policy Program.* Washington, D.C.: Brookings Institution.

Kochhar, Rakesh, Richard Fry, and Paul Taylor. 2011. "Wealth Gaps Rise to Record Highs between Whites, Blacks, and Hispanics." Pew Research Center, July 26. https://www.pewresearch.org/wp-content/uploads/sites/3/2011/07/SDT-Wealth-Report_7-26-11_FINAL.pdf.

Kozol, Jonathan. 2012. *Savage Inequalities: Children in America's Schools.* New York: Broadway Books.

Krivo, Lauren J., Heather M. Washington, Ruth D. Peterson, Christopher R. Browning, Catherine A. Calder, and Mei-Po Kwan. 2013. "Social Isolation of Disadvantage and Advantage: The Reproduction of Inequality in Urban Space." *Social Forces* 92(1): 141–64.

Krogstad, Jens Manuel, and Richard Fry. 2015. "Analysis Shows Fewer Hispanic Young Adults Disconnected from School, Jobs." Pew Research Center, August 17. https://www.pewresearch.org/fact-tank/2015/08/17/analysis-shows-fewer-hispanic-young-adults-disconnected-from-school-jobs/.

Krogstad, Jens Manuel, Jeffrey S. Passel, and D'Vera Cohn. 2017. "Five Facts about Illegal Immigration in the U.S." Pew Research Center, June 12. https://www.pewresearch.org/fact-tank/2019/06/12/5-facts-about-illegal-immigration-in-the-u-s/.

Lamont, Michèle. 2002. *The Dignity of Working Men: Morality and the Boundaries of Race, Class, and Immigration.* Cambridge, Mass.: Harvard University Press.

Lardier, David T., Jr., Kathryn G. Herr, Veronica R. Barrios, Pauline Garcia-Reid, and Robert J. Reid. 2019. "Merit in Meritocracy: Uncovering the Myth of Exceptionality and Self-Reliance through the Voices of Urban Youth of Color." *Education and Urban Society* 51(4): 474–500.

Lareau, Annette. 2003. *Unequal Childhoods: Class, Race, and Family Life.* Berkeley: University of California Press.

Lee, Hyein, and Margaret M. Chin. 2015. "Navigating the Road to Work: Second-Generation Asian American Finance Workers." *Asian American Policy Review* 26: 20–29.

Lee, Jennifer, and Min Zhou. 2014. "The Success Frame and Achievement Paradox: The Costs and Consequences for Asian Americans." *Race and Social Problems* 6(1): 38–55.

———. 2015. *The Asian American Achievement Paradox*. New York: Russell Sage Foundation.

Lee, Matthew T., and Ramiro Martinez. 2009. "Immigration Reduces Crime: An Emerging Scholarly Consensus." In *Immigration, Crime, and Justice*, edited by William F. McDonald. Bingley, U.K.: Emerald Group Publishing.

Lee, Sara S. 2004. "Class Matters: Racial and Ethnic Identities of Working- and Middle-Class Second-Generation Korean Americans in New York City." In *Becoming New Yorkers: Ethnographies of the New Second Generation*, edited by Philip Kasinitz, John H. Mollenkopf, and Mary C. Waters. New York: Russell Sage Foundation.

Leventhal, Tama, and Jeanne Brooks-Gunn. 2000. "The Neighborhoods They Live In: The Effects of Neighborhood Residence on Child and Adolescent Outcomes." *Psychological Bulletin* 126(2): 309–37.

Lewis, Oscar. 1961. *The Children of Sanchez: Autobiography of a Mexican Family*. New York: Viking.

———. 1966. *La Vida: A Puerto Rican Family in the Culture of Poverty—San Juan and New York*. New York: Random House.

Livingston, Gretchen, and Joan R. Kahn. 2002. "An American Dream Unfulfilled: The Limited Mobility of Mexican Americans." *Social Science Quarterly* 83(4): 1003–12.

Logan, John R., Brian J. Stults, and Reynolds Farley. 2004. "Segregation of Minorities in the Metropolis: Two Decades of Change." *Demography* 41(1): 1–22. DOI: 10.1353/dem.2004.0007.

Long, Bridget Terry, and Michal Kurlaender. 2009. "Do Community Colleges Provide a Viable Pathway to a Baccalaureate Degree?" *Educational Evaluation and Policy Analysis* 31(1): 30–53.

Lopez, David E., and Ricardo Stanton-Salazar. 2001. "Mexican-Americans: A Second Generation at Risk." In *Ethnicities: Children of Immigrants in America*, edited by Alejandro Portes and Ruben Rumbaut. Berkeley: University of California Press.

Lopez, Edward M., Alison Wishard, Ronald Gallimore, and Wendy Rivera. 2006. "Latino High School Students' Perceptions of Gangs and Crews." *Journal of Adolescent Research* 21(3): 299–318.

López, Ian F. Haney. 2009. *Racism on Trial: The Chicano Fight for Justice*. Cambridge, Mass.: Harvard University Press.

Lopez, Mark Hugo, Rich Morin, and Jens Manuel Krogstad. 2016. "Latinos Increasingly Confident in Personal Finances, See Better Economic Times Ahead." Pew Research Center, June 8. https://www.pewhispanic.org/2016/06/08/latinos-increasingly-confident-in-personal-finances-see-better-economic-times-ahead/.

Louie, Vivian. 2004. *Compelled to Excel: Immigration, Education, and Opportunity among Chinese Americans*. Stanford, Calif.: Stanford University Press.

———. 2006. "Second-Generation Pessimism and Optimism: How Chinese and Dominicans Understand Education and Mobility through Ethnic and Transnational Orientations." *International Migration Review* 40(3): 537–72.

———. 2012. *Keeping the Immigrant Bargain: The Costs and Rewards of Success in America*. New York: Russell Sage Foundation.

Ludwig, Jens, Greg J. Duncan, Lisa A. Gennetian, Lawrence F. Katz, Ronald C. Kessler, Jeffrey R. Kling, and Lisa Sanbonmatsu. 2013. "Long-Term Neighborhood Effects on

Low-Income Families: Evidence from Moving to Opportunity." *American Economic Review* 103(3): 226–31.

Lynch, Mamie, Jennifer Engle, and Jose L. Cruz. 2010. "Subprime Opportunity: The Unfulfilled Promise of For-Profit Colleges and Universities." Education Trust, November. https://edtrust.org/wp-content/uploads/2013/10/Subprime_report_1.pdf.

Ma, Jennifer, and Sandy Baum. 2016. "Trends in Community Colleges: Enrollment, Prices, Student Debt, and Completion." *College Board Research Brief.* College Board Research, April. https://trends.collegeboard.org/sites/default/files/trends-in-community-colleges-research-brief.pdf.

MacLeod, Jay. 1995 [1987]. *Ain't No Makin' It: Aspirations and Attainment in a Low Income Neighborhood.* Boulder, Colo.: Westview Press.

Macmillan, Ross, and John Hagan. 2004. "Violence in the Transition to Adulthood: Adolescent Victimization, Education, and Socioeconomic Attainment in Later Life." *Journal of Research on Adolescence* 14(2): 127–58.

Marcelli, Enrico A., and Wayne A. Cornelius. 2001. "The Changing Profile of Mexican Migrants to the United States: New Evidence from California and Mexico." *Latin American Research Review* 36(3): 105–31.

Margolin, Gayla, Katrina A. Vickerman, Michelle C. Ramos, Sarah Duman Serrano, Elana B. Gordis, Esti Iturralde, Pamella H. Oliver, and Lauren A. Spies. 2009. "Youth Exposed to Violence: Stability, Co-occurrence, and Context." *Clinical Child and Family Psychology Review* 12(1): 39–54.

Martinez, Cid. 2016. *The Neighborhood Has Its Own Rules: Latinos and African Americans in South Los Angeles.* New York: New York University Press.

Martinez, Cid, and Victor M. Rios. 2011. "Conflict, Cooperation, and Avoidance." In *Just Neighbors? Research on African American and Latino Relations in the United States,* edited by Edward Telles, Mark Sawyer, and Gaspar Rivera-Salgado. New York: Russell Sage Foundation.

Martinez, Ramiro, Jr. 2002. *Latino Homicide: Immigration, Violence, and Community.* London: Routledge.

Martinez, Ramiro, Jr., and Abel Valenzuela Jr. 2006. *Immigration and Crime: Ethnicity, Race, and Violence,* New York: New York University Press.

Massey, Douglas S. 1990. "Social Structure, Household Strategies, and the Cumulative Causation of Migration." *Population Index* 56(1): 3–26.

———. 1996. "The Age of Extremes: Concentrated Affluence and Poverty in the Twenty-First Century." *Demography* 33(4): 395–412.

———. 2007. *Categorically Unequal: The American Stratification System.* New York: Russell Sage Foundation.

Massey, Douglas S., and Nancy Denton. 1993. *American Apartheid: Segregation and the Making of the Underclass.* Cambridge, Mass.: Harvard University Press.

Massey, Douglas S., Jorge Durand, and Nolan J. Malone. 2002. *Beyond Smoke and Mirrors: Mexican Immigration in an Era of Economic Integration.* New York: Russell Sage Foundation.

Massey, Douglas S., and Kristin E. Espinosa. 1997. "What's Driving Mexico-U.S. Migration? A Theoretical, Empirical, and Policy Analysis." *American Journal of Sociology* 102(4): 939–99.

Massey, Douglas S., and Mary J. Fischer. 2003. "The Geography of Inequality in the United States, 1950–2000." In *Brookings-Wharton Papers on Urban Affairs: 2003*, edited by William G. Gale and Janet Rothenberg Pack. Washington, D.C.: Brookings Institution.

Massey, Douglas S., and Audrey Singer. 1995. "New Estimates of Undocumented Mexican Migration and the Probability of Apprehension." *Demography* 32(2): 203–13.

Mateu-Gelabert, Pedro, and Howard Lune. 2003. "School Violence: The Bidirectional Conflict Flow between Neighborhood and School." *City and Community* 2(4): 353–69.

———. 2007. "Street Codes in High School: School as an Educational Deterrent." *City and Community* 6(3): 173–91.

Mazelis, Joan Maya. 2017. *Surviving Poverty: Creating Sustainable Ties among the Poor.* New York: New York University Press.

McPherson, Miller, Lynn Smith-Lovin, and Matthew E. Brashears. 2006. "Social Isolation in America: Changes in Core Discussion Networks over Two Decades." *American Sociological Review* 71(3): 353–75.

Menchaca, Martha. 2001. *Recovering History, Constructing Race: The Indian, Black, and White Roots of Mexican Americans.* Austin: University of Texas Press.

Menchaca, Martha, and Richard R. Valencia. 1990. "Anglo-Saxon Ideologies in the 1920s–1930s: Their Impact on the Segregation of Mexican Students in California." *Anthropology and Education Quarterly* 21(3): 222–49.

Menjívar, Cecilia. 2000. *Fragmented Ties: Salvadoran Immigrant Networks in America.* Berkeley: University of California Press.

Mickelson, Roslyn Arlin. 1990. "The Attitude-Achievement Paradox among Black Adolescents." *Sociology of Education* 63(1): 44–61.

Ming, William, Jr. 1949. "Racial Restrictions and the Fourteenth Amendment: The Restrictive Covenant Cases." *University of Chicago Law Review* 16(2):203–38.

Molina, Natalia. 2006. *Fit to Be Citizens?: Public Health and Race in Los Angeles, 1879–1939.* Berkeley: University of California Press.

———. 2014. *How Race Is Made in America: Immigration, Citizenship, and the Historical Power of Racial Scripts.* Berkeley: University of California Press.

Moore, Joan W. 1989. "Is There a Hispanic Underclass?" *Social Science Quarterly* 70(2): 265–85.

Moore, Joan W., and Raquel Pinderhughes, eds. 1993. *In the Barrios: Latinos and the Underclass Debate.* New York: Russell Sage Foundation.

Moore, Joan W., and James Diego Vigil. 1987. "Chicano Gangs: Group Norms and Individual Factors Related to Adult Criminality." *Aztlan* 18(2): 27–44.

———. 1993. "Barrios in Transition." In *In the Barrios: Latinos and the Underclass Debate,* edited by Joan Moore and Racquel Pinderhughes. New York: Russell Sage Foundation.

Morando, Sarah J. 2013. "Paths to Mobility: The Mexican Second Generation at Work in a New Destination." *Sociological Quarterly* 54(3): 367–98.

Morenoff, Jeffrey D., and Marta Tienda. 1997. "Underclass Neighborhoods in Temporal and Ecological Perspective." *Annals of the American Academy of Political and Social Science* 551(1): 59–72.

Moynihan, Daniel Patrick, Lee Rainwater, and William L. Yancey. 1967. *The Negro Family: The Case for National Action.* Cambridge, Mass.: MIT Press.

Mulvaney-Day, Norah E., Margarita Alegria, and William Sribney. 2007. "Social Cohesion, Social Support, and Health among Latinos in the United States." *Social Science and Medicine* 64(2): 477–95.

Musick, Kelly, Ann Meier, and Sarah Flood. 2016. "How Parents Fare: Mothers' and Fathers' Subjective Well-Being in Time with Children." *American Sociological Review* 81(5): 1069–95.

Newman, Katherine S. 2009. *No Shame in My Game: The Working Poor in the Inner City.* New York: Vintage.

Newman, Katherine S., and Victor Tan Chen. 2007. *The Missing Class: Portraits of the Near Poor in America.* Boston, Mass.: Beacon Press.

Noguera, Pedro. 2003. *City Schools and the American Dream: Reclaiming the Promise of Public Education.* New York: Teachers College Press.

O'Conner, Carla. 1999. "Race, Class, and Gender in America: Narratives of Opportunity Among Low-Income African American Youth." *Sociology of Education* 72: 137–57.

Orfield, Gary, Jongyeon Ee, Erica Frankenberg, and Genevieve Siegel-Hawley. 2016. "'Brown' at 62: School Segregation by Race, Poverty, and State." Civil Rights Project/ Proyecto Derechos Civiles, University of California–Los Angeles, May 16.

Orfield, Gary, and Chungmei Lee. 2007. "Historic Reversals, Accelerating Resegregation, and the Need for New Integration Strategies." Civil Rights Project/Proyecto de Derechos Civiles, University of California–Los Angeles, August 29.

Ortiz, Vilma. 1996. "The Mexican-Origin Population: Permanent Working Class or Emerging Middle Class?" In *Ethnic Los Angeles*, edited by Roger D. Waldinger and Mehdi Bozorgmehr. New York: Russell Sage Foundation.

Ousey, Graham C., and Charis E. Kubrin. 2018. "Immigration and Crime: Assessing a Contentious Issue." *Annual Review of Criminology* 1: 63–84.

Owens, Ann. 2010. "Neighborhoods and Schools as Competing and Reinforcing Contexts for Educational Attainment." *Sociology of Education* 83(4): 287–310.

Owens, Ann, Sean F. Reardon, and Christopher Jencks. 2016. "Income Segregation between Schools and School Districts." *American Educational Research Journal* 53(4): 1159–97.

Papachristos, Andrew. 2009. "Murder by Structure: Dominance Relations and the Social Structure of Gang Homicide." *American Journal of Sociology* 115(1): 74–128.

Papachristos, Andrew, David M. Hureau, and Anthony A. Braga. 2013. "The Corner and the Crew: The Influence of Geography and Social Networks on Gang Violence." *American Sociological Review* 78(3): 417–47.

Pastor, Manuel, Rhonda Ortiz, Vanessa Carter, Justin Scoggins, and Anthony Perez. 2012. "California Immigrant Integration Scorecard." University of Southern California, Center for the Study of Immigrant Integration, September 12. https:// dornsife.usc.edu/assets/sites/731/docs/California_Immigrant_Integration_ Scorecard_web.pdf.

Patten, Eileen. 2016. "The Nation's Latino Population Is Defined by Its Youth." Pew Research Center, April 20. https://www.pewhispanic.org/2016/04/20/the-nations-latino-population-is-defined-by-its-youth/.

Patterson, Orlando. 2015. *The Cultural Matrix: Understanding Black Youth.* Cambridge, Mass: Harvard University Press.

Pattillo, Mary. 2013. *Black Picket Fences: Privilege and Peril among the Black Middle Class.* Chicago: University of Chicago Press.

Pedraza, Silvia. 1991. "Women and Migration: The Social Consequences of Gender." *Annual Review of Sociology* 17: 303–25.

Peguero, Anthony A., Nadine M. Connell, and Jun Sung Hong. 2018. "Introduction to the Special Issue "School Violence and Safety." *Youth Violence and Juvenile Justice* 16(2): 119–23.

Peguero, Anthony A., and Zahra Shekarkhar. 2011. "Latino/a Student Misbehavior and School Punishment." *Hispanic Journal of Behavioral Sciences* 33(1): 54–70.

Peguero, Anthony A., Zahra Shekarkhar, Ann Marie Popp, and Dixie J. Koo. 2015. "Punishing the Children of Immigrants: Race, Ethnicity, Generational Status, Student Misbehavior, and School Discipline." *Journal of Immigrant and Refugee Studies* 13(2): 200–20.

Perlmann, Joel. 2005. *Italians Then, Mexicans Now: Immigrant Origins and Second-Generation Progress, 1890 to 2000.* New York: Russell Sage Foundation.

Perlmann, Joel, and Roger Waldinger. 1997. "Second Generation Decline? Children of Immigrants, Past and Present—A Reconsideration." *International Migration Review* 31(4): 893–922.

Pessar, Patricia. 1999a. "Engendering Migration Studies: The Case of New Immigrants in the United States." *American Behavioral Scientist* 42: 577–600.

———. 1999b. "The Role of Gender, Households, and Social Networks in the Migration Process: A Review and Appraisal." In *The Handbook of International Migration: The American Experience*, edited by Charles Hirschman, Philip Kasinitz, and Joshua DeWind. New York: Russell Sage Foundation.

Pew Research Center. 2011. "Wealth Gaps Rise to Record Highs between Whites, Blacks, and Hispanics." Pew Research Center, September 12. https://www.pewresearch.org/fact-tank/2011/09/12/wealth-gaps-rise-to-record-highs-between-whites-blacks-and-hispanics/.

———. 2013. "Modern Parenthood Roles of Moms and Dads Converge as They Balance Work and Family." Pew Research Center, March 14. https://www.pewsocialtrends.org/2013/03/14/modern-parenthood-roles-of-moms-and-dads-converge-as-they-balance-work-and-family/.

———. 2015. "The American Middle Class is Losing Ground." Pew Research Center, November 9. https://www.pewsocialtrends.org/2015/12/09/the-american-middle-class-is-losing-ground/.

———. 2016a. "America's Shrinking Middle Class: A Close Look at Changes within Metropolitan Areas." Pew Research Center, May 11. https://www.pewsocialtrends.org/2016/05/11/americas-shrinking-middle-class-a-close-look-at-changes-within-metropolitan-areas/.

———. 2016b. "Five Facts about Latinos and Education." Pew Research Center, July 28. https://www.pewresearch.org/fact-tank/2016/07/28/5-facts-about-latinos-and-education/.

———. 2019. "Latinos' Incomes Higher Than Before Great Recession, but U.S.-Born Latinos Yet to Recover." Pew Research Center, March 7. https://www.pewhispanic.org/2019/03/07/latinos-incomes-higher-than-before-great-recession-but-u-s-born-latinos-yet-to-recover/.

Pong, Suet-Ling, and Lingxin Hao. 2007. "Neighborhood and School Factors in the School Performance of Immigrants' Children." *International Migration Review* 41(1): 206–41.

Portes, Alejandro. 1998. "Social Capital: Its Origins and Applications in Modern Sociology." *Annual Review of Sociology* 24: 1–24.

Portes, Alejandro, and József Böröcz. 1989. "Contemporary Immigration: Theoretical Perspectives on Its Determinants and Modes of Incorporation." *International Migration Review* 23(3): 606–30.

Portes, Alejandro, Patricia Fernández-Kelly, and William Haller. 2005. "Segmented Assimilation on the Ground: The New Second Generation in Early Adulthood." *Ethnic and Racial Studies* 28(6): 1000–1040.

Portes, Alejandro, and Patricia Landolt. 1996. "The Downside of Social Capital." *American Prospect* 26(May-June): 18–22.

Portes, Alejandro, and Rubén Rumbaut, eds. 2001. *Legacies: The Story of the Immigrant Second Generation.* Berkeley: University of California Press.

Portes, Alejandro, and Julia Sensenbrenner. 1993. "Embeddedness and Immigration: Notes on the Social Determinants of Economic Action." *American Journal of Sociology* 98(6): 1320–50.

Portes, Alejandro, and Min Zhou. 1993. "The New Second Generation: Segmented Assimilation and Its Variants." *Annals of the American Academy of Political and Social Science* 530(1): 74–96.

Purser, Gretchen. 2009. "The Dignity of Job-Seeking Men: Boundary Work among Immigrant Day Laborers." *Journal of Contemporary Ethnography* 38(1): 117–39.

Putnam, Robert D. 2016. *Our Kids: The American Dream in Crisis.* New York: Simon and Schuster.

Rainwater, Lee. 1970. "The Problem of Lower Class Culture." *Journal of Social Issues* 26(2): 133–48.

Reardon, Sean F. 2011. "The Widening Academic Achievement Gap between the Rich and the Poor: New Evidence and Possible Explanations." In *Whither Opportunity: Rising Inequality, Schools, and Children's Life Chances,* edited by Greg J. Duncan and Richard Murnane. New York: Russell Sage Foundation.

Reardon, Sean F., and Kendra Bischoff. 2011. "Income Inequality and Income Segregation." *American Journal of Sociology* 116(4): 1092–1153.

Reardon, Sean F., and Ann Owens. 2014. "60 Years after Brown: Trends and Consequences of School Segregation." *Annual Review of Sociology* 40: 199–218.

Reid, Lesley Williams, Harald E. Weiss, Robert M. Adelman, and Charles Jaret. 2005. "The Immigration-Crime Relationship: Evidence across U.S. Metropolitan Areas." *Social Science Research* 34(4): 757–80.

Rendón, María G. 2013. "Drop Out and 'Disconnected' Young Adults: Examining the Impact of Neighborhood and School Contexts." *Urban Review* 46(2): 169–96. DOI: 10.1007/s11256-013-0251-8.

———. 2014. "'Caught Up': How Urban Violence and Peer Ties Contribute to High School Noncompletion." *Social Problems* 61(1): 61–82.

———. 2015. "The Urban Question and Identity Formation: The Case of Second-Generation Mexican Males in Los Angeles." *Ethnicities* 15(2): 165–89. DOI: 10.1177/1468796814557652.

———. 2019. "'There's Nothing Holding Us Back': The Enduring and Shifting Cultural Outlooks of Inner City Second Generation Latinos." *City and Community* 18(1): 151–72.

Rendón, María G., Adriana Aldana, and Laureen D. Hom. 2018. "Children of Latino Immigrants Framing Race: Making Sense of Criminalisation in a Colour-Blind Era." *Journal of Ethnic and Migration Studies.* DOI: 10.1080/1369183X.2018.1486181.

Rich, John A., and Courtney M. Grey. 2005. "Pathways to Recurrent Trauma among Young Black Men: Traumatic Stress, Substance Use, and the 'Code of the Street.'" *American Journal of Public Health* 95(5): 816–24.

Rios, Victor. 2011. *Punished: Policing the Lives of Black and Latino Boys.* New York: New York University Press.

Riosmena, Fernando, and Douglas S. Massey. 2012. "Pathways to El Norte: Origins, Destinations, and Characteristics of Mexican Migrants to the United States." *International Migration Review* 46(1): 3–36.

Roffman, Jennifer, Carola Suárez-Orozco, and Jean E. Rhodes. 2003. "Facilitating Positive Development in Immigrant Youth: The Role of Mentors and Community Organizations." In *Community Youth Development: Practice, Policy, and Research*, edited by Francisco A. Villarruel, Daniel F. Perkins, Lynne M. Borden, and Joanne G. Keith. Thousand Oaks, Calif: Sage Publications.

Rosales, Rocio. 2014. "Stagnant Immigrant Social Networks and Cycles of Exploitation." *Ethnic and Racial Studies* 37(14): 2564–79.

Rosenbaum, James E. 2001. *Beyond College for All: Career Paths for the Forgotten Half.* New York: Russell Sage Foundation.

Rosenbaum, James E., Caitlin E. Ahearn, and Janet Rosenbaum. 2017. *Bridging the Gaps: College Pathways to Career Success.* New York: Russell Sage Foundation.

Rosenbaum, James E., Stefanie DeLuca, Shazia R. Miller, and Kevin Roy. 1999. "Pathways into Work: Short- and Long-Term Effects of Personal and Institutional Ties." *Sociology of Education* 72(3): 179–96.

Rosenblum, Marc R. 2012. "Border Security: Immigration Enforcement between Ports of Entry." Washington: Congressional Research Service, January 6.

Roux, Ana V. Diez, and Christina Mair. 2010. "Neighborhoods and Health." *Annals of the New York Academy of Sciences* 1186(1): 125–45.

Royster, Deidre A. 2003. *Race and the Invisible Hand: How White Networks Exclude Black Men from Blue-Collar Jobs.* Berkeley: University of California Press.

Rugh, Jacob S. 2014. "Double Jeopardy: Why Latinos Were Hit Hardest by the U.S. Foreclosure Crisis." *Social Forces* 93(3): 1139–84.

Rugh, Jacob S., and Douglas S. Massey. 2010. "Racial Segregation and the American Foreclosure Crisis." *American Sociological Review* 75(5): 629–51.

Ruiz, Vicki L. 1998. *From Out of the Shadows: Mexican Women in Twentieth-Century America.* New York: Oxford University Press.

Rumbaut, Rubén G. 1997. "Assimilation and Its Discontents: Between Rhetoric and Reality." *International Migration Review* 31(4): 923–60.

Rumberger, Russell W. 2011. *Dropping Out: Why Students Drop out of High School and What Can Be Done about It*. Cambridge, Mass.: Harvard University Press.

Rumberger, Russell W., and Daniel J. Losen. 2016. "The High Cost of Harsh Discipline and Its Disparate Impact." Civil Rights Project-Proyecto Derechos Civiles, June 2. https://www.civilrightsproject.ucla.edu/resources/projects/center-for-civil-rights-remedies/school-to-prison-folder/federal-reports/the-high-cost-of-harsh-discipline-and-its-disparate-impact/UCLA_HighCost_6-2_948.pdf.

Sabogal, Fabio, Gerardo Marín, Regina Otero-Sabogal, Barbara Vanoss Marín, and Eliseo J. Perez-Stable. 1987. "Hispanic Familism and Acculturation: What Changes and What Doesn't?" *Hispanic Journal of Behavioral Sciences* 9(4): 397–412.

Sampson, Robert J. 2008. "Rethinking Crime and Immigration." *Contexts* 7: 28–33.

———. 2012. *Great American City: Chicago and the Enduring Neighborhood Effect*. Chicago: University of Chicago Press.

Sampson, Robert J., Jeffrey D. Morenoff, and Thomas Gannon-Rowley. 2002. "Assessing 'Neighborhood Effects': Social Processes and New Directions in Research." *Annual Review of Sociology* 28: 443–78.

Sampson, Robert J., and Stephen W. Raudenbush. 2004. "Seeing Disorder: Neighborhood Stigma and the Social Construction of 'Broken Windows.'" *Social Psychology Quarterly* 67(4): 319–42.

———. 2005. "Neighborhood Stigma and the Perception of Disorder." *Focus* 24(1): 7–11.

Sampson, Robert J., Stephen W. Raudenbush, and Felton Earls. 1997. "Neighborhoods and Violent Crime: A Multilevel Study of Collective Efficacy." *Science* 277(5328): 918–24.

Sampson, Robert J., and Patrick Sharkey. 2008. "Neighborhood Selection and the Social Reproduction of Concentrated Racial Inequality." *Demography* 45(1): 1–29.

Sanbonmatsu, Lisa, Jeffrey R. Kling, Greg J. Duncan, and Jeanne Brooks-Gunn. 2006. "Neighborhoods and Academic Achievement: Results from the Moving to Opportunity Experiment." *Journal of Human Resources* 41(4): 649–91.

Schwartz, David, and Andrea Hopmeyer Gorman. 2003. "Community Violence Exposure and Children's Academic Functioning." *Journal of Educational Psychology* 95(1): 163–73.

Segura, Denise A., and Jennifer L. Pierce. 1993. "Chicana/o Family Structure and Gender Personality: Chodorow, Familism, and Psychoanalytic Sociology Revisited." *Signs: Journal of Women in Culture and Society* 19(1): 62–91.

Sharkey, Patrick. 2006. "Navigating Dangerous Streets: The Sources and Consequences of Street Efficacy." *American Sociological Review* 71(5): 826–46.

———. 2008. "The Intergenerational Transmission of Context." *American Journal of Sociology* 113(4): 931–69.

———. 2010. "The Acute Effect of Local Homicides on Children's Cognitive Performance." *Proceedings of the National Academy of Sciences* 107: 11733–38.

———. 2012. "An Alternative Approach to Addressing Selection Into and Out of Social Settings: Neighborhood Change and African American Children's Economic Outcomes." *Sociological Methods and Research* 4(2): 251–93.

———. 2013. *Stuck in Place: Urban Neighborhoods and the End of Progress toward Racial Equality.* Chicago: University of Chicago Press.

———. 2018a. *Uneasy Peace: The Great Crime Decline, the Revival of City Life, and the Next War on Violence.* New York: W. W. Norton & Co.

———. 2018b. "The Long Reach of Violence: A Broader Perspective on Data, Theory, and Evidence on the Prevalence and Consequences of Exposure to Violence." *Annual Review of Criminology* 1: 14.1–14.17.

Sharkey, Patrick, and Felix Elwert. 2011. "The Legacy of Disadvantage: Multigenerational Neighborhood Effects on Cognitive Ability." *American Journal of Sociology* 116(6): 1934–81.

Sharkey, Patrick, and Gerard Torrats-Espinosa. 2017. "The Effect of Violent Crime on Economic Mobility." *Journal of Urban Economics* 102: 22–33.

Sherman, Jennifer. 2006. "Coping with Rural Poverty: Economic Survival and Moral Capital in Rural America." *Social Forces* 85(2): 891–913.

Shildrick, Tracy, and Robert MacDonald. 2013. "Poverty Talk: How People Experiencing Poverty Deny Their Poverty and Why They Blame 'The Poor.'" *Sociological Review* 61(2): 285–303.

Silva, Jennifer M. 2013. *Coming Up Short: Working-Class Adulthood in an Age of Uncertainty.* New York: Oxford University Press.

Singer, Audrey, and Douglas S. Massey. 1998. "The Social Process of Undocumented Border Crossing among Mexican Migrants." *International Migration Review* 32(3): 561–92.

Skiba, Russell J., and Kimberly Knesting. 2001. "Zero Tolerance, Zero Evidence: An Analysis of School Disciplinary Practice." *New Directions for Youth Development* 92(Winter).

Small, Mario Luis, and Jessica Feldman. 2012. "Ethnographic Evidence, Heterogeneity, and Neighborhood Effects after Moving to Opportunity." In *Neighborhood Effects Research: New Perspectives*, edited by Maarten van Ham, David Manley, Nick Bailey, Ludi Simpson, and Duncan Maclennan. Dordrecht, Netherlands: Springer.

Small, Mario Luis, David J. Harding, and Michèle Lamont. 2010. "Reconsidering Culture and Poverty." *Annals of the American Academy of Political and Social Science* 629(1): 6–27.

Small, Mario Luis, and Katherine Newman. 2001. "Urban Poverty after the Truly Disadvantaged: The Rediscovery of the Family, the Neighborhood, and Culture." *Annual Review of Sociology* 27: 23–45.

Smith, James P. 2003. "Assimilation across the Latino Generations." *American Economic Review* 93(2): 315–19. DOI: 10.1257/000282803321947263.

Smith, Robert Courtney. 2006. *Mexican New York: Transnational Lives of New Immigrants.* Berkeley: University of California Press.

———. 2008. "Horatio Alger Lives in Brooklyn: Extrafamily Support, Intrafamily Dynamics, and Socially Neutral Operating Identities in Exceptional Mobility among Children of Mexican Immigrants." *Annals of the American Academy of Political and Social Science* 620: 270–90.

———. 2014. "Black Mexicans, Conjunctural Ethnicity, and Operating Identities: Long-Term Ethnographic Analysis." *American Sociological Review* 79(3): 517–48.

Smith, Sandra S. 2000. "Mobilizing Social Resources: Race, Ethnic, and Gender Differences in Social Capital and Persisting Wage Inequalities." *Sociological Quarterly* 41(1): 509–37.

———. 2007. *Lone Pursuit: Distrust and Defensive Individualism among the Black Poor.* New York: Russell Sage Foundation.

Solis, Hilda L., and John M. Galvin. 2012. "Labor Force Characteristics by Race and Ethnicity, 2011." Washington: Bureau of Labor Statistics. https://www.bls.gov/opub/reports/race-and-ethnicity/archive/race_ethnicity_2011.pdf.

Solorzano, Daniel. 1992. "Chicano Mobility Aspirations: A Theoretical and Empirical Note." *Latino Studies Journal* 3(1): 48–66.

Stack, Carol B. 1974. *All Our Kin: Strategies for Survival in a Black Community.* New York: Basic Books.

Stanton-Salazar, Ricardo D. 2001. *Manufacturing Hope and Despair: The School and Kin Support Networks of U.S.-Mexican Youth.* New York: Teachers College Press.

———. 2011. "A Social Capital Framework for the Study of Institutional Agents and Their Role in the Empowerment of Low-Status Students and Youth." *Youth and Society* 43(3): 1066–1109.

Stepick, Alex, and Carol Dutton-Stepick. 2010. "The Complexities and Confusions of Segmented Assimilation." *Ethnic and Racial Studies* 33(7): 1149–67.

Suárez-Orozco, Carola, and Marcelo Suárez-Orozco. 1995. *Transformations: Immigration, Family Life, and Achievement Motivation among Latino Adolescents.* Stanford, Calif.: Stanford University Press.

Suárez-Orozco, Carola, Marcelo M. Suárez-Orozco, and Irina Todorova. 2008. *Learning a New Land: Immigrant Students in American Society.* Cambridge, Mass.: Harvard University Press.

Sullivan, Mercer L. 1989. *"Getting Paid": Youth Crime and Work in the Inner City.* Ithaca, N.Y.: Cornell University Press.

Swidler, Ann. 1986. "Culture in Action: Symbols and Strategies." *American Sociological Review* 51(2): 273–86.

Sykes, Brooks, and Sako Musterd. 2011. "Examining Neighborhood and School Effects Simultaneously: What Does the Dutch Evidence Show?" *Urban Studies* 48(7): 1307–31.

Symonds, William C., Robert Schwartz, and Ronald F. Ferguson. 2011. *Pathways to Prosperity: Meeting the Challenge of Preparing Young Americans for the 21st Century.* Cambridge, Mass.: Harvard University Graduate School of Education. Pathways to Prosperity Project.

Telles, Edward, and Vilma Ortiz. 2008. *Generations of Exclusion: Mexican Americans, Assimilation, and Race.* New York: Russell Sage Foundation.

Telles, Edward, Mark Sawyer, and Gaspar Rivera-Salgado. 2011. *Just Neighbors? Research on African American and Latino Relations in the United States.* New York: Russell Sage Foundation.

Thompson, Theodore, Jr., and Carol Rippey Massat. 2005. "Experiences of Violence, Post-Traumatic Stress, Academic Achievement, and Behavior Problems of Urban African-American Children." *Child and Adolescent Social Work Journal* 22(5/6): 367–93.

Tran, Van C., and Nicol M. Valdez. 2017. "Second-Generation Decline or Advantage? Latino Assimilation in the Aftermath of the Great Recession." *International Migration Review* 51(1): 155–90.

Treviño, Roberto R. 2006. *The Church in the Barrio: Mexican American Ethno-Catholicism in Houston.* Chapel Hill: University of North Carolina Press.

Trujillo-Pagan, Nicole Elise. 2012. "Boundary Work at the New Corner: Latino Workers in New Orleans." *International Review of Modern Sociology* 38(1): 1–24.

Turner, Margery Austin, Diane K. Levy, Claudia L. Aranda, Robert Pitingolo, Robert Santos, and Douglas A. Wissoker. 2013. "Housing Discrimination against Racial and Ethnic Minorities 2012." Washington: U.S. Department of Housing and Urban Development, Office of Policy Development and Research (June).

Tyson, Karolyn, William Darity, and Domini R. Castellino. 2005. "It's Not 'a Black Thing': Understanding the Burden of Acting White and Other Dilemmas of High Achievement." *American Sociological Review* 70(4): 582–605.

Valencia, Richard R., Martha Menchaca, and Rubén Donato. 2002. "Segregation, Desegregation, and Integration of Chicano Students: Old and New Realities." In *Chicano School Failure and Success: Past, Present, and Future,* 2nd ed., edited by Richard R. Valencia. London: Routledge.

Valenzuela, Angela. 2010. *Subtractive Schooling: U.S.-Mexican Youth and the Politics of Caring.* Albany: State University of New York Press.

Valenzuela, Angela, and Sanford M. Dornsbusch. 1994. "Familism and Social Capital in the Academic Achievement of Mexican Origin and Anglo Adolescents." *Social Science Quarterly* 75(1): 18–36.

Van Hook, Jennifer, and Frank D. Bean. 2009. "Explaining Mexican-Immigrant Welfare Behaviors: The Importance of Employment-Related Cultural Repertoires." *American Sociological Review* 74(1): 423–44.

Velez-Ibanez, Carlos. 1993. "U.S. Mexican in the Borderlands: Being Poor without the Underclass." In *In the Barrios: Latinos and the Underclass Debate*, Joan Moore and Raquel Pinderhughes. New York: Russell Sage Foundation.

Venkatesh, Sudhir Alladi. 2008. *Off the Books: The Underground Economy of the Urban Poor.* Cambridge, Mass.: Harvard University Press.

Verdery, Ashton, and Colin Campbell. 2019. "Social Support in America: Stratification and Trends in Access over Two Decades." *Social Forces.* DOI: 10.1093/sf/soz008.

Vigil, Diego James. 1988. *Barrio Gangs: Street Life and Identity in Southern California.* Austin: University of Texas Press.

———. 2002. *A Rainbow of Gangs: Street Cultures in the Mega-City.* Austin: University of Texas Press.

———. 2017. *The Projects: Gang and Non-Gang Families in East Los Angeles.* Austin: University of Texas Press.

Viruell-Fuentes, Edna A., Jeffrey D. Morenoff, David R. Williams, and James S. House. 2013. "Contextualizing Nativity Status, Latino Social Ties, and Ethnic Enclaves: An Examination of the 'Immigrant Social Ties Hypothesis.'" *Ethnicity and Health* 18(6): 586–609.

Wacquant, Loïc. 2007. "Territorial Stigmatization in the Age of Advanced Marginality." *Thesis Eleven* 91(1): 66–77.

Waldinger, Roger, and Cynthia Feliciano. 2004. "Will the New Second Generation Experience 'Downward Assimilation'? Segmented Assimilation Re-assessed." *Ethnic and Racial Studies* 27(3): 376–402.

Waldinger, Roger, Nelson Lim, and David Cort. 2007. "Bad Jobs, Good Jobs, No Jobs? The Employment Experience of the Mexican American Second Generation." *Journal of Ethnic and Migration Studies* 33(1): 1–35.

Warikoo, Natasha Kumar. 2011. *Balancing Acts: Youth Culture in the Global City.* Berkeley: University of California Press.

Warren, Robert. 2016. "U.S. Undocumented Population Drops below 11 Million in 2014 with Continued Declines in the Mexican Undocumented Population." *Journal on Migration and Human Security* 4(1).

Warren, Robert, and John Robert Warren. 2013. "Unauthorized Immigration to the United States: Annual Estimates and Components of Change, by State, 1990 to 2010." *International Migration Review* 47(2): 296–329.

Wasem, Ruth Ellen. 2012. "Unauthorized Aliens Residing in the United States: Estimates Since 1986." Congressional Research Service, December 13. https://fas.org/sgp/crs/misc/RL33874.pdf.

Waters, Mary C., Van C. Tran, Philip Kasinitz, and John H. Mollenkopf. 2010. "Segmented Assimilation Revisited: Types of Acculturation and Socioeconomic Mobility in Young Adulthood." *Ethnic and Racial Studies* 33(7): 1168–93.

Wellman, Barry, and Scot Wortley. 1990. "Different Strokes from Different Folks: Community Ties and Social Support." *American Journal of Sociology* 96(3): 558–88.

Wilkes, Rima, and John Iceland. 2004. "Hypersegregation in the Twenty-First Century." *Demography* 41(1): 23–36.

Wilson, William Julius. 1987. *The Truly Disadvantaged: The Inner City, the Underclass, and Public Policy.* Chicago: University of Chicago Press.

———. 1996. *When Work Disappears: The World of the New Urban Poor.* New York: Vintage Books.

Wodtke, Geoffrey T., Felix Elwert, and David J. Harding. 2016. "Neighborhood Effect Heterogeneity by Family Income and Developmental Period." *American Journal of Sociology* 121(4): 1168–1222.

Wodtke, Geoffrey T., David J. Harding, and Felix Elwert. 2011. "Neighborhood Effects in Temporal Perspective: The Impact of Long-Term Exposure to Concentrated Disadvantage on High School Graduation." *American Sociological Review* 76(5): 713–36.

Wojtkiewicz, Roger A., and Katherine M. Donato. 1995. "Hispanic Educational Attainment: The Effects of Family Background and Nativity." *Social Forces* 74(2): 559–74. DOI:10.2307/2580492.

Wolkow, Katherine E., and H. Bruce Ferguson. 2001. "Community Factors in Development of Resiliency: Considerations and Future Directions." *Community Mental Health Journal* 37: 489–98.

Yosso, Tara, William Smith, Miguel Ceja, and Daniel Solórzano. 2009. "Critical Race Theory, Racial Microaggressions, and Campus Racial Climate for Latina/o Undergraduates." *Harvard Educational Review* 79(4): 659–91.

Young, Alford A., Jr. 2004. *The Minds of Marginalized Black Men: Making Sense of Mobility, Opportunity, and Future Life Chances.* Princeton, N.J.: Princeton University Press.

Zhou, Min. 1997. "Segmented Assimilation: Issues, Controversies, and Recent Research on the New Second Generation." *International Migration Review* 31(4): 825–58.

Zhou, Min, and Carl Bankston. 1998. *Growing Up American: How Vietnamese Children Adapt to Life in the United States.* New York: Russell Sage Foundation.

———. 2006. "Delinquency and Acculturation in the Twenty-First Century: A Decade's Change in a Vietnamese American Community." In *Immigration and Crime: Ethnicity, Race, and Violence*, edited by Ramiro Martinez Jr. and Abel Valenzuela Jr. New York: New York University Press.

Zuniga, Victor, and Rubén Hernández-León. 2001. "A New Destination for an Old Migration: Origins, Trajectories, and Labor Market Incorporation of Latinos in Dalton, Georgia." In *Latino Workers in the Contemporary South*, edited by Arthur D. Murphy, Colleen Blanchard, and Jennifer A. Hill. Athens: University of Georgia Press.

INDEX

....

Boldface numbers refer to figures and tables.

acculturation: cross-racial ties and, 133, 231, 294*n*7; delayed assimilation and, 190–191; exposure to native-born racial minorities and, 7, 27, 36, 37–38, 231, 252, 292*n*10; gang activity and socialization, 93, 278*n*24, 292*n*10; neighborhood effects and, 8, 24; in schools, 292–293*n*17. *See also* downward assimilation

African Americans: college graduation rates, 12; cross-racial ties and, 133, 231, 294*n*7; employment discrimination for, 62; gangs and gang activity of, 95–96, 98, 292*n*10; life outcomes compared, 252, 294*n*8; meritocracy and, 292*n*16; millennials, 284*n*129; neighborhood effects and, 15, 36, 281*nn*71–72; racialization of, 205; unemployment and social isolation, 17, 56, 281*n*81; violence and, 43, 47–48

Alba, Richard, 10, 278*n*29

American Dream: Asian Americans and, 240, 280*n*64; education leading to, 55, 204; housing goals and, 195–196; individual responsibility for, 9, 187, 189–190, 198–200, 240–241; inner-city Latinx and, 9–14, 240; lost faith in, 192, 202, 209; necessary sacrifices for, 175; parental sacrifice and, 114; power and deception of, 226–228; segregation and, 192, 198, 246; self-blame for lack of achievement, 14, 202, 240; self-efficacy and, 192; shifted understanding of, 202–203, 207–209; social isolation and, 18, 187. *See also* success

Anderson, Elijah, 18, 205

Asian Americans: American Dream and, 240, 280*n*64; cross-class ties and employment, 135, 234; millennials, 284*n*129; narrow frames for success and, 279*n*40; social capital of, 20

assimilation. *See* downward assimilation; integration of second-generation Latinx

Bachmeier, James, 163

Bankston, Carl, 20, 282*n*97

Bean, Frank, 163

border enforcement, 11, 71, 83–84, 290*n*35, 290*n*36

Border Patrol, 71, 289*n*24, 290*n*35

bracero program, 67–68, 288–289*nn*17–18, 289*n*21

Briggs, Xavier de Souza, 20, 167–168

Britton, Marcus, 282*n*85

Brown, Susan, 163

California: foreign-born population in, 26, 284*n*127; higher education attainment in, 147; Latinos as percentage of working poor in, 294*n*15; minimum wage in, 281*n*66; segregation in, 5, 136. *See also* Los Angeles

Center for Migration studies, 284*n*127

Chin, Margaret, 157

churches. *See* neighborhood institutions

cognitive frames, 24–25, 30, 52, 65, 191.
    See also cultural outlooks

Coleman, James, 65, 283*n*101

collective efficacy, 46, 64, 232

college and higher education: challenges
    in navigating, 23, 145–148, 151, 156,
    234–235, 244, 295*n*30; community
    colleges and vocational training programs,
    144–149, 168–171; counseling for,
    146, 244; "Dreamers" and, 208–209;
    experience outside of segregated
    neighborhoods, 204–210; graduation
    rates, 10–11, 12, 243–244; institutional
    support of, 22–23, 149, 157–158, 160,
    164, 167–169, 234–235, 244–245;
    limited returns on, 143, 145, 155–158, 164,
    209–210, 244; readiness for, 149–150, 204,
    233–234, 236, 296*n*42; social leverage
    ties and, 22–23, 149, 155–160, 168–175,
    233–234; social mobility and, 138–139;
    success standards and, 142; universities,
    147–148, 149–160, 171–175; work ethic
    and, 153

community colleges and vocational
    training programs, 144–149, 168–171

community organizations.
    See neighborhood institutions

crime and delinquency: as barrier to
    social capital, 218; as barrier to social
    mobility, 7, 36; decrease in, 61; fear
    of reporting, 44; immigrant effect on
    urban neighborhoods and, 36–37, 46;
    neighborhood cohesion as deterrent
    to, 45–49, 64; peer influence and, 6,
    25; research confidentiality and, 263;
    resistance to, 49–51, 61. *See also* gangs
    and gang activity; incarceration

criminalization of young men: gang tattoos
    and, 225; police surveillance in schools
    and, 5, 18–19, 105–106, 128, 236; racial
    segregation and, 5, 12, 199–200, 207

cross-class relations, 135, 174–175, 234,
    241–242

cross-racial relations: acculturation and,
    133, 231, 294*n*7; gang conflicts and, 95–96,
    98, 183, 292*n*10, 292*n*13; neighborhood
    cohesion and trust, 48; policies for
    integration, 241–242; segregation and,
    136–137; violence and, 43–44

cultural outlooks, 32, 188–228; cognitive
    frame types, 25, 32, 191–192, **191**;
    determined young men, 202–214;
    false inner-city narrative and, 189–190;
    integration of second-generation Latinx
    and, 239–241; oppositional culture and,
    190–191; resolute optimists, 192–202

culture: barriers of, 295*n*30; as context
    for Latinx inner city, 25–26, 36–37;
    oppositional, 7, 26, 190–191, 231, 253;
    of poverty, 24, 190; segregation as
    barrier to, 137; underclass, 6, 15, 36–37,
    281*n*71. *See also* acculturation; American
    Dream

cumulative causation, 289*n*19

Curran, Sara, 291*n*41

Deferred Action for Childhood Arrivals
    (DACA), 28, 208–209, 213, 284–285*n*137

delayed assimilation, 191, 278–279*n*29

Denton, Nancy, 6, 15, 17

determined young men: American Dream,
    shifted understanding of, 202–203,
    207–209; experience outside of segregated
    neighborhoods, 204–210; overview, 25,
    32, 191–192, **191**; perseverance attitude of,
    202–203; social capital of, 210–214

discrimination: classism and, 207–209;
    in employment, 62, 177, 208–209;
    experience outside segregated
    neighborhoods and, 204–207; gang
    tattoos and, 225; in housing, 4, 12;
    racialization of Mexicans and, 205–207,
    237, 280*n*54; reception of immigrants
    and, 11, 232; self-blamers and, 225–226.
    See also race and racism

downward assimilation: disconnection and marginalization leading to, 24, 55–57, 166; lack of social leverage ties and, 166–167, 185–186; lack of work ethic and, 52; risks for, 7–9, 26; second-generation Latinx, contradictions of, 133, 189–190, 230–231; social capital to mitigate, 19, 22, 31, 64, 70, 160, 164, 237–238

drug sales and use, 36, 95, 99, 118, 180–181, 223–224

Durand, Jorge, 288n14, 288–289n18, 290n32

education and schools: alternative schools, 104–106, 293n19; American Dream and, 55, 204; college readiness and, 149–150, 204, 233–234, 236, 296n42; desegregation busing and magnet programs, 115–116, 236, 293n26; downward assimilation and, 7; employment and work ethic, 55, 58–59, 134, 139–144, 190; gang activity, detrimental effects of, 102–104, 128; gatekeepers for, 164, 167, 176–177; gender differences in attainment, 27; meritocracy and, 103, 139, 292n16; noncompletion of, 4, 11, 58–59, 102–107, 160–162, 293n23; police surveillance and, 5, 18–19, 104–106, 236; quality of, 3, 26, 136; restorative justice programs through, 243; rural Mexican migrants and, 68, 71; second-generation Latinx improvements in, 10, 133, 137, 231, 279n40; segregation of, 3, 5, 26, 136, 233; social capital and, 283n101, 292–293n17; social leverage ties and, 22–23, 135, 149, 155–160, 233–234; social mobility and, 134–135, **134**, 139–144, 149–160; spatial inequality and, 5, 17, 243, 278n18; success standards and, 142; violence and, 16–17, 92, 102–107, 233, 293n23. See also college and higher education

employment: avoiding job loss, 54; barriers to advancement in, 134, 138; bracero program, 67–68, 288–289nn17–18,

289n21; circular flow of migrants and, 288n16; discrimination in, 62, 177, 208–209; education leading to, 55, 58–59, 134, 139–144, 190; gang violence as barrier to, 42–43; of high school graduates, 139–144; improvement in rates of, 284n133; of Mexican immigrants, 36, 51–52, 56; oppositional culture and, 7; quality of, 137–138; of second-generation Latinx, 133; social capital and, 21, 52, 62, 139; social isolation and, 17, 56, 281n81; social mobility through, 12, 138, 294–295n21, 298n16; spatial inequality and, 17; of undocumented immigrants, 58, 68, 201, 209, 288n16, 289n21, 289n24; university mechanisms for, 157, 172; of women, 291n43; work agencies for, 144, 158. See also work ethic

employment networks: as alternative to work agencies, 144; higher education institutions and, 22–23; high school noncompleters and, 161–162; limitations set by, 141, 159–160; low-skilled ties for, 138; migrant networks and, 52, 62, 68; for post-college jobs, 155–156, 159–160; social leverage ties and, 22–23, 133, 135, 169, 212, 294n2; of study participants, 295n25; undocumented immigrants and, 163, 238; at universities, 157

ethnic neighborhoods, 37–38, 135, 165. See also segregation; social capital

familism, 65, 81, 287n5

family ties. See social capital

fathers and father figures: absence of, 119–120; employment networks and, 238; frames of success and, 194–195, 297–298n16; gender roles, 123–124, 293n28; neighborhood effects, mitigating, 111–112; self-blamers and, 221

Ferguson, Ronald, 147

Fernández-Kelly, Patricia, 19, 282n95

fictive kin, 73, 75, 78, 84–85, 87

Flores-Yeffal, Nadia, 290–291nn39–40

gangs and gang activity: as barrier to employment, 42–43; as barrier to school completion, 102–104, 128; clothing and appearance, 97, 224–225; fear of reporting, 44; lack of social capital and, 23, 218; lack of social leverage ties and, 179–186; in Los Angeles, 35–36, 39; moral boundaries against, 30, 55–57, 97, 140, 177, 232; neighborhood cohesion as deterrent to, 45–49; nongang member relations, 94–98; percentage of youth joining, 64; racial exclusion and isolation, 12; racial tension among, 95–96, 98, 183, 292*n*10, 292*n*13; resistance to, 49–51; as social capital, 100–101; social capital as deterrent to, 77–78; socialization to, 93, 278*n*24, 292*n*10; social reciprocity and, 31, 102–103, 106–107, 233; tagging crews, 98–100, 250, 291*n*46; transitioning out of, 175–179, 184–185, 225; violence and, 16–17, 35–36, 40–45, 92

Gans, Herbert, 7, 230
Garip, Filiz, 65, 283*n*101, 287*n*9, 287–288*n*12, 291*n*39, 291*n*49
gatekeepers, 22, 164, 167, 176–177
gender: gender roles, 74–76, 123–124, 293*n*28; migration and settlement processes, 66, 68, 291*nn*41–43; neighborhood experiences and, 250
generational reproduction: housing issues, 162; social class and poverty, 6, 8, 165, 230, 246, 296*n*46; social isolation, 6, 187
Goldsmith, Pat, 282*n*85
Gonzales, Roberto, 28, 226
Great Recession (2008): employment and, 9, 59, 171; housing issues and, 142, 188, 295*n*22, 297*n*1; predatory lending and, 12; recovery from, 277*n*4

Haller, William, 19, 279*n*31, 282*n*95
Harding, David, 25
health. *See* physical and mental health
Hernández-León, Rubén, 70–71, 290*n*33

home ownership, 12, 69, 295*n*27
Hondagneu-Sotelo, Pierrette, 76
housing costs and issues: discrimination and, 4, 12; gentrification and, 247; Great Recession and, 142, 188, 295*n*22, 297*n*1; increase in costs, 135, 295*n*21, 295*n*28; intergenerational and multifamily, 81–82, 138, 162, 163, 196–197, 211–212, 238, 295*n*22; predatory lending and, 12; social capital and, 211
human capital, 67–68, 288–289*nn*17–18, 289*n*21

Iceland, John, 284*n*132
immigrant bargain, 3–6, 10, 84, 113–114, 193–194, 300*n*50
immigrant effect on urban neighborhoods, 36–37, 46, 51
immigrant rights movement, 208–209
Immigration and Customs Enforcement (ICE), 174, 201, 290*n*35
Immigration Nationality Act (1965), 6
immigration policy legislation and reform, 6, 67–69, 71, 241, 245–246, 300*n*50
Immigration Reform and Control Act (IRCA, 1986), 69, 257, 288*n*12, 289*n*21, 289*n*24
incarceration: as barrier to social mobility, 36, 242–243; mass incarceration era, 61, 242; neighborhood effects and, 4, 236–237; police surveillance in schools and, 5, 18–19; school-to-prison pipeline, 19, 128, 236
income inequality, 229, 241–242
individualism, 167, 189–190, 198–202, 240. *See also* self-blamers
integration of second-generation Latinx, 32, 229–248; cultural outlook and, 239–241; delayed assimilation and, 190–191; future outlook for, 246–248; inner-city neighborhoods and, 14–15, 36–37; neighborhood effects and, 4, 230, 232–237; policy landscape and, 241–246; race and, 136; segregation

and, 136; social capital and, 65, 66, 235–239; social isolation and, 18, 238–239; social mobility and, 229, 246–247; spatial inequality and, 229–232. *See also* segmented assimilation
internships, 153, 157, 173–174
interviews. *See* research study

Jack, Anthony, 156, 204, 240

Kahn, Bonnie, 7
Kasinitz, Philip, 7, 10, 234, 294*n*8
kin ties. *See* social capital
Krivo, Lauren, 136

Lamont, Michèle, 25
Lareau, Annette, 114
Lee, Hyein, 157
Lee, Jennifer, 20, 279*n*40, 279*n*46, 297*n*15
life outcomes: neighborhood effects and, 3–6, 13, 281*n*69; oppositional culture and, 231; poverty and, 252; second-generation Latinx vs. African Americans, 252, 294*n*8; social capital and, 8–9; undocumented status and, 28
Los Angeles: characteristics of research neighborhoods in, 267, **268**; choice of research neighborhoods in, 252–253; inner-city life in, 37–39; Los Angeles Unified School District (LAUSD), 115; median income in, 26, 294*n*9, 296*n*5; Mexican American population in, 25–26; minimum wage in, 281*n*66. *See also* gangs and gang activity; housing costs and issues
Louie, Vivian, 22, 279*n*40, 280*n*64
Lynch, Scott, 279*n*31

Massey, Douglas: on bracero program, 288–289*n*18; on class division, 16; on cumulative causation, 289*n*19; on eras of migration, 68, 288*n*15; on origin of migrants, 288*n*14, 290*n*32; on social isolation, 17; on underclass culture, 6, 15

mass incarceration era, 61, 242
Menchaca, Martha, 280*n*54
Menjívar, Cecilia, 238
mental health. *See* physical and mental health
meritocracy: education and, 103, 139, 292*n*16; individual responsibility for, 167; optimism for success and, 13–14, 24, 190, 240; segregation and, 18, 198–202, 227; self-blamers and, 214, 216, 222–226, 227–228. *See also* work ethic
Mexican Americans: in Los Angeles, 25–26; racialization of, 205–207, 237, 280*n*54. *See also* migrant streams; second-generation Latinx
Mexico: economic crisis in, 70–71; origin of migrants from, 288*n*14; rural migrants from, 67–70; urbanization of, 70, 290*n*32; urban migrants from, 70–74; U.S. border wall with, 11
micro-agressions, 207, 234, 244
middle class: assimilation of immigrants into, 7, 10–11, 229, 278–279*nn*28–29; college education and, 172–175, 210; necessity of social leverage ties for, 155–156, 167–168; shrinking of, 4; social isolation as barrier to entry, 164, 231–232
migrant streams: decrease in, 245, 290*n*34; diversity within, 86, 291*n*49; gender and, 74–76; kin ties facilitating, 86; from rural Mexico, 67–70, 288–289*nn*14–24, 290*n*32; from urban Mexico, 70–74, 290*nn*32–36, 290–291*nn*39–40
migration and settlement processes: cognitive frames for, 30; cumulative causation and, 289*n*19; eras of migration, 68, 288*n*15; ethnic neighborhoods and, 37–38; history of, 67–70, 288–289*nn*14–24; neighborhood institutions and, 85; social capital and, 21, 23, 30, 65, 66, 86–87, 235, 287–288*n*12
millennials, 12, 197, 277*n*5, 284*n*129
moral boundaries: avoiding marginalized peers and, 133, 139–140; decline in crime

and violence, 61–62; gang activity, buffering, 30, 55–57, 97, 140, 177, 232; negative effects of, 62, 232–233; public assistance and, 59; shame of self-blamers and, 222, 226; undocumented immigrants and, 58. *See also* work ethic
mothers and mother figures, 123–124, 195–196, 293*n*28

Nee, Victor, 278*n*29
neighborhood effects: acculturation and, 8, 24; father figures as buffer against, 111–112; incarceration and, 4, 236–237; inner-city neighborhoods and, 15–19; integration of second-generation Latinx and, 4, 230, 232–237; life outcomes and, 3–6, 13, 281*n*69; magnet schools as buffer against, 115–116, 293*n*26; in Mexican vs. African American neighborhoods, 15, 36, 281*nn*71–72; police surveillance and, 3, 18–19, 38, 61, 62, 107, 122–123, 236–237; schools, impact of, 292–293*n*17; social capital as buffer against, 77–78, 235–237; social integration and, 5–6, 18; social isolation and, 16, 232–235; social mobility and, 4, 15, 231
neighborhood institutions: decline in crime and violence, 61; disconnection and marginalization from, 23–24; gatekeepers in, 22, 164, 167, 176–177; migration and settlement processes, 85; neighborhood effects and, 18–19; policies to strengthen, 242; resolute optimism, support for, 197–198; self-blamers and, 221; social capital through, 65, 73, 75, 78, 84–85, 87, 235–236; social leverage ties in, 22–23; social mobility and, 167–168; sports participation and, 19, 112–114, 118; violence, buffering, 109, 112–119, 129, 232. *See also* education and schools; police and law enforcement
neo-liberal economics, 4, 13, 238, 247
non-family ties. *See* social leverage ties

oppositional culture, 7, 26, 190–191, 231, 253
oppositional pessimists, 191–192, **191,** 216
Ortiz, Vilma, 8, 135, 230, 233, 280*n*49, 297*n*6

parental support: intergenerational housing, 81–82, 138, 162, 163, 196–197, 211–212, 238, 295*n*22; mothers and mother figures, 123–124, 195–196, 293*n*28; single-parent homes, 23, 119, 241, 252. *See also* fathers and father figures; social capital
peer influence: avoiding negative, 133, 139–140; as barrier to school completion, 103–104; in college, 153–154; crime and, 6, 25; drug use and, 118; social capital and, 16–17, 94–97
Perlmann, Joel, 281*n*72
physical and mental health: abuse and, 83, 186, 219, 264; neighborhood effects and, 3–4; poverty and, 21; research study and, 262, 264–265; social support and, 21, 283*n*101; violence and, 16, 92, 181–182, 233
police and law enforcement: corruption and neglect of, 44–45, 49, 50, 242; gang tattoos and criminalization of young men, 225; involvement in parent-child conflicts, 120, 181, 237; racial profiling of, 199–200, 207; social isolation and, 120, 181; surveillance in neighborhoods, 3, 18–19, 38, 61, 62, 107, 122–123, 199–200, 207, 236–237; surveillance in schools, 5, 18–19, 104–106, 236. *See also* incarceration
Portes, Alejandro: on American Dream, 10; on reception of immigrants, 11; on segmented assimilation, 6, 7, 279*n*31; on social capital, 19, 64, 282*n*95
poverty: culture and, 24, 190; generational reproduction of, 6, 8, 165, 230, 246, 296*n*46; health and, 21; increase in, 4–5, 16; lack of social leverage ties and, 179–186; life outcomes and, 252;

navigating higher education and, 156; policies to counter, 241–242; resilience and, 205; segregation and, 3, 15–16; social capital and, 21; social isolation and, 17; straining relationships, 66, 163; violence and, 16. *See also* social class; social mobility; spatial inequality

public assistance, 59–60, 224, 247

race and racism: American Dream and, 192, 202; criminalization of young men and, 199–200, 207; educational performance and, 192; employment and, 62; experience outside segregated neighborhoods and, 204–207; gang activity and, 95–96, 98, 292*n*10, 292*n*13; inner city and racialization, 205–207, 237, 280*n*54; micro-aggressions, 207, 234, 244; racialization of Mexicans, 205–207, 237, 280*n*54; racial profiling, 199–200, 206–207; racial slurs and insults, 105, 207, 293*n*21; self-segregation and, 27; social mobility and, 4. *See also* discrimination; segregation

racial integration, 241–242

reactive identities, 189, 191, 253

reception of immigrants, 11, 232, 245–246, 300*n*50

reciprocity and social obligation, 23, 31, 66, 102–104, 106–107, 233

research study, 249–266; design of, 25–27, 284*nn*126–127; ethical dilemmas in, 261–262; interviews and analysis, 254–258, 264–266; Latino males as focus of, 27–29; longitudinal cases, 260–261, 269–275; as multigenerational, 258–260; neighborhood and sample choices for, 252–254; personal safety and, 262–264; positionality and, 249–252; socioeconomic characteristics of study neighborhoods, 267, **268**

resolute optimists: integration of second-generation Latinx and, 239–240; meritocracy beliefs and, 198–202;

overview, 25, 32, 191–192, **191**; role models and, 192–193; social capital and, 193–198

Rivero-Fuentes, Estela, 291*n*41

Rosenbaum, James, 147

Rumbaut, Rubén, 7, 11

rural Mexican migrants: education of, 68, 71; migrant streams of, 67–70, 288–289*nn*14–24, 290*n*32; social capital of, 72, 235

schools. *See* education and schools

Schwartz, Robert, 147

second-generation decline, 128, 160–161, 163–164, 186–187, 231. *See also* downward assimilation

second-generation Latinx, 91–130; American Dream and, 9–14, 240; avoiding violence, 107–109, **109**; buffered young men of, 109–119; cultural logics of, 25, 32, 191–192, **191**; educational attainment of, 10, 133, 137, 231, 279*n*40; exposed young men of, 119–128; gang activity and, 97–98; high school noncompletion of, 103–107; immigrant bargain of, 3–6, 10, 84, 113–114, 193–194, 300*n*50; institutional ties of, 112–117; kin ties of, 110–112; neighborhood effects and, 3–6; optimism of, 190, 227, 297*n*6; social capital and gang activity, 100–101; social obligations of, 102–107; tagging crews and, 98–100; third generation compared, 279–280*n*49; violence, effect of, 92–97, 128–130. *See also* cultural outlooks; integration of second generation Latinx

segmented assimilation: criticism of theory, 237, 278–279*n*29; cultural context for Latinx inner city and, 25–26; exposure to native-born racial minorities and, 27, 36, 37, 231, 252, 292*n*10; gang involvement and, 93; of Latinx, 6–9, 14, 231, 278–279*nn*28–29, 279*n*31; social capital and, 19, 129, 237; types of, 278*n*28. *See also* acculturation segregation: American Dream and, 192, 198, 246; as barrier to social leverage ties, 137; criminalization of young men and, 5, 12, 199–200, 207; discrimination, buffer against, 204–207; of education and schools, 3, 5, 26, 136, 233; hypersegregation, 26, 200–201, 284*n*132; of Los Angeles neighborhoods, 25–26; meritocracy beliefs and, 18, 198–202, 227; police surveillance and, 3, 18–19, 38, 61, 62, 107, 199–200; poverty and, 3, 15–16; self-blamers and, 222–226; social mobility and, 133–137, **134,** 165, 246–247; violence and, 3, 16–17. *See also* social isolation

self-blamers: future outlook for, 247–248; lack of achievement of American Dream, 202, 240; lack of social capital, 214–222, 227–228; overview, 25, 32, 191–192, **191**; segregation and meritocracy, 222–226

Sharkey, Patrick, 61

single-parent homes, 23, 119, 241, 252

Small, Mario, 25

Smith, Robert C., 10, 294*n*7

social capital, 30–31, 63–87; American Dream and, 226–228; of determined young men, 210–214; as deterrent to gangs, 77–78; disconnection and marginalization from, 23–24; downward assimilation, buffering, 19, 22, 64, 70, 160, 164, 237–238; education and, 283*n*101, 292–293*n*17; employment and, 21, 52, 62, 139; for empowerment, 149, 167; ethnic, 7–8; fictive kin, 73, 75, 78, 84–85, 87; fragility of, 81–84; gangs as, 100–101; gendered migration and female isolation, 74–77; housing and, 211; housing opportunities and, 135, 138, 294–295*nn*21–22; inner-city neighborhoods and, 19–24; integration of second-generation Latinx and, 65, 66, 235–239; lack of, gang involvement and, 23, 218; life outcomes and, 8–9; loss of, immigration policies and,

245–246, 300*n*50; marriage and, 79–81; migration and settlement processes and, 21, 23, 30, 65, 66, 86–87, 235, 287–288*n*12; neighborhood cohesion and, 45–49; neighborhood effects, buffering, 77–78, 235–237; neighborhood institutions as, 65, 73, 75, 78, 84–85, 87, 235–236; peers influence and, 94–97; reciprocity and, 23, 66; reconceptualization of, 64–66, 86–87; resolute optimists and, 193–198; rural Mexican influence and, 67–70, 235; in schools, 283*n*101, 292–293*n*17; seeking, 84–86; of self-blamers, 214–222, 227–228; social isolation and lack of, 23–24, 181–182, 238–239; social leverage ties as, 22–23; social mobility and, 14, 19–21, 226–228, 282*n*95, 282*n*97, 283*n*101; social support as, 21–22, 64–66, 283*n*105; urban Mexican influence and, 70–74; variations in, 66–67, 77–78; violence, buffering, 109, 110–112, 117–119, 129. *See also* social leverage ties

social class: cross-class relations and, 135, 174–175, 234, 241–242; discrimination and, 207–209; ethnic ties across, 20; generational reproduction of, 8, 165, 230, 246, 296*n*46; neighborhood effects and, 13, 16; underclass culture and, 6, 15, 36–37, 281*n*71; working class poor, 136, 138, 230, 294*n*15. *See also* middle class; poverty; social mobility

social isolation: abuse and broken trust, 83, 182, 219–220; as barrier to middle-class entry, 164, 231–232; in college, 204, 206; defined, 17; exposed youth and, 125–128; fear of violence and, 44; generational reproduction of, 6, 187; integration of second-generation Latinx and, 233–235; lack of social capital and, 23–24, 181–182, 238–239; lack of social leverage ties and, 186; neighborhood segregation and, 16, 17–18, 282*n*85; police involvement in parent–child conflicts and, 120, 181, 237;

poverty and, 17; of self-blamers, 216–222, 228; of urban vs. rural Mexican migrants, 72–73, 235; of women, 75–77. *See also* segregation

social leverage ties, 32, 166–187; defined, 20; disconnection and marginalization from, 23–24; education and, 22–23, 135, 149, 155–160, 168–175, 233–234; lack of, 155–160, 166–167, 179–186; middle class entry and, 155–156, 167–168; segregation as barrier to, 137; social capital and, 22–23; social isolation and, 18; social mobility and, 21, 138; transformative nature of, 175–179; value of, 186–187, 237–239. *See also* employment networks

social mobility, 31, 131–165; alternatives to college for, 147; of community college students, 144–149; crime and incarceration as barriers to, 36, 242–243; of "Dreamers," 208–209; education and, 134–135, **134,** 139–144, 149–160; employment opportunities and, 12, 138, 294–295*n*21, 298*n*16; of European white immigrants, 4; of high school graduates, 139–144; of high school noncompleters, 160–162; inequality as barrier to, 296*n*46; integration of second-generation Latinx and, 229, 246–247; neighborhood effects and, 4, 15, 231; neighborhood institutions and, 167–168; routes of, 138–139; segregation and, 133–137, **134,** 165, 246–247; social capital and, 14, 19–21, 226–228, 282*n*95, 282*n*97, 283*n*101; stagnation of, 8, 137–138, 231; of undocumented immigrants, 69, 208–209; of university students, 149–160; violence and, 16–17, 31, 93, 128, 182, 231–232. *See also* American Dream; downward assimilation

social support: for college success, 151, 296*n*43; defined, 20, 64, 283*n*101; disconnection and marginalization from, 23–24, 163–165, 182, 216–222; marriage and, 79–81; neighborhood effects,

buffering, 77–78, 235–237; neighborhood institutions for, 75, 87; social capital and, 21–22, 64–66, 283*n*105; social mobility and, 21, 31, 166–168, 231; value of, 186–187, 227, 231, 238. *See also* migration and settlement processes

spatial inequality: education and schools, 5, 17, 243, 278*n*18; employment and, 17; integration of second-generation Latinx and, 229–232; policies to counter, 241–242; race and class segregation, 136

Special Supplemental Nutrition Program for Women, Infants, and Children (WIC), 59–60

Stanton-Salazar, Ricardo, 22, 149, 168

stereotypes, 60, 164, 173, 176–177, 206, 207–209

structural assimilation, 135, 235, 278*n*28

structural barriers, 200–202, 203, 209–210

Suárez-Orozco, Carola, 22

success: Asian American standards for, 279*n*40; fathers and father figures, 194–195, success 297–298*n*16; individual responsibility for, 167, 189–190, 198–202, 227; self-efficacy and, 192; standards for, 10, 142, 212, 279*n*40, 279*n*46; stereotypes as barriers to, 207–209. *See also* American Dream; meritocracy

Swidler, Ann, 97

Symonds, William, 147

tagging crews, 98–100, 250, 291*n*46

tattoos, 224–225

Telles, Edward, 135, 233, 280*n*49, 297*n*6

Trump, Donald, 11, 245–246, 300*n*50

trust: broken, social isolation and, 83, 182, 219–220; research study and, 265; social cohesion and, 46–47, 64; social networks and, 65, 66, 281*n*81, 290–291*nn*39–40

underclass culture, 6, 15, 36–37, 281*n*71

undocumented immigrants: caging effect of border enforcement and, 71, 83–84, 290*n*36; in California, 284*n*127; Deferred

Action for Childhood Arrivals (DACA) program for, 28, 208–209, 213, 284–285*n*137; employment connections via, 163, 238; employment of, 58, 68, 201, 209, 288*n*16, 289*n*21, 289*n*24; life outcomes and, 28; limitations for, 28, 200–201, 298*n*22; in Los Angeles, 26; public assistance and, 59–60; racial slurs, 105, 293*n*21; rates of migration, 290*n*34; in research study, 71; self-blamers and, 226; social mobility of, 69, 208–209; threat of deportation and, 11, 245–246, 280*n*53, 300*n*50; U.S. hostility towards, 245–246; work ethic of, 58, 201

United States: border enforcement of, 11, 71, 83–84, 289*n*24, 290*n*35; decline of violence in, 61, 242, 247; immigration legislation and reform of, 6, 67–69, 71, 245–246, 288*n*12, 300*n*50; Latinx population in, 277*n*1; policies and integration of second-generation Latinx, 241–246; racialization of Mexicans in, 206–207, 237, 280*n*54; reception of immigrants in, 11, 232, 245–246, 300*n*50 universities, 147–148, 149–160, 171–175. *See also* college and higher education upward mobility. *See* social mobility urban Mexican migrants, 70–74, 290*nn*32–36, 290–291*nn*39–40

Vigil, Diego James, 65, 278*n*24
violence: co-occurrence of, 125–128, 181–183, 219, 293*n*29, 297*n*9; cross-racial, 43–44; decline of, 61, 242, 247; differential exposure to, 107–109, **109**; dominant narrative of inner-city neighborhoods and, 6; effect of, 92–97, 128–130, 233; exposed youth and, 125–128; gang activity and, 16–17, 35–36, 40–45, 92; immigrant effect on urban neighborhoods and, 36–37, 51; immigrant experience with, 40–45; institutions as

buffers against, 109, 112–117, 129, 232; integration of second-generation Latinx and, 232–233; navigating, 93–97; neighborhood effects and, 3–4, 6, 16–17, 49; poverty and, 16; resistance to, 49–51, 61; response to, 25–26; school noncompletion and, 102–107, 293*n*23; social capital as buffer against, 109, 110–112, 117–119, 129; social mobility and, 16–17, 31, 93, 128, 182, 231–232

Viruell-Fuentes, Edna, 287*n*9
vocational training, 144–149, 168–171

Wacquant, Loïc, 18, 205, 237
wages: median income, 26, 134, 294*n*9, 296*n*5; minimum wage, 281*n*66; second-generation Latinx improvements in, 138; stagnation of, 4–5, 247

Waters, Mary, 10, 20
wealth gap, 229, 241–242
welfare, 59–60, 224, 247
Wellman, Barry, 283*n*101
Wilkes, Rima, 284*n*132
Wilson, William Julius, 6, 15, 17, 36, 62, 252
work ethic: American Dream and, 9, 187, 189–190, 198–200, 240–241; children and, 53–55, 111; college success and, 153; disconnection and idleness, 55–57; employment searches and, 171; fathers and father figures, 194; as identity marker, 52–53; of Mexican immigrants, 36, 51–52; moral worth of, 25, 140–142, 232; public assistance and, 59–60; school dropouts and, 58–59; social support and, 21; success standards and, 10, 279*n*40, 279*n*46; of undocumented immigrants, 58, 201. *See also* meritocracy
working class. *See* social class
Wortley, Scot, 283*n*101

Zenteno, Rene M., 288–289*n*18, 290*n*32
Zhou, Min, 20, 64, 279*n*40, 279*n*46, 282*n*97